THE POLITICS OF ELECTORAL PRESSURE

The Politics of Electoral Pressure

A STUDY IN THE HISTORY OF VICTORIAN REFORM AGITATIONS

D. A. HAMER
Professor of History
Victoria University of Wellington
New Zealand

THE HARVESTER PRESS LIMITED
HUMANITIES PRESS INC.

First published in England in 1977 by
THE HARVESTER PRESS LIMITED
Publisher: John Spiers
2 Stanford Terrace, Hassocks, Sussex, England
and in the U.S.A. in 1977 by
Humanities Press Inc.,
Atlantic Highlands, N.J. 07716, U.S.A.

The Harvester Press Limited
ISBN 0 85527 839 0

British Library Cataloguing in Publication Data

Hamer, David Allan
    The politics of electoral pressure: a
    study in the history of Victorian reform
    agitations.
    Index.
    ISBN 0–85527–839–0
    1. Title
    329'.03'0941   JN955
    Pressure groups—Great Britain—History

Humanities Press Inc.,
ISBN 0–391–00682–7
Library of Congress Number 76–49478

Printed in Great Britain by
Latimer Trend & Company Ltd, Plymouth

Contents

Preface

The purpose of this book is to examine an important but hitherto rather neglected aspect of the history of the extra-parliamentary reform agitations of the Victorian period in Britain. This is the employment by some of them of one particular kind of agitational technique, namely the organisation of electoral power and the mobilisation of electoral pressure for the purpose of persuading political parties and candidates for seats in Parliament to promise to promote legislation along the lines advocated by these movements.

There were four organisations during the Victorian period which used electoral pressure in a more or less systematic way. These were the Anti-Corn Law League, the Liberation Society, the National Education League, and the United Kingdom Alliance. In the following pages the history of the electoral campaigns and strategies of each of these is considered—why they adopted and used this particular technique, how their campaigns were mounted, what impact they made on the political scene. The book traces one important part of the tradition of the Anti-Corn Law League, that is the inspiration given to reformers in the mid- and late-nineteenth century by the great triumph which that organisation appeared to have secured in 1846. The Liberation Society was founded (as the Anti-State-Church Association) in 1844, at the peak of the League's campaign, while the United Kingdom Alliance was set up in 1853. The organisers of both bodies naturally sought the secret of the League's success, and they clearly believed that a substantial part of it was to be found in the electoral pressure mobilised by the League. They therefore endeavoured to emulate the League in this regard. In time they developed forms of electoral activity appropriate to their own objectives and philosophy and diverged markedly from the techniques utilised by the League. But, nevertheless, although each pressure group's electoral strategy had its own distinctive characteristics, the employment of electoral pressure by reform movements can be seen as constituting a continuing theme in the history of Victorian politics.

It is not a theme which has hitherto been given much prominence by historians. This is partly no doubt because of the ultimate failure of these movements to achieve their objectives, partly because this kind of pressure has not been a conspicuous feature of the campaigns of reform organisations in our own time, and partly also because of the fact that so much of this activity was organised and carried on outside the realm of 'high politics'. The mobilisation of electoral pressure by Victorian reform movements left no legacy for the twentieth century in the form either of substantial legislative achievement or of techniques to be adapted and refined by later generations of reform crusaders. It looks like a dead end in British political history. Yet it is an aspect of the politics of the nineteenth century which deserves to be rescued and which has to be rediscovered if we are adequately to comprehend the development of 'popular politics' in Britain. This study is intended as a contribution not just to the history of pressure groups but also to electoral history. It reveals a Victorian political sub-culture, a world which is very different from the political world in which we live today and yet one which was in some respects more democratic, more open to popular participation and influence. It was an age in which the uses of the vote were only just being discovered and in which a sense of the liberating potential of electoral power inspired many to make these discoveries the basis of a great widening of the scope of popular influence over government.

But it is part of the story also that the involvement of the people in the electoral process was later to be largely confined within the channels afforded by the party system which came to dominate the process and stifle the independent electoral life of the pressure groups. In tracing this development this book is therefore also a contribution to the history of the Liberal party. It is designed to be in that respect complementary to my earlier work, *Liberal Politics in the Age of Gladstone and Rosebery* (Clarendon Press, Oxford, 1972), in which I examined the ways in which the leaders of the party between 1868 and 1900 tried to combat what they saw as the problems of 'sectionalism' or 'faddism' within the party. For them a major part of the work of Liberal leadership had to be the imposition of order and discipline on the enthusiasts for various reform causes or 'fads' who congregated in the party, looked to it to take up these causes and promote legislation embodying their demands, and competed with one another for priority of attention from the leaders and within the party programme. In *Liberal Politics* I studied the impact on Liberalism of the phenomenon of competing sections. In this present work I examine the origins of that phenomenon and in particular what was one of the most troublesome aspects of it as far as the Liberal leaders were concerned, namely the electoral difficulties which the pressure groups threatened to create, and at times did create, if their demands were not met. I seek to trace the connection between this electoral pressure and the development of Liberal politics in the country at the constituency level in order to show how the relationship of the reform movements to the Liberal party changed from being largely external, aggressive, and coercive to being mainly internal, dependent, and integrated.

The people whom I studied and quoted in my previous work were the politicians and party leaders to whom the faddists were a problem which had to be dealt with in some way or other in the interests of the maintenance of party strength and unity. In this present work I turn away from the world of Parliament and high politics to enter the world of the faddists themselves, to see politics from their point of view. Much of my research has been done in the minute books and the newspapers of their organisations, and in the process I have discovered a substantial amount of material bearing on Liberal politics in the constituencies which might not now be obtainable from any other source or else would have to be retrieved by a laborious search through the files of dozens of local newspapers over many years. John Vincent in his *Formation of the Liberal Party 1857–1868* (1966, 2nd ed., The Harvester Press, Hassocks, 1976) and *Pollbooks, How Victorians Voted* (Cambridge University Press, 1967) has already done much to add this third or popular dimension to the history of Liberal politics in the Victorian era through his use of such unconventional sources as pollbooks and the minute books of the Liberation Society. I hope that this book may add to this work of redressing the balance in our appreciation of Liberal history which he—and Brian Harrison in his *Drink and the Victorians; The Temperance Question in England 1815–1872* (1971)—have so well begun.

In order to define what this book is about I must also define what it is not about. The reader is referred to *Liberal Politics in the Age of Gladstone and Rosebery* for a full discussion of the response of the

Liberal leaders to the problems created by the application of electoral pressure by these movements. I do not discuss the defensive electoral strategies organised by the threatened vested interests, notably the drink trade and the Church of England. A study of these would require, and needs, a book to itself and would contribute a great deal to our understanding of the development of *Conservative* politics in the constituencies. It should be noted also that I study only parliamentary elections and have omitted other forms of electoral activity in which some of the reform movements engaged, such as School Board elections in the early 1870s in the case of the National Education League and municipal elections in the case of the temperance movement.

In the course of my research I incurred many debts which I must acknowledge here. First and foremost I wish to thank the Council of the Victoria University of Wellington for granting me the period of leave during which I was able to undertake the preparation of this book and the President and Governing Body of Corpus Christi College, Oxford, for awarding me a Visiting Fellowship for two terms and thus providing me with extremely congenial conditions for research. In this regard I wish to give my particular thanks to Brian Harrison for his very generous assistance in the arranging of my leave and while I was in Oxford. During my period of leave I was grateful for the opportunity to discuss aspects of my work with numerous Oxford historians and to present papers bearing on it to various seminars.

I wish also to express my gratitude to the Rev. G. Thompson Brake for giving me permission to consult the records of the United Kingdom Alliance and to the staff of the Alliance for their constant kind assistance during the many hours which I spent at Alliance House; to the staff of the Greater London Record Office for guiding my research in the papers of the Liberation Society; to the Librarian of the Bishopsgate Foundation in connection with the Howell Collection; and to the staff of the Birmingham University Library, the Birmingham Central Reference Library, the Bodleian Library, the Department of Manuscripts in the British Library, Dr. Williams's Library, the Manchester Public Library, the Leeds City Archives, and the Sheffield Public Library. I must also thank Mrs. G. Biggs for typing the manuscript of this book.

D. A. HAMER
Victoria University of Wellington

February 1977

CHAPTER I

The Faddists and Victorian Liberal Politics

The terms 'fad' and 'faddist', 'crotchet' and 'crotcheteer', abound in the political controversies and the political rhetoric of mid- and late-Victorian Britain. They are pejorative words, used in particular by Conservatives and hostile Liberals to describe certain reform causes and their supporters. The distinguishing characteristic of a faddist was that he was an enthusiast for the cause and that his enthusiasm was so strong that he tended to feel very impatient with others who did not share it. This impatience was, above all, what determined his political style. Lack of enthusiasm was often attributed, for example, not to an honest difference of opinion but to the sinister workings of the influence of the particular vested interest which was the movement's enemy. The faddist was someone who attached an exalted significance to the reform for which he was struggling. If it was secured, it would, according to him, have the effect of a universal panacea, ending a great number of the evils to which society had become subjected. To the faddist it was his possession of this faith and this vision which both explained and justified his extreme commitment to the cause. But what the outsider saw in him was crankiness and fanaticism and a refusal to see or take into account points of view other than his own.

Many of the reforms which appeared on the programmes of Victorian Radical and Liberal organisations were promoted by movements consisting of such faddists, people to whom the promotion of them became an obsession, sometimes the object to which their lives were consecrated. Examples are the various organisations which agitated for temperance legislation, the Anti-Corn Law League, the peace movement, the agitation against the Contagious Diseases Acts, the movement opposed to compulsory vaccination, and Nonconformist pressure groups, notably those which sought disestablishment and the removal of the allegedly privileged position of the Church of England in the sphere of education. All were ostensibly non-party movements operating outside Parliament, but since they were all seeking changes that could only be brought about, even if public opinion was in their favour, by the passage of an Act of Parliament, they could not help but become very involved in politics and gravitate in the process towards closer association with the Liberal party which they saw as their main hope for the enactment of such legislation, especially once the Conservatives became unmistakably identified with the protection of the vested interests and institutions to which they were opposed. This meant that not only the reforms which they were demanding but also faddism itself became a major political issue. Faddism was seen as a political problem which needed remedying, quite apart from the causes for which the faddists were agitating. The Tories endeavoured to foster an image of the Liberals as a party not fit to be entrusted with the responsibilities of government because it was controlled by fanatics and extremists. Since these tactics appeared to have some success, and since the behaviour of the Liberals when in office seemed more and more to lend credence to this thesis, there developed a strong current of anti-faddism within the Liberal party itself, as worried Liberals sought to dissociate themselves and their party from this unattractive image.

Nevertheless, in spite of the prominence both of faddism and of the controversy to which its existence gave rise in Victorian politics, there has, at least until quite recently, been remarkably little serious investigation of the subject by historians. The reasons for its neglect are fairly obvious. Faddism is most emphatically not a twentieth-century subject. Quite early in this century the whole world of faddism seemed suddenly to collapse. What was left of it and of the structure of nineteenth-century political Dissent within which so much of it had been rooted was largely overwhelmed by the political and social upheavals of the First World War. The great new fact of twentieth-century British politics was the rise of Labour, and this came to receive a great deal of attention from historians who have seemed to be much more interested in looking back into the nineteenth century to trace the origins of major twentieth-century political phenomena than in studying phenomena which were important then but have since greatly diminished in importance. Faddism became an unfashionable and irrelevant subject, especially as so many of the faddist movements were agitations which failed. It must also have seemed unattractive and unglamorous. The world of the faddists was a crude world of fanatics, and the fanaticism is of a peculiarly dated kind. The mental world of someone who believed passionately that the key to the transformation of society was the prohibition of liquor is very difficult for us now to enter. Another and very practical problem has been that of source material. The disappearance of most of these movements, and their apparent irrelevance to our own age, no doubt account for the paucity of the records which now survive. For a long time very few people cared that they should survive. Evidence that can now be used to reconstruct the world of the faddists is not easily accessible. The references in Brian Harrison's *Drink and the Victorians* give some idea of the diversity and obscurity and amount of the material that has to be used.

Faddism is a negative and pejorative term, the invention of opponents. What now needs rescuing and re-emphasising is the positive side of the politics of the faddists, what these pressure groups contributed to nineteenth-century political life. One way of assessing this is to look at the programmes and manifestoes of late Victorian Liberal associations, including the National Liberal Federation. Behind many of the reforms listed in these, and indeed behind many of the reforms that were proposed by the party's leaders and undertaken by Liberal governments, can be found the pressure of one or more organisations whose purpose it was to promote that reform or at least reform in that particular area. The faddists, through their pressure at the constituency level—which it is one of the main purposes of this book to discuss—undoubtedly played a major role in getting these reform proposals on to the Liberal agenda and then in conducting propaganda and agitation on their behalf and mobilising support for the Liberal party as it set about trying to secure their enactment.

This mobilising of voters, including, as we shall see, much basic work in connection with electoral registration, represented a significant channel whereby life was injected into Liberal politics. Until the late nineteenth-century the Liberal leadership was drawn almost entirely from the aristocracy and the upper reaches of the middle classes, and the party itself was essentially a parliamentary party with no systematic organisation behind it in the constituencies. The leaders had at their disposal no machinery for establishing contact with the new middle-class and working-class voters and little understanding of how to go about creating and using such machinery. The pressure groups, inspired 'from below', filled this vacuum. An outstanding example of the Liberal leadership's discovery and exploitation of their significance in this regard is the relationship between G. G. Glyn, the Chief Whip, and the Reform League in the period preceding the general election of 1868.[1]

The great positive force which the faddists had to contribute to Liberal politics was enthusiasm, stemming from their very strong devotion to their particular causes. If the Liberal party appeared to them a vehicle for the accomplishment of the desired reforms, then it itself received a share of this enthusiasm and devotion. The effect could be very advantageous for the party. For example, it provided bands of people who were willing to volunteer their services as local party organisers, canvassers, and supporters and to work very hard for the cause. The availability of these enthusiastic and unpaid party workers became especially important with the decline in the funds available from wealthy private donors, the growing costs of electioneering owing to the increase in the size of electorates, and the Elimination of Corrupt Practices Act of 1883 which placed a limit on the amount which a candidate could legally spend at an election. The great reform movements could offer not only party workers but also voters, good voters who could be relied on to turn out and vote for a party which showed sympathy with their cause, voters who took politics seriously. 'Liberalism' was an abstract concept for many voters, and very remote from their daily lives, especially when sponsored by a party that was led by Whig aristocrats and other members of the governing class; but its identification with some cause such as temperance or disestablishment gave it relevance for people who had been constantly worked on, through lectures and meetings and many other forms of publicity, by the organisations promoting these causes.

The enthusiasm of the faddists could be a powerful and positive force from harnessing which the Liberal party had much to gain. But it could also be a disruptive force. Much of what follows in this book will concern that aspect of its involvement in Liberal politics. The enthusiasts for particular reforms were often impatient people, inclined to lack sympathy for the claims of other questions and for considerations of political expediency. If their enthusiasm was to be utilised, it had to be controlled and disciplined, but not to such an extent that as a result it was choked. The challenge for the Liberal leaders in the late nineteenth-century was to maintain and benefit from this devotion and commitment and yet avoid the disruptiveness which was so often the price that had to be paid.

Faddists were people who were possessed of a vision and also filled with indignation at the fundamental wrongness, indeed the evil, of the existing state of affairs. They tended to be intolerant of others who shared neither vision nor indignation and to have little time for the politician who gave excuses for not devoting himself immediately to the fulfilment of their demands. Another reason why they were so difficult to deal with politically was that the organisations to which they belonged derived much of their strength from their unity. This was, as we shall see, particularly true of electoral power where the main weapon was the *bloc* vote. In order to maintain unity and hence strength they strove to suppress, or minimise scope for, internal divisions. This meant, for instance, that their objectives were often stated in as unqualified, extreme, and simplified a manner as possible. It was always dangerous for a pressure group to admit the possibility that lesser or alternative modes of reform would be acceptable, even as stepping stones to the ultimate goal. That might well open the floodgates to the host of theories and schemes which always proliferate in reform crusades and lead rapidly as a result to quarrels, fragmentation, and loss of effective power. The history of many of these movements reveals frequent conflict between advocates of concentration on the achievement of a single, ultimate change and those who, perhaps because they had grown doubtful of the possibility of this happening in the foreseeable future, pressed for acceptance of lesser and intermediate reforms. Examples are the early history of the Anti-Corn Law League and the divisions in the United Kingdom Alliance over the recommendations of the Peel Commission in 1899 and 1900.[2]

The problem was that no government ever had popular support for proceeding to legislate at the extreme points at which these movements often pitched their demands. But attempts to enact lesser measures often encountered open hostility and resistance from the pressure groups. Compromise was not a part of their political vocabulary. They had to be given one hundred per cent. of what they wanted, and he who offered or was prepared to accept less than that was regarded as an enemy or a traitor to the cause.

Another major difficulty which these movements created for Liberal politics was their competition with one another. They helped to construct the agenda of the Liberal party in the late nineteenth century, but, once they had done so, there then arose the problem of priorities. Given that Liberal governments could not attend to all the desired reforms at the same time or even within the lifetime of a single Parliament, in what order were they to be attended to? Whatever decision was made, several powerful organisations were certain to feel offended and frustrated.

For the greater part of the nineteenth century the relationship between the Liberal leaders and parliamentarians, on the one hand, and the reform movements, on the other, was a distant one and characterised by a substantial gulf of incomprehension and suspicion. Most of the Liberal leaders had little or no direct connection with the pressure groups and dealt with them from the outside, often seeing them as a problem, something rather awkward and even distasteful that needed suppressing or combatting. The reasons why they had become Liberal leaders usually had little or nothing to do with the pressure groups. Pressure-group leaders seldom ascended into the ranks of the governing class. A barrier to this was constituted partly by social factors and partly by the nature of the faddist himself whose 'opposition mentality' has been well analysed by B. Harrison in his description of the career of Sir Wilfrid Lawson, the temperance leader.[3] Even those Nonconformists who attained prominent positions in the Liberal party were usually strongly anti-faddist. It is true that a few Liberals, especially Nonconformist Radicals such as Joseph Chamberlain, did use the pressure groups as, or at least found that they became, means for the advancement of their political ambitions and the acquisition of wider reputations. But such men usually left their faddism behind as they rose up the political ladder. Chamberlain made a national name for himself in the early 1870s as a militant Nonconformist through his association with the National Education League and the Liberation Society, but in the later stages of his career anti-faddism was one of his main characteristics, and he sought to solve several of the 'faddist questions' without any reference to the pressure groups themselves. He tried to develop a brand of Radical politics that assumed that they did not exist or could be ignored.[4] The career of Lloyd George follows a very similar pattern.

Two of the Liberal leaders deserve special mention in regard to their relationship to the reform movements. One is Sir William Harcourt. He was one of the few leaders who perceived the problem of the need to maintain the faddists' enthusiasm and tried to shape policy in relation to this need. The other is Gladstone. He was very remote from them and their world. He had very little direct contact with them and never spoke at their meetings. He disliked them very much, because he felt that they selfishly placed the satisfaction of their own special demands above consideration of the common interest. It was Gladstone who administered one of the most famous rebukes to them—to Edward Miall on the third reading of the Education Bill in July 1870. He praised them only when, as in 1879–80, they were expressing a readiness to subordinate their special causes to some greater national interest. He often despaired over the impact of 'selfish' sectionalism on Liberal politics, constantly tried to turn his policies into vehicles for countering it, and at the end of his career referred to it as the greatest problem facing the party.[5] Nevertheless, some of the pressure-group leaders seemed almost hypnotised by him. His overtures to Nonconformity, and the way in which he became a hero for so many Nonconformists because of his style of leadership and stress on the moral factor in politics and in national life, created an important bridge and led Nonconformist faddists often to make much greater allowances for him than they were prepared to make for his colleagues.

The party Whips did little to connect the two worlds. G. G. Glyn, Chief Whip from 1868 to 1873, did at least become aware of the value of using a pressure group such as the Reform League to make contact with the new voters, but he did nothing to bring its leaders into a more permanent and organic relationship with the Liberal party. His successor, W. P. Adam, was concerned particularly with one form of faddism, the movement for Scottish disestablishment, and then only as a disruptive and disorganising influence in Scottish Liberalism. Lord Richard Grosvenor came from the Whig side of Liberal politics, and Arnold Morley (1886–92) was the son of Samuel Morley, the prominent Nonconformist political leader who had long since broken with and repudiated faddist politics of the kind practised by the Liberation Society and the United Kingdom Alliance. Tom Ellis, Chief Whip from 1894 to 1899, was the exception. His principal connection was with Welsh politics, but he knew the disestablishers and temperance advocates, appeared on their platforms, and corresponded with them. He alone tried to act as an intermediary between them and the Liberal leadership, but there was little that he could do against the tide of reaction in the party away from the Newcastle Programme and sectionalism. His successor, Herbert Gladstone, was militantly anti-faddist and devoted the major part of his tenure of the office to curbing and controlling the influence of the sections in Liberal politics.

Large numbers of Liberal MPs at one time or another during the late nineteenth century professed adherence to the causes which were being promoted by the major reform movements. But political opportunism or electoral necessity created by the electoral pressure of the faddists often accounted for such 'conversions'. The only really reliable intermediaries between the pressure groups and the Liberal party were those pressure-group leaders and organisers who succeeded in becoming Liberal MPs. But very few did, and, with the notable exceptions of Wilfrid Lawson and Alfred Illingworth, their careers were usually brief and frequently interrupted. For example, J. Carvell Williams of the Liberation Society won a seat in Parliament in 1885, lost it in 1886, and only came back in 1892 for eight years at the very end of his career as the Society's principal organiser and when the Society's fortunes were in serious decline. Edward Miall experienced very great difficulty in obtaining and retaining seats in Parliament. Many prominent figures in the Alliance, such as J. H. Raper, F. R. Lees, J. Kempster, and J. Hargrove, stood for Parliament, but almost none of them ever succeeded in winning election. The result was that there were few men who moved between the two worlds, explaining each to the other, making Liberal politicians more aware of and sensitive to the views of the faddists and endeavouring to persuade the faddists to make allowances for the effect of wider political circumstances and exigencies on the ability of the politicians to give them what they demanded. In the absence of such harmonising and connecting influences it is not surprising that the relationship was so frequently one of electoral warfare.

CHAPTER II

Electoral Strategies

Although there are now numerous studies of nineteenth-century pressure groups, there are few analyses on a comparative basis of the methods which they employed.[1] This book is a study of one category of agitational technique resorted to in the Victorian period—the creation and utilisation of electoral influence for the purpose of persuading candidates and parties to promote particular reforms advocated by pressure groups.

The electoral strategy came to be a very important form of agitation in the nineteenth century as major measures of parliamentary reform continually opened up new opportunities for pressure groups to transmit their demands to Parliament via the electoral system. More indirect and traditional forms of pressure persisted, however, and were sometimes deployed by a movement in conjunction with an electoral strategy. These included mass meetings and demonstrations, petitioning, the issuing of tracts and propaganda, and behind-the-scenes lobbying of ministers, MPs, and civil servants. Each of these could acquire or be given an electoral dimension. Mobilising people as voters gave a crowd or a demonstration additional potency and provided an alternative, constitutional sanction to the threat of violence which crowds were traditionally feared, and sometimes intended, to represent. As for petitioning, there is a transition from petitions asking Parliament to enact a certain reform to the signing of petitions and pledges signifying a resolve to use one's vote in a particular way if MPs did not assist in this enactment. Publicity on behalf of reform causes was often concentrated on by-elections and general elections which were felt to give excellent opportunities for drawing attention to them. Lobbying, especially of MPs, was more effective if those engaged in it had in reserve the possibility of bringing electoral pressure to bear should it not prove fruitful.

There were many ways in which a reform movement could exploit the nineteenth-century electoral system to promote and publicise its cause. Much of the work of pressure groups—and, of course, of the political parties as well—consisted of finding out what these opportunities were. The constant alterations to the franchise and the procedures governing elections meant that the electoral system was characterised by very great fluidity. Changes wrought by the Reform Bills were ill understood even by those who enacted them, and each Bill proved to be riddled with anomalies and ambiguities. Furthermore, each Bill brought in large numbers of new voters who could be assumed to have little or no attachment to the existing parties and might therefore be more easily recruited for the particular electoral campaigns of pressure groups.

The heyday of the electoral strategy conducted by a reform movement was probably the period between the first and second Reform Acts when the constituencies were, in the main, of just the right size to make effective the mobilisation of small blocs of dedicated voters—large enough to make possible escape from the influence of large landowners, yet small enough to give such minority groups some real prospect of being able to hold the balance and of not being swallowed up in vast numbers. One particularly important feature of that era was open voting. Prior to 1872 elections were very public affairs in which voters were obliged to give a highly visible indication of their political commitment. This suited reform movements admirably in two ways. First, it provided a further means whereby adherents could give a public demonstration of their commitment to the cause. An election was a chance for an individual to prove the reality of that commitment and his readiness to make sacrifices for it, such as refusing to vote for the candidate of the party which he normally favoured. Secondly, open voting enabled blocs of voters to be much more apparent as a real political force, for example as reserved votes not available except to candidates who gave specific promises. It was known for whom people voted. Therefore, if somebody adhered to a particular movement and yet voted for a candidate who did not support its demands, he knew that he had to be ready to justify his conduct afterwards. After the introduction of the secret ballot, the relationship between pressure groups and the behaviour of voters became rather more ambiguous. A candidate could no longer relate so precisely the claim that a bloc vote existed to the actual way in which particular people voted and so had to proceed much more by trial and error. The ambiguity was centred on the phenomenon of abstention from voting. There were all sorts of possible interpretations for the decline in the turn-out of voters in a specific poll and it was not easy either to refute or to verify a pressure group's claim to the major responsibility for this.

In one important respect reform movements went against the grain of early- and even mid-Victorian politics. By entering constituencies and endeavouring to mobilise voters for or against candidates on account of their views on questions of national policy, they challenged the reality of many electoral contests which would otherwise have been determined solely by local influences. They undoubtedly did a great deal to advance the real working in the constituencies of the idea of the general election, and even the by-election, as an occasion to register a verdict on national issues. Down to the late nineteenth century large numbers of seats were left uncontested at general elections.[2] Pressure groups from the Anti-Corn Law League on challenged the assumptions about elections which led to this state of affairs. For doing so they were often reviled and accused of introducing 'alien' influences into local contests.[3]

One of the main areas of electoral activity by reform movements was registration.[4] After 1832 one could vote only if one had a claim to possess the requisite qualification to vote accepted and had then been placed on the register. The initiative in all this had to come from the individual or from an organisation acting on his behalf. The procedure by which the electoral rolls were compiled and revised was very elaborate and complicated. There was an annual timetable prescribing certain dates by which claims must be submitted, objections made to claims, and so forth. The individual would-be voter desperately needed help if he was to make his way through this labyrinth. Given the complexity of the registration procedures, the existence of many people qualified to vote but not able to vote because unregistered, and the apathy consequent on the meaningless-ness of many electoral contests, there was abundant scope for parties and reform organisations to acquire considerable electoral power by campaigns to get their supporters on to the register. The major pressure groups devoted a large amount of effort to helping their supporters to become voters and one, the Anti-Corn Law League, went into the business of helping them to acquire the property which conferred the qualification.[5] Assiduous attention to this work could yield substantial electoral dividends from which the Liberal party ultimately benefited even more than the reform movements. Some of the pressure groups developed very great expertise in this area. Electoral strategies ranged well beyond the registration of supporters, but that always had to be their basis.

The fluidity of the electoral system gave much opportunity for the exercise of imagination and innovatory boldness on the part of electoral strategists. One senses in some of them at times a feeling almost of exhilaration as they experiment and discover new electoral possibilities and new ways of influencing voters. There were in the nineteenth century very large numbers of people who could have voted but did not, either because, although qualified, they had not registered, or because, although registered, they saw little point in voting in the prevailing electoral circumstances. Here was a vast potential but hidden voting power. The reform movements always placed great emphasis on the rewards to be derived from entering virgin political territory and recruiting new voters.

It would not be accurate to see electoral pressure as relevant as an agitational technique only for people who already possessed the vote and for movements which represented them. The distinction between voters and non-voters was far from clear or rigid, and a man who did not possess the vote might very easily be converted into a voter by the manipulation of electoral procedures and regulations. Non-voters were potential voters and therefore had some kind of electoral significance. Some of the pressure groups gave them a role to play in their electoral activities. Sometimes movements representing the unenfranchised invented substitutes for an electoral strategy and even for the electoral system. The Chartists put up their own candidates at the hustings and also organised an electoral system of their own for their Conventions.[6]

The reasons for the decision to engage in electoral action varied considerably from one movement to another, as also did the form which that action then took. These differences were related closely to the nature of each movement and of the policy which it was seeking to promote. An electoral strategy was most likely to be effective and to engage the attention and sustained commitment of the adherents to a movement if it did have a relationship to the basic objectives of the movement. For such strategies had to be worked out and maintained over lengthy periods, for example between general elections, and the effort involved was often laborious and unexciting. It was not at all easy to induce volunteers to sustain this unless they felt it to be integrally related to the wider commitment which they had originally made to the movement. In any case, when pressure groups had to choose a form of electoral action, they naturally preferred the one that made the most sense to them in terms of their own basic philosophy.

Some examples will illustrate this. It is in the temperance movement that one finds the most elaborate and systematic effort to gain and use electoral power in order to further the movement's ends. This is not at all surprising. The major political aim of the prohibitionists, notably in the United Kingdom Alliance, was itself electoral—the achievement of prohibition through local polls or referenda. Much time was spent in debating what the machinery for these should be, how often they should be held, what sort of majority should be required, and so forth. It was natural, therefore, that prohibitionists should be very interested in and sensitive to opportunities for the utilising of existing electoral procedures. If, by their action, parliamentary elections were turned into trials of strength between themselves and the liquor interest, this could be regarded as no more than a trial run for, a foreshadowing of, the type of electoral situation which they were agitating to inaugurate on an official basis throughout the country. Temperance electoral activity was natural for another important reason. The enemy of the movement, the drink trade, was already established as a powerful force in electoral life. The influence of the public house in election contests, its central position in campaigning (until this was checked by law), and the debauchery and corruption which resulted, constituted a standing provocation to the temperance movement and made it virtually inevitable that a part of its crusade against liquor would take place within the electoral sphere. Another aspect of the movement which clearly shaped the electoral action in which it engaged was the way in which temperance became a complete way of life for many of its adherents. It followed from this that efforts were made to include even the electoral part of a temperance enthusiast's existence. Temperance went considerably further than other movements in endeavouring to isolate and organise its voters and provide them with a thorough temperance political identity. Finally, there was, as we shall see, a connection between the basis of teetotalism, the taking of a pledge to abstain from intoxicating liquor, and the basis of temperance electoral activity, the taking of a pledge to abstain from voting for candidates who would not promise to assist the crusade against this great evil.[7]

When one turns to the electoral activity of movements specifically related to the interests of Nonconformity, one finds different motives and forms of action corresponding to the general philosophy of nineteenth-century 'Political Dissent'. Underlying all Nonconformist involvement in elections can be seen the emphasis placed by so many Nonconformist leaders—of whom George Dawson and R. W. Dale are perhaps the best known—on 'the duties of Christian citizenship', the obligation of the Nonconformist to play a part in the public life of the community.[8] A positive attitude to politics followed from this, and especially a disposition to take elections very seriously and to regard with disgust the rioting, intimidation, bribery, and drunkenness which were a feature of many election contests. The high-minded attitude of Nonconformists to electioneering, and the novelty which it was felt to be, can be illustrated by this account given by Edward Miall of his candidature at Halifax in 1847:

My committee is composed almost wholly of religious men, who make every day's work a matter of prayer. I have had much talk with the different electors almost wholly upon spiritual subjects. Many of them are startled by my views . . . In short, the contest is a most novel and extraordinary one, and compels respect from all quarters. Our committee room is at a private house; we have no colours—we go to no expense. Every one works gratuitously. We meet every evening to sum up results; and if pure motives, thorough earnestness, good organisation, and minute attention to details can carry me, I shall be safe enough.[9]

The Nonconformist was urged to regard his vote as a sacred trust conferred on him by God. Miall often described it in these terms in his addresses to Liberationists in the 1860s. 'We ought not to trifle with our votes,' he would say. 'We ought to consider that we have that power placed in our hands by the wisdom of God to bring advantage to his church.'[10] A Nonconformist who accepted this point of view was bound to ponder very seriously the question of how to use his vote and to be susceptible to appeals to place it at the service of some great moral cause.

Another influence over Nonconformists' interest in the use of electoral power was undoubtedly the memory of centuries of 'exclusion' and discrimination, a memory which constituted a major part of their collective identity in the nineteenth century.[11] To many of them the active and conspicuous deployment of the vote was clearly a way of demonstrating that they were now citizens, now belonged. To take an attitude of indifference or passivity to the possession of the vote might have been taken to imply that the years of exclusion had left their permanent mark, that Nonconformists were still 'excluded' at least in their own minds, or that the exclusion had been correctly based on an unwillingness or unfitness to participate in public life. One may also sense that the more radical Dissenters at least enjoyed Nonconformist electoral action as a means of publicly displaying Nonconformist power, especially when it was used to bring to heel or control the conduct in Parliament of Anglican politicians. There is one distinctive feature of Nonconformist electoral practice which would seem to be very much a product of Nonconformist history—a strong current of distaste for negative tactics, such as abstaining from voting.[12] This one may attribute to an overwhelming desire now to play a positive part in public life.

We shall see also how the electoral strategies of the Anti-Corn Law League and of Labour and Socialist movements closely reflected their own particular ideologies.[13]

A major theme in the history of the electoral strategies of reform movements is the conflict between the enthusiasm of those who alone could carry these out and make them effective and the need for realism which was just as important from the point of view of effectiveness. The strategy which was most likely to succeed was one which balanced these two considerations and ensured that neither became so predominant as to stifle the other. This was an extremely difficult exercise and required great skill and talent for leadership on the part of the organisers of a movement.

Enthusiasm was a vital ingredient in any effective electoral strategy—vital as the force that would inspire people to put a particular cause first in their use of their votes, often against strong pressure from the political parties and from the great issues which are raised at general elections, and even to obey instructions to stay at home on election day and not vote at all. This required great discipline amongst the voters who supported the movement, something which could come only from feeling very strongly about the objective to which all these electoral efforts were related. But realism was also essential. No electoral strategy could hope to succeed unless it was founded on a very clear understanding of the working of the electoral system, an ability to assess realistically the strength and reliability of the material at the movement's disposal, and the capacity to perceive where and how that material could be used to maximum effect. There had to be a readiness to recognise weaknesses and to check the growth of false hopes and excessive optimism, for disappointment consequent on the deflating of such hopes could be very demoralising.

The problem was that these two ingredients were seldom compatible. Optimism and the concealing or minimising of setbacks and weaknesses had often to be encouraged in order to maintain enthusiasm. Passionate commitment to a cause at times seriously affected the ability to perceive reality and also to see matters from the point of view of others who lacked this enthusiasm but whose co-operation was nevertheless essential if the ultimate goal was ever to be attained. Furthermore, an electoral strategy usually needed much time and patience and behind-the-scenes organisation and negotiations. Enthusiasts looked for quick results and were apt to be disillusioned when these did not occur. In a highly complex electoral system trial and error was the only way to proceed, and only the patient, systematic accumulation of electoral information could provide a sound foundation for effective intervention in election contests.

Devotion to causes which were usually highly moral in emphasis had one major disadvantage for those who sought to promote them by means of electoral action. This was that there was frequently resistance when the faithful were invited to allow considerations of political expediency to influence their political conduct. There was much debate over whether the end justified the means or whether the employment of expedients fatally contaminated the cause itself. Suspicion of normal electioneering practices was naturally strong among high-minded reformers in an age when these included much corruption and intimidation, and electoral strategists often had to work hard to break this down. An example of this debate between the proponents of morality and of realism can be found in the Alliance in 1873 when Handel Cossham attacked that organisation's strategy for its political impracticality. William Hoyle, a leading temperance publicist, replied by arguing that 'questions of right and wrong are involved, and therefore political-expediency doctrines, which under some circumstances might perhaps be recognised, cannot, except in a secondary way, be taken into the account'. The Alliance question, he said, 'is a question which cannot be judged by the ordinary rules of political strategy—it is too sacred and important for this'.[14] The issue came up again in the correspondence columns of the *Nonconformist* in 1878 when criticism of the Alliance's impracticality was expressed. J. Hayward of Bristol wrote that 'true men and patriots must use their political influence according to the light God has given them. Certain it is, that even if as a result of this action a political party had to perish, that the principles of truth and justice would survive the shock, and win their way, and finally secure the victory.' To this 'Argus' replied:

Mr. Hayward speaks of conscience in this connection which cannot be laid aside even in political operations. I firmly hold that there is a conscience in man, and that it has a sphere of action in the practical affairs of mankind; but that sphere is the morally right, not the expedient. I think that many religious and philanthropic men in the present day endow their own crotchets or opinions on matters of mere utility with the sacred authority of conscience, and quote this authority in support of measures of mere party organisation. I do not see what conscience, properly so-called, has to do with the question whether I should vote for a man who will support the Permissive Bill or some other measure intended to interfere with the drinking system.[15]

The influence of enthusiasm was all the greater because of the way in which electoral strategies were formulated and reviewed. The basis of this was usually resolutions passed at annual conferences and public meetings. These gatherings were not satisfactory as occasions on which strategy could be frankly debated and defects realistically acknowledged. Their main purpose was to rally the faithful and provide them with inspiration and encouragement to carry on the crusade. The predominant atmosphere had to be one of enthusiasm and optimism. Speakers who ventured to suggest that all was not well tended to encounter hostility.[16] Electoral strategies were formulated in sweeping resolutions which excited by their boldness, and there was not enough frank assessment of obstacles and difficulties.[17] It was sometimes observed that resolutions passed at conferences with enthusiasm proved to be worthless in practice, since few who voted for them had thought through their possible practical implications.[18] There was too much of a complacent attitude that the passing of a resolution was all that needed to be done, like the waving of a magic wand. As the *Nonconformist* observed in 1877, the trouble with 'strong resolutions passed by crowded public meetings' was that 'nobody in particular is bound' by them.[19] Individuals in a crowd, carried away by the euphoria of the occasion, voted for resolutions without feeling any sort of personal commitment to them. For this reason temperance enthusiasts for electoral action gave up relying on resolutions 'pledging' mass meetings and turned instead to seeking out individuals in their own homes and pledging them there on a personal basis.[20]

To be effective an electoral strategy had to be conceived and co-ordinated from the centre, but put into operation by local people in the constituencies. Therefore it was necessary that there be a very careful definition of the roles of the national and local organisations and that these be delicately balanced.[21] This was an area, after all, in which personal sensitivities were particularly likely to be involved. It was essential not to give the local people any cause to think that everything would be done by the national organisation. But, on the other hand, all the surviving minutes of pressure groups show the importance of constant surveillance and intervention from the centre. Local branches were prone to become entangled in very complex local situations and to be subject to powerful local pressures and so often experienced considerable difficulty, if unaided, in implementing any general strategy. The most realistic strategies were those which allowed for this. In some movements there was a considerable amount of independent local electoral activity which provided a basis for the promotion of action at parliamentary elections. This is particularly true of the temperance movement which became very involved in municipal politics.

One of the most important aspects of the relationship between pressure groups and constituencies was their work in placing candidates. Several of them—the U.K. Alliance, the Liberation Society, the National Education League—became, in effect, major national electoral agencies on whose lists of men available to become candidates it was highly advisable for an aspiring Radical or Nonconformist politician to have his name placed. These organisations developed a great network of contacts throughout the country, and, as a result, were able to provide an entrée into many places for men who had political ambitions but lacked local roots of their own or professed a brand of politics that transcended localism. They also developed an immense fund of knowledge about local politics, an asset of considerable value to politicians who were connected with them. Local Liberal parties often needed candidates who would be acceptable both to themselves and to the major 'sections' in the constituency, and so they would consult the local leaders or representatives of these movements. They, in their turn, would appeal to the national headquarters for suggestions.[22]

Pressure groups engaged in this kind of work because they were anxious to see elected men who were sympathetic to themselves and not just have to rely on bullying others who were not. This was Miall's policy in the Liberation Society, for instance. He advocated attention less to issues than to persuading, or if necessary forcing, the Liberal party to give candidatures to men of broad Nonconformist sympathies in areas where Nonconformists were strongly represented on the register.[23]

The linkage between the national organisation and the local branches was usually provided by the organisation's agents, superintendents, and lecturers. Such people often had electoral work as one of their major responsibilities. Indeed, some movements created a special and separate network of electoral agents and organisers.

CHAPTER III

Types of Electoral Action

1. BY-ELECTIONS AND GENERAL ELECTIONS

Each type of election had its advantages and disadvantages from the point of view of a pressure group.

The pressure groups did a great deal of their work at by-elections. 'They are always instructive', said W. S. Caine; 'they are always valuable to any great agitation. There is no opportunity like a bye-election for bringing any political principle before the country . . .'.[1] Much of the complicated manoeuvring between pressure groups and the Liberal party took place at by-elections, so that tactical positions assumed at general elections were very often the representation of conclusions arrived at as a result of this series of trials of strength and will over the previous five or six years. The party tested and discovered the electoral implications of particular policy positions: how many votes might be withheld, for instance, or how many extra votes secured from people who might otherwise abstain or even vote for the other side. It balanced the electoral forces for and against a proposal and tried to gauge the point at which the gains might be expected to outweigh the losses. For their part, pressure groups discovered how far their adherents were prepared to support particular forms of electoral action. A by-election was more suitable than a general election for operations of this kind because it could not easily be dominated by a great national issue. It was much easier at by-elections to persuade voters to do what pressure groups always most wanted them to do—give the special question priority over considerations of party in their exercise of the vote. Since the fate of the government was never at stake, as it always is at a general election, disgruntled supporters could give their party a warning and a fright in a manner that was at the same time dramatic and safe. As isolated events, by-elections could provide excellent opportunities for gaining publicity for the cause and even for carrying some spectacular *coup* that could overnight transform the political status of the question. By-elections were also better suited than general elections to organisations with only limited resources. The major drawback to by-elections was that a pressure group had no control over their location, whereas in a general election some degree of discrimination could be exercised in the selection of constituencies on to which efforts could be concentrated. A sequence of by-elections in unfavourable localities could do damage to a pressure group's reputation. Organisations such as the Anti-Corn Law League ran into trouble when they raised high expectations concerning a strategy based on contesting every by-election.[2]

General elections, it was recognised, came in two varieties. There was the election at which there was no major national issue and so it was possible to wage electoral war on behalf of the cause without fear of its being overshadowed or large numbers of its supporters being distracted. Those of 1865 and 1874 were widely claimed to be elections of this kind. On the other hand, there were elections when such national issues were raised. A movement took a considerable risk in asserting its question under such circumstances, for many of those who were normally its adherents might not on this occasion follow its electoral instructions and so its electoral credibility might be damaged considerably. The argument that it was unpatriotic to put one's sectional interests above those of the nation was a powerful one and often heard at general elections.[3] Nonconformists seem to have been particularly sensitive to the 'peace' question. It was often referred to in the period 1872–4 as the one factor which would justify a suspension of militant electoral tactics, while in 1879–80 Gladstone commended Nonconformists for their patriotism in putting first the objective of extirpating immorality in foreign policy.[4]

Nonconformists took electoral pledges very seriously. The recognition that there could be transcending national issues at general elections led to refusals to give pledges in case an election should then turn out to be of this kind and the voter would have to choose between breaking an oath and refusing to take a stand in a great question involving the national interest. Some Nonconformists opposed strategies based on taking pledges to vote henceforth only in a certain way for this reason.[5] It was often necessary, therefore, in order to secure adequate support for an electoral strategy, to have written into it an escape clause, recognising that the commitment to the particular form of electoral action that was proposed would not be binding in the case of a general election where there was an issue of overriding national importance. This first appeared when Miall proposed a new strategy for the Liberation Society in 1863 and various Nonconformists demanded more flexibility with regard to general elections. This was quickly conceded. Dale had to do the same in 1872 in connection with the new militant tactics of the Nonconformists.[6]

Such escape clauses were potentially inimical to the effectiveness of an electoral strategy. They gave virtual *carte blanche* to an individual to make up his own mind whether or not to vote as his pressure group requested. This was all the more critical because one feels that elections of the kind referred to in the escape clauses increasingly did not just happen. They were willed into happening, as more and more Liberals came to long for great, overriding issues that would provide them with an excuse for not making any binding pledges.[7] This applied both to candidates who required protection from the pressures of the faddists and to Liberals who were associated with pressure groups and desired honourable relief from the conflict of loyalties that sometimes arose. For example, a correspondent wrote in the *Nonconformist* in August 1878 about the disruption caused by sectionalism in Liberal politics 'in nearly every borough in the kingdom': 'it is to be feared that it will continue to exist until some burning question demands for its solution the united strength of the Liberal party. When that time comes, as come it will, crotchets and crotchet-mongers will be imperiously thrust aside.'[8] Before long it seemed as if all general elections involved such 'burning questions' —or at least Liberals were told that they did by their leaders. The insertion of escape clauses into electoral strategies and pledges was a virtual invitation to Liberal leaders who saw their party disorganised by sectionalism to adopt a certain style of leadership and make all campaigns appear to focus on a great national issue. Miall himself believed that leaders would not scruple to raise questions of foreign policy as a diversion.[9] J. Guinness Rogers, than whom no pressure-group leader was readier to accept and promote the subordination of a special question if this was asked for by the Liberal party, wondered in retrospect whether there might not have been some deliberate 'shunting' of disestablishment by Gladstone on the two occasions, in 1876–80 and 1885, when agitation for it was reaching a peak.[10]

2. FORMS OF PRESSURE

Almost every pressure group in the nineteenth century engaged in a basic form of electoral action. This consisted of submitting to candidates a list of questions as to their attitudes to the policies of the pressure group. What electoral strategies were all about was the question of the further action to be taken whenever one or more of the candidates returned answers which did not satisfy the requirements of the pressure group. Deputations were often sent to candidates to put the questions to them and to discuss their answers and also in many cases to make them aware of the electoral sanctions which might follow should these answers continue to be unsatisfactory. Much pre-election manoeuvring involved the use of threats of various kinds of sanction in order to persuade the candidate and his party managers to change their position on the particular policy issue. In all this there was often undoubtedly a sizeable element of bluff, and candidates had to gauge how far they dared go in calling this bluff in any particular set of circumstances. In the following discussion the various forms of electoral sanction are reviewed.

A. *Independent candidatures*

One might have expected this to be the predominant form of electoral action engaged in by pressure groups whenever none of the candidates of the regular parties satisfied their demands. But it is surprising how infrequently it is resorted to. Preference was usually given to forms of action which might induce a change of mind and policy on the part of the existing candidates. One pressure group, the Liberation Society, explicitly ruled out independent candidatures and confined itself to securing greater influence over the selection of Liberal candidates and withholding support where that influence was not allowed.[11]

The classic case of a strategy based on the promotion of independent candidatures was that of the Anti-Corn Law League. Its formula, that electors should always have the opportunity to vote for free-trade principles and therefore a free-trade candidate would be brought forward whenever none of the candidates already in the field espoused these, was adopted later by both the National Education League and the U.K. Alliance. Neither seemed to appreciate that the League had had a great deal of trouble over implementing this policy and had had to abandon it in the end.[12]

B

There were various risks and drawbacks associated with independent candidatures. For one thing, it was not at all easy to find good men to undertake them. They were, by and large, not attractive to politicians of ambition or reputation who looked to or already had careers within the established parties and feared the damage to these which a low vote might inflict. But, as the Anti-Corn Law League found, obscure men were no good advertisement for a movement and were no help in attracting voters.[13] Independent candidatures on behalf of pressure groups almost never succeeded. Because they appeared to be such definite assertions of an organisation's claims and strength, failure could be very harmful to its reputation and to the morale of its members. They were seldom accepted and supported by all the local adherents to a cause and tended to have a divisive effect whenever attempted.

The independent candidature was usually a failure if taken the full distance, but often the intention was not that it should be carried right through to polling day. The tactical use of such candidatures was far more important than any expectation that they should actually result in the gaining of the seat. They were often started, like the threat to withhold votes, as a tactical manoeuvre in the hope that fear of a possible loss of votes would lead one of the main parties to make concessions which would enable a last-minute withdrawal to take place.[14]

B. *Abstaining from voting*

This was the major form of electoral action engaged in by pressure groups. The candidate who did not provide satisfactory answers to the questions put to him was told that the supporters of the particular movement would not vote for him, and, since most pressure groups were dealing with Liberal candidates and had no hope of doing anything about the Tories, this threat usually meant that they would abstain from voting altogether.

Advocates of this strategy argued that it alone made meaningful and effective any attempt to persuade a politician to promote a particular reform. There had to be this ultimate sanction of the withholding of votes or he would not take any notice of demands. A politician is subjected to many pressures and invited to take up a great variety of questions. In this competition for his time and attention the victory was likely to go to that organisation which offered him the most attractive incentive to take up its question—

or made the most impressive threats, according to which way you looked at it. The *Alliance News* put it this way in an editorial in 1864: 'The only way to convince a candidate that you are in earnest, that you mean something, that you want him to do something, is to decline to vote for him except on condition. That, and that alone, in most cases, brings the mere politician to reason.'[15] The *Nonconformist* argued that 'at some point or other restraining force must be exercised' in relations between a politician and Nonconformists, and this was constituted by a refusal to vote for him whenever he 'transgresses the boundary which separates permissible from non-permissible opposition' to their demands.[16]

The threat to withhold one's vote meant that a pressure group fixed the terms of its relationship with a politician by refusing to vote for him unless he came up to a standard which was defined by the pressure group. If the possibility of not voting was not brought into the equation, then this meant that one was going to vote even if the candidate did not reach that standard and so he was left much freer to determine for himself how far he would go in the direction of the ideal. The alternative to abstaining was to vote for the better or best man amongst the candidates, and, once the Conservative party became the total opponent of most of the demands being made by reform movements, such a criterion was tantamount to allowing a Liberal to get away with anything from 99 per cent. down to 1 per cent. of the commitment that was asked for.

The most persuasive set of arguments in favour of abstention as an electoral strategy for a pressure group is to be found in an essay by William Canning of Manchester which won first prize in a temperance competition in 1890.[17] Canning argued that the strength of a movement resided above all in its unity, and that the greatest enemy of this was loyalty to party. Party ties set up 'claims, to ignore which involves to many a severe struggle and a great sacrifice'. Consequently, temperance men needed to have an objective which was powerful enough to enable them to withstand such claims. This was not provided by a strategy of voting for 'the best man'.

Men cannot be bound in advance to vote for a candidate who is only, by some undefined shade, more favourable than a foe. A party formed on such a basis would find the relative importance of each candidate's concessions very difficult to determine amid the excitement of a contest, and materially biassed by the influences I have named. A definite demand determined upon in the cool judgment of peaceful time would command respect and ensure unity, while the assessment of comparative excellence by a majority vote in the heat of a contest could not ensure the consent and obedience of the minority or of those who were not present at the division. Men are willing to bind themselves by their own deliberate judgment, but not by a chance vote that may be swayed by the prejudices and politics of other people. This is what in actual practice has repeatedly occurred.

The election of the 'best man' would result in an immense diversity of opinion on temperance reform among MPs, and the liquor trade would be able to exploit this to its own advantage. The only way in which unity, which alone confers strength, could be secured both among one's own followers and also among the men whom they help to elect is to insist on a definite level of commitment and to abstain from voting unless it is reached. 'This "best man" policy would level us down to the candidates' standard; one definite minimum equivalent for our votes would tend to raise the candidate to ours. . . . An agreement to withhold our votes from every candidate who will not vote for this law is the essential condition of unity and power.'

One major objection to this particular form of electoral action was that it meant asking people to disfranchise themselves, to refrain from using a right and a power which had been secured only after long and arduous struggle. As we shall see, abstention was not a popular strategy amongst Nonconformists and labour people because the right to participate in political life had long been one of their principal demands.[18] But there were some, notably Edward Miall, who did advocate abstention as a positive way of expressing political opinions, much more positive, indeed, than the mindless and bribe-controlled voting which was a feature of so many nineteenth-century elections. Miall put it this way:

The mere abstaining from giving a vote was not disfranchisement. The power exercised by refusal was surely quite as great as the power exercised by giving a vote. Indeed, in some cases he should say it was greater, and a man was disfranchising himself by obliging himself to vote between two persons where there was no difference of principles, and where he was not consulted whether those principles were approved by him or not.[19]

'There was as great a power in abstaining from voting as in voting', said a delegate to the Alliance Council Meeting in October 1885.[20]

Tactical non-voting is a very sophisticated idea. To carry it out effectively requires a considerable amount of organisation and discipline which can only be derived from feeling very strongly about the issue involved, and yet one aspect of the strategy is that people who have these feelings must be prepared if necessary to stay at home on polling day and not exercise their right to vote. As Handel Cossham once put it, the people who were usually asked to abstain in the interests of these strategies were amongst the country's 'most earnest and independent voters'.[21] Was there not something immoral, even unpatriotic, in urging such men to refrain from voting? Sir Wilfrid Lawson in a speech to the Alliance Council in October 1872 acknowledged and tried to counter the unattractiveness of abstaining as an election strategy:

I know it is a very painful and very difficult process. I know that you who are keen politicians—and most Alliance men are keen politicians, because they are intelligent men—(cheers)—I know that when a battle is raging and the speeches are being made, and the processions are marching about the town, it is very painful for you to sit quiet and seem to be doing nothing to fight the matter out. But many a regiment has done good service by lying down on the cold damp ground and doing nothing during the battle, being held in reserve; yet, they have done as good service as those who have been fighting in the bloody fray. Think of that, and use a little resolution in this matter.[22]

However, very often it was not the intention of those who organised strategies based on threatening to abstain from voting that the men who made these threats should actually have to carry them out on polling day. The threat was what mattered. It became a tactical device very similar in function to the independent candidature. The real significance of the strategy of withholding votes was usually to be found in the bargaining process prior to election day or prior even to the selection of the Liberal candidate. If the threat had to be put into effect and the electors involved did have to stay at home and not cast their votes, then more often than not this meant that the strategy had failed because the candidate had not given the policy pledge which was what it had all been about. Voters who were reluctant to disfranchise themselves, to 'give up their citizenship', were reassured that the threat to abstain would probably suffice to bring the candidate to his senses. The pledge to abstain therefore became a major weapon in the armoury of the pressure groups.

C. *The voter's pledge*

Securing pledges from voters to abstain unless certain concessions were made was a form of electoral action much favoured in the temperance movement. Teetotallers were people who had taken abstinence pledges and were therefore accustomed to the notion of the pledge to abstain from doing something as a way of demonstrating personal commitment to the cause. Indeed, there are instances of abstinence and electoral pledges being taken at the same meeting.[23]

There were two basic kinds of pledge, the positive and the negative. The positive pledge bound a voter to vote for a candidate who made a particular promise but left entirely open and at the voter's own discretion what he should do if there were no such candidate standing. The negative pledge stated that the voter would not vote for any candidate who did not make the required promise. This committed the voter much more fully. If no candidate would satisfy the demand, then the only way in which the voter could fulfil his pledge was to abstain. Negative pledges could become extremely tortuous as they depended on a sequence of negatives for their meaning. For example, a conference at Bath in August 1874 resolved that 'we will not vote for a candidate who will not promise he will not vote against the Permissive Bill'.[24] The form of the pledge was often debated in the temperance movement, not everyone by any means favouring the negative version. A positive pledge was seen as more attractive as a propaganda device, the negative as a half-way house which would enable Conservative and (after 1885) Liberal Unionist voters to record a protest against their party without being obliged to vote *for* a Liberal who was sound on temperance but obnoxious on other questions.[25] The 'Direct Veto Party' movement which developed in the late 1880s became militant advocates of the negative pledge.[26] William Canning wrote in his prize essay:

This negative form of pledge is a necessary matter of policy, because by agreeing to vote for any man who gives the required promise, we may be at the mercy of any who chooses to qualify for our support, even if he were the veriest humbug and charlatan. It enables us to detach from the political parties men who would not join our ranks with a positive pledge that might involve them absolutely in more than neutrality to a political foe. Their abstinence from voting is a material gain when the votes are counted.

A positive pledge was founded on the theory 'that if there is no candidate who gives [the required] pledge we cannot promote any Temperance Legislation by abstinence from voting, and that in such circumstances our votes should justly be influenced by other questions'. 'This', Canning argued, 'would simply deliver us into the hands of our adversaries and let them so control the parties that the candidates could by mutual consent refuse to grant our demands. It would announce to all that we would surrender should the candidate resist.'[27]

D. *The organisation of a bloc vote*

Pledge-taking and electoral canvassing were among the methods employed to identify and isolate a bloc vote. Electoral strategies usually involved complex pre-election manoeuvring in which the bargaining counter was votes. It helped to be able to tell a candidate precisely what it was that one had to offer—or to withhold. Election agents treated with contempt vague threats based on no knowledge of how many voters were actually committed to carrying them out.[28]

Some electoral strategists in the pressure groups, especially in the temperance movement, had a vision of a great bloc vote, completely detached from all other parties and issues, that could be placed at the disposal of whatever strategy seemed at any particular time to be best calculated to advance the cause.[29] The problem was how to organise this and keep it separate from and uncontaminated by all other political influences and pressures. Very strenuous efforts were made to segregate and coop up a 'temperance vote' through pledges and Electoral Associations which asked signatories and members to accept political isolation until the desired reform was secured. An entire temperance electoral way of life developed: canvassing, pledges, meetings. To some people this was not only impractical but also immoral and dangerous. Handel Cossham wrote in September 1873:

We are not only temperance reformers, we are citizens of a free country, and bound by every obligation of duty and self-interest to express our opinions through our representatives in Parliament on all questions that affect the well-being of society; but how can this be done if we only vote for Permissive Bill men. Surely, because I feel it right to abstain from intoxicating drinks I do not cease to hold opinions on other questions.[30]

One thing that had to be accepted was that it would be impossible to persuade all temperance supporters to pool their votes. Debates on the idea of a pledged and isolated temperance vote often showed that Cossham's views were widely held.[31] But that did not matter. What did matter was the existence of a bloc vote which could hold the balance at elections.[32]

The attempt to create and utilise a bloc vote was probably a tactic that was best suited to the period before the Ballot Act of 1872 when such a vote could be held in reserve on polling day—perhaps physically cooped up in a hall or church—and dangled before candidates who knew how the vote was proceeding during the day and might be very tempted by, say, early afternoon to produce a form of words that would satisfy the controllers of this vote. In the 1860s temperance voters were sometimes isolated on polling day and then marched along *en bloc* to cast their votes.[33] In the days of open voting it was much harder for a pledged voter to evade fulfilling his pledge. A bloc vote was always likely to be most effective when there was an even balance between the parties. The problem was that it was on these occasions that party feeling was likely to be at its most intense and therefore the strain on efforts to preserve detachment greatest. Making a bloc vote an effective electoral force required great discipline and very thorough organisation. Above all, there had to be a very clear understanding as to who was to make the final decision as to what should be done with the bloc vote.

E. *Playing the parties off against each other*

The most attractive position in which a pressure group could find itself was one where it had a good prospect of inducing either of the main parties to take up the reform for which it was agitating. The ideal situation was one in which the Liberal and Conservative parties competed for the pressure group's vote and by their competition accelerated the process of attaining the desired goal.

But this seldom happened. Only the Irish were believed to have fostered such a state of genuine competition between the parties, and then only for a very short time. The fallacy was the assumption that a political issue produces only that kind of response. A two-party system tends rather to polarisation of viewpoints, and, since every one of the reforms desired by pressure groups threatened a substantial vested interest which had its own political influence, it was natural that in electoral terms the parties should polarise for and against the reform. Each standpoint brought its own corps of supporters who tended to flock to the party which seemed to be *more* favourable to their own interests and so accelerated the process by which it became completely favourable.

For the disestablishers and the temperance reformers the close identification between the Conservative party and the Church of England and the drink interest from the 1870s on made any genuine balancing strategy impossible to take seriously. The dialogue had to be between the pressure group and the Liberal party, with the Tories acknowledged as implacable foes.

Voting Conservative was sometimes advocated for tactical reasons, similar to those which lay behind independent candidatures and organised abstention. At the Durham by-election in July 1898 there were two candidates, one of whom, the Conservative, was totally unsatisfactory from the Alliance's point of view, and the other of whom, the Liberal, was satisfactory to some extent but not completely. In spite of this difference E. Tennyson Smith, a prominent figure in the Alliance, urged temperance electors to vote for the Conservative. He justified this advice by saying that 'I fail to perceive any difference in principle in effecting the defeat of the Liberal candidate by passive means, by abstaining from voting for him, or by active means, by voting for his opponent. The only difference that I can see is that the latter method is far more likely to achieve the result aimed at.'[34] Alfred E. Boal of Plymouth wrote to the *Alliance News* expressing agreement with this. He opposed abstention because 'it is hardly fair to ask an elector to practically disfranchise himself after he has taken the trouble to get on the voters' list'. Voting Conservative doubled the effectiveness of abstaining as a method of putting pressure on the Liberal because it meant not only a loss of one of his votes but a gain of one for his opponent. This greatly extended the range of Liberal majorities which could be put at risk.[35]

The purpose of coercive strategies of all kinds—whether threatening to abstain or to vote for another candidate—was usually to induce a Liberal candidate to come up to the mark. The threat was that he might lose the contest as the result of these tactics. Those who made the threat therefore did so in the knowledge that, if they had to put it into effect, they might facilitate the election of his Conservative opponent and perhaps even help a Conservative government to take office. In other words, they were organising action which would advance the electoral prospects of a party far worse and far less sympathetic to their cause than the party against which that action was directed. Taking this risk was also justified on tactical grounds. The Liberals would quickly learn their lesson, perhaps as soon as they appreciated that the threat was real, and so the gain which the Conservatives would derive would be very short-lived. But the possibility of 'letting in the enemy', especially when the Conservatives became so strongly identified with the attacked interests, was a major stumbling-block to many, and so any electoral strategy which might have this result aroused considerable controversy.

3. THE DEBATE ON THE MORALITY AND EFFECTIVENESS OF ELECTORAL STRATEGIES

The techniques so far described in this chapter were coercive, that is they threatened candidates and parties who might not otherwise have decided to support a particular reform with dire electoral consequences if they failed to make this decision. The morality of such methods was often questioned and debated, especially in those movements which claimed to have as their main aim the increase of morality in public life. Did the end justify the means? In the first place, there was the immorality of tactics which might result in the acquisition of power by 'the enemy', the Tories and their allies, the vested interests. In February 1872 the *Nonconformist* published a letter of protest against the strategy of the National Education League:

I and many other Nonconformists do not believe in doing evil that good may (possibly) come. We do not believe in such a doctrine of contrarieties. We regard the Liberal party as represented by Mr. Gladstone to be squeezable, and capable of being 'educated' up to our views. The Tories are unimpressionable, our unplacable foes, and one of the first things they would do if they succeeded to power would be to make us feel that power. Reaction and repression is the Tory creed, and I am loth to believe that Nonconformists are so unpatriotic as to wish, from feelings of pique, to see their country exposed to the evils of Tory misrule even for an hour.[36]

The *Nonconformist* in an editorial in July 1873 attacked the idea of 'ruling by Tory votes' and said that 'those who call in their opponents to coerce their friends may well be left to the tender mercies of those opponents in the hour of need'.[37]

Secondly, some regarded as immoral the manipulation of small minorities to force or tempt politicians to give a pledge.[38]

Thirdly, there was the basic question of the morality of forcing a man to change his opinions by the employment of techniques of electoral intimidation. The stand which one took on this depended very much on how one viewed 'the politician', his psychology, and his place in society and in the constitution. At one extreme were those who saw the MP as a special kind of person, 'corrupted' by the life which he led at Westminster.[39] Nonconformists noted what happened to their own men when they entered the House of Commons. Too many of them seemed to grow suspiciously ready to uphold the privileges of the Church of England. An MP simply could not be trusted. W. S. Caine told the Alliance Council meeting in October 1892: 'It is an evil place, is the House of Commons. (Hear, hear.) It is an evil place.'[40] The argument was often advanced that a politician's main motivation was his greed for power. He would do anything to gain and keep it, and a pressure group not only should exploit this characteristic of his but had to in order to communicate meaningfully with him. The Rev. Charles Stovel declared at the Liberation Society's conference in May 1871: 'I expect, therefore, always that the man who holds the seat of power and profit, and whatever emolument or honour may tie him to it, will cling to it, and in proportion as he clings to it he will be ready to concede something to those who may wish to shift him. . . .'[41] Those who held this view argued that the politician responded only to brutal tactics that threatened him with loss of, or inability to gain, power.[42] The only thing that he respected, the only language that he understood, was votes. This was not necessarily something to be deplored. Votes were his stock in trade. If he neglected them, he ceased to be effective as a politician, ceased indeed to be a true representative of the people. Therefore, if a movement wished to gain his adherence to its cause, it had to offer the only price that he could afford to ask for it—votes. The politician was not like ordinary men and certainly was very unlike the enthusiasts for reforms. He took up questions for 'political reasons'. This impression of a politician's motivation may be illustrated by the following item which appeared in *The Liberator* in January 1874:

A Hint to Nonconformist Electors.—Lately, a Liberal member was privately told that, unless he came out for disestablishment at the next election, he would not have the support of Nonconformists, who were the backbone of the Liberal party. His reply was 'Well: if I thought they meant it it would determine my course.'[43]

It was therefore misguided to rule out as 'immoral' the application of methods of electoral coercion to a politician. He was a virtual machine, an agency for the transmission of electoral pressures, and his own personal convictions had nothing to do with the matter. Dr. J. Murray McCulloch said in 1875 that 'the ruck of them [MPs] are influenced by votes and by votes alone, and the knowledge that there was a phalanx of pledged and inflexible temperance voters outnumbering the liquor traffic votes in their constituencies, would convince them of the excellence of the Permissive Bill with marvellous rapidity!'[44]

An additional reason that was sometimes given to explain why most politicians could only be dealt with from outside by a coercive electoral strategy was their remoteness, in social class and in religion, from the world of the pressure groups. The relationship was an external one in so much else that it could not help but be so in electoral matters as well. The *Nonconformist* in an editorial in December 1863 argued that, 'as the representative class consists, for the most part, of men whose birth, education, traditions, and sympathies attach them to the Church as by law established, we have the best reason for expecting that, relieved from all pressure, they will seldom spontaneously expose themselves to the reproach of treating with indifference the privileges of the Church to which they belong'.[45]

Others, however, queried both the wisdom and the morality of trying to coerce politicians by electoral pressure. They doubted whether the psychological assumptions on which this coercion was based were altogether correct. For instance, was it so certain that a politician's response to intimidation would be to retreat and yield? Some argued that the reverse might well prove to be the case, especially as a politician cannot afford to be seen to give way to threats lest he thereby creates a precedent. Another difficulty that coercive tactics were bound to lead to was insincerity. They seemed just the way to attract to the support of one's cause the worst kind of politician, the man who would sell his soul and pledge himself to anything just in order to get votes.[46] Might not the best kind of politician, the man most worthy of admiration by movements professing to wish to promote morality, be the man who would refuse to yield to such pressure and such temptation but would hold out until he himself was convinced?[47]

The alternative, non-coercive philosophy was that supporters of a cause were treated generously by a politician if they adopted a positive attitude towards him and, instead of threatening and intimidating him, acted in such a way as to make him grateful to them. This was a totally different interpretation of the politician's psychology. It was argued by advocates of it that it was better to help a politician who showed even a glimmer of sympathy for one's cause in the hope that gratitude and a recognition of what the adherents to it could do positively on his behalf would move him further in one's direction. Loyal service earns gratitude, coercion breeds resentment. Politicians should be thanked for whatever they do for a cause and thus encouraged to go further, not cursed and condemned for failing to go every inch of the way.[48] A politician who is helped feels under an obligation to give a reward. The outstanding exponent of this philosophy in the Alliance was Thomas Whittaker.

They knew the adage, [he said in 1873] 'He who would have friends must show himself friendly'; and from his experience he had this fact to give, that by making himself useful politically to gentlemen who had sought his help as candidates, when they were not quite friendly to our movement, that service had laid them under obligations and had ultimately made them think one good turn deserved another, and they had become friends.[49]

The advocates of the non-coercive approach stressed the value of fostering an atmosphere of mutual respect and trust between a politician and those who desired his support. This kind of bond was more durable and worked far better in the long run. Whittaker wanted temperance people to work to change the atmosphere surrounding a politician so that he would find it natural to be in sympathy with the movement.[50] In March 1878 a correspondent in the *Nonconformist* expressed thus the alternative to electoral coercion: 'surely reason and conscience in a candidate, and character in the voter, count for something. Candidates can be moved by the spectacle of men so true to their convictions that even neglect and unfair treatment will not drive them from their duty.'[51] George Howell much preferred to try to 'impress and move' politicians than to put electoral pressure on them. The criterion which should be applied was 'the whole tone of a man's character and life' and not his readiness to give pledges.[52] The placing of relations on a coercionist basis seemed to some to be dishonourable and demeaning to all concerned. One of H. J. Wilson's correspondents wrote to him in 1873 concerning the temperance opinions of Joseph Chamberlain, then being promoted as a candidate for Sheffield: 'I don't like the idea of questioning & pledging, especially the latter. If the statement [about the Permissive Bill] came freely from a gent[leman] in Mr. C's. position, it would accord more with my idea of what is manly & respectful on both sides.'[53]

Coercive methods were regarded as dangerous in that they created a very fragile bond between a politician and the movement which they had been used to induce him to support.[54] It was one that was all the more fragile because the way in which it was imposed was calculated to cause resentment. If someone is coerced or blackmailed into taking up a cause, he has not undergone a genuine conversion of mind and heart and so he is not likely to prove a very effective or convincing spokesman and worker for it. Indeed, he is likely to be looking for the earliest opportunity to wriggle out of the commitment. Electoral coercion involved the risk of delivering a cause into the hands of dishonest and unscrupulous men who would tarnish it and be as ready to betray it as they were to be insincere in the first place.

Edward Miall was one who believed in the vulnerability of advances made solely by coercive electoral methods. When in 1863 he urged the Liberation Society to adopt a new kind of strategy, he pointed out that a recent decline in the Society's 'prestige' had suddenly exposed the 'impatience and resentment' which MPs felt at the 'moral coercion' to which the Society had subjected them in the past. 'A reaction of feeling against what came to be looked upon as a dictatorial power sprang up. Measures tending, however slightly, towards religious equality, were opposed, not on their merits, but on account of our supposed connection with or interest in them. . . .'[55]

Another reason frequently given for opposing strategies that were based on electoral coercion or manipulation was that they might result in forcing on a question too rapidly for its own ultimate good. The danger was of getting a measure enacted by Parliament before public opinion was ready to accept it, simply because a majority had been manufactured by such methods. Then there might be a violent reaction from the public when the government attempted to enforce the new law, and the cause would be set back disastrously. There was often in reform movements a conflict between the advocates of electoral tactics and those who preferred a concentration on educating public opinion. The former would argue that the public was on their side and that electoral pressure was no more than the most natural and efficacious way of making politicians aware of this. The latter maintained that politicians are always ready to follow trends in public opinion and could be relied upon to do so whenever they saw a movement gaining popular support without any need to coerce them.

Why did negative, coercive tactics have so strong an appeal in spite of the plausibility of the arguments against them? Enthusiasts who were convinced that what they were fighting was a great social evil were not likely to think that it was any less an evil because they did not have the majority of the public on their side. Part of their case was often that the public itself was in need of being rescued from that evil. Consequently, they were not very worried about methods that brought nearer the day when some legislative action might be taken to suppress it. Many of them were opposed, in any case, to allowing considerations of expediency to influence their action. Reason and logic might point one way, but emotion suggested rather the wrongness of supporting any politician who refused to recognise the evil and join in the crusade against it.

CHAPTER IV

Pressure Groups and Liberal Politics

The ostensible purpose of electoral strategies that were mounted by pressure groups was to promote the interests of the particular reform which they advocated. However, some had an additional and deeper purpose which was to influence Liberal politics in general. This was Edward Miall's aim in the 1860s. He wished to utilise the electoral agency and power of the Liberation Society in order to revitalise the Liberal party by creating a new relationship between it and its rank-and-file supporters in the country.[1] Since these were assumed to include very large numbers of Nonconformists, a far greater interest on the part of the Liberal party in questions of specific interest to them could be expected to emerge naturally from such a transformation. Chamberlain and his Radical associates took a similar view of the electoral activities of the National Education League. These were to force not merely a reconsideration of the Liberal leaders' education policies but also a fundamental re-organisation of Liberal politics that would give Radicalism a greatly enhanced influence.[2]

Some movements, or factions, or individuals within movements, saw themselves as having an essentially internal and organic relationship to the Liberal party and sought to define and develop electoral strategies which were appropriate to such a relationship and in which the employment of electoral methods to promote the cause would be controlled by a basic recognition that only the Liberal party could in the end enact the desired reform. One such strategy was to concentrate on convincing the Liberals that they would gain electoral advantage from taking up the question and giving it prominence in their programme.[3]

If a movement had to rely on the Liberals for the accomplishment of its objective and had no other party to which it could turn, the logical strategy seemed to be for it to integrate itself as far as possible into the machinery of the Liberal party and to work from within to procure an influence over its policy. The advocates of 'working within the Liberal party' were strong in most movements and in some, like the Reform League and the Liberation Society, gained the upper hand. It was the strategy which Nonconformists normally preferred. It consisted principally of encouraging supporters to join the Liberal Associations in the constituencies and take an active part in their work, particularly the selection of candidates. In July 1873 the *Nonconformist* published an editorial condemning the National Education League's electoral policy and defining an alternative. This was that Nonconformists should seek an

embodiment of their own principles in the candidate of the Liberal party in proportion to their strength. They must, in fact, insist on having the best candidate they can get, and having got him must give him undivided support. It is in the domestic arrangements of the party in the previous selection of the candidates that their power can be exerted to most effect; and if it is wisely used in these preliminary negotiations a vast step may be made in securing representation in Parliament, and a strong guiding influence be brought to bear on the Liberal leaders without fatally dividing the party or driving it from power.[4]

This policy had a positive, non-disruptive emphasis and was indeed intended as a contrast to coercionist 'external' strategies. But it could be associated with electoral threats. For instance, the Liberation Society's strategy of the 1860s, as formulated by Miall, was fundamentally about the acquisition of influence over the selection of Liberal candidates but did involve the threat of abstention if the Liberals did not permit the Nonconformists to have that influence where they seemed fairly entitled to it. The subsequent development of representative Liberal Associations, where membership was open to as many individuals as cared to join, seemed to remove the need for any such threats. If the candidate was then not to the liking of the supporters of a movement, this could be construed as the fault of the movement itself, either because its adherents had not taken the trouble to join the Association and participate in its work or because they really were in a minority and so could not expect to have their question taken up by the candidate.

It could be and was argued that action at the candidate-selection stage was far preferable to applying pressure only after the candidate had been chosen. The difference lay in the two types of contest. More often than not in an election contest itself a Liberal candidate, in order to secure enough votes to get elected, had to appeal to un-committed voters and to people who might be inclining to vote Conservative or had done so in the past. The effect of this electoral necessity might be to offset or even outweigh any pressure that a reform movement could bring to bear at that stage. But these non-Liberal voters were not participants in the 'primary' election. Then the would-be candidate was competing with other Liberals to prove that he was more 'liberal' than they were and was naturally anxious to conciliate and win the support of the sections within the party. In addition, it was obvious that, if threats had to be resorted to, they would cause much less friction and unpleasantness in an internal poll than if subsequently directed against a Liberal who was fighting a Tory.[5] Electoral coercion of a Liberal candidate was seldom sup-ported by all the adherents to a movement, for many preferred at that stage to put first their loyalty to the party, especially when the opponent was strongly hostile not only to the party but to the move-ment itself. From many points of view, therefore, it made very good sense for a reform movement to concentrate on influencing the selection of Liberal candidates.

However, the strategy of working from within had its critics who felt that the disadvantages were considerably greater than the benefits. If a group limited itself to being a section within the Liberal party, it thereby deprived itself of political leverage and indepen-dence that were perhaps essential to real effectiveness. It alienated 'independent' and non-Liberal voters who were considered in the temperance movement at least to be very important. Once a move-ment became the mere appendage of a party, it could safely be ignored. Its adherents were drawn into the world of Liberal politics and became accustomed to voting Liberal, and so, the critics argued, their votes would prove to be less and less easily withdrawable should the Liberal attitude to the particular reform demand begin to show a weakening of commitment and concern.

There was, of course, a fundamental difference between belonging to a movement which was fighting for a cause and supporting a party which professed sympathy for that cause. The difference was that the movement was devoted to that cause alone, whereas the party and its candidates had other interests as well and might support the cause but give it a low priority as compared to some of these. Conflict arose when a movement called for support for candi-

dates because they supported the reform which it advocated. In doing this it was asking its adherents to be indifferent to all the other political attitudes held, and causes supported, by these candidates. This imposed a very considerable strain on them, especially when party feeling was running high on other issues, for example Irish Home Rule in the period after 1885. It was naïve in the extreme to imagine that there was a 'temperance vote' which could be preserved completely uncontaminated by the uses to which it was put. Yet the Alliance claimed that there were Conservatives who responded election after election to appeals to vote for men who were Radicals but sound on the temperance question. One wonders in what sense they could still be regarded as Conservatives after having done this for four or five successive general elections. The evidence is of a steady erosion of the Tory temperance vote but of the maintenance of the concept of it by the Alliance because of the usefulness of its alleged existence as a bargaining counter in dealings with the Liberal party. The Conservative voter who was prepared to cross the party lines and vote Liberal if the Liberals were sounder on temperance was a bait perpetually dangled before the Liberal party.[6]

Opponents of working from within the party believed that it was a suicidal strategy because it gave the supporters of a cause a new loyalty which would subvert that which they felt to the cause. Another contaminating consequence of close identification with one party which became evident as time went on was that a cause acquired for itself the enemies of all the other policies which that party advocated. This in its turn weakened a movement by introducing internal divisions. Thus the Alliance was torn by strife between opponents and supporters of Home Rule because it normally supported Gladstonian candidates, even although the reason for its doing so was supposed to be solely the fact that they alone endorsed the Local Option.[7]

There was one fundamental weakness in the integrationists' strategy which only gradually became apparent. The strategy was to infiltrate and influence local Liberal Associations, gain a control over the choice of Liberal candidates, and persuade them to pledge themselves to the support of the desired reform. As Brian Harrison has noted, the Alliance concentrated its efforts on candidates and private Members of Parliament.[8] The proudest boast of a pressure group was usually its tally of MPs returned at each general election who were committed to its cause by pledges made during the campaign. What was only slowly appreciated was that this 'success' was far from representing a completion of the work that needed to be done to 'convert' the Liberal party. Perhaps too late the disestablishers and the prohibitionists became aware that beyond the political plateau to which they had so triumphantly ascended, that of the convictions and commitments of ordinary MPs, lay a further and much more difficult barrier, namely the power of the party leaders, the control which they could exercise over the progress of a question. This was a power above all to determine the ordering of priorities for legislative attention and to find excuses that could almost indefinitely delay the commencement of any serious effort to enact a reform.[9] Pressure groups would find that they had 'converted' the great majority of Liberal MPs and yet were still not making any legislative progress. This was a deadlock which they were never able to find a way of breaking—although in 1884-5 thought was given by some Alliance people to a new form of electoral strategy for this purpose.[10]

Various reasons may be suggested for this fatal flaw in the pressure groups' political calculations. One is that it reflects the great social —and ecclesiastical—gulf between the faddists and the Liberal leaders. As R. W. Dale pointed out on one occasion, 'they did not belong to that class which had the most intimate personal relations with the chiefs of the Liberal party, who were therefore easily misled with regard to their position and policy'.[11] These were not men whose mental outlook or way of life the enthusiasts could begin to understand and so they had no idea of how to set about influencing them or even of the need to do so.[12] The men whom they did feel at home with were the members of local Liberal Associations and the aspiring middle-class and working-class candidates. Consequently it was on them that they focused their efforts. Secondly, there was the confusion as to what 'the Liberal party' really was or might become.[13] Edward Miall and other Radicals and Nonconformists felt that they were participating in the emergence of a new kind of party which would be a popular and democratic alternative to the dominance of the old ruling class and to the executive-oriented parliamentary system. The National Education Leaguers strongly believed that theirs was the revolt which would bring the parliamentary leadership under the control of the rank and file in the country.[14] Thirdly, there was the dilemma that a really ruthless strategy designed to force the Liberal leaders to take immediate action on a question would have had to involve the electoral coercion of Liberal candidates and MPs who supported those leaders but also supported the desired reform. This would have been almost impossible to make effective, given the apparent absurdity of opposing one's own sympathisers and the very close links which one's adherents would have developed with many of the Liberal Associations which had been 'advanced' enough to nominate such candidates.

There was a constant debate in the reform movements between the advocates of these two types of relationship with the Liberal party, between those who believed that getting inside it and becoming an organic part of it constituted the only way of ensuring that it would become genuinely committed to a reform and those who insisted that a movement had to maintain its independence and adopt an essentially external relationship to the party.[15] The existence of this debate was in itself sometimes a weakening factor. For instance, one finds some local temperance 'parties' being torn apart by quarrels between the two factions. Some people advocated independence precisely for this reason, that it seemed the only way to avoid the debilitating quarrels that so often followed any move towards closer relations with the Liberal party.

One result of this divergence of opinion was a tendency towards inconsistency on the part of the reform movements. They would swing from one strategy to the other and so put considerable strain on the tolerance of their Liberal 'allies'. The reason for this was an imperfect acceptance of the fact, that in return for the numerous benefits to be derived from involvement in Liberal organisation at the local level, there was a certain price that had to be paid. This was that they must be prepared to abide by the rules of the Liberal Associations, especially the principle of acquiescence in decision by the majority. Acceptance of this principle meant that supporters of a particular reform had to be prepared to be 'loyal' to the party in a situation in which the majority had decided in favour of a candidate whose attitude to that reform was not regarded by them as satisfactory. The reward for such loyalty was the prospect that, if the majority endorsed the candidature of a man who supported the reform, he would then be given the support of a united Liberal party, including that of some Liberals who personally felt no enthusiasm for this item in his programme. Under Miall's guidance, the Liberation Society accepted the basic principle of democratic Liberal organisation. The claims which Nonconformists were to regard themselves as entitled to make on their local Liberal parties were to be in proportion to their actual strength on the register and within the local party membership.

The trouble came with those people who wanted to have it both ways, that is to conduct their own independent electoral strategy after having failed, as a minority section, to control the selection of the Liberal candidate. Miall would tolerate such behaviour only in one situation—when the Liberal selection procedure had been unfair and undemocratic. Temperance people were sometimes sharply divided over what to do when ballots to select Liberal candidates failed to produce winners who were acceptable to them. At Bath in 1873 Handel Cossham refused to stand as an independent temperance candidate after failing to win the ballot for the Liberal nomination and was highly indignant when Charles Thompson was then put up as such a candidate by a section of the local temperance party. Cossham told the Alliance Council meeting in October 1875 that they must accept the principle of majority rule:

when he acted with a political party he must act with common sense and go with that party, otherwise he could not get from them that which he wanted to get. ('Principle.') Yes, he was talking of principle, and of the only way men could carry out principle. . . . We could not accomplish our end without combining to do it.[16]

Most of the Alliance leaders who intervened in constituencies in connection with Liberal nominations were scrupulous about obeying the Liberals' rules.[17] It was local enthusiasts who were more inclined first of all to get drawn into the affairs of Liberal Associations and then to rebel if they failed to get their own way. A correspondent of the *Nonconformist*, writing in August 1878, described what had happened in one constituency—Dudley. Here the Liberal member was not a supporter of the Permissive Bill and was suspected by some of being 'too amenable to publican influence'. The teetotallers had abstained from voting in 1874 and at a subsequent by-election, when the member had been unseated on petition but had been eligible to stand again, they had voted for the Tory candidate who had given them some sort of promise on the Permissive Bill. Then in 1877 a Liberal Association was founded in Dudley, and the teetotallers joined it, some of their leaders attaining positions of influence.

The association is modelled to that of Birmingham, and the rule is, that the general committee selects the candidate. Notwithstanding their having given their assent to this rule by joining the association, several have declared that they will not support the sitting member should he be the selected candidate; and one, at least, has publicly announced that he will support a man of any politics, provided he will promise to vote for the Permissive Bill. Here, then, we have a section of a constituency numbering about 300 votes out of 15,000, and forming, perhaps, a thirtieth part of the Liberal party in the borough, coolly asking the Liberals to accept their policy, an acceptance which would assuredly end in seating a Tory. And this is not all. They have hawked a declaration about the borough asking people to pledge themselves not to vote for any candidate who will not support Sir Wilfrid Lawson's measure. From what I can hear they have obtained a number of signatures which, supposing all who have signed abide by their pledge, is just sufficient to secure the defeat of the Liberal candidate.[18]

Why was it that, in spite of all these difficulties and obstacles in the path of its smooth operation, the philosophy of an integrated and internal relationship to the Liberal party prevailed, in the sense that by the last two decades of the century most Radical pressure-group activity had ceased to have any genuinely independent political sphere of its own and was being carried on within the structure of Liberal party politics? Part of the reason is to be found in the way in which the Liberal party itself responded to the challenge of sectionalism. This is discussed elsewhere in this book.[19] But several reasons for the triumph of integrationism are suggested by studying the question from the point of view of the sectionalists and faddists.

In the first place, many of the supporters of particular reforms did not belong to any monolithic bloc vote attached to one reform alone, as the leaders of pressure groups and some extreme enthusiasts often wrongly assumed, but were supporters of a wide range of such causes. They needed help in controlling and ordering the variety of sometimes conflicting political pressures to which they were as a result subjected, and such relief they could find only beneath the umbrella of a 'representative' Liberal Association. Secondly, there was the fact that in some places there was a vacuum in Liberal politics which the enthusiasts for reform causes were able to fill, thus in effect themselves becoming the Liberal party.

Thirdly and undoubtedly extremely important, there was the influence of Nonconformity which was strongly in favour of an integrated involvement in the affairs of one of the country's two major political parties.[20] Nonconformists did not wish to place themselves in political isolation and thus in effect voluntarily restore their centuries-old exclusion from public life. Their main desire was to show that they could be and were good citizens, prepared to co-operate with others and to enjoy that recognition of status which such 'partnership'—as Miall described it—would confer.[21] Miall's strategy of the 1860s was aimed at the use of electoral influence to secure a political acknowledgement of the status of Dissent within the community and a fairer definition of the 'partnership' within the Liberal party. Nonconformists took great pride in being described as the 'backbone' of the Liberal party and were therefore not disposed to be sympathetic to strategies which were based on the notion of a completely external relationship to it.

Integration into Liberal politics was also facilitated by the development of polarisation as the Tories became the party of the interests which were under attack, the Church of England and the liquor industry. Within the pressure groups there were always those who were anxious to force on such a polarisation and arrive at a situation in which the parties were ranged for and against their question. Better, they argued, to have one party unequivocally for the cause than to have neither. Many temperance people rejoiced at the coming of an identification of the Tories with the drink interest because of the likely effect of this on the Liberals. An Alliance agent said in March 1874:

They had seen one of the great political parties taking the publican under their wing, and the lesson to be derived from this fact was just this, that the other party must fight the publicans. There was no escape from this alternative. If the Tories allied themselves with the brewers and the publicans, as had been the case throughout the country at the recent contests, the Liberals, whether teetotalers or not, must combine to fight publicans and brewers; there was no help for it. . . . [22]

The practical political realities were that the reforms for which these movements were pressing could only be effected by Act of Parliament. The objective of any strategy had therefore to be to persuade one of the parties which had a chance of forming a majority in Parliament to take up the reform. It was natural for many to regard the commitment of the Liberals to their cause as a triumphal culmination to their efforts. Their tactics had worked.

To some, however, this development inaugurated a new era of dependence on one party and represented a fatal loss of flexibility and freedom. There was rejoicing at the 'capture' of the Liberal party by the movement. Only gradually was it realised that the movement could just as plausibly now be depicted as the prisoner of the Liberals.[23] The 'conversion' of one party was accompanied or preceded by the identification of the other with the enemy. This diminished considerably the political leverage which the pressure groups could exert. It meant that their adherents were much less

likely to wish to co-operate in any electoral action, including abstention from voting, that might have the effect of 'letting the Tories in'.
The Liberals discovered as time passed that they could get away
with weaker pledges and still effectively invoke the nature of the
Conservative enemy as a check on potential desertion. Therefore
the Liberal party acquired the upper hand in the relationship.

But was there any realistic alternative as far as the pressure groups
were concerned? The 'realists' repeatedly attacked those who
seemed to want to cling to an illusion of independence. They should
recognise who their only friends were and support them even if they
were not prepared to go quite as far as they wished. Nobody else
who was in a position to do anything effective for them was willing
to go any distance with them at all. And, while one tried to keep up
a pretence of independence, real power, the power that could come
only from influence over the Liberal party, went to one's competi-
tors, the groups which did work wholeheartedly within that party.[24]

The integration of the faddists into Liberal party politics was
greatly facilitated by the concern which many Liberals themselves
felt about gaining some control over them and minimising their
disruptiveness. During the 1870s in particular Liberal Associations
tried to come to terms with the pressure groups and to integrate
them into local Liberal politics. Indeed, the establishment of discipline in local Liberalism was quite often one of the main reasons
why these Associations were founded in the first place.

Integration was carried out in two principal ways. First was the
inclusion of the reform which the pressure group advocated in the
programme of the Association. Second was the attempt to ensure
beforehand that a candidate when finally decided on would be
someone who would not offend any of the major pressure groups and
thus cause electoral trouble which might lose the Liberals the seat.
Quite often the local temperance 'party', in particular, would be
consulted in advance as to the acceptability of a proposed candidate
or even invited to nominate someone whom they would be prepared
to recommend to their supporters. Local people would then turn to
the Alliance's headquarters for a suggestion as to a possible candidate
who would have an appeal both to Liberals in general and to
temperance enthusiasts in particular.

In the majority of cases some kind of 'concordat' or arrangement
in which there was on both sides a readiness to compromise and not
press extreme demands was possible. Many temperance people were

pleased to be relieved of the need to make a choice between loyalties to the Liberal party and the prohibitionist cause, especially if they had taken a pledge to uphold the latter. For their part, many Liberal candidates and organisers felt that, as Anglican and 'drink-traffic' support for the Conservative grew, they would be well advised to make sure of having on their side the full countervailing strength of the local Nonconformists and teetotallers. As A. J. Mundella once put it, 'one thing is certain, the publicans will not forgive us, and we may as well fill our sails with the enthusiasm of the other side'.[25]

Enthusiasm and willingness to work hard for the cause were great assets which the faddists could offer to the Liberals. Once a candidate had been selected of whom it approved, it was important for a pressure group to demonstrate very clearly that the adoption of somebody who was identified with their cause made a great deal of difference to a party's electoral fortunes. Temperance people in particular therefore often flung themselves into electioneering on behalf of Liberal candidates.[26]

In a minority of cases there was the problem of the importunate pressure group. The spirit of give and take required that demands should not be taken to the point where a section would be appearing to dictate to the party and to force it to yield. This could create an embarrassing precedent. If a group were to be listened to and given the right to an influence over candidates and policy, then it must come into and work within the party's structure and respect its rules. It must not give the appearance of having an external relationship to the party. An example of the 'correct' way of handling a pressure group's demands is the response of the Central Hackney Liberal and Radical Association to a letter which it received in April 1886 from the secretary of the Central Hackney Local Option Union advising it that no candidate would be acceptable to the Union unless he promised to vote for the Direct Veto. A meeting was held to consider what reply to make.[27] The first speaker argued that such questions could be dealt with only if 'brought before them in an ordinary way'. Therefore they should simply acknowledge the letter and inform its writer 'that the members of the Local Option Union were eligible to become members of the association and might thus materially attain the object they had in view'. The Chairman agreed that the basic principle was that only members of the Liberal Association were entitled to raise the matter. A. F. Robbins suggested that they tell the Local Option Union that 'a candidate had been chosen, that certain leading members of the general committee were also members of the union, and that they had resolved to ask Major Hume [the candidate] to meet them and discuss with them Liberal questions generally. That would be a favourable opportunity for such as were Local Optionists to attend and put such questions as they desired.' Another speaker, J. R. Jones, 'questioned the propriety of giving the teetotalers more favour than any other interest that might demand to question the candidate. There were at least a dozen members of the committee who were teetotalers. If they allowed the teetotalers to come, the representatives of all the churches and chapels would want to have their deputations.' The meeting finally decided that the Local Option Union should be informed 'that they would have an opportunity of asking questions at the forthcoming conference; and if they wished further to influence the association on their particular subject, they could become members, and at the next election of the general committee they could get a larger representation thereon'. That the Central Hackney Liberals had to proceed with great caution and 'propriety' in their handling of the local 'interests' is indicated by two subsequent reports, first that Major Hume had retired from the candidature because of opposition to him by Nonconformists on the question of disestablishment, and, secondly, that he had resumed it and had been promised support by a deputation from the Alliance.[28]

How did the Liberal candidates themselves cope with the pressure to give pledges? Many gave them very readily, no doubt often reminding themselves that they and their leaders retained an enormous amount of discretion as to when these actually would have to be given legislative effect. W. S. Allen, MP for Newcastle-under Lyme, remarked in 1877 on 'the state of feeling with a great many candidates at the time of a general election—they are in such an amiable frame of mind that they feel very kindly disposed to all the electors, and are quite ready to pledge themselves as far as they conscientiously can'.[29] Some gave pledges and then subsequently tried to devise all sorts of ingenious excuses for evading them,[30] but candidates learned in time to rely on the party leaders to provide these for them. MPs, harassed to fulfil the pledges so readily handed out at elections, were very much in need of the type of argument so often employed by Gladstone and other Liberal leaders in support of their major policies, that these were of overriding importance because they represented the clearing away of an obstruction that prevented anything being done about any other reform question.[31]

There were some Liberal politicians who refused to give any pledges on principle. Notable examples are Edward Baines, William Rathbone, J. J. Colman, and W. E. Forster.[32] A. J. Mundella wrote in 1874 after an unhappy experience with the Irish voters: 'I am resolved that no section of my constituents shall ever squeeze me again. I mean to act perfectly square and independent and follow out my own convictions.'[33] Leaders of the reform movements who themselves moved into Liberal politics and became MPs often turned against pledges. In October 1885 W. S. Caine told the Alliance Council of his unwillingness to

give pledges with regard to my conduct in the House of Commons. I will give no pledges to any constituency on this subject. (Hear, hear.) . . . I will not, by pinning myself to one particular application of any principle, run the risk of not getting some valuable instalment which I might otherwise secure. (Cheers.) Therefore, I once more urge upon you not to pledge your candidates too much to details and methods. . . .[34]

George Howell, one of the most experienced of all pressure-group electoral organisers, regarded pledges exacted from candidates as largely valueless and resisted having to give them himself.[35]

As the applause for Caine's remarks indicates, there was some sympathy even within the Alliance for resistance to pledges by candidates. They became an increasingly controversial issue within the reform movements, especially as a closer *rapport* developed with candidates and it seemed unnatural to display distrust of one's own people in this way. The insincerity and opportunism that were often involved in candidates' pledges worried high-minded advocates of moral reform. Was it not more fitting that a man should be allowed to be true to himself and take up a position only when he was really persuaded that it was right?[36] One Liberationist said that 'he did not care for such [candidates] as only evinced a teachable disposition on the eve of an election'.[37] It was sometimes preferred that a candidate should withdraw rather than change his opinions just because he was subjected to electoral pressure. 'Such rapid conversions have taken place,' commented the *Nonconformist* on one occasion when a candidate did withdraw, 'but not in men who afterwards do much service, or who are much to be trusted. Pledges exacted from unwilling persons are seldom very honourably fulfilled. . . .'[38] In January 1871 H. S. Winterbotham, MP for Stroud, made a most moving plea not to be coerced by electoral pressure into changing his position on disestablishment after having previously told his

constituents that he did not agree with Miall's proposal for bringing
it about:

> If I changed now, and supported Mr. Miall, I *might* be charged with mis-
> leading my constituents. Yet, if I had changed my opinion, I would not
> hesitate to say so. I will never sacrifice to consistency what I know to be
> true.
> I value my seat for Stroud very much, but I would not consent to occupy
> it for an hour unless I might follow the dictates of my conscience freely.
> You do not know how hard it is for a young man, without rank or fortune,
> to be true to his convictions in the House of Commons. It is so much
> pleasanter and easier to echo a popular opinion to please one's constituents,
> or to refrain from opposing a measure to please a Minister, that it needs
> constant watchfulness, and even obstinacy, to do what one knows to be
> right. I am too inexperienced a man to put any opinion on the shelf. I am
> open to conviction, but not with a pistol at my head.[39]

There was a growing awareness among pressure-group leaders
that MPs who were pledged as the result of electoral blackmail were
of little real value to a cause, especially in the House of Commons
where far more work was needed to advance a question than just
recording an annual vote in favour of a disestablishment or local
option resolution. Such MPs often did not really understand the
question and so were not much use at the committee stage of a Bill
for instance. Their commitment was likely to be enforced and shallow
and affected by feelings of resentment. In April 1879 Henry Richard
urged the Council of the Liberation Society to try to get 'a considerable addition to the small band of earnest Nonconformists in
the House of Commons'. 'You cannot have any adequate conception,' he said, 'of the difficulty that those who espouse and advocate
your cause in the House of Commons have to contend with.' Out-
siders saw only the pledged MPs who voted 'right' on divisions, but
many of these in fact 'do so grudgingly and reluctantly, growling
and grumbling at us all the time'.[40] As F. J. Thompson of Bridg-
water put it, such men 'are not worth much in a time of trial'.[41]

The Liberals detested pledges. Many reformers came to feel that
they were not worth the effort and friction often involved. Gradually
they fall into disuse and are replaced by much more flexible and
subtle methods. The party puts the various reform proposals in a
very generalised form into its programmes, such as those of the
N.L.F., and then candidates can say that they adhere to the party
programme and are absolved from the need to give any specific
pledge unless they wish to put part of it 'in italics'.[42] As for the
pressure groups, they find that they do much better if they send

deputations to candidates and have lengthy interviews at the end of
which they can make recommendations based on their impression
of the candidates' state of mind. This allows for much negotiating
over the nuances of different forms of words and gives candidates
and pressure groups that room to breathe and to be flexible to
which both Caine and Winterbotham were, from their different
points of view, referring.

For Liberal politicians one of the most obvious and disturbing
facts about the reform organisations was their competition with one
another for priority of legislative attention. But this vision of the
world of reform politics as one in which there were many different
reform pressures and interests which needed to be kept in some kind
of balance and harmonious interrelationship was utterly alien to the
outlook of many of the people who were actually involved in these
movements. They were enthusiasts who were convinced of the
supreme importance of their own particular cause and were prepared
to devote their time and energies to achieving its triumph. For them
it was sometimes as though no other politics existed. This is seen, for
example, in the habit of claiming credit for an MP's election simply
because he happened to have included a particular question—
amongst many others—in his platform.

This appearance of complete self-containment is, however, deceptive. There was often resentment when other reform movements
tried to secure priority for their questions. The Alliance frequently
clashed with the Nonconformist organisations, especially the
Liberation Society, at times when its disruptive electoral tactics
threatened to obstruct the return to power of a Liberal government
pledged to act in ways highly favourable to Nonconformist interests
or points of view.[43] In particular, in the 1890s, after the Liberals'
commitment to the Newcastle programme, the rivalry became quite
intense.

The most common way of justifying priority for a question was to
claim that there was a difference between it and all other questions
which required or entitled it to first place. For example, an organisation would say that the accomplishment of the reform which it
advocated was an essential preliminary to the passage of all other
reforms. When J. A. Picton addressed Liberal Clubs on 'Disestablishment considered as a question of practical politics', he would
review all the leading items in the Liberal programme, 'showing
how impossible of attainment many of them were unless preceded by

Disestablishment'.[44] Temperance people made much of the need to procure a sober population before any other reform could be expected to operate as hoped. E. Jacobs wrote in June 1868: 'We cannot understand how the disendowment of the Irish Church can help the Permissive Bill, but we do understand how the settlement of the liquor traffic question would help to secure sober elections, and we clearly see that the masses of the people would then become so powerful as to be able to get *all* that they ought to have.'[45] Some members of the Alliance were very annoyed when the National Education League put its cause above that of temperance on the grounds that education would sweep drunkenness 'off the face of the earth'. They retorted that it was well known that teetotallers always educated their children.[46] William Hoyle argued that temperance reform 'will ensure the solution of most of the other social questions of the day, and that, without its solution, these other reforms can never be realised, and therefore, in the interest of these other reforms, it is important to press forward this one'.[47] Sir Wilfrid Lawson declared:

What I want above everything is to get a sober people, and if we get that, all these questions about county franchise, disestablishment, &c., we shall fight out much better and in a much better spirit than if we refer them to the decision of an intoxicated people. (Applause.) You can have no reform, no great amendment in any way until this matter is put upon a right foundation. (Applause.) ... It is in vain to talk politics or religion or anything else with any satisfactory result to a nation which is in that state.[48]

Advocates of disestablishment placed stress on the immense social and political power of the Church of England and claimed that this would have to be destroyed before any other reform could have a hope of success. Thus Picton said:

they would see that if they could sweep the one obstacle out of the way, all the other things would follow as a matter of course. The Church Establishment was an intensive rock around which all manner of abuses accumulated; and until they got rid of it there would be an amount of resistance to every reform which in these times they really ought not to be exposed to. ... With the doubtful exception of the liquor traffic reform, which he called a doubtful exception because he remembered a certain association of beer and bible, he was firmly persuaded that none of the reforms he had mentioned could be thoroughly carried out without the Establishment was first taken out of the way.[49]

It was one thing, however, to advance such arguments in order to convince the Liberal party that it ought to take up a particular question first and quite another to use militant and coercive electoral

methods to force it to do so. The great danger then was one of
escalation. If one movement resorted to such methods, the others
might well feel obliged to follow suit, simply in order to protect their
own position, and chaos would ensue. If all organisations insisted on
'exclusive voting' by their adherents, the situation would become
intolerable for candidates and voters alike. The dilemma of the voter
who happened to be an ardent supporter of several reform causes
was expressed by Thomas Snape of Liverpool in opposing a proposal
to ask Nonconformists not to vote for any candidate who would not
pledge himself to support the amendment of the Education Act
when this was moved at the Manchester conference of Nonconformists
in January 1872:

> The supporters of many movements which appealed chiefly to Noncon-
> formists for their support had already adopted that principle, and if the
> different sections of the Liberal party went on with it a little while longer
> they would find themselves so pledged that it would be impossible to find
> any member of Parliament for whom they could vote. They were simply
> attaching fetters to themselves, which they would find very difficult to
> remove. ('Hear, hear,' and 'No, no.')[50]

Many individuals did, for instance, belong to both the Liberation
Society and the U.K. Alliance and were faced with the possibility of
conflict between pledges. In April 1879 George Palmer, MP for
Reading, told the annual conference of the Liberation Society of the
kind of situation which could develop:

> Some time ago in the town in which he lived an Independent minister,
> when addressing a Liberation meeting, wished to pledge everybody to this
> —that at the next election they would not be represented by a man who
> would not vote for the separation of Church and State. About a fortnight
> afterwards, the same gentleman asked a meeting in the Town Hall to
> support no candidate at the next election who would not pledge himself
> to vote in favour of the Permissive Bill. (Laughter.) The two positions were
> absolutely absurd and absolutely unsound.[51]

There can be no doubt that the fear of individuals that they would
be torn between the conflicting electoral demands of the various
movements to which they adhered was a factor working against the
adoption of 'exclusive' electoral strategies. 'Look at this platform,'
said the Rev. G. M. Murphy at a temperance convention in February 1887 which was debating the merits of such a scheme; 'there
were gentlemen who were teetotallers and prohibitionists; but they
were many other things besides. Some were members of the Peace
Society. Supposing that society were to have a national convention

and form a national organisation, we should be split up into pieces.'[52] F. W. Newman strongly opposed the principle of advising abstention when there was no candidate favourable to the Alliance's demand, because such advice

may be hurtful aid to evil, when the voter desires to forbid Compulsory Vaccination, with possible extinction of leprosy, or to forbid Opium Traffic or Overtaxation in India with starvation, or the C.D. Acts by stealthy evasion, or to forbid unjust war. In short, I think it not the duty of our Alliance, when it cannot win an M.P. for itself, to damage other good causes from getting an M.P. available for them, though against us. I am solicited by several other societies, *which I respect*, to refuse my vote to all who will not support *them*![53]

In October 1885 the Alliance Executive decided to put before the Council a resolution calling for support for candidates who were in favour of the Direct Veto. In effect, this was the positive pledge, leaving open the question of how the voter would vote if in his constituency there was no such candidate. But an amendment was moved to insert the word 'only', thus converting the motion into a recommendation to abstain in these circumstances. J. H. Raper attacked this as leaving the way open 'for a great cessation from voting, not on this question, but upon all other questions'. It was an incitement to others not to vote for a man who 'was wrong in his views on vaccination, or on vivisection, or on ecclesiastical questions, although he was right upon this question'. What Raper—and Newman—preferred was that they should confine themselves to the positive form of recommendation, 'to vote for a man who was right as to the Direct Veto, whatever his views on other subjects were'.[54]

The characteristic answer to these objections can be illustrated by remarks made to the Alliance Council in October 1877 by Dr. J. M. McCulloch. He gave two arguments in response to the claim that, 'if you vote exclusively for the Permissive Bill, then all other crotchetmongers have a right to do the same, thus rendering it impossible, especially for the Liberal party, to attain power'. The first was that 'the liquor interest has voted and does vote exclusively, and unless you fight them with the same weapon of precision your success must be indefinitely postponed'. The second was the moral obligation to use such methods arising from the fact that 'our measure is of such vast importance to the welfare of the people economically, socially, physically, morally, and religiously'.[55]

Sometimes pressure groups would become entangled when they happened to be trying to mount an aggressive and exclusive electoral

c

campaign in the same place at the same time. This was particularly the case in the period 1869–74 when one movement after another— even including the agitation for the repeal of the Contagious Diseases Acts—decided to organise its own electoral strategy. Here, undoubtedly, imitation was an important factor and was based partly on the feeling that in such circumstance any movement needed to become electorally militant in order to safeguard its own interests. The kind of turmoil which could ensue in individual constituencies can be illustrated by places such as Bradford and Leeds. Edward Baines listed half-a-dozen and more 'sections' which had simultaneously embarked on electoral war and thereby made completely untenable the position of many Liberal candidates, including himself.[56] A group could condemn a candidate who was approved by another, and this could lead to much ill will as well as confusion among voters who sympathised with all good Radical causes. Sometimes it was considered advisable for an organisation to keep clear when another was already in the field.[57] A classic case of entanglement and confusion was the three by-elections at Bath in 1873 when the pressure groups seemed to vie with one another in their bombardment of the hapless electors.[58] At the second of these, in June, J. C. Cox was brought forward by the National Education League. But the other movements were not willing to allow their questions to be ignored. Cox attended a meeting at the residence of Miss L. Ashworth who condemned the stand taken by the Liberal candidate, Hayter, on the Contagious Diseases Acts and women's suffrage as well. The chair was taken by the president of the Bath Temperance Association who echoed these sentiments and threw in Hayter's views on the Permissive Bill for good measure. At this Cox was moved to point out that he had not come 'at the request of the Temperance party in any way'.[59]

The establishment of representative Liberal Associations in many constituencies reflected to a considerable extent the development of an agreement among the people who were involved in this kind of electoral competition that, in their own interests, they would have to find a way of learning to get on together.[60] The conflicting pressures were often within the individual Radical who could resolve and harmonise them only in this way. An example is H. J. Wilson of Sheffield. His papers show him caught up in almost every reform movement in the early 1870s and terribly confused and distracted as a result. 'I am almost torn to pieces in my own mind', he wrote in 1872 after the apparent failure of one attempt to unite the local party. 'I do so regret that nobody comes up to work at & cement the rads. & the teetotallers & trades unions & I do not see how I can dare to try to do it.'[61] Relief was found in the end in participation in the creation of a popular Liberal Association in Sheffield.

There was certainly a good deal that separated the reform movements. Many of their members were enthusiasts who believed passionately in the supreme value and importance of their particular reform and were therefore impatient with others who felt the same way about theirs.

But there was also much that linked them and their members. The popular impression of the faddists as monomaniacs, exclusively devoted to the pursuit of individual crotchets, was far from accurate, as Brian Harrison's analyses of the biographical data concerning them have shown.[62] H. J. Wilson once remarked that people thought that men such as himself were 'men of one idea' 'when in truth we have too many'.[63] There was a very considerable overlap of membership. As the preceding part of this chapter has indicated, the debate over electoral strategies was often between those who were genuine enthusiasts for one cause alone and therefore favoured 'exclusive voting' on its behalf and those who were involved in several such movements.

Another force that bound the pressure groups together was the awareness of many of the people in them that they belonged to a tradition which transcended their own particular movement. This tradition was summed up in the innumerable references to the Anti-Corn Law League as the great precedent and exemplar for the kind of political activity in which they were engaged. The history of the nineteenth-century pressure groups appears to be that of a series of separate and self-contained movements. But this was not really the case at all. There was a continuous growth of expertise and sophistication, a continuous process of refining and improving organisational and electoral methods, from one movement to the next. Each movement learned from the mistakes and the achievements of its predecessors. The role of the professional lecturers and agents in this was especially important. For them organisational, electoral, and propaganda work on behalf of reform movements became a career, and they moved on from one movement to another in search of employment.[64] An outstanding example of this is George Howell who, after his efforts as secretary to the Reform League, gave his services in the 1870s to a wide range of 'sections' and reform organisations, including the Liberation Society, the National Education League, the Alliance, the trade unions, and the Liberal party itself.

CHAPTER V

The Anti-Corn Law League

An electoral strategy had never before been mounted in Britain on the scale or with the apparent effectiveness of that of the Anti-Corn Law League. But it was not the first attempt by a pressure group to mobilise electoral power in the constituencies as a means of promoting its objectives. Prior to 1832 such strategies were naturally very limited in scope and in accomplishment, for the unreformed electoral system provided little material that could be used by a Radical movement. Much of the Radicalism of the late eighteenth and early nineteenth centuries related to the demands and interests of the unenfranchised, and so could not include electoral power within the range of agitational instruments at its disposal. However, there were occasions when possessors of the franchise themselves were anxious to promote reforms. It is then that one first sees appearing—in very embryonic form—the concept of an electoral strategy.

The 1760s has traditionally been regarded by historians as the decade which witnesses the birth of modern British Radicalism, and it is there that we can begin our survey of the history of the utilisation of electoral power by reform movements. The immediate cause of the upsurge of Wilkite Radicalism in the late 1760s was electoral, the government's attempt to set aside the election of Wilkes for the county of Middlesex. The issue became an electoral one, the right of electors to choose whom they wished to represent them in Parliament. And the agitation itself concentrated on organising electors— the forty-shilling freeholders whose signatures were canvassed for the great petitions of 1769. In various constituencies, mainly in London, Wilkite candidates appeared, but efforts to turn the main Wilkite organisation, the Society of the Supporters of the Bill of

Rights, into a national electoral movement came to very little. However, Wilkite Radicalism does show certain very early signs of what are later to become characteristic features of the electoral strategies of pressure groups. Wilkite candidates were fond of giving pledges to their electors as to their conduct if elected, and a great deal was made of the notion of 'instructing' MPs as to the course which their constituents wished them to follow in Parliament. An extension of this was the idea that constituents should place before candidates a list of pledges which they required them to make before the electors would agree to vote for them. As early as 1768 such lists are appearing in Radical publications. The programme which the Society of the Supporters of the Bill of Rights issued on 11 June 1771 included a proposal for a pledge to be put to every candidate at a general election. Members of the Society or supporters of its principles would vote only for those candidates who were willing to subscribe to it. In the same year Obadiah Hulme in his *Historical Essay on the English Constitution* advocated the organisation from London of a network of associations throughout the constituencies pledged to support only those candidates who would promise to work for parliamentary reform if elected.[1]

Within a few years another movement had developed which similarly gave expression to the grievances of people who already possessed the franchise and therefore could also think of ways of utilising this power—the Association movement, focused on Yorkshire. Like most of the early reform organisations, it found great difficulty in co-ordinating electoral activity beyond that which was initiated by Radical electors acting independently within particular constituencies, but the aspiration to do so was there and also some of the general principles and techniques which are to become so important in the nineteenth century. The basic and original purpose of the Association movement was to petition Parliament for what became known as 'economical reform'. But there was a contradiction at the very heart of this objective. Could a Parliament which was allegedly so seriously corrupted by the exercise of Crown patronage and influence be expected voluntarily to reform itself and cast off this corruption? But, if it could not, what sanction was there behind the petitions that might nevertheless oblige the House of Commons to take notice of them? It was this crucial question that began to divide the Association movement between radicals and moderates, for the logical consequence of a refusal by Parliament to heed the demands of those whom it was supposed to represent seemed to be a recourse to force or the turning of the 'Associated Counties' into an 'anti-Parliament' that would represent them. In London the radicals who favoured these alternatives became vociferous and numerous.

It is against this background that one must assess the development of the Association's electoral strategy. Herbert Butterfield has interpreted this as forced on Christopher Wyvill, the major figure in the Yorkshire Association, as a necessary device to hold the movement together by reassuring the more conservative or, as he puts it, 'timorous' adherents to it that there did exist a constitutional and therefore legitimate form of sanction and that the Association intended to adopt this. In February 1780 Wyvill had published in the *York Chronicle* a letter in which he indicated that he understood that the plan was simply to ask people 'to support the Petition, by engaging not to vote for any Candidate for a seat in Parliament at any further Election, who will not promise to support the Reform requested by the Petition'. Such explanations seem to have reassured the Rockingham Whigs—at least for the time being.

This electoral strategy was planned by a subcommittee of the Yorkshire Association in a paper drawn up early in 1780 prior to the grand meeting of deputies from the 'Associated Counties' in London. This paper listed the reforms to be asked for in the petition and then went on to propose that 'the application for those salutary regulations be supported in a legal and pacific way, by engaging not to vote for any candidate at any future election for this county, or any other county or place in Parliament, who shall not first have made a public promise, signed with his name, in the words, or to the effect following'. This was certainly the most elaborate plan yet conceived for voters' and candidates' pledges. When the deputies met at the St. Alban's Tavern in March 1780 they resolved to incorporate in the 'association' to which adherents would subscribe an undertaking to vote only for candidates who were prepared to give adequate assurances that they would work for the objects of the movement in Parliament. Wyvill's plan now was, on the basis of this, to develop a nation-wide campaign of resistance by electors to candidates who would not agree to support the movement's programme. In Yorkshire by the beginning of 1780 about 5,800 freeholders had taken a pledge not to vote for any candidate who declined to give undertakings to support the Yorkshire Association's programme. But only there and in the now thoroughly radicalised metropolitan constituencies did the idea catch on and make any sort of impact at the general election of 1780. Few candidates or electors elsewhere accepted it. Wyvill tried to put it into operation against the Whig-supported candidates in the borough of York and failed completely. Territorial influence was still all-pervasive and the force which controlled most elections, and to the landed class the notion of making a pledge the bond between MP and constituents was quite abhorrent. Lord John Cavendish, for instance, declared at a meeting that 'to engage not to vote for any man they did not think would support these several objects, was such a restraint upon men's private friendships & interests, as I thought would drive many away'.[2]

In the days before the 1832 Reform Bill some spectacular episode involving an election seemed to be necessary in order to jolt men into an awareness of the possibility of the use of electoral power. Such was the Middlesex elections of the 1760s. But after the flurry of interest in electoral action which these partly inspired, Radical pressure groups fell back once again on the more traditional forms of agitation—petitioning, mass demonstrations, propaganda and publicity. Interest in electoral action as a major instrument of pressure does not seem to revive until another highly dramatic episode of electoral history—the election of Daniel O'Connell for county Clare in 1828. This was significant because it represented the culmination of the agitation of a reform movement, the Catholic Association, and was clearly the immediate cause of the government's decision to concede the main demands of that organisation. The Catholic Association had discovered in existence large numbers of forty-shilling freeholders, 'created' for quite different political purposes, and had utilised them as an electoral lever to force attention to their demands. Here was a revelation of the political potential of the forty-shilling freehold qualification which the Anti-Corn Law League was later to develop so dramatically. There were other features of the county Clare by-election which pointed the way to later developments. It revealed the dramatic political impact which a pressure group could make through intervention in a by-election, particularly a by-election of the kind which has now disappeared from the British electoral system—one consequent on the conferring on an MP of a ministerial post.[3] It provided one of the nineteenth century's most striking instances of an independent candidature on behalf of a pressure group. And it demonstrated the effect on a government of fear of a large-scale electoral strategy which might end by entirely subverting the nation's social and political system.

Although the 1832 Reform Bill included numerous features which could be exploited by reform movements, these were by no means immediately apparent. What was needed was a great deal of investigation of potentialities and of exploration and experimentation, a readiness to proceed by trial and error. This work was carried out above all by the Anti-Corn Law League during the period 1839 to 1846. It set a pattern for the exploitation of opportunities presented by the electoral system for the promotion of a reform cause which was to be followed by numerous other pressure groups later in the century. The history of the League shows a record of constant electoral experimentation and improvisation and adaptation of strategy to correspond to the discovery of new features of the electoral system. This could be a fascinating and exciting type of agitational activity. Fortunately the League possessed in Richard Cobden a leader who both revelled in it and displayed a very great aptitude for this kind of work. He became one of the nineteenth century's greatest electoral strategists. His zest for this side of the League's agitation was manifest. But it is also clear that his interest in it reflected his own basic understanding as to what was needed to sustain amongst the adherents of a movement such as the Anti-Corn Law League enthusiasm for a commitment to its campaign of pressure and agitation. Cobden ended by concentrating on electoral work as the League's major sphere of activity not just because he himself enjoyed engaging in it but also because he came to appreciate that, more than any other form of agitation, it kept the supporters of the movement interested and involved and therefore provided the fuel that maintained its onward momentum.

At first the Anti-Corn Law League was much like any other pressure group, concentrating on educating public opinion and petitioning Parliament. But gradually, as such methods proved slow to produce results, interest grew in more directly political and electoral action. Almost from the beginning Cobden was highly sceptical as to the efficacy of petitioning and looked rather to a campaign based on the organisation of electoral pressure. In February 1839 he wrote to J. B. Smith arguing that the construction of the existing House of Commons

forbids us hoping for success. *That House must be changed before we can get further.* All our efforts then must be directed upon the constituencies, &, to strike a blow that will be responded to by every large town, let us begin in Manchester.
I propose that on the return of our delegates [from a League meeting in

London], (unsuccessful of course) our association call a meeting of the electoral body of Man[cheste]r, by which a pledge shall be entered into, & published to the world, not to return any man to represent them in future, who will not vote for the total & immediate repeal of the corn & provision laws. An appeal must then be put forth to all the manufacturing & commercial bodies represented in parliament, to adopt the same course. Wherever, as in Stroud, or Notts, or Tiverton, or North Cheshire, or West York, cabinet ministers, & others in the administration are returned, lectures must be delivered, & correspondence entered into, for the purpose more especially of operating upon those constituencies.[4]

But in this respect Cobden was well in advance of the thinking of most of his colleagues. As Norman McCord has shown, for much of 1839 and 1840 the League's policy remained that of avoiding political methods to the greatest possible extent and concentrating on publicity and lecture tours and the now traditional extra-Parliamentary techniques for influencing Parliament, petitions and large-scale demonstrations and conferences.[5]

Eventually, in late 1840, the evident futility of such a strategy enabled Cobden to persuade the League's Council to commit itself to something along the lines of the plan which he had described in his letter to Smith—a campaign to persuade anti-Corn Law electors to band themselves together on the basis of a pledge to support only thorough-going free-trade candidates.[6] But the problem which this raised was what the League and its adherents should do in situations where there were no such candidates standing.

Should the strategy be to recommend and organise the abstention of free-trade electors, or to take steps to promote a free-trade candidature, or to accept that candidate whose views were closest to those of the League? It was, as we shall see, a choice which every pressure group was to have to make from this time on. The first challenge came in connection with a by-election at Walsall at the beginning of 1841. The Whig candidate was not a free trader, and the League decided to put up a candidate against him. As usually happened in pressure groups, such a decision was not accepted unanimously, some supporters arguing that its effect would be to split the Liberal vote and thus let in a Conservative who was far more of an opponent of free trade than the Whig. The Whig withdrew and left the field to the League which was embarrassed by its inability to find a good candidate. This was partly on account of another problem which pressure groups were often to come up against—resentment by local people at interference by an outside body. No prominent local Liberal wished to stand and so appear as the tool of an external agency. Finally J. B. Smith, one of the League's officials, agreed to stand. The League poured its resources into the campaign, and, in spite of all the obstacles and criticisms, very nearly won the seat.[7] Walsall was not merely a great publicity success for the League. It was a major turning-point in the history of the employment of electoral tactics by nineteenth-century pressure groups.

There were two possible courses now open to the League. One was to adopt a general electoral strategy and apply the Walsall principle in every constituency. The other was to see the lesson of Walsall as being the publicity value of concentrating effort and resources on a small number of constituencies. The League Council at first seemed to prefer the former of these and declared its intention of opposing any candidate anywhere who refused to subscribe to the 'total and immediate' repeal of the Corn Laws. This would have meant a virtual declaration of electoral war on the Whigs who modified their Corn Law policy considerably in 1841 but were still not in favour of the League's policy.[8] And a universal strategy risked over-extending the League's resources and exposing their cause to elec-toral humiliation as many free-trade supporters put party loyalty first.[9] Therefore, in practice in the 1841 general elections the League did not, as John Morley, Cobden's biographer put it, display 'that inflexibility in electoral policy which afterwards marked their operations'. League efforts were concentrated on those constituencies where free traders dominated Liberal politics and could hope to get a free trader selected and returned as the Liberal candidate. In others, supporters of the League were advised to vote for candidates who at least went as far as the Whig government's policy of a fixed duty on corn imports.[10]

By this time the League was already engaged in continuous elec-toral work in numerous areas, especially to consolidate and increase the electoral basis of free trade. In Walsall, for instance, immediately following the by-election, a registration society was set up to make sure that all possible qualified free-trade electors were placed on the register in that constituency.[11] Cobden was quickly interested in the possibilities inherent in this kind of activity and began to consider how it could be systematised into a general electoral strategy. It is clear that electoral work appealed to him because of the effect it would have in sustaining the interest and enthusiasm of the sup-porters of the anti-Corn Law campaign. In October 1841 he wrote to George Wilson:

It strikes me after a day or two of respite from the turmoil of London politics that the League wants a *revival* of some kind to give us a fresh impulse. I hardly know what to suggest but shall merely offer my opinion of the necessity of *doing something*. . . . If we could find some *work* for our friends in all parts *that* would be the best plan for uniting us. But I question if the work of getting up petitions is a sufficient excuse for calling them together. I confess I feel at fault, & I wish our friends would talk the matter over, & try to devise some plan of action. Of one thing I am certain, that a new move is necessary.[12]

An agitation such as that against the Corn Laws depends for its vigour, and therefore its effectiveness and the seriousness with which it is regarded by those on whom it is exerting its pressure, upon the enthusiasm of its adherents and their determination to go on devoting their time and energies to it. But such excitement can very rapidly be deflated by the effects of boredom or of apparent lack of progress towards the desired goal. There is the danger that, unless the enthusiasts are kept constantly occupied by work that is interesting, varied, and capable of producing tangible evidence of such progress, their enthusiasm will either run into the sands or else become diverted into alternative channels which weaken the impact of concentrated attention on a single aim.[13] The problem was very well put by James Wilson in a letter to George Wilson in November 1841:

If I may judge by the attendance at our meeting yesterday, either by its size or the zeal which was manifested, I must conclude that not only are we making great progress here, but that the liveliest interest is felt in your proposed meeting in the hope that some very decided and active course of action leading to practical results, will be recommended:—there appeared among them a strong desire and considerable impatience to be called into some more stirring and active existence than hitherto:—they become organised, they distribute tracts, they get up lectures, which are every where well attended, but this they think only a means to an end; and as you know that men who take the lead in such matters are generally of a very ardent character, they want to see some more tangible action towards an end:— . . . we must devise something of an active and stimulating character to keep up an interest:—and in doing so our great object must be, usefully to direct this energy, and not allow it either to chill or run riot.[14]

Despondency and discouragement frequently affected the adherents to the League. It is clear that Cobden saw electoral work as more suited than any other form of agitational activity to be the antidote to this tendency. The registration side of it provided abundance of occupation for the enthusiasts, and occupation that could be seen statistically to be making a contribution to the attainment of the goal. But election work was also exciting and dramatic. Involvement in by-elections and general election contests in individual constituencies could be turned into the substance of a constantly varying drama of conflict with the forces of 'feudalism' and 'monopoly'.

In February 1842 Cobden wrote to Geoge Wilson setting out his ideas as to 'the course which the League should henceforth pursue'. This letter showed that already he was considering elevating electoral tactics to principal place amongst the League's methods of carrying on its operations. Thus he advised a public renunciation of any further petitioning of the present Tory-controlled House of Commons. 'It involves great trouble and expense, and will do no good.' What he advised instead was a three-stage electoral campaign based on the boroughs—which for the next couple of years he was to regard as more important that the counties, a calculation for which two main reasons may be adduced: the fact that they seemed to be the urban part of the electoral system where free-trade support would be concentrated, and the numerical superiority which they continued to possess.[15] The first stage would be the work of investigation, carried out mainly by the League's lecturers and agents, as to 'the state of all the boroughs in the kingdom in reference to our question'. This having been done, the second stage would be the work of analysis and classification: the boroughs would be 'put into lists of *safe, tolerably safe, doubtful, desperate, hopeless*'. The third and final stage would be action. The League's 'whole strength should be then thrown upon the doubtfuls'. In every borough a working committee should be set up to 'look after the registration'. Cobden ended his letter by expressing his opinion that 'old and regular methods' would not suffice to beat down the power of the aristocracy. His ingenious mind is leading him to pioneer new forms of agitation.[16]

This plan implied a lengthy period of patient, laborious behind-the-scenes work before the commencement of large-scale electoral action, and this is in fact the course which the League follows. During 1842 and 1843 the basis is laid for action through the massive accumulation of information at League headquarters concerning electoral conditions, the state of the registers, the existing electoral strength of free traders in individual constituencies, and so forth.[17] During the later part of 1842 and the early part of 1843 the strategy which is to make use of all this information is debated and by May a plan has been agreed on although it is not announced by Cobden until September.[18] The main debate seems to have been between two types of electoral strategy, one focusing on the next general election by announcing well in advance that free-trade candidates will be run in certain constituencies and commencing to mobilise support for them, the other looking rather to by-elections and the exploitation of such opportunities as they offer from time to time. An illustration of this debate is afforded by a letter which Colonel Perronet Thompson wrote to Cobden in October 1842. He raised against the idea of 'declaring the intention of standing for a place at the next general election' some of the objections which pressure-group electioneers often regarded as applying to general-election as distinct from by-election activity:

The chance of what may happen at *one* place half a dozen years hence, is always like betting on one card; it is all very well if it turns up. At the same time a determination on this ground, is always very much at the control of actual circumstances. There may always be *some* prospect which may make it right to cast all others into the shade.

His preference was therefore for a by-election-based strategy:

Were I called to be counsellor to the League, I would certainly advise them, barring local fitnesses or unfitnesses, to try to raise an understanding for putting forward the candidate of their approval in any of the places under their influence where the vacancy should occur. On an average I think there is a vacancy in the House of Commons about once a fortnight (or six-and-twenty in the year); so that if the League could reckon upon one-thirteenth of the boroughs as under their influence, they might calculate on putting a man in, every six months. And where they were put, they would probably stick. Which seems more hopeful than posting them to boroughs for the chance of succeeding six years hence.[19]

The plan which the League did decide to adopt was in accordance with Thompson's advice. Briefly, it consisted of an undertaking by the League's Council to ensure that there would be a candidate who was pledged to the 'total and immediate' repeal of the Corn Laws at every borough election henceforth. This meant that, if the local free traders were unable to find such a candidate, the League itself would supply them with one. The League had committed itself to making electoral work its main sphere of operations from now on. In its manifesto to the people of the United Kingdom issued on 28 September the Council indicated its determination to concentrate on influencing and educating electors. There was to be no more petitioning of Parliament but instead an emphasis on direct action by voters. The League would obtain copies of all registration lists, maintain a correspondence with electors, send deputations to visit every borough, and take measures such as canvassing to ascertain the opinions of all electors on the free-trade question. As for by-elections, the critical paragraphs read as follows:

6. Whenever a vacancy occurs in the representation of any borough, the electors will be recommended to put a Free-Trade Candidate in nomination; and the League pledges itself to give such candidate every possible support, by deputations, lectures, and the distribution of publications.

7. In the event of any borough being unable to procure a suitable candidate, the League pledges itself to bring forward candidates, so as to afford every elector an opportunity of recording his vote in favour of Free Trade, until the question be decided.[20]

Thus the main strategy which the League decided to adopt was one of independent candidatures. The strategy which appealed to many later pressure groups, that of pledging adherents to abstain from voting unless one of the candidates of the regular parties came up to their standard, does not become a prominent feature of the League's operations. There was some canvassing for signatures to pledges, but these were usually much weaker than those used by pressure groups later in the century. For example, at Gateshead in 1845 333 electors were canvassed and 100 signed a pledge which simply affirmed their conviction that the Corn Laws and all other protective duties should be immediately abolished and declared that they would work together to accomplish this. It is interesting that 12 of the canvassed electors rejected the pledge as too weak.[21] Meetings occasionally passed resolutions in the form of electoral pledges. A meeting of free-trade electors at Yarmouth in July 1844 pledged itself to support only such candidates as were in favour of total and immediate repeal of the Corn Laws and the principles of free trade.[22] But the League's preferred strategy was positive—to ensure that the question of not voting need never arise.

One other feature of the Council's manifesto is worthy of note. The League was undertaking to impart into elections a novel kind of electoral influence at a time when 'influence' in elections was largely understood to mean the massive expenditure of money on bribery and intimidation, corrupt practices and the buying of votes. The League was asking for funds for its electoral campaign, and the danger was that it would have trouble in raising these because people would think that it too was intending to engage in these traditional modes of influencing voters—a call on funds to which there could be no end, escalation of expenditure being a well-known feature of Victorian electoral contests. The League's leaders were very sensitive on this issue. In October 1842 Colonel Perronet Thompson wrote to Cobden opposing 'the applying any of the League's 50,000 to the imitation of the enemy's courses'. 'We must', he wrote, 'keep ourselves clear of the accursed thing; or we shall be beaten at our own weapons. There will always be plenty of use for the sum in question, in conducting agitation; and even if applied in the other way, it would only be like a drop in the bucket.'[23] At the time of the Walsall by-election Cobden, when writing to Joseph Sturge about his plan to raise 'a national subscription like the Catholic rent', was careful to add: 'Do not be alarmed that the League will do anything to injure its moral weight at the day of election. I would not consent to an act of illegal bribing to save the election'.[24] In September 1843, in order to reassure subscribers and place a firm line between its form of influence and other forms, the Council promised that it would, as part of its electoral work, take strong action against bribery and intimidation in the elections in which it was engaged and even undertake prosecution. Cobden placed great stress on this commitment in his Covent Garden speech of 28 September. Another reason for this was no doubt to give heart to League supporters who might otherwise feel that the proposed electoral action—which so depended on whole-hearted co-operation—was doomed from the start because of the normally overwhelming impact of bribery and intimidation.

The by-election strategy was put into operation at once. The aim was to make the free-trade electors in every borough where a vacancy occurred feel that they were not isolated but had behind them the support of free traders throughout the country and would be regarded as heroes of the cause if they won the election. Thus, when an early challenge emerged in the City of London, the Liverpool Anti-Monopoly Association passed a resolution calling on the City electors to vote for an advocate of the repeal of the Corn Laws, and W. J. Fox, the League orator, said that every vacancy must now be contested 'as if the fate of this country depended solely on each particular election'.[25]

The League could expect to do well in a large urban constituency such as the City of London. Much more worrying in terms of the League's commitment was the large number of small and often highly corrupt boroughs such as St. Albans and Sudbury where vacancies also began to occur. Cobden addressed himself to this problem in a speech at Manchester on 19 October 1843.[26] If such boroughs were impenetrable, then Cobden's strategy lay in ruins. He therefore had to act quickly to deny that they were. The electors there, he argued, were just as intelligent and opposed to monopoly as the electors of Manchester or Birmingham;

but they are not placed in such a favourable position for giving expression to their opinions. How is that to be remedied? I say, lay Manchester and Birmingham alongside of St. Alban's and Sudbury, and you will give them a moral influence and support, and, by persevering in a local way, you will beat down the influence of the local monopolist squire who has been hitherto able to domineer over the inhabitants of those small boroughs. I speak of these boroughs merely as a type of others, where there has been no countervailing power to step in and prevent the neighbouring tyrants from domineering over the constituencies.

Cobden then went on to reveal more details of the electoral strategy. The aim was to select enough boroughs to give the League a majority in the House and then to concentrate fire on the electors in these. The entire campaign would be run from London by means of deputations and propaganda sent to electors. There would be a rigorous attempt to keep free of involvement in the complexities of local politics and party feuds: 'there shall be no party work, the business shall not go into the hands of local cliques at all. We will take a room, and meet the electors by appointment there, without the co-operation of any local leaders, so as to excite no jealousy on either side.' This determination to avoid contamination by local feuds was laudable, but it remained to be seen whether there were yet many local voters who could similarly detach themselves. Cobden also made an even more emphatic and sweeping pledge concerning corruption. The League would prosecute all who offered bribes: 'we intend, as one of the glorious objects of the Anti-Corn Law League, to put down for ever the system of bribery in this country.' Most League speakers at this time did in fact place great stress on this crusade against corruption. Placards were issued offering rewards of £100 to anyone giving evidence which led to conviction for bribery.[27] The League was committed to proving that reform could be obtained through the existing parliamentary and electoral system—something which was denied by the Chartists, Joseph Sturge, and other radicals. The appearance of the impossibility of obtaining reform in this way could be explained by the existence of corruption and a remedy therefore could be offered in the form of the attack on corruption promised by the League. Cobden wrote to Bright in May 1842 urging him to make 'a swinging assault upon the corruptions of the last general election, & [to] argue from the disclosures made by the House of Commons itself that we the anti-corn law party were not defeated but virtually swindled & plundered of our triumph at the hustings'.[28]

A free trader was returned for the City of London, and this was hailed as proof of the correctness of the League's strategy. In an editorial on 4 November 1843 *The League* made the first major attempt to assess its significance in the history of extra-parliamentary agitation. It was the first movement whose agitation had behind it an ultimate sanction other than violence (a point that Wyvill had, of course, arrived at over sixty years before):

All previous agitations have implied insurrection as their ultimatum. The Duke of Wellington avowedly conceded Catholic Emancipation as the alternative of civil war. The Reform struggle came to the verge of a refusal to pay taxes . . . Mr. Roebuck once defined 'moral power' to be 'physical force in perspective'. Under the plan of the League, this definition breaks down. A fulcrum is indicated for the lever of moral power, whereby the stoutest resistance may be overcome, *if the agitation be founded in truth and justice*.[29]

The League had reached a crisis by 1843. Were the Chartists and Joseph Sturge right in maintaining that reforms such as the repeal of the Corn Laws were not possible until Parliament was much more drastically reformed?[30] And, since the existing Parliament had rejected the Chartist petitions and was clearly adamant against further parliamentary reform, was 'physical force' now the only means left for obtaining an end to the economic power of the monopolistic landed class? Already some League members had flirted with the notion of coercive action. Would the League collapse as its adherents—and especially its subscribers—lost confidence that its ends could ever be peacefully attained?[31] To all these questions the League's electoral strategy was the answer. Reform was possible by means of the existing electorate if its character was elevated, and not just the repeal of the Corn Laws.

The timid will grow courageous. . . . There is a contagion of good not less than of evil. . . . When the Corn Laws shall have vanished, a constituency will remain, capable of restraining legislative authority within its just limits, of preventing future abuses, and of enforcing its wise and beneficent direction.

For the present, however, Cobden remained particularly worried about the possible effect of the new electoral strategy on the flow of funds to the League. Speaking at Manchester on 14 November, he urged League supporters not to suppose,

because we require money for an electoral agitation, and to enter into election contests, that therefore we are contemplating an expenditure of an objectionable kind. The very principle of contested elections in this country has been so tainted, that it is difficult to bring ourselves to the belief that people can go into a borough, and spend money there, without spending it in an illegal, or, at all events, in an impure way.

The money, he explained, was needed for printing tracts for electors, deputations, public meetings—and prosecuting people who indulge in bribery. It was an expensive business to reach and educate the 700,000–800,000 electors whose votes were needed to fulfil the League's aim 'to carry a Free-Trader at every borough election'.[32]

Pursuing this policy, Cobden went down to Salisbury in late November to speak on behalf of a free-trade candidate and issued very strong warnings as to the action which the League would take against persons who gave or received bribes.[33] This was all very well, but comment soon began to be made on the fact that the League had not actually launched any prosecutions. James Wilson wrote in great alarm to George Wilson:

If we really have evidence of treating and bribery, I sincerely trust there will be no hesitation about prosecuting—the more so as the election is in our favour. The League must not hold out a *threat* without performance. Its future moral influence depends on the conviction being maintained which is at present prevalent—that what the League says—it means.
We have the country in our hands if we can convict on this occasion. The effect on Liverpool and such places will be great.
It is of course of the first consequence that we should be quite clear that we have good ground:—to prosecute and fail would no doubt damage us;—but if you are quite sure of your evidence we must not hesitate.[34]

At the League's monthly meeting on 30 November Cobden had to explain that there were proving to be considerable legal difficulties involved, especially in relation to the obtaining of evidence.[35]

Here was a crisis undoubtedly. If the forces of corrupt influence which appeared to hold a large part of the existing borough electorate in thrall could not be suppressed, what hope was there for the League's great electoral strategy? Indeed, far from being suppressed, they seemed to be contaminating the League's own electoral operations. The kind of temptation to which the League was exposed can be illustrated by this letter which G. Wilson received from James Coppock, the Whig parliamentary agent:

I am told that there are nearly fifty voters in Salisbury, who had been promised £3 per head at the last Election, & that the promises being un-fulfilled the same fifty expectants are in a very dissatisfied state. To pay them is dangerous. Not to promise to pay them may be dangerous for their voting . . . Win Salisbury & every place is open to you.[36]

R. Moore wrote to Wilson some months later in connection with a contest at Hastings: 'Coppock should be kept at arms length from us *he is not honest.*'[37] Cobden grew very uneasy about the electioneering activities of James Acland. 'There is a general opinion', he wrote to Wilson, 'that there is a wild expenditure going on, & there is an objection to the *principle* of our taking upon ourselves to appoint election agents or paid canvassers, & taking on ourselves also the general management of the contest.' What particularly concerned him was 'the agreement to pay the non-electors (which Acland says he has entered into)'. Cobden hoped that this

does not turn out badly. If it be generally known amongst the non-electors that some of their body are receiving pay, it will excite jealousy amongst the rest. And if the electors discover it, it will take away the reality of the move-ment altogether, & deprive it of any force.[38]

Nor was the problem of corrupt electioneering the only threat to the League's effectiveness. The determination to fight every borough vacancy was leading to many defeats. This was bound to damage morale among supporters and the credibility of the League itself since such great expectations had been built up concerning the strategy. The League had seriously underestimated the number of borough seats which were, to use Cobdens terminology of 1842, 'desperate' or 'hopeless'.[39] Cobden, always very sensitive about the effects of electoral setbacks on the movement, was coming to the conclusion by February 1844 that the strategy would have to be greatly modified. For example, he had to plead with the Leeds Liberal leader, Baines, to ask the Liberal candidate at a by-election to 'use the peace maker "if" ' so as to save the League from the necessity of opposing him.[40] In public he abandoned the ambition of working towards a numerical majority in the Commons and shifted his emphasis towards 'moral power'. At a Covent Garden meeting on 8 February he explained that the question 'cannot be carried *pro* or *con* by such insignificant boroughs as Devizes'. What the League should concentrate on doing was winning the large urban seats. Once this was accomplished, 'there is no Minister to be found who can maintain office to carry on a system of monopolies upon the strength of a mere numerical majority of the House of Commons, and by the aid of the representatives of such places as Devizes or St. Alban's'.[41] John Bright pointed to another weakness in the by-election strategy. Hopeless seats such as Hastings and Christchurch were not the battle-fields on which the League would have chosen to make a test of the support for its principles, and there was growing evidence that the government was deliberately avoiding creating vacancies through ministerial appointments in seats where free-trade sentiment was strong.[42]

Nevertheless, the commitment remained. The abandonment of such a pledge carried its own risk, after all, of damage to morale and reputation. It could be seen as a retreat before the enemy and so had to be handled very discreetly. Supporters were reminded by Bright that 'we did not pledge ourselves to do that which is an impossibility —to return Free-Trade candidates on *every* occasion, especially on the first occasion of our contest in these boroughs'. By late March the policy was still to contest every borough vacancy, but for a different purpose—to *start* a process of 'weakening the monopolist party'. Contested elections gained publicity and formed the nucleus of a free-trade party which would grow and ultimately triumph.[43] 'The League', it was pointed out, 'is most securely fixed in those boroughs where it first encountered defeats; Stockport, Durham, and Walsall were lost before they were won.'[44]

Another problem was that local people proved much more reluctant than expected to put the strategy into operation. It was not easy to find good local men willing to stand as League candidates, and there was a great deal of resentment at outside interference. Cobden discussed the problem in a letter to George Wilson:

We are in a most awkward predicament with these approaching vacancies. We can't find candidates—that's certain. And our only course is to let some of them go by default, & get out of the dilemma afterwards with the best excuse in our power. At Huntingdon no local man can be found. I wrote to Captn. Duberly, but he won't stand. I have written to Acland to desire that he will not nominate any person without previous directions from the Manch^r. Council, & I have told him not to promise a candidate beyond the general pledge we have (perhaps unwisely) given. The fact is I am afraid of his standing himself which must on no acc[oun]t be permitted. It will make our electioneering a farce if we put up men to fight an unreal battle. Unless a local man could be found he would be placed in a ludicrous position at the poll. At Horsham there is a Whig landowner of the neighbourhood a Mr. Hurst who is going to stand, but I hear is a decided advocate of the corn law. Now if we could possibly find a man (not one of our own staff, *that* must not be repeated) to cut in between the two aristocrats, & spoil the

Whig game *that* is the course I should like. But I know not where to find a
man who will be set up to be knocked down. . . . Woodstock is a pocket
borough. If Follett stands again for Exeter, nobody can best *him*, but a contest should if possible be had. We have sent Paul down to try to look up a
local man but I fear even that is hopeless. I know not where to apply. . . .
Whatever you do, pray interdict Acland from setting up himself or any of
our own people. Moore ought not to stand again. I think we can get a good
excuse for letting some of these vacancies go over by default. It is at the best
a sad mess.[45]

Cobden's policy of coming in to a borough and acting independently
of local interests had clearly been too extreme and had underestimated the need for local effort and initiative. On 13 April 1844 *The
League* urged local people to be active when vacancies occurred,
choose their own candidate, organise their own committees, and
'guard against their own peculiar dangers'. The League, it said, 'is
more anxious to act as the ally of the Free-Traders in each borough
than to assume the place of principal'.[46]

Here we see the emergence of the decisive shift of emphasis which
was to free the League finally from its commitment to fight every
vacant borough. In mid-April another round of 'hopeless' contests
loomed—Horsham, Huntingdon, Woodstock. Speaking at Covent
Garden on 17 April, Cobden reverted to the problem of how the
battle-fields were determined and made a statement which both
relaxed the League's commitment and suggested a way in which
free traders could regain control over that determination:

We have been charged with dictating to constituencies. Gentlemen, we
only proffer to 'co-operate' with constituencies (cheers)—we go to boroughs
to offer our co-operation to the local members of the League resident in
those boroughs to which we go; and if you hear in any case of a contest
passing over without a League candidate being proposed, you may conclude that it was because the League Council did not choose to dictate to
the local Free-Traders, but deferred to their feelings not at present to contest the borough, but to leave it for future organization.[47]

Thus the retreat from the pledge was skilfully camouflaged under a
proposal to transfer the initiative in selecting electoral battle-fields
from the Tory government to the rank-and-file free traders. At
Horsham the free traders declined the Council's offer to supply a
candidate and it looked as if they were not going to run one of their
own. At Huntingdon the Council would bring someone forward
only if the local people allowed them to.[48] And so the pledge of
September 1843 was quietly abandoned.

Huntingdon, Horsham, and Woodstock were not contested by

free-trade candidates. The League had to admit that there were many such corrupt and backward boroughs in the south of England.[49] But Cobden would not acknowledge that those who said that repeal could not be obtained through existing constitutional arrangements were right. Instead his reaction to this new crisis was typically positive. In a letter to G. Wilson of 2 April he explained what he and Bright had agreed should be the nature of the League's future operations:

We must now concentrate our efforts upon those Boroughs that may be won. Abandon the Counties & the farmers as hopeless. I should not be sorry if the whole Council of the League were to resolve itself into a Borough Registration Society. . . . I think it will be better to come to an understanding that we (I mean Bright & myself particularly) will not visit any places except *Boroughs* which may be possibly won, & that we do not leave them without an efficient organization for registration purposes. If there be any exception to this rule it must be only where money is in the question as at Wolverhampton. If we call County Meetings again they must be held in boroughs where the constituency may be acted upon in the same way & at the same time.[50]

In the light of subsequent developments what is especially striking about this is the almost total rejection of electoral operations in the counties.

In a speech at Covent Garden on 1 May Cobden concentrated on the theme of borough registration. He estimated that there were 40–50,000 people in the metropolitan boroughs alone who were qualified to vote but were not on the register. A massive registration drive could transform the electoral system.[51] The League had been attending to the registration of its supporters and objecting to the registration of its opponents in various constituencies for some time.[52] But over the next two years this campaign was to be greatly intensified. The League, with the aid of numerous sympathetic lawyers, developed enormous expertise in this area which enabled it to cut through and master the complexities of the registration procedures established after 1832. In August 1844 George Wilson explained how the League proceeded:

We selected 140 boroughs upon which we thought, with reasonable exertions, an impression might be made. We selected for our visiting agents to such boroughs men fully acquainted with the subject of registration in all its parts . . . In some instances they found the registration had been totally neglected—in many partially attended to, whilst in others it had been entirely in the hands of local agents . . . They then formed committees where none existed, and exacted a pledge from the free traders in many boroughs, that the subject be fully attended to hereafter . . .[53]

The new policy concerning both registration and by-elections was stressed by W. J. Fox at Covent Garden on 8 May. He referred to *'the necessity of attending to the registration'*: enthusiasm at an election was inadequate to carry it unless the registration had been seen to. Then he outlined the revised by-election strategy:

> Remember that the elections which occur now, from time to time, are not a true test of what our question will be when its forces are in the field. We look to the elections that pass now as to their *moral*, not as to their *numerical* results. We have no dream in the present Parliament of adding such a number of Free-Traders upon these particular occasions, as can make any impression whatever on the divisions there. Our time will come by-and-by. Now, the occasions are to be taken when victory, as it was in London, is great by its moral strength, by the electrical stroke which it gives the country.[54]

As luck would have it, an opportunity was immediately at hand to demonstrate the wisdom of these new departures—the South Lancashire by-election, in which William Brown stood as free-trade candidate. Brown was defeated, but this time a by-election loss could be used to reinforce the existing electoral strategy. First of all, the margin of defeat was narrow—590—and a moral victory could plausibly be claimed on a number of grounds.[55] Brown did poll 6,972 votes, he came first in six out of ten districts, and, so Cobden claimed, would have won but for the £50 tenants-at-will who were herded in to vote for his opponent. The nearness of victory caused Cobden to see as justified the strategy of concentrating on the large constituencies where alone 'public opinion' could freely be expressed and enabled him at last boldly to say in public: 'We will leave Launceston, Huntingdon, and Aylesbury; we will give up Hastings too, if you like.' But what is most significant of all is his perception in the South Lancashire result of the most striking electoral innovation to be made by the League. Two things impressed him about the result: the critical importance of attention to the register in relation to the narrowness of the defeat, and the contrast between the £50 tenants-at-will and the independent freeholders, many of them urban people who qualified for the county franchise, and whose votes, he claimed, were strongly in Brown's favour. The conclusion to be drawn from these facts seemed to come to him in a flash of inspiration. The free traders had been too obsessed with boroughs as urban seats and had ignored the potentially very strong urban element in the county seats. In the counties, not the boroughs, was their salvation.

It has been wholly lost sight of [said Cobden] that the first duty of men in the towns of Lancashire who have the means to become freeholders is to arm themselves with electoral weapons with which to fight the enemy in the polling booths. Every one must become a freeholder who can afford to invest £50 at four per cent. per annum. It requires only £50 to bring you 40s. [a] year; and it is the duty, and is felt to be so, of every man, whether here, the West Riding, or in South Lancashire, to become a freeholder and entitled to vote at a county election; and we have it in our power to carry the repeal of the Corn Laws by that simple means.[56]

The 1832 Reform Act had allowed for persons who lived in boroughs but possessed the county qualification, the forty-shilling freehold, to vote in the counties. This was heatedly debated at the time and was recognised as an urban intrusion into the counties which Lord John Russell justified both as a means of avoiding excessively rigid barriers between the worlds of industry and agriculture and as a counter-weight to the dependent £50 tenant farmers who were enfranchised by the Chandos clause. Now this provision seemed to have delivered into the League's hands a weapon of enormous and exciting electoral potential.

Cobden often wrote the editorials in *The League*, and that of 15 June 1844 which explores the political implications of this discovery is surely by him.[57] It starts by directly taking up the Chartist challenge and asserting that the League has nothing to do with the merits and demerits of the Reform Bill. What does concern it are the 'capabilities' of that Bill, never yet tested, but likely to lead, if so tested, to an addition, for example, of nearly a million borough voters.

Only a pitiful fraction of the possible constituency, under the Reform Act, has ever yet existed. In many counties, the mass of unrepresented property is enormous; much of it, too, is of a kind, or belongs to a class, comparatively free from the electoral tyranny of landlords. Why should not this legalized power be called into existence and active operation against monopoly. Why should not the errors of voters *in esse* be corrected by the mass of voters *in posse*?

Two significant features of this editorial may be noted. One is the suggestion that the campaign should be to enrol as many new voters as possible and not to try to confine those registered to known free-trade supporters, the assumption being that most of them will be free-trade supporters anyway. We may see here the early signs of Cobden's growing tendency to see what he calls 'experimenting on the Reform Act' as the great means for overthrowing the power of 'feudalism', more important perhaps even than the repeal of the Corn Laws. Secondly, there is the claim that as a result of the 1832 Reform Bill all pressure groups have to adopt an election strategy involving long-term and systematic attention to registration as their main *modus operandi*. The politics of sudden enthusiasm and popular demonstrations are now unable to have any effect on an election which will be determined by the state of the register, something which is decided long before an election is held.

It is wrong to think of Cobden as believing that there had to be a straight choice between the programmes of the Chartists and the Anti-Corn Law League, between an extension of the suffrage and the repeal of the Corn Laws as objectives for reformers to pursue. He did oppose Joseph Sturge's Complete Suffrage movement which attempted to combine the two. But his reasons for opposing Sturge can easily be misunderstood. His views are seen in his letter to George Wilson of 27 February 1842. This makes it clear that it is the *combination* which he objects to because it will alienate from the movement for the repeal of the Corn Laws the great majority of middle-class people who are not yet ready to support a suffrage extension. This does not mean that Cobden himself was opposed to that extension, for he goes on: 'at the same time I think the more that individuals connected prominently with the League join the suffrage party the better. I shall take the first opportunity in the House of avowing myself for the suffrage for every man.' 'After all,' he adds, 'I hardly entertain a hope that we shall effect our object by old & regular methods—accidents may aid us, but I don't see my way in the ordinary course of things for beating down the power of the aristocracy.'[58] The fact that Cobden appeared, nevertheless, to show little sympathy over the next few years for the Chartist and Complete Suffrage programmes is not because he had ceased to believe that an extension of the suffrage was necessary but because he had discovered a means of achieving it that differed from that which was advocated by the supporters of those programmes.

The by-election strategy was now steadily breaking down. In August 1844 a vacancy occurred at Cirencester. The League offered to put up a candidate, for the commitment of September 1843 had not been formally rescinded. But a meeting of Liberal electors at Cirencester passed a resolution, 'That, in the present circumstances of the borough of Cirencester, and especially considering the aristocratic and undue influence which can be brought to bear on the electors, this meeting is of opinion, that for the Anti-Corn Law League to send a candidate at the present vacancy would be an expenditure of energy and means, without any prospect of success.' An editorial in *The League* commented that the League Council had scarcely understood the extent of the evil represented by such pocket boroughs when it made its engagement to contest all borough vacancies.[59] Cobden, for his part, had now thoroughly rejected the small boroughs. 'In many of the small boroughs,' he said at Manchester in October, 'there is no increase in the numbers; there is no extension of houses; the whole property belongs to a neighbouring noble, and you can no more touch the votes which he holds through the property than you can touch the balance in his banker's hands.' By contrast, 'the county constituency may be increased indefinitely'. His vision now was of a conquest by the League of every county with a large urban population within three years.[60]

The strategy for increasing the county constituencies was in full swing by the end of 1844. Cobden and Bright toured the counties addressing special county registration meetings to explain the scheme and exhort people to participate in it.[61] The League did not itself buy the properties which conferred the qualifications.[62] It simply provided advice for those who wished to acquire such properties and put them in touch with lawyers who could help them do so. Most of the detailed work was done by local people, and much therefore depended on the vigour of the local free-trade movement and the willingness of the local Liberals to associate themselves with the registration campaign. In the West Riding, for instance, much of the work was carried out by the regular Liberal party agents. *The League* carried a series of articles on 'How to Win Counties', drawing attention to the techniques most appropriate to local conditions. Cobden stressed how easy and cheap it was to obtain a county vote and reassured audiences constantly as to the legality of the scheme. In fact, it was more than legal. It was deeply conservative in that it encouraged men to save their money in order to acquire property and the right to vote.

Cobden also appealed to Chartist sympathisers who were by this time disillusioned by the collapse of that movement:

Don't let us merely talk about theories for getting the franchise in some great sweep, which can be carried some day, I don't know when; but let us do something as well as talk. . . . There has been a great clamour for an extension of the suffrage. Now, there are two ways to get it: one way is to get Parliament to come down, and the other is to get the people to raise themselves up to the suffrage.[63]

He tried to stir up local pride and competition by setting targets for increases in the register and extolling those towns which exceeded them. He was full of ingenious ideas for the campaign. Employers should obtain qualifications for their employees. Non-electors should put pressure on neighbours. Even women could acquire electoral influence, for example by cajoling husbands to obtain freeholds, refusing to marry fiancés until they did so, and buying property themselves and then bestowing it on men in order to qualify them. But above all Cobden appealed to the skilled operative, the toolmaker and artisan, whom he described as 'the aristocracy of your class'. They should forget about borough qualifications which were very difficult to obtain and expensive and feel it 'a matter of pride and a matter of duty, to qualify for the county'. It was their duty because—and here was a direct thrust at Chartism —it would enable them 'to give the benefit of your vote to those poorer classes of your countrymen who cannot buy the qualification'. Indeed, he went so far as to predict that in a few years' time 'the election for the county of Lancaster will be more in the hands of the operative classes than it is now in the hands of the squirearchy and the farmers', that 'there will be such a vast number of skilled artisans and better paid operatives on the county register, that it will be impossible . . . to return a man for South Lancashire unless he be acceptable in the main to that class of voters'. He admitted that people were already saying to him about this strategy, ' "This is a very dangerous political game you are playing: you are going to democratise the constituencies of this country".' To that his answer was that it was far preferable to have political power in the hands of a democracy consisting of 'that class of people who can afford £50 or £60 out of their earnings for an investment' than to leave it with 'the landed aristocracy who have so much abused their power'.[64] To the League orators one of the great attractions of the forty-shilling freehold was the 'moral good' which it would effect: 'It tends to act upon the character of the entire labouring population of the country,—the working classes,—the more toilsome section of the middle classes; it holds out to them a hope, promise, and incitement of the most desirable and elevating description.'[65]

Thus the League's electoral strategy was seen as a way of resolving one of the most agonising dilemmas of mid-nineteenth century Radicals—how to secure that 'safe' enfranchisement of working men which many realised was necessary to break the continuing ascendancy of the landed class. It provided a mechanism for ensur-

ing that only 'respectable' working men, only men who had proved
their moral worthiness by being prepared to make the sacrifice of
saving their earnings and investing in property in order to secure the
right to vote, were admitted to the franchise.

This was not the only aspect of contemporary Radical ideology
for which the electoral strategy might become the principal vehicle
of expression and fulfilment. The League rested its case for the repeal
of the Corn Laws in part on the claim that Britain was now an
industrial country, a country whose wealth largely depended on the
well-being of her trade and manufactures, and that her economic
policy and political arrangements ought to be altered to reflect this
new state of affairs. The multiplication of county freehold qualifications for urban property-owners was justified as a most important
instrument in this campaign to make the nation's politics reflect the
basic fact of the dependence of the countryside on the towns. Thus
W. J. Fox spoke of it as a crusade to infuse 'the lifeblood of city
thought and independence into the constituencies':

Are not most counties made by the towns and cities which are in them? Do
they not rise as the crown of the richness and fertility of the more productive
counties? Where there is no such fertility, but mineral treasures exist below
the surface, or ports and harbours are found along the coast, why, there
towns and cities make counties by a work almost to be compared with that
of creation, giving them numbers, wealth, grandeur, and importance,
which Nature seems to have forgotten or overlooked. What would Middlesex be, if you were to strike London out of it? (Hear, hear.) Nay, what
would the most rural counties be, if you were to take from them the advantage of towns, if not in them, at least in their vicinity, and within an easy
reach—and what are not now within easy reach? . . . Towns and cities are
the heart of counties—the last portion of them that should be left unrepresented.[66]

The League argued that the acquisition of forty-shilling freeholds
would result in the formation of 'an industrial landed interest'.[67]

While the new electoral strategy was being thus promoted, the old
one was still further eroded. On 15 February 1845 *The League* announced that henceforth no by-election occasioned by a ministerial
change would be contested. This was because the government was
making sure that such vacancies now arose 'only in those boroughs
in which the material of a contest—viz., a constituency—does not
exist'. Far from being a retreat, such a revision of strategy represented another electoral triumph for the League: 'The League have
virtually *vetoed* the acceptance of office by monopolist members who
sit for popular constituencies.'[68] Cobden was now very outspoken

about any attempt to go on fulfilling what he called 'the ridiculous pledge of 1843'. In April 1845 he quarrelled with the Council and with George Wilson over their determination to contest Leominster. He told Wilson that he had consulted Coppock and Parkes and discovered from them 'that Leominster has from time immemorial been one of the most rotten boroughs in England'. A League candidate would stand no chance whatever. 'I most heartily regret,' wrote Cobden, 'that the Council should send Mr. Acland on such errands; I think it a waste of money, time, & energy, to say nothing of the fame of the League . . .'.[69]

Attention to the register was now the key-note of the League's campaigning. On 7 June 1845 *The League* declared its belief that the work of educating public opinion was now complete. But that opinion would be of no value unless it was registered. 'The approaching general registration will, essentially and really, be a general election. It will, in all probability, decide the character of the next Parliament. . . . Registration is now really almost all that we have to do.' A careful, patient, long-term electoral strategy based on registration now had yet another vast claim made for it: it had become, as a result of the very peculiar nature of the 1832 Reform Bill, the key to securing control over the government of the country. *The League* thus attempted to define the new post-1832 nature of government in Britain:

a government where the popular will is practically everything, if it express itself through the medium of certain complicated technical forms, compliance with which must precede, by months or years, the actual exercise of the powers which those forms authenticate—and next to nothing, if those forms are neglected; a government where popular elections take place by anticipation, under another name, noiselessly, indirectly, almost privately, and in the entire absence of all the ordinary excitements of popular feeling. . . .[70]

The claims were very large indeed. But how much impact did the League's registration campaign really make? Here it is of great importance to distinguish between the League's stated ambitions and its actual achievements, not only because there was a very marked discrepancy but also because that discrepancy was itself intended to have major political implications.

The most important point to bear in mind when assessing the League's electoral strategy in 1845–6 is that it had now, largely owing to the collapse of its earlier borough strategy, abandoned any idea of attaining its goal by 'numerical' power. 'It is not necessary,' declared *The League* of 15 February 1845, 'to the carrying of our question that we should proselytise, man by man, a numerical majority of the House of Commons.'[71] The emphasis was now on 'moral power', and that meant, as far as the counties were concerned, not attempting at once to conquer them all, but rather selecting a few where early success was most likely and concentrating resources on winning them as an example of what *could* be done in the others.

To begin with, three county constituencies were chosen for predominant attention—South Lancashire (to build on the by-election foundation), North Cheshire, and the West Riding of Yorkshire—while efforts were made to develop interest in a registration drive in a fourth, South Staffordshire.[72] By June 1845 registration operations were also under way in East Surrey and Middlesex. And by September a registration campaign was beginning in East Gloucestershire. As if to underline the wisdom of this strategy, which naturally caused some frustration among League supporters as so much of the work was laborious and legalistic and the benefits were only likely to be seen in the long term, the League suffered a humiliating setback when it hurled its resources into the Sunderland by-election of August 1845 on behalf of Colonel Perronet Thompson against Hudson, the 'railway king'. Hudson, who spent lavishly, won by a large majority, and the local Liberals did not unite behind Thompson, their leaders in particular considering him too extreme.[73]

In October the first conquest of a county seat was claimed. Registration efforts had now converted the 'monopolist' majority of 600 against Brown at the South Lancashire by-election into a free-trade majority of 3,000. The power of the great landed families to determine the representation of South Lancashire had been shattered. *The League* made the significant comment on this that it was sure that it would impress Peel.[74] Then at Manchester on 28 October Cobden reported another gain. The free traders of the West Riding had exceeded their target and added 2,300 electors to the register. As a result, there was now a free-trade majority of 1,600 in that constituency. Just to make sure, Cobden was asking for 2,000 more by 31 January 1846. Cobden predicted that neither South Lancashire nor the West Riding would be contested now by the 'monopolists' who would not wish to waste their money. He also claimed that a free-trade majority had been attained in North Cheshire, Middlesex, South Staffordshire, and possibly North Lancashire.[75] The most spectacular confirmation of these claims was to come in February

1846 in the West Riding when Lord Morpeth, the Liberal free-trade candidate, was returned unopposed at a by-election, the Protectionists having acknowledged that they were now hopelessly outnumbered on the register.[76]

The question now was what use the League would make of these new electoral facts in pressing its campaign for the repeal of the Corn Laws. In his Manchester speech Cobden made the main point abundantly clear: they were a token of much more to come *if* the government did not carry out repeal. He foreshadowed an extension of the county freehold campaign to cover the entire country. The League had now drawn up a list of twenty counties and intended to visit each and organise them on the same plan as had been so successful in South Lancashire. The object, he stressed, was to 'alarm the monopolists' by undermining what they believed to be the very base of their social and political authority.

The League orators now began making the most sweeping claims as to what their campaign would lead to. Bright claimed that 'there has never been in the lifetime of the oldest man amongst us, nor for generations back, any lever so potent, so all-overturning of evils in legislation, as this scheme of the 40s. freeholds for the counties'. He called it 'the strong and irresistible weapon before which the domination of this hereditary peerage must at length be laid in the dust'.[77] Cobden said that it was 'an avenue by which we may reach the recesses of power'.[78] From now on the entire campaign was geared to stressing the implications of *what might be* for the political and social system of the country. To heighten the tension, a further refinement of the county freehold strategy was announced. On 15 November 1845 *The League* referred to the problem of those county constituencies where 'the means of self-emancipation afforded by a numerous and free-spirited town population, do not exist to a sufficient extent within the boundaries of the county or division itself'. The idea was that free traders should take out qualifications not just in their own counties, as had so far mainly been the practice, but in neighbouring counties as well. It was an idea which had already been applied—in Manchester, where a prosperous man's 'complement of county votes is regularly understood to be *four*, at least'.[79] Here was a device of immense possibilities, especially in light of the fact that in 1845 alone about £500,000 was being spent in the purchase of county freeholds. *The League* gave many suggestions as to what might be done. Birmingham should look to North Warwickshire and East Worcestershire and get control over 'that great district which its own marvellous and many-handed industry has made what it is'.[80] The free traders of London should buy qualifications in Hertfordshire and so end the control of landlordism there, for it is to London that, 'by commercial dependence and local proximity, Hertfordshire naturally belongs'.[81]

As events quite other than the League's electoral campaign took over and impelled the politicians and especially Peel towards conceding the League's demands, Cobden continued to warn of the menace which that campaign would represent if that concession were not made. Speaking at Manchester on 23 December 1845, he declared that if the question were not settled in the coming parliamentary session the League 'would plant registration agents in every county in the kingdom' and as a result within three years they would be in a position to unseat one hundred 'monopolist' county members.[82] His ultimate warning, however, came in a speech at Leeds on 14 January 1846 when he suggested that, if Peel did not decide on prompt repeal of the Corn Laws, there was a danger that he and Bright would be discredited through their failure to attain their goal and more extreme men would rise up in their place and use the weapon of the forty-shilling freehold as a means of waging class war against the landed aristocracy. In ten years this could effect a revolution in constitutional arrangements as complete as that of 1688.[83]

Peel gave as one of his main reasons for coming out in favour of repeal his desire to avert a confrontation between town and country.[84] By far the most striking evidence available to him to lead him to the conclusion that such a confrontation was imminent was the electoral strategy of the League. Cobden himself believed that repeal was brought about more by what the League had achieved in the four or five counties than by any other single factor.[85] But the real meaning of that was, of course, the demonstration of what the League might be able to accomplish in many other places. The League's electoral policy acquired the status of a myth in later nineteenth-century politics because it ended so ambiguously. The real power in 1846 was the threat of the realisation of an alleged potential, but that potential remained unrealised and so no one was able to say exactly either what effect it did have on the decision reached by Peel and Parliament in 1846 or what the electoral power of the League might have become. It is such ambiguity that is the substance of potent political myths.

There is a further interesting ambiguity about the League's

electoral strategy as it stood in 1846 when Peel's decision to repeal the Corn Laws terminated its *raison d'être*. Did Cobden and Bright really mean what they said about its possible use as a weapon for purposes ranging well beyond this particular reform? Or were their statements merely bluff, designed to frighten Peel and the landed class into surrender? About Bright, it seems, there can be little doubt. According to Morley, he was always to maintain that the forty-shilling freehold scheme would never enfranchise enough voters permanently to make any real and effective change in the representation.[86] In his later career he was to be involved in more traditional and direct forms of agitation for the extension of the suffrage.

But Cobden is a different matter. It seems that he really did believe that the multiplication of county voting qualifications could be made the instrument of a peaceful revolution in the political system of the country. Indeed, in 1861 he expressed regret that the Protectionists had not resisted repeal of the Corn Laws for another three or four years after 1846. The extra votes that would have been created during that time would have enabled many other reforms to be secured as well as repeal.[87] After that reform had been accomplished, the League was wound up, and its superb election machinery continued for many years, under the control of George Wilson, to play an important role in the Liberal politics of South Lancashire.[88] But Cobden wanted more than that. He was very anxious to carry on the forty-shilling freehold side of its work throughout the country.[89] When in 1848–51 he and Bright and other Radicals discussed what they should embark on next, he persistently recommended the forty-shilling freehold plan to them—until the point was reached when Roebuck, for one, came to feel that it was an obsession: 'Cobden is a poor creature with one idea—the making of county voters. He is daunted by the county squires, and hopes to conquer them by means of these votes.'[90] His views are set out in a series of letters which he wrote to Bright.[91] He argued that none of the reforms which Radicals advocated could be carried until there was 'an increase in the popular element in the House of Commons' and that the only way to achieve that was 'by local exertions in the registration courts, and above all by the forty shilling votes in the counties'. Many men who would not support the Radicals on 'any large scheme of sudden organic change' would associate themselves with the forty-shilling freehold movement as a way of extending the suffrage because of all the 'moral and social benefits' that it involved. Such a movement, if zealously promoted, could double the electorate in under seven

D

years, and at that point, with a phalanx of forty-shilling freeholders of whom nine-tenths would be 'teetotallers, nonconformist and rational Radicals', an ideal electorate would have been attained for the securing of 'thorough practical reforms'. To Joseph Sturge Cobden wrote:

> . . . the more I reflect on the subject the more am I convinced that our only way of taking another step in advance against the oligarchy is by beginning with the instrument which the League resorted to at the end of our struggle viz the 40/- freehold qualification. With that instrument, & quiet persevering work under the sanction of men of character, any & every good object may be attained in this country. . . . I have no doubt that the next movement will take almost exclusively this shape. The Chartists have thrown a discredit upon the more exciting mode of effecting reforms by public meetings, & they have to some extent brought even petitioning into ridicule.[92]

What Cobden seemed for a time to be trying to achieve was to interest the adherents of particular reform sections in the county qualification movement so as to make it the unifying basis for Radicalism and to prevent the disintegration of Radicalism which appeared to be setting in after the passing of the cohering issue of the repeal of the Corn Laws. Thus he wrote to Sturge in connection with the peace movement:

> . . . the only way to make your principles triumph is by entering the arena of politics & doing as you did in your anti-slavery efforts. You must make yourself troublesome in the registration Courts, & induce all your partisans to qualify as County members with 40/- freeholds. . . .[93]
> . . . The only way in which we can reduce our own armaments, or bring Lord Palmerston heartily to cooperate in persuading other nations to disarm is by making ourselves strong in the polling booths, particularly of the *Counties* whose representatives are almost to a man against us & the mere nominees of the aristocracy. . . .[94]

For the militant voluntarists among the Nonconformists, whose disruptive and weakening effect on the Liberalism of the West Riding Cobden constantly condemned during this period,[95] Cobden had a similar message. He wrote to John Bright in August 1848 urging him to get in touch with their leader, Edward Baines.

> I wish you would impress upon him the entire powerlessness of the independent liberals in the House—that *we the representatives of the dissenters* are in the power of the three other parties, who at any time by uniting upon the endowment of Irish Catholics or any other question touching the consciences of dissenters, can set us at defiance & treat us as nobodies—& that this must

always be the case so long as the representation remains as it now is, giving to the landlords & parsons in the Counties & the aristocracy in little boroughs the power of returning 3/4ths of the members of the House.[96]

Then again, when the agitation for government retrenchment began to gather momentum, Cobden wrote: 'I am for throwing ourselves into the retrenchment movement & *importing into it the means on which we are all agreed viz the registration & qualification means.*'[97]

But Bright did not share Cobden's enthusiasm. He felt that Cobden was so obsessed with the idea that he was no longer interested in any broad and thorough reform of Parliament. Cobden denied that this was so. To him it was the only way of assailing the immensely powerful forces of privilege. The power of the aristocracy must be struck at 'in their strongholds'. Normal methods of agitation were useless in any campaign for parliamentary reform.

Our enemy is as subtle as powerful, and I fear some of us have not duly weighed the difficulties of our task. The aristocracy are afraid of nothing but systematic organization and step-by-step progress. They know that the only advantage we of the stirring class have over them is in habits of persevering labour. They fear nothing but the application of these qualities to the business of political agitation. I prize the privilege of our platforms, and the power of public discussion and denunciation as much as anybody; but public meetings for Parliamentary Reform which do not tend to systematic work (as was not the case in the League), will be viewed by the aristocracy with complacency as the harmless blowing off of the steam.[98]

When in 1851 Joseph Sturge once again called for universal suffrage, Cobden's response was identical with that which a similar appeal by Sturge had evoked from him in the days of the League: 'I look to the forty shilling freehold movement as the surest guarantee of our being able to break down the power of the aristocracy without an appeal to violence.' He longed to be given the opportunity to try again the electoral strategy which had led to the League's triumph in 1846: 'A county or two quietly rescued from the landlords by this process will, when announced, do more to strike dismay into the camp of feudalism and inspire the people with the assurance of victory, than anything we could do.'[99]

No electoral strategist of the Victorian reform movements carried as far as did Cobden this understanding of the deeper significance of electoral policy. Indeed, it may be argued that Bright was correct, that it did become for Cobden an end in itself. When this happened, he left behind him almost all of those who had worked with him as long as the goal had appeared to be the specific one of the repeal of the Corn Laws. Cobden came to see his great electoral policy as the essential prerequisite for the accomplishment of every one of the reforms which contemporary Radicals were advocating. But in his mind those reforms declined in vividness and urgency, while the electoral policy itself became the vehicle for the accomplishment of Cobden's ideal state of society. It ended up by being for him not just a means to an end but a reform which, if achieved, might well render unnecessary the particular measures, including a direct, frontal attack on the question of extending the suffrage, in which Bright and other Radicals believed.

In various districts Radicals founded Freehold Land Societies in order to carry on the work which had been begun by the Anti-Corn Law League. Thus in 1847 John Taylor, a Birmingham Radical, helped to found the Birmingham Freehold Land Society 'for the purpose of procuring qualifications in the County for the representation of North Warwickshire'. In 1849 these numerous local societies were federated in the National Freehold Land Society and a journal, the *Freeholder*, was issued. In the same year was also founded the National Parliamentary and Financial Reform Association, involving Bright, Cobden, and other Radicals. One of its aims was to attend to the registration of voters and to promote the freehold movement. A conference held in London in April 1850 issued an address outlining plans for attention to the register, promotion of the purchase of forty-shilling freeholds, and independent action at the polls. But no great national campaign such as Cobden envisaged came out of this. The business side of the Freehold Land Societies soon overshadowed the political and they became important precursors of the modern Building Societies. The most that can be said about the county qualification campaign is that by 1852 significant gains had been made in a few counties where a sound foundation had already been made in the days of the Anti-Corn Law League.[100] Electoral strategies become an increasingly important feature of pressure-group agitation, but the techniques employed prove to be very different from those favoured by Cobden and the League.

CHAPTER VI

Nonconformist Electoral Policy prior to 1870

The involvement of Nonconformists in the politics, especially the Radical politics, of particular constituencies can be documented from an early stage. But before the 1840s there is little sign of the development of pressure groups seeking to mobilise the electoral power of Nonconformists on a wider basis in order to secure redress of their grievances by Parliament. The most that one can find is the occasional effort to get candidates to subscribe to pledges. This happened during the agitation for the repeal of the Test and Corporation Acts in the 1820s. In 1830 the Anti-Slavery Society, which attracted the support of many Nonconformists, issued an *Address to the Electors* instructing supporters to seek from candidates a solemn undertaking to vote for the abolition of slavery. In 1833, it is estimated, 150 candidates took such pledges as the result of the work of the Society's Agency Committee. In the same year the Baptists of Yorkshire issued *An Appeal to the Christian Electors of the United Kingdom on Their Obligations in Reference to the Ensuing Elections*, asking voters to seek pledges from all candidates on the redress of religious grievances as well as the abolition of slavery.[1]

But the first major impetus for the formation of a national Nonconformist electoral policy came from two developments in the mid-1840s: the establishment of the Anti-State Church Association (Liberation Society from 1853) in 1844, and the strong Nonconformist reaction against the Peel government's decision to increase the grant to the Roman Catholic seminary at Maynooth.[2] Having been made aware of the strength of Nonconformity by the successful protest against the obnoxious educational provisions in Graham's factory legislation in 1843, many Nonconformists now began taking an interest in a concerted electoral campaign. In the summer of 1845 the Executive Committee of the Anti-State Church Association passed a resolution committing them to seek to get at least half a dozen of their own men elected to represent their principles in Parliament.[3] The Maynooth Grant and other recent episodes seemed to demonstrate a dangerous absence of representation for the Nonconformist point of view in the House of Commons. In various constituencies electoral associations were formed.[4] In Bristol there was an Anti-State Church Electoral Association which aimed at getting 'Voluntary' candidates elected to Parliament.[5] Plans became remarkably ambitious, stimulated no doubt by the contemporaneous activities of the Anti-Corn Law League. There was talk of a campaign involving no fewer than 350 constituencies. But, like the League at this time, the Association soon found that intervention at by-elections was a hazardous foundation for an electoral strategy. A vacancy occurred at Southwark in August 1845 and the new policy was given its first test when Edward Miall, editor of the *Nonconformist* and one of the founders of the Association, accepted an invitation to stand from local Dissenters and Liberals who found unacceptable the official Liberal candidate, Sir William Molesworth. Miall attached much significance to his candidature. It would enable Dissenters 'to read an impressive lesson to a powerful political party that the insults they have heaped upon principles dear to their former supporters are remembered and resented'. But the result was a humiliation. Miall polled only 353 votes to Molesworth's 1,942 and, because Molesworth's majority over the Conservative was nearly 800, Miall had not even put the Dissenters in the position of appearing to hold the balance of power. At other by-elections local Liberals showed the same resentment towards 'outside' interference as they were manifesting at this time towards the League, and so the Nonconformists' first attempt at an electoral strategy soon petered out.[6]

In 1847 there was, however, a great revival of interest in electoral action, and we see the first major attempt at a Nonconformist strategy in connection with a general election. The immediate cause was a new political 'insult' to Dissenters—proposals by Lord John Russell's Whig government for an increase in aid for Anglican schools. The decisive step was the creation of a national co-ordinating committee—the Dissenters' Parliamentary Committee, set up by a conference of Dissenters in April 1847 for the purpose of promoting the candidature of 'Voluntaries'. Its chairman was Samuel Morley, the immensely wealthy Nottingham industrialist, who was to be one of the dominant figures in Nonconformist politics for the next thirty years. The electoral strategy which this Committee devised took several forms.[7] First was an interesting early attempt to do what later became commonplace with pressure groups, draw up a list of sympathisers available to stand as candidates. On 25 May the Committee sent a letter to selected persons asking them to allow their names to be placed on this list. They included many names which are to become familiar in pressure-group politics.[8] The appeal put great emphasis on the duty of Christians to undertake this kind of work. Secondly, an address to electors was issued. This suggested two types of action: the return of members who would give direct expression to the Nonconformist point of view, although it is admitted that this may be possible in only a few constituencies; and, more broadly, action that would at least

convince the Legislature that there exists a large body of constituents, numerous enough to turn the balance of parties, with whose interests it is unsafe to tamper—who have sufficient self-respect to resent gratuitous insult; attachment enough to their principles to stand by them against any and every political confederacy; and resolution enough to cast off allies who have thought fit to betray them.

What this meant was that Dissenters should not support any candidate who held Russell's views on ecclesiastical questions. Where there was no candidate standing on behalf of the principle of religious liberty, abstention was recommended. But 53 candidates were specifically recommended. There were other interesting developments in electoral action. A periodical, the *Nonconformist Elector*, was published to give guidance to all Dissenting electors. A campaign was opened to raise £50,000 not only to help with the expenses of Voluntary candidates but also to secure freehold voting qualifications.

Specific action in the constituencies owed much still to local initiative, although the increase in national co-ordination is impressive. Action that was concentrated on notorious anti-Voluntarists was very successful, Macaulay being ousted at Edinburgh and Roebuck at Bath. In London the lead was taken by the Dissenting Deputies who issued electors with five pledges to seek from candidates. Their bid to eject Lord John Russell himself from the City failed, but Voluntarists defeated junior Whig ministers at both Lambeth and Tower Hamlets. There was also vigorous electoral action in Lancashire and Yorkshire, although Miall again failed to gain election, this time at Halifax where the threatened Whig minister, Sir Charles Wood, made a pact with the local Peelites.[9]

The overall results were claimed as a Voluntarist triumph. Sixty MPs were alleged to be pledged against any endowment of religion by the State. Nonconformists naturally began thinking of developing a longer-term strategy and concentrating in particular on registration. The Anti-State Church Association began to develop its electoral organisation, setting up a network of local committees one of whose purposes was to organise electoral abstention. In 1852 it set up a General Election sub-committee which gave help to various candidates including Miall who at last won election to Parliament— at Rochdale.[10] This gave Miall new authority in the movement. He began pressing for the Liberation Society, as it became in 1853, to 'bring systematic and continuous effort to bear upon our electoral bodies' in order to increase the anti-state church element in the House of Commons. The Executive Committee debated this and finally submitted to a soirée held in London in February 1854 a major plan for electoral work. They indicated that they looked forward confidently to emulating the success of the Anti-Corn Law League through the adoption of similar methods. The proposal, which was adopted, was to set up two committees. One, the Parliamentary Committee, was to concentrate on parliamentary work, lobbying, preparation of legislative proposals, and so forth. But the other, the Electoral Committee, was given the duty of 'inquiry into the state of the constituencies, to ascertain where attempts might properly be made to obtain the return of representatives holding the Society's principles, to suggest suitable candidates, and in other ways to work electoral machinery as far as possible for anti-state-church purposes.'[11]

On 3 July 1854 the Executive Committee took a step further in its creation of electoral machinery when it adopted a recommendation of its Income Sub-Committee to appoint a Travelling Agent who would be employed 'in making those local inquiries, & in having those conferences with parties among the various constituencies, which must form an essential feature in any successful electoral scheme'. In October the Rev. E. S. Pryce accepted the offer of this position.[12] Consultations were now proceeding with regard to the composition of the Electoral Committee, especially its chairmanship, and in the meantime Dr. C. J. Foster, chairman of the Parliamentary Committee, attended to electoral work. It is interesting to see how this was developing. There was a by-election at Frome, and some of the Society's friends there sought advice as to how they should vote. Foster then interviewed Donald Nicoll, one of the candidates, and he was able to advise them that his views on ecclesiastical questions justified their support.[13]

The composition of the Electoral Committee was decided in March 1855 when Samuel Morley agreed to be its chairman. Pryce was to act as secretary, and Foster was included among its members.[14] The committee then began the task of collecting information about the state of the constituencies. But planning also now began as to the use to which this information would be put. In September 1855 *The Liberator* called on Dissenters to utilise the machinery provided by Freehold Land Societies in order to get themselves on to the register.[15] On 6 December Foster spoke at a meeting of friends of the Liberation Society and explained why this was so important: 'They had found out that wherever there was a respectable element of dissent in point of numbers and influence, it was almost a matter of certainty that they could mould the voice of the members representing that constituency in favour of any particular question in which they took interest.' He then described the information which the Committee had been collecting and the conclusions they were drawing from it. They had taken Church attendance statistics and used these to construct tables giving the electoral strength of Dissent in every county constituency in England and Wales. These demonstrated that in Hertfordshire, for instance, where the three Tory MPs had won by very narrow margins, Dissenters could become a majority of the voters. Here was a great opportunity to enable Liberals to gain seats on condition of adhesion to 'the Religious Liberty party', and he called on London supporters—as the League had done—to invest money in Hertfordshire freeholds 'in order to turn the balance'. He listed counties in which, according to these tables, Dissenters were in the majority. Yet 32 out of their 50 members, as things stood, voted against the Dissenters on every division. The remedy was obvious.[16]

And so we see the emergence of an electoral strategy, one in which the influence of the Anti-Corn Law League is still strongly evident. The interest of rank-and-file Liberationists was now being aroused, as is seen in the keen debate on the subject at the triennial conference in May 1856.[17] Both Foster and Pryce read papers. Pryce indicated that the Society had decided, like the League, to concentrate on the counties where there existed a vast potential but so far 'inert' body of Dissenting voters who needed to be aroused. The Committee were preparing two lists—one of 'localities where attention to the registering of votes was most likely to reward their efforts', the other of 'gentlemen who united principle and practical ability, the gift of speech, leisure, and social position', and were available as candidates. Thus Morley revived the idea which he had originated in 1847. Pryce warned against three influences which could disrupt the election strategy—internal disagreements, 'sectarian exclusiveness' such as refusing to vote for sympathetic non-Dissenters, and existing ties of personal friendship and party connection. In the ensuing debate one delegate who said that he personally had added 500 names to the register in South Essex advocated the same principle as the League had favoured—registering as many more people as possible without specifying that they must be Dissenters. Foster stressed the particular advantage of registration work in counties that were unaccustomed to contested elections: if the party that came in first did its registration work quietly, it would not have its claims resisted or claims on the other side sent in. He advised delegates to set to work systematically within their own congregations to get all those qualified on to the register. In this way they could build up enough votes to turn the scales at most contested elections. Delegates suggested attendance at registration courts as well. One said that he had started this kind of work six years before in Hertfordshire, had established 1,400 claims, purged about as many from the register, and virtually wiped out the Tory majority. Again and again delegates insisted that it need not be taken for granted that great families controlled counties. This idea was 'a mere chimera', a myth that crumbled as soon as any aggressive electoral action was undertaken.

Following the conference, the Electoral Committee began a drive to increase the number of 'religious liberty voters' on the register in a selected list of counties. One novel feature of this was that agents were being advertised for to undertake this work and a fee was being offered of one shilling for every Dissenting voter placed upon the register.[18] Meanwhile, Pryce made a series of visits to different parts of the country. He also kept a careful watch on by-elections. When early in 1857 adverse reports were received on the views of Wykeham Martin, Liberal candidate at West Kent, Pryce and another agent were dispatched to endeavour to extract from him satisfactory pledges on Sir William Clay's Tithes Bill and the withdrawal of the Maynooth grant. They were successful on the former only.[19]

A general election now loomed. In spite of the dominance of foreign policy questions, the Electoral Committee claimed that it had succeeded in mobilising enough electoral pressure to force numerous candidates 'to consider subjects which they had neglected, and to adopt and pronounce unmistakeable opinions'. One form of electoral pressure was the widespread issuing of circulars setting out the votes of MPs on ecclesiastical questions. Nonconformist votes, as organised by the Liberation Society and its agents, were claimed to be responsible for numerous Liberal victories.[20] J. Vincent has argued that the Society may well be entitled to a considerable amount of credit for the Liberal landslide in the counties in the 1857 elections.[21] The county electoral strategy was certainly impressive and very shrewdly devised. It showed what could be achieved by patient, long-term planning. It began in December 1855 when the Liberals were publicly advised that there were 25 county constituencies which they could recover if they brought forward candidates acceptable to Nonconformists. Then Dissenting ministers and correspondents in these 25 were sent material to help them to qualify new voters. This was followed up by a more intensive campaign in 11 county constituencies. Apart from Berkshire, Dorsetshire, and Herefordshire, all the counties gained by the Liberals were on the Society's list.[22]

This was very encouraging, and Foster came before the annual conference of the Society on 6 May with a new plan for increasing the Nonconformist electorate in the counties.[23] For several months *The Liberator* contained a great quantity of information on county registration and advice on how the campaign should be conducted.[24] But, unfortunately, all was not well in other areas of the Society's electoral work. Carried away by their excitement over the counties, the strategists had perhaps unduly neglected the boroughs. Maill had been defeated at Rochdale, a serious blow as he was not to be able to get back into Parliament, in spite of repeated attempts, for twelve years.[25] Another important parliamentary leader, Sir W. Clay, was ousted at Tower Hamlets, and unpleasant recriminations ensued at the annual conference.[26] And then a major reconstruction of the electoral organisation had to be undertaken. Pryce resigned as Travelling Agent in June, although he agreed to stay on as secretary to the Electoral Committee. In February 1859 he resigned from that post as well. Following this second resignation, the Electoral Committee—which in 1857 had been amalgamated with the Parliamentary Committee—was itself dissolved and replaced by a new Committee to prepare for the general election. Responsibilities were divided between Foster who was to look after the introduction of candidates to constituencies and the Society's secretary, J. Carvell

Williams, who was to superintend 'the more general action among the constituencies'.[27] It is not surprising in view of all these upheavals that the Society played a much more subdued role in the general election of 1859. A new departure was plainly needed, one that would tackle the problem of the boroughs. It was to this task that Edward Miall now turned his attention. Since the time of the League, which had largely abandoned the boroughs as a field of operation, electoral strategies had become heavily oriented towards the counties, all the more so because in the Freehold Land Societies existed excellent facilities for carrying on the kind of strategy popularised by the League. The challenge of the 1860s for all pressure groups was to redress the balance.

During 1860 one can see the early signs of a feeling among Liberationists that a much more aggressive electoral policy was needed than that which had been pursued in the previous decade. At the annual meeting in May there were numerous calls for constituents to put more pressure on their members, especially those who were failing to fulfil their pledges to vote for Trelawny's Bill for the abolition of Church rates.[28] The Society's main campaign on this question continued, however, to be based on the traditional technique of mass petitioning. But there was much debate on how to translate this into votes in the House of Commons. At a conference on the Church rates question on 12 February 1861 Samuel Morley told Dissenters that they must not vote for any Liberal candidate who was not in favour of the abolition of Church rates. 'He felt sure that they would never be thoroughly understood as being in earnest until they carried out the earnestness in something like the way he had ventured to indicate.'[29] An opportunity for doing this seemed to be at hand—the South Wiltshire by-election, where T. F. Grove, the Palmerstonian candidate, was refusing to support unconditional abolition. The *Nonconformist* called on Dissenters to abstain, but Grove withdrew before the election.[30]

By May 1861 the *Nonconformist* was calling on Dissenters for an all-out war at the next general election against 'vacillating Whigs' and Liberals who tried to stay on the fence—even if this meant letting Tories in.[31] In July occurred a by-election which was critical in this respect. Lord John Russell, the sitting member, had had a stormy electoral relationship with the Dissenters in the City of London, being alternately opposed and supported by them and sometimes seriously dividing them as to what attitude they should take towards him. But he had at last, as the *Nonconformist* put it, 'been screwed up to voting and speaking for total abolition' of the Church rates. Now he was elevated to the House of Lords, and his City of London seat was vacant. The Liberal candidate, Western Wood, was not satisfactory on the rates question, refusing to support unconditional abolition, and for him to replace Russell would be a conspicuous setback for the Dissenters. There were many predictions of large-scale Nonconformist abstentions. In the event, Wood was victorious, but there was a smaller poll than in 1857, the last contested election. The *Nonconformist*'s advice to Dissenters to abstain produced one of the first instances in Nonconformist electoral politics of controversy over whether or not it was a 'suicidal policy' to withhold support from an indifferent candidate 'when the result would be the return of a worse one'. It argued that the City of London by-election was a very special test of opinion in which such tactics were thoroughly justified, but it did admit 'that on ordinary occasions an indifferent Liberal is to be preferred to a zealous Tory.' 'We are not at all insensible to party obligations. We are no advocates of thrusting isolated crotchets into positions of primary importance.' But abstention had been advised in this case in order to warn the Whigs of the danger of running candidates such as Wood and trying to trifle with the Church rates question. The problem for the Liberation Society was that its basic purpose was the disestablishment of the Church of England but that this was a goal that was far too remote to be practicable as an electoral test question. The way was open as a result for a great deal of uncertainty as to which intermediate stages on the way to this ultimate destination were, and which were not, acceptable in the platforms of Liberal candidates. Should a man be accepted by the Dissenters because he was further along this road than his Conservative opponent? Thus the Chairman of the City of London Liberal Registration Association said that his support for Wood was in accordance with the policy of the Liberation Society of which he was a member. As the Society became in effect the electoral umbrella organisation for Dissenters, concerting electoral strategy on behalf of all the various causes in which they were interested, it became increasingly important to define exactly what that policy was. In this instance the *Nonconformist* justified making Church rates a test question on the grounds that a man's attitude to it could be taken to exemplify the state of his mind on the whole range of questions connected with 'religious equality'.[32]

A special sub-committee of the Society's Executive Committee now prepared a report on the Society's future operations. The critical question was the reason for the Society's failure through its traditional methods of agitation—petitioning, propaganda, lobbying—to secure increased votes in Parliament. The sub-committee had before it a report, which seems to reflect Miall's views very strongly, advocating a public announcement 'that we decline wasting our energies upon the present Parliament, and that we shall concentrate them upon the formation of a Parliament more in unison with our wishes'. It was deemed inadvisable to state this change of strategy publicly, but the main lines of the report were accepted. The main thrust of Liberationist tactics was now to be 'the creation and direction of power amongst the Constituencies', in other words the conversion of the House of Commons into 'a more efficient instrument for our designs, by bringing to bear upon its election, a fuller and weightier volume of public opinion, operating through the agency of the constituent bodies'. The Parliamentary Committee was instructed to begin preparing for the next general election and to pay particular attention to Wales in this regard.[33]

Numerous articles in the Nonconformist press at this time discussed what should be done to oblige the Liberal party to pay more attention to the Nonconformists both in the selection of candidates and in the promotion of legislation in the Commons. Especially influential was an article in the *British Quarterly Review* which advocated exploiting the breaking up of the old arrangements whereby Tory and Whig families divided the representation of counties. The Tories were now much weaker in Parliament and were desperate to win every seat that they could. Thus there were more county contests, and Dissenters could exploit this by abstaining in the case of an unsatisfactory Liberal candidate. In many counties Dissent 'can make itself, if it chooses, master of the situation as between itself and the Liberal party'. Dissenters would not need to vote for a Tory. All that was required was that the Tory party managers should get to know that, 'as at present advised, the present Liberal member will not be supported by the Dissenters at the next election'. The Tories would then hasten to take advantage of this impending Liberal split, and the Liberal would have to protect himself by conceding what the Dissenters demanded.[34]

Wales was the most glaring instance of discrepancy between Nonconformist strength in the community and weakness in parliamentary representation, and it was there that the Society concentrated its electoral efforts. In September 1862 a great conference was held in South Wales at which plans were laid for a massive Welsh campaign to get Nonconformists on to the electoral register and to lay the foundations for the election of a large number of Welsh Liberal Nonconformists at the next general election. Carvell Williams now begins to emerge as a significant electoral strategist. In a most impressive paper which he presented to this conference he analysed electoral conditions in South Wales and estimated how many members the Nonconformists could elect. The conference was followed by numerous district meetings and conferences in other regions in most of which Williams played a prominent part.[35]

The development of a more systematic electoral strategy was seen in another direction. The Parliamentary Committee decided to meet 'on the occasion of each parliamentary vacancy, to consider what steps should be taken in connexion with it'.[36] The significance of by-elections was that they enabled warnings to be given in advance as to the type of action that might be taken at a general election and thus encouraged the making of arrangements that could forestall the need for such action. Preparation for the next general election became all the more urgent when the defeat of the Church Rates Bill in Parliament in 1863 indicated that, far from advancing, Nonconformist strength in Parliament was now in decline.[37] At the annual meeting in May one delegate called for the creation of electoral committees in all parts of the country 'to promote the return of suitable members'.[38] Writing to the *Nonconformist*, 'A Political Dissenter' suggested action to promote three kinds of candidatures: first, that of their leader, Miall (there was much dissatisfaction with Trelawny's handling of the Church Rates Bill); secondly, in opposition to any Liberal who refused to support the Church Rates Bill; and thirdly, wherever there were men ready to 'break new ground, or break afresh old but lost ground, such as the counties and boroughs of Wales, "single-handed" against a Tory, even though their return at the first contest may be almost hopeless'. Above all, they must 'be rid of the bugbear of dividing the "Liberal interest" ' and be prepared to run their own candidates and allow Tories to win. Since this was a novel idea 'which it will take a long time to make clear, even to many Dissenting electors', the work of educating the constituencies to accept it should begin as soon as possible. Here was the problem. Nonconformists had been deplorably ready in the past to accept and vote for totally unsatisfactory Liberal candidates. They must be educated to see that letting in Conservatives would be only the prelude to the growth of a new, a 'real' Liberalism in which their interests would at last be fairly represented.[39]

So far there had been many ideas put forward but little attempt to have them debated or to secure agreement on which should be implemented. There was, for instance, much confusion as to whether the aggressive electoral action should take the form of independent candidatures or of mass abstention of Nonconformist voters. It was imperative that, if the Nonconformists were to play a significant role in the Liberal party's electoral calculations, these crucial decisions should be reached and supporters educated to understand, agree on, and implement them well in advance of the next general election. By late 1863 it was probable that less than two years remained before Parliament would next be dissolved.[40]

An opportunity now arose for someone to take the whole matter in hand. Back in 1861 the Parliamentary Committee had been entrusted with the work of preparing for the next elections. So far this work had proceeded mainly on traditional lines with the emphasis on registration.[41] But in late 1863 even this threatened to be disrupted, and the Society's hopes for making an impact at the general election shattered, by the resignation of the Committee's Chairman, Dr. Foster, who had decided to go to New Zealand. Here was Edward Miall's great opportunity. Miall had been out of Parliament since 1857 and had grown very frustrated over both his own impotence and that of the movement so long as its action continued to be narrowly parliamentary in its focus. He now persuaded the Executive Committee to set up a sub-committee under his chairmanship to investigate the situation following Foster's resignation. Its report which he wrote and which was presented at the Executive Committee meeting on 23 October 1863 is one of the major documents of pressure-group electoral policy.[42]

Miall's paper begins by stressing the dismal state of the Society's parliamentary position and prospects. The Society's 'prestige' had been shattered by the way in which once large majorities in favour of Trelawny's Bill had 'dwindled down to a tie vote'. Members who had supported the Society in its parliamentary work, not because they felt any real interest in its immediate objects or approved of its ultimate design, but because it seemed to be succeeding, to be the bandwagon on to which all ambitious politicians needed to jump, were now hastening to dissociate themselves from it. In other words, success breeds success and failure breeds failure, and the

deterioration was now proceeding at an accelerating pace:
the *prestige* of our earlier successes fading, if not faded—all our measures
rejected by growing rather than by diminishing majorities—none of them
placed by their promoters upon a broad, intelligible principle which it is
worth many defeats to ensure—a melancholy meagreness of debating power,
and an utter want of commanding qualifications for the successful lead
even of a forlorn hope.

An entirely new political strategy was therefore called for, and it
is a measure of Miall's genius as an electoral strategist that he
grasped at once that this must not be the merely negative kind for
which so many angry Nonconformists were calling. One lesson of the
parliamentary débâcle was precisely that coercion did not work,
that it built up among the members who were obliged solely for
electoral reasons to pledge themselves to vote in a certain way
'impatience and resentment' which burst forth in an avalanche of
reaction against the Society and its objects as soon as something
occurred to break the spell of the Society's prestige. The new
strategy must therefore be one that would establish reliable and
strong foundations, that would contain within itself 'the germ of
future power—a new life to become developed, *pari passu* with the
decay of the old—which in process of time shall constitute an independent political party, strong in its own strength, capable of indefinite expansion, and vitalized and united by the broad principles
which this Society aims to embody in Legislation'.

They should abandon the present Parliament and devise a
strategy to determine the character of the next one. This meant
rejecting the principle of supporting at all costs the Liberal party as
it at present existed, for in such a strategy lay no hope of any advance
for Nonconformist interests. The stage had arrived when the friends
of the Society should give its interests precedence in their use of their
electoral power. Hitherto they have let themselves be influenced
primarily by their attachment and loyalty to the Liberal party, and
this has been on the whole a reasonably successful strategy. 'We
have hung on, as it were, to strength greater than our own, and, in
return for the preponderance given by our support to the Liberals
in Parliament, we have extracted from them some few concessions.'
But that phase is now at an end. The Liberals have nothing more to
offer, and so the supporters of religious equality ought now to
'reverse the rule of their political action by giving primary importance to their object, and only subordinate importance to the
ascendancy of the Liberals'.

What Miall then proposes is that in future all electoral co-operation should be withheld from the Liberals in any constituency where they are not prepared to grant to Nonconformists that share of influence over the representation to which they are entitled by virtue of their local strength. He describes how this principle would work in practice:

> if, in a constituency returning two members, we contribute the larger number or a full half of the votes which give them their seats, we are entitled to claim for ourselves the nomination of one of the two accepted candidates. Should the proportion of those who sympathise with us be too inconsiderable to justify a claim to that extent, it may yet be large enough to warrant their demanding, in return for their co-operation, the recognition of some, at least, of the practical measures they desire.

The basic rule he defined as follows:

> that we should act with the Liberal party in future Elections on the well understood but indispensable condition, that *up to the measure of our strength on the local register the objects about which we are interested shall be advanced by the Election*—that as a part of the Liberal force in each constituency, and in due proportion to that part, we should be recognised in the political programme of the candidate who wishes to receive our assistance—and, if this measure of justice be denied us, that we *resolutely withhold our co-operation*—our 'vote and influence'—*whatever may be the consequences of our abstention to the Liberal party.*

This, he stressed, was not merely a coercive strategy. Its effect would be, in fact, to plant 'the beginning of a healthy and vigorous electoral life in the very heart of incipient electoral death': 'It will gradually, perhaps more rapidly than we dare anticipate, but surely, absorb into itself the best elements of the Liberal party, and effect a transition from the no creed of to day, to the heart-stirring creed of to-morrow.'

But would it work? Miall considers two possible sources of resistance to it. First is the Liberal party managers, but, although they may 'wince', he is convinced that it will take no more than one general election for them to come around. 'They need us quite as much as we need them.' Far more serious is the problem of 'the almost insurmountable difficulty we shall meet with in persuading those who sympathise with us in sentiment to stand by us firmly in this kind of electoral action'. However, it was not essential to win over all sympathisers to it nor to make it work in every constituency:

> In most places, the balance between parties is so even that a comparatively small proportion of votes withdrawn from one of the scales will determine on which side the preponderance shall be. And the two sides of the House

of Commons are so near to an equality of strength, that the loss of a few seats will make all the difference between the ins and the outs.

Miall's principle provided basic guide-lines, but he insisted that it should do no more than that. The maximum of flexibility should be allowed for each constituency to determine their own mode of implementing it. The Liberation Society would collect all available information and advise the local people as to 'the practical inferences which it warrants'. But the final decision as to the action to be taken must be theirs. Miall provided one of the best definitions ever arrived at by a pressure-group electoral strategist of the proper relationship between central headquarters and local branches:

Our plans will have to embrace a two fold purpose—first, to create about our friends a general atmosphere of thought and sentiment favourable to Electoral self-appreciation—and secondly, to adapt and apply the stimulative process locally, so that each constituent body may feel an influence emanating from the centre & touching it in that way which is best suited to its circumstances.

Miall called on the Society to make this policy its major work from now on until the next general election. So important were the issues raised that the Executive Committee desired to refer the report to conferences of friends of the Society. The first and most important of these was held in London on 11 November 1863. At this Miall read his report, and then three resolutions were debated and passed. The first of these called on all who accepted the Society's principles 'to attach to them paramount importance in the use of the electoral power with which the constitution of the country has invested them'. The second declared the opinion that the present was a time when party claims could safely be subordinated without injury to any single issue of national policy. The third endorsed Miall's basic principle by asking the Executive Committee to act so as to persuade all electors who 'concur in the general objects of the Society henceforward to make such demands on behalf of their principles as may be warranted by their strength on the local Registers, and, in the event of a refusal, to withhold their support from candidates for their suffrages'.[43]

Miall then commenced a tour of the country during which he presented his paper at a series of regional conferences. The first was at Manchester on 18 November when a resolution compounding the three adopted at the London conference was passed with only two dissentients. The mood was generally enthusiastic, George Hadfield, MP, asking, 'Why could they not as a Liberation Society do as the

Corn-Law League did?' But a sour note was struck by Hugh Mason of Ashton who moved an amendment to delete the words, 'and, in the event of a refusal, to withhold their support from candidates for their suffrages'. He objected to any policy which might lead to a severance from the Liberals to whom they owed so much already and who could, he was sure, be won over to do more by a process of 'reason and argument'. The proposed *coup de main* would only drive the Liberals away and lose the Nonconformists valuable friends. He objected to what seemed to him a pledge to abstain from voting irrespective of what the issue of the general election might happen to be. He also raised the crucial dilemma which was so often to divide members of pressure groups: whether to support the better party or only that one which came completely up to the ideal. 'He would rather have half a loaf than no bread at all,' Mason declared; 'and so if he found a party in power disposed to give a considerable amount of support to them; and if, by displacing that party, as he believed it was in the power of the Nonconformists to do, he brought in a party who would not give them the same support, he certainly was not wisely supporting the principles with which he was identified'. In reply Miall insisted that the proposed strategy was far more flexible than Mason alleged, and the amendment was soundly defeated. But Mason's point of view was one which was widely held. It is significant to find it being supported by the Rev. J. Guinness Rogers who is to play a major role in the shaping of Nonconformist electoral strategy over the next thirty years.[44] And at a meeting in Birmingham the previous day the Rev. R. W. Dale, who is to be the great disestablishment agitator with Rogers in the 1870s, had spoken out strongly against any aggressive electoral action aimed at the Liberals, especially if it would have the effect of handing government over to the Tories.[45] Much adverse criticism of Miall's proposals also appeared in the Nonconformist press.[46]

The next conference was at Bristol on 25 November. Handel Cossham moved the same composite resolution, but it was strongly opposed by Herbert Thomas largely on the grounds that such action would break up the Liberal party by giving other sections, 'with whom he also sympathised', the feeling that they would have to make similar demands on it in order to protect their own position. F. J. Thompson said that, although he generally supported the resolution, he felt that the phrase 'paramount importance' was 'rather too strong'. J. H. Leonard then admitted that the local committee had been divided over the wording of the resolution. He moved to replace 'paramount' by 'increased' and to omit the clause about withholding support. He opposed any strategy which might cause the Tory party to gain power. Miall's answer was to stress that he was not intending to be purely negative and disruptive in his attitude to the Liberal party. The strategy was likely to 'infuse new life' into the party and to 'put within it the germ of a new existence'. He also appealed to the Nonconformist conscience by telling them that their political power had been given them by God and that therefore they ought not to trifle with their votes and allow them to be 'at the beck and call of any member of the aristocracy who comes forward and suits his creed to the constituency'.

We ought to consider that we have that power placed in our hands by the wisdom of God to bring advantage to his church. And if we do not make our principles "paramount" in the use of this power, I fear we do not apprehend the greatness of the question to which we have put our hands.

But this did not mollify his critics. Indeed, Thomas and Leonard extended the amendment so that it asked also for the omission of the statement that no national issue would be injured by the proposed policy. The Rev. D. Thomas said that he feared harm to the Liberation Society's influence in Bristol if they became regarded as extremists. Like Mason at Manchester, he expressed anxiety over the effect of the resolution on their freedom at a general election if a major issue of policy such a reform bill or a war should come up. The amendment was finally defeated by 54 to 20 and the resolution carried by 58 to 10.

At the public meeting following the Bristol conference Miall emphasised again the God-given nature of the Nonconformists' political power. He used another argument which was also likely to appeal to his audience: the methods proposed were the same as those which had made the Anti-Corn Law League a political power. The aim of the strategy was not to disrupt the Liberal party but to seek a fairer share for the friends of religious equality within the tripartite partnership of which that party was made up, the other partners being the Liberal Churchmen and 'the politicians as such'. It was a flexible strategy: 'We don't intend to say, "Vote for that at the next election, whatever it may be, or we shall have nothing to do with you"; we don't intend to run the line sharply through all the constituencies of the country, nor do we intend to neglect a fair appreciation of what may be up at the time an election comes.'[47] But the major force against which he had to contend was clearly that of Nonconformist fear of splitting the Liberal party. An editorial in the *Nonconformist* for 9 December 1863 explained why the withholding of votes had to be available as an ultimate sanction. Most politicians were Anglicans and therefore their natural course was not to do anything which would interfere with the privileges of their Church. If they were given to understand that their liberty to resist the claims of their Dissenting constituents was without limit, then 'it may easily be foreseen that such questions, for example, as the abolition of Church-rates, will very speedily be thrust back into a position of neglect and contempt'. Nonconformists could not allow politicians of the type which predominated in Britain to feel that they would always be supported: 'at some point or other restraining force must be exercised. A refusal to vote for the member who thus transgresses the boundary which separates permissible from non-permissible opposition, constitutes the restraining force.'[48]

By the beginning of 1864 the new electoral strategy was coming under attack from many directions. The Rev. John Gordon, a member of the Executive Committee, resigned because of his disagreement with it, and many Nonconformist and Liberal journals expressed strong disapproval.[49] One of the main fears was that the policy would only lead to the complete isolation of Nonconformists, especially if the Liberals and Tories agreed not to compete against each other for their votes.[50] The *Nonconformist* denied that Liberationists were seeking to 'isolate themselves from the political world', a claim that was made by W. E. Forster.[51] The counterattack took the form of trying to show Nonconformists that the proposed action was in fact the proper form of action for them to take as Nonconformists. Thus the *Liberator* declared in an editorial on 'Electoral Action':

Our duty arises directly out of our position. The possession of the franchise gives every man an opportunity of 'witnessing for his principles'. If he is in earnest in anything, he should be in earnest with respect to this. It is a personal duty which can no more be escaped or carelessly performed with impunity than any other duty. It is our business to see to it that, as far as possible, just and honourable men are returned to the Legislature. If we return, or allow men to be returned, who are neither, we do dishonour to our principles and stain our reputations.[52]

Meanwhile Miall was continuing on his round of visits to District Conferences. The next was at Norwich on 20 January 1864. This turned out to be strongly influenced by indignation over the conduct of Colonel Coke, the Liberal member for East Norfolk. According to

J. H. Tillett, the mover of the resolution endorsing the new electoral strategy, some of the Dissenting voters had told Coke at the last election that they would not support him unless he gave a written declaration of his principles on the Church rates question. Coke accordingly promised to vote for Trelawny's Bill and so received the Nonconformists' support. Having voted once for the Bill, he then announced that he had thereby fulfilled his pledge and 'had done all he promised to do'. It was obvious that opinion in East Norfolk was likely to be strongly in favour of the new strategy. Many speakers swore that they would not again vote for Coke—and Coke was indeed defeated in 1865, coming bottom of the poll, 156 votes behind the other unsuccessful Liberal, and 991 behind the second Conservative, whereas in an 1858 by-election Coke had had a majority of 213 over his Tory opponent.

The mood at the Norwich conference was accordingly very militant, and the resolution was carried unanimously, delegates being most disinclined to heed the Rev. T. A. Wheeler's plea to them to 'remember that they had won their privileges not from their own strength, but from the gradual influence they had brought to bear upon the Liberal party'. The prevailing mood was more accurately expressed by J. Fletcher who said that 'they must familiarise their minds to the idea of letting in the Tories': 'The old policy had been to vote for the man who under all circumstances was the best. He thought if the candidate did not represent the truth as it appeared to them, the right policy would be not to give him their votes'.[53]

The next conference was at Halifax on 27 January. Carvell Williams attended this in place of Miall. An amendment was moved to delete all reference to coercive action but received only a few votes.[54] Then in late February six meetings in leading Scottish towns passed resolutions endorsing the new policy.[55] On 25 February a Midland Counties conference was held at Leicester. Once again an amendment was moved which offered a much milder and completely non-coercive approach to the Liberal party. The mover, the Rev. R. W. McAll, expressed anxiety about any possibility of separation from that party. But only three delegates voted for the amendment.[56] At Sheffield the resolution, as moved by R. Leader of the *Sheffield Independent*, was worded rather differently, obviously in order to forestall objections of this kind from strongly Liberal Nonconformists:

That the course pursued by the leader of the Tory opposition in the House of Commons in making resistance to measures for the extension of religious liberty the distinctive policy of his party, is an especial call to the friends of religious liberty and equality to accept the challenge thus given, and to maintain, as the leading principle of their electoral policy, that all the various classes of her Majesty's subjects should be impartially dealt with by the laws of the realm, without regard to distinctions of religious faith.[57]

At Plymouth on 10 March Miall defined the two points which should be regarded as the minimum that could be accepted from a Liberal candidate: support for the abolition of Church rates, and support for allowing Nonconformist ministers to officiate in parochial burial-places.[58]

At the annual meeting of the Society on 5 May the Executive Committee reported on what it had done so far to implement the new policy. An electoral history of every constituency over the last thirty years had been drawn up, and local information was being accumulated. But they were most anxious to avoid the impression that all that needed to be done would be done centrally. Most of the action which would be needed to ensure the success of the electoral policy would have to come from the efforts of people in the constituencies. It was clearly at the constituency level that the strategy was most likely to break down. One delegate suggested that some means should be thought of 'to bring their own electors together in the various constituencies, whenever elections took place'.[59] There was growing anxiety that a dissolution of Parliament could occur at any time and find the local people quite unprepared with any electoral policy for their own particular local situations. Editorials in the *Liberator* again and again emphasised the critical importance of early preparation for an election. A letter in the *Nonconformist* on 20 July 1864 pointed out that candidates were now being selected and so action was needed if the 'great mass of moral opinion' elicited at the conferences in favour of the new policy was to be of any avail.[60]

By-elections and selections of candidates now became critical. The first test of the new policy seemed to arise at Halifax where Sir Charles Wood was talking of retiring and Edward Akroyd was being promoted as his successor. Wood's vote had been for the Nonconformists in Parliament, but Akroyd's would not be. He was a strong Churchman and opposed to concessions to Nonconformists, but he did support the Liberal government. Nonconformists in Halifax were urged to seek a candidate of their own to run against Akroyd lest his 'evil example' infect other Liberal constituencies. 'Of what use', asked one correspondent of the *Nonconformist*, 'is the inauguration of an electoral policy, if in such a borough it is deliberately reversed?'[61]

The supineness of the Halifax Dissenters was ominous indeed, but fortunately an event occurred at this time which did a great deal to restore the credibility of the electoral strategy—the Exeter by-election. Edward Divett had held one of the two Exeter seats for the Liberals continuously since 1832. In 1864 he died, and at the ensuing by-election the Conservatives gained the seat, thus holding both Exeter seats for the first time since the Reform Bill. The Liberal candidate, J. D. Coleridge, lost by 26 votes, and his defeat was generally attributed to the abstention of some Nonconformist voters in protest against his refusal to support the total abolition of Church rates. The result was hailed as the first major test of the new policy, a portent of what could happen if a handful of Nonconformists abstained in numerous other very evenly balanced constituencies. Another encouraging feature was the role of local initiative. One Exeter elector wrote: 'I had little idea that our abstaining from voting would produce so much excitement, and cause our conduct to be so extensively canvassed.' The editor of the *Nonconformist* drew the appropriate moral in an editorial entitled 'To Whom It May Concern—A Warning'. The warning—to 'Whig whips'—was that 'they will find some such intractable zealots *in every borough*, and that the nearer parties are to an even balance, the more dangerous it will be to treat their convictions as of no moment. *Do they want fifty Exeters next year?*' The important point was that it took only a handful of intransigent Dissenters to do the damage, so that the Whips should not feel reassured upon discovering other 'politically childish' Nonconformists who can be 'gulled by high sounding generalities'.[62]

It was these normally strongly Liberal Nonconformists who were now the focus of attention. Some were very worried over this impending tug of loyalties and urged early peace talks between Nonconformists and local Liberal managers.[63] But then came another by-election which took a good deal of the gloss off the Exeter result and revealed that these Nonconformists could not be quite so contemptuously dismissed as Miall had claimed. This was at Hastings where the Liberal candidate, George Waldegrave Leslie, was an opponent of the abolition of Church rates. News of his candidature brought immediate calls for the Nonconformists of Hastings to mobilise their forces against him. On 23 September the Liberation Society's Executive Committee decided to obtain further local information 'with a view to determining what, if any, action should

be taken by the Society'. Accordingly W. Skeats visited Hastings.
But he had to report back that 'it had been found impossible to
induce a sufficient number of the Electors to adopt the Society's
Electoral policy, & that Mr. Waldegrave Leslie had been returned
by a majority of 29'. The *Nonconformist* carried an angry editorial
entitled 'Eating Dirt' condemning Nonconformists such as those at
Hastings who were ready to accept any Liberal candidate, even if
they had to put their own principles in abeyance in order to do so.[64]

This setback seemed to suggest that co-operation was a safer
course to pursue than trying to provoke local Nonconformists into
confrontation with the Liberals. In some places both sides proved
ready to come to terms. For example, at Southampton Nonconformists were reported to have been given a voice in the preliminary
arrangements for the selection of the Liberal candidates and, as a
result, the Liberal party there was united behind the two men who
had been chosen.[65] It was not only the Liberals, after all, who
suffered from the divisions caused by militant Dissenters. The
Liberationist cause itself was weakened by the divisions among
supporters over the new electoral policy, especially if an attempt
was made to invoke the ultimate sanction of the withholding of
votes, and so the Liberationists too, having made their gesture and
shown what disruption they could cause, had every incentive now to
seek to come to terms with the Liberals. In an editorial in its
November issue the *Liberator* emphasised 'the necessity for mutual
consultation and timely arrangement' and 'the importance of
avoiding as far as possible the severance of existing political ties'.
Nonconformists should discover and organise their own electoral
strength in each constituency and then open communications with
other sections of the Liberal party. Detailed advice was given to
them on how they should deal with Liberal members with unsatisfactory voting records. The stress was on getting involved as far as
possible in the process that led up to the selection of the Liberal
candidate.[66]

The Executive Committee now began its own serious preparations
for the general election. On 7 October 1864 it adopted a recommendation of the Electoral Committee that a special agent be engaged to visit certain critical constituencies prior to the elections,
and two weeks later it was decided to appoint J. M. Hare to this
position.[67] A list of thirty-three boroughs was finally arrived at after
a special sub-committee had scrutinised the electoral situation in all
200 English boroughs. 'In some of these', it reported, 'a very moder-

ate, or inconsistent supporter may apparently be either turned out, or made to pledge himself to more active support of Religious Equality measures.' Boroughs which were not selected included those under predominant Conservative influence where effort would be entirely wasted, and those where action against one weak member 'would have the effect of weakening & endangering the position of a firm friend'.[68] Hare now began a series of visits to the selected boroughs.

One of the boroughs which were selected and which Hare visited was Aylesbury. Here in January 1865 another success for the electoral policy was claimed. The prospective Liberal candidate, Frederic Calvert, could not bring himself to promise to support the abolition of Church rates. Local Nonconformists therefore interviewed him and told him that he would not receive their support at the general election. Calvert realised that he could not succeed without this support and so retired from the contest. He was praised for doing so rather than being prepared, like Coke of East Norfolk, to give an insincere pledge.[69]

The Parliamentary and Electoral Committee now commenced a massive electoral campaign. This was both public and behind the scenes. Constituencies were bombarded with literature, giving details of members' voting records and information on registration, voters' qualifications, and so forth. Much of the campaign consisted of electoral education. H. S. Skeats, for instance, published a volume which set forth the results of every election in every constituency over the last thirty years.[70] The minutes of the Committee show it as hard at work many months before the election promoting the candidatures of sympathetic persons, prodding local 'friends' to take firmer electoral action, and making enquiries about the opinions of proposed Liberal candidates.

Nevertheless, at the triennial conference of the Liberation Society on 2 May 1865 some delegates argued that progress was still far from satisfactory. The Rev. C. Vince of Birmingham admitted that it was 'unpleasant and disagreeable' work and that those who engaged in it were 'called narrow-minded, bigoted, pig-headed, and all sorts of hard names'. Many of the Society's friends could not stomach this and so succumbed and accepted weak Liberal candidates. He suggested therefore that 'it would be better to concentrate our threatenings at ten or twenty places' and let those who were carrying them out 'know that they have the whole body at their back, and that they have the hearty sympathy and thanks of those who are pledged to the carrying out of this great question'.[71] An editorial in the *Nonconformist* also acknowledged that the weakest part of the strategy was 'the electoral conduct of our friends in small constituencies'.[72] Accordingly the Electoral Committee decided to make a second investigation of each of the selected constituencies and to make further efforts to establish links with the 'friends of religious equality' in them.[73] Pressure was stepped up on weak candidates. On 15 June the Committee heard that the Liberal candidate for North Yorkshire had agreed under pressure from local electors to support the Church Rates Bill. It was decided to dispatch H. A. Skeats to Reigate to organise opposition to G. W. Leveson-Gower who had voted against the Oxford Tests Bill and to send circulars to South Shropshire and North Hampshire urging that no support be given there to Liberal candidates who were not prepared to vote for the abolition of Church rates. A week later the Rev. Mark Wilks was sent to Reigate as well to lecture against Leveson-Gower (who, nevertheless, was re-elected).[74]

The general election was held during July 1865. On its eve the *Liberator* claimed that almost all Liberal candidates were now satisfactory on the Church rates question. One who was not, Lord Albert Gower, had held out almost to the end at North Shropshire, but had finally withdrawn after being 'well plied with letters' which made him appreciate that he could not be returned.[75] Throughout the elections the Electoral Committee kept a very close watch on constituencies, intervening wherever it saw weakness in a candidate or the need for stronger local support for a sound one. It became something of an agency for candidates, on the one hand trying to find seats for prominent supporters of the cause including Miall, on the other trying to help local friends who asked for names of good people whom they could run. The Committee's report on the elections claimed a large measure of success.[76] Its strategy had been, it explained, to concentrate effort on certain seats—the selected boroughs, plus the county and borough seats of Norfolk, Suffolk, and Essex, and Cardiganshire, where an attempt was made to promote Henry Richard as Liberal candidate, Banbury, where the Society was particularly anxious to secure the re-election of Sir Charles Douglas, and Hastings, where further pressure was put on Waldegrave Leslie. Although Richard did not in the end stand at Cardiganshire because local Nonconformists objected to his opposing Sir Thomas Lloyd, the Liberal who was already in the field, and Douglas was defeated at Banbury, most of the results were satisfactory. A particular triumph was the defeat of Frederick Peel, 'a hostile voter on nearly all the

Society's questions', by a much sounder Liberal at Bury. At Walling-
ford and Frome, two of the selected boroughs, Tories had been
replaced by Liberals. At Hastings Leslie had been compelled to
abandon his opposition to the total abolition of Church rates and
had saved his seat. At Lichfield, Wareham, and Northallerton, all
selected boroughs, Tories had ousted Liberals who had never voted
for 'religious equality measures'. At East Norfolk Colonel Coke had
come bottom of the poll, being replaced by an 'independent Conservative' who had been proposed by J. H. Tillett, the Norwich
Nonconformist Radical. Efforts in West Norfolk were also rewarded
by the defeat of J. Brampton Gurdon, a Liberal but an unsatisfactory voter in the House of Commons. 'These are changes', admitted
the report, 'which will for a time involve hostile votes, but they will,
it is believed, pave the way for future changes which will be decisive
gains; while the moral influence of Liberal defeats under such circumstances will be of a wholesome kind.' Only at Salisbury and
Exeter did specific efforts to defeat Liberals with unsatisfactory views
on the Church rates question fail. In most of the selected boroughs
'the precise results at which the Committee aimed, have been
achieved, in some instances mainly, and in all partly, through their
instrumentality'. For this much credit was given to J. M. Hare, the
special agent, who had 'placed the Committee in possession of
valuable information concerning the precise weight & character of
the leaders of the Liberal party in the constituencies'.

The Committee did not, however, confine its efforts to the selected
constituencies. In numerous other places friends of the Society were
communicated with and advised on appropriate action as soon as a
Liberal candidate appeared with unsatisfactory views on Nonconformist questions. Only in Reigate, West Kent, and North and South
Wiltshire did these candidates successfully resist this intervention.
Most of the others gave satisfactory private or public assurances
after having been communicated with by local electors. In the Isle
of Wight a very special form of action was taken, a vigorous campaign by the Society to persuade local Dissenters to vote for Sir
John Simeon, a Liberal but a Roman Catholic. This was successful,
Simeon retaining the seat for the Liberals.

Above all, it was claimed, the electoral strategy had been successful in fulfilling Miall's pledge that its effects on the Liberal party
would be positive and not merely disruptive and coercive. The
Liberator put it thus:

If Liberalism is especially indebted to any one influence for its recent victories, we venture to assert that it is to the stern determination of Non-conformists to attach due importance to their principles in the electoral struggle. That has braced up languid reformers, and generated enthusiasm which has carried the ablest and most advanced politicians triumphantly at the poll.[77]

Even former Nonconformist critics were mollified. R. W. Dale told a Liberation Society conference at Manchester that, while he had at one time feared that the electoral policy 'might prove injurious to the interests of Liberalism, he was glad to acknowledge that, except, possibly, in one or two cases, it had worked most advantageously'.[78]

The Society was anxious, however, not to rest on its laurels but to exploit the strengths and remedy the defects revealed during the election campaign. An appeal was at once launched for a continuation of the supply of electoral information which had proved so useful. 'Having been at some pains and cost to construct efficient electoral machinery, we mean to keep it bright, and in good order.'[79] The failure to get Richard accepted as candidate for Cardiganshire particularly rankled, and in June 1866 the Executive Committee instructed the Parliamentary Committee to make arrangements 'for improving the Cardiganshire Register, with a view to the return of a Nonconformist candidate'.[80] Wales did in fact now seem the area both of greatest backwardness and of greatest opportunity, and in 1866 a series of Welsh County Conferences were held at which Carvell Williams and Miall spoke, papers were read on electoral conditions, and committees were appointed to organise a massive registration drive. In mid-1867 a South Wales Liberal Registration Committee was set up after a conference at Carmarthen, attended by Miall and Richard. This work was to bring spectacular results and great benefit to the Liberal party in the 1868 and subsequent general elections.[81]

But, as was to be the frequent experience of pressure groups in the nineteenth century, the Liberation Society now found that just as it had mastered the rules of one set of electoral conditions it had to adapt to a drastically altered electoral situation. 1867 brought a new Reform Bill and with it the challenge of many new voters, enormously increased urban constituencies, many altered boundaries, and baffling new prescriptions for the qualification of voters. Accordingly, at the annual meeting of the Society's Council in May

1867 a motion was passed asking the Executive Committee to 'be prepared to adopt measures for so influencing the newly enfranchised class in the several constituencies as to induce them to exercise their electoral power in furtherance of the Society's objects'. The Rev. Edward White argued that this new situation presented the Liberationists with a great opportunity since the new voters 'were without formed opinions, except upon their own special questions'. Consequently the Nonconformists might exercise great influence over them if they made the first effort to form their opinions, and he suggested a conference with working-class leaders at which they would put before them 'the arguments on which Nonconformists relied'.[82] The *Nonconformist* launched appeals for an early start to preparation for the crucial first election under the new franchise. Registration work was particularly emphasised.[83]

Uncertainty over the right electoral strategy to pursue at the forthcoming general election was entirely dispelled by Gladstone's decision to take up the issue of the disestablishment of the Irish Church. This at once became the focus of all Liberationist planning for the election—whole-hearted electoral support for Gladstone and all Liberal candidates who supported him and his Irish policy. Liberals who would not give this support to Gladstone were warned that, if their seats depended on the suffrages of Dissenters, they might as well spare themselves the trouble and expense of standing for them.[84] Immediate steps were taken to bring unsatisfactory Liberal candidates into line. For example, South Essex now looked a very good prospect for the Liberals. Both seats had been won by Conservatives in 1865 but in 1868 they were to let in the Liberals unopposed. One of the Liberal candidates, R. B. Wingfield Baker, however, would support only the reform, not the disestablishment, of the Irish Church. On hearing of this the local Dissenters held meetings of protest, and Baker deemed it wise to fall into line with Gladstone. A correspondent of the *Liberator* was most impressed by what happened in South Essex:

It was quite refreshing to hear the speeches of the new voters, and amusing to see how difficult it was for the old type of rich dissenting Liberals to get out of the ruts. This little spurt of electoral activity has convinced me that it is within the faculty of any two or three determined men to make Dissent a power even in a county. Dissenting shop-keepers and dissenting working-men are the people brought into power by the new Reform Act.[85]

Liberal unity was now the pressing need, and much anger was expressed over the independent and potentially disruptive temper-

ance electoral strategy.[86] On 12 June the Executive Committee
adopted its Parliamentary Committee's recommendations for its
own election campaign. It was agreed that Irish disestablishment
should be the one point to be insisted on and that other Nonconformist questions should be regarded as of subordinate importance.
It was decided to accumulate electoral information once again from
the constituencies and to prepare a list of potential candidates to be
recommended to the Society's friends.[87] The new electoral situation
was extremely complicated, and the Society was very dependent on
its local supporters for detailed information on the altered circumstances in the constituencies. A circular sent out to them in July
indicates the kind of information which it was anxious to obtain:

1. What changes have been effected in the constituency by the new Reform
and Boundary Acts, so far as they can be ascertained, and what will be the
probable result of the approaching election?
2. Who are likely to be the candidates, and to which political party do they
belong?
3. Is there any Liberal registration, or electoral, committee in existence?
If not, is the formation of one contemplated?
4. Who may be communicated with on electoral matters, as the recognised
official, or other, representative of the Liberal party?
5. Who are the most influential Liberal electors—distinguishing Nonconformists from others?

By early September replies had been received to this from 62 county
and 104 borough constituencies in England.[88]

The Liberation Society's role in the 1868 general election was a
curious one, at once subordinate and very important. It was subordinate in that it concentrated all its efforts on helping the Liberals
to obtain a majority in Parliament, but also critical in that its own
propaganda campaign on behalf of the Irish Church issue helped
enormously to educate electors and Liberal politicians as to the main
arguments to be used to promote that policy on which the Liberal
leader had chosen to base his appeal to the people. As the Electoral
Committee admitted, it was a novel kind of election for the Society.
There was very little call on the Committee either to find suitable
candidates or to help obtain satisfactory pledges. The readiness of
Liberal candidates to support Gladstone's ecclesiastical policy 'made
any pressure on the part of the Society's supporters almost needless'.
The Society's main impact on the election was as a 'centre of information' and 'an educational agency'. Particularly important were
the publications which it supplied to voters and to Liberal speakers
and writers on the subject of the Irish Church. The Society poured

forth tracts and mounted a vast lecturing campaign throughout the country. In the twelve months preceding the election the Society's 27 paid lecturers gave 515 lectures on the Irish Church. 44 different pamphlets and tracts were prepared, and of these over a million copies were distributed.[89] The enormous asset to the Liberal party of a cause in which a major pressure group happened to be interested was graphically revealed by the 1868 elections.

During the next six years the electoral side of the Liberation Society's work was almost completely overshadowed by the 'revolt of the Nonconformists' in which its role was a strictly subsidiary one and which will be described separately in the next chapter. The enormous effort which the Society had put into the Irish disestab-lishment campaign, and then the rapid resolution of that issue, left Liberationists very confused and divided over their next course of action. Some wanted to follow the same line of policy as had just proved so successful and promote agitations for the disestablishment of the Welsh and Scottish Churches. But Carvell Williams opposed this and urged concentration on the major Establishment with the aim of making its abolition ultimately 'a test question at the hust-ings'.[90] The decision to adopt this strategy was reflected in the general disestablishment motion which Miall, once again an MP, brought forward for the first time in 1870. Efforts were made to get Nonconformist voters to put pressure on their MPs to persuade them to vote for this or at least not to vote against it.[91] At the trien-nial conference in May 1871 Alfred Illingworth, MP for Knares-borough, suggested that once certain additional measures of parlia-mentary reform had been carried disestablishment should be made 'a *sine qua non* of adhesion to the great Liberal party'.[92] One proposal for electoral action which had been rather submerged in the great Irish Church campaign of 1868 was now revived. This was that a special effort should be made to appeal to the new working-class voters. A Working-Men's Committee for promoting the Separation of Church and State was set up under George Howell's chairman-ship, and the Executive Committee of the Liberation Society issued a statement giving as its electoral justification for supporting this 'the conviction that the recent extension of the franchise—the results of which are likely to be seen at the next General Election to a greater extent than in that of 1868—has placed in the Society's hands a powerful leverage, the value of which will be dependent on previous efforts to acquaint the newly-enfranchised classes with the

E

merits of the question which they will presently be called on to decide'.[93]

During the 1860s the Liberation Society had been able to mount an at times highly effective electoral strategy because it had done so on behalf not of its major aim, the disestablishment of the Church of England, but of certain intermediate reforms—Irish disestablishment, abolition of Church rates, abolition of University tests—about which many Nonconformists felt strongly, and the achievement of which in the reasonably near future was sufficiently likely to encourage them to undertake the hard work and make the temporary sacrifice of normal political allegiances which the electoral strategy often necessitated. But by the early 1870s most of these 'lesser' grievances felt by Nonconformists had been redressed, and the Liberation Society was thrown back upon its ultimate objective, which now seemed all the more remote and unattainable because there was no longer available to be focused on it the mass of grievance against the Church of England which had been caused by these particular instances of discrimination or privilege. The efforts of the 1860s had converted the Liberation Society into a very efficient electioneering organisation. Miall had, after all, called on the Liberationists in 1863 to make electoral work their main concern. And yet it would be obviously futile now to try to mount the same kind of electoral strategy on behalf of disestablishment itself. Nonconformists would not believe in the likelihood of its succeeding and so would not be prepared to co-operate in it, and it would be a humiliating fiasco. That the Society did not now know what to do is illustrated by the vagueness of the electoral resolution moved by E. S. Robinson at the annual conference on 30 April 1873:

That, in view of the approaching general election, it is a duty incumbent on the Society's friends to prepare without delay to avail themselves of the opportunity presented by such an event, both for successfully advocating their principles, and for securing their better representation in Parliament. It, therefore, trusts that there will be a prompt response to the appeals of the Executive Committee for the increased funds, and for the improved organisation which will be essential for electoral purposes, together with a resolve to exercise the electoral franchise in the way best calculated to secure the ultimate triumph of the policy of disestablishment.

Unlike Miall in the 1860s, Robinson had no guide-lines to offer by which these platitudes might be translated into an effective practical electoral strategy. All that he could do was to praise the resolution for its 'moderate tone', for having 'no hard and fast line drawn in it', and for allowing 'full discretion', and then give this gem of unhelpful advice: 'While he himself could not say that he might not vote for a member who would not follow Mr. Miall into the lobby, he would say that candidates should be pressed very hard.' His seconder, J. S. Wright, did observe that 'they had not used their electoral machinery to the extent that they should have done', but he had little to offer as to the use to which it might now be put.

The irony is that at this time Nonconformist electoral militancy seemed to be flourishing as never before. But it had passed almost entirely out of the orbit of the Liberation Society. In some ways this was most unfortunate, for the discipline and shrewd realism displayed by the Liberationists in the 1860s were often sadly lacking in the electoral interventions of the 'revolt of the Nonconformists' in the 1870s.

CHAPTER VII

The National Education League and the 'Revolt of the Nonconformists'

The great Liberal election victory of 1868 was very widely attributed, not least by Nonconformists themselves, to the massive support which they had given to Liberal candidates in expectation of the election of a government whose policies would be directed largely towards promoting Nonconformist interests. Therefore, when Forster's Education Bill of 1870 revealed that the government was far readier to conciliate the Church of England and protect *its* interests than many Nonconformists found acceptable, it was natural that thoughts should quickly turn towards making the withdrawal of that electoral support one of the principal methods of protest against this alleged Liberal 'betrayal' of those who had been mainly responsible for placing Gladstone in power in 1868.

For this the machinery was immediately available in the National Education League, an organisation originally set up to campaign for the establishment of a non-denominational system of elementary education but now capable of conversion into a machine for electoral retaliation against a government which had failed to fulfil this programme. Joseph Chamberlain, the ambitious Birmingham Radical and one of the leading figures in the Birmingham-based League, was aware of these possibilities almost from the start. As early as July 1870 he was writing that the League would test the opinion of the country 'at every by-election that takes place' and was helping to form branches with the deliberate intention of using them to create trouble for the Liberals at the next general election.[1] The electoral potential of Nonconformist dissatisfaction with the Education Bill was soon revealed by some dramatic government losses in by-elections, most notably at Shrewsbury in September 1870. For the next year or so the League methodically built up its organisation—a network of branches throughout the country linked to the headquarters by a system of full-time travelling agents.[2] These agents developed an important electoral function. For instance, at the Truro by-election in September 1871 Francis Adams, senior, the League's travelling agent in the southern counties, was instructed by the Central Committee to intervene actively on behalf of the Radical candidate, Edward Jenkins, who was understood to support the League's principles. Adams did so, but Jenkins was defeated.[3]

That Truro was thus lost to the Conservatives, no doubt because Jenkins alienated some of the more moderate Liberal voters, did not worry the militant Nonconformists at all. In fact, the reverse was the case. This was exactly the kind of polarisation that they were anxious to promote, and if it could come about only through an initial phase of Liberal defeat and Tory success, that would have to be accepted. By late 1871 the volume of Nonconformist enthusiasm for a militant electoral strategy along these lines was clearly increasing. Thus at a meeting of Cambridgeshire and Huntingdonshire Nonconformists on 26 October some of the leading speakers 'threatened that if the Government does not administer the Education Act more in conformity with religious equality, they will do all they can to turn out the Government and replace it by a Tory Administration'.[4] Alfred Illingworth told a Liberation Society conference at Manchester on 6 November that 'where a special election occurred, and Nonconformists could not get a man to go the whole length of their principles, they should abstain from voting, and let a Conservative go into the House of Commons'. This form of electoral action was the only way to make the government consider the claims and grievances of Nonconformists, and it might have to be taken as far as to force the Liberals into opposition.[5]

The man who did most to develop support for this new Nonconformist militancy was R. W. Dale. He appealed for adherence to a specific electoral strategy: refusal to vote for any candidate who would not support the repeal of clause 25 and the amendment of clause 74 of the Education Act.[6] Particularly influential was his address on 'The Politics of Nonconformity' which he delivered in numerous centres and which was extensively reprinted.[7] The main theme which he expounded was that the present crisis proved that the traditional methods of agitation on which Nonconformists had relied to promote their educational policy were not adequate and would have to be supplemented by a definite line of electoral action. In effect, he reverted to Miall's strategy of 1863 and renewed the

demand that in those constituencies where Nonconformists constituted the overwhelming majority of Liberal electors they should
have the right to insist 'that Liberal candidates shall accept our
principles in all their breadth, and be prepared to carry them to
their ultimate issue as the condition of our support'. In other constituencies where they were less numerous but still essential for
Liberal success, Liberal candidates should at least pledge themselves
to resist any new violations of the principles of religious equality.
Nonconformity should cast off its ties with the Liberal party, and a
network of Nonconformist organisations should be formed throughout the country

through which, should the occasion arise, the country and the House of
Commons may learn that the party ties between ourselves and the Liberal
leaders are finally dissolved, and that Liberal members who shrink from
using the first opportunity for showing their want of confidence in the
Ministry, and dislodging it from power, must expect to lose the confidence
of their Nonconformist constituents.

No electoral strategy had ever gone quite this far before. What Dale
was proposing was the mobilisation of electoral power in such a way
as to cause it to become the leverage for a virtual *coup d'état*, the
bringing down of the government by extra-parliamentary pressure.

Dale having devised an electoral theory on which a strategy could
be based, the next stage was to work out the details. This was done
at a conference of Nonconformists held at Manchester towards the
end of January 1872.[8] Chamberlain presented a paper on 'The
Political Organisation of Nonconformists' which revealed for the first
time to a national audience the emergence of another very talented
electoral strategist in the tradition of Cobden and Miall. The main
strategy which he advocated was abstention. He pointed out that of
the 110 Liberal borough members who were returned after a contest to the present Parliament sixty per cent. were returned by
majorities of less than one-tenth of the electors and ninety per cent.
by majorities of less than one-fifth. Therefore, the withdrawal of
Nonconformist votes could virtually destroy Liberal representation
of boroughs, and if the result was to give power to Conservatives,
'open enemies are better than traitorous friends'. To prepare for the
implementation of this strategy Nonconformists should set up special
committees in every borough.

J. J. Stitt, a Liverpool delegate, then moved a resolution appealing
to Nonconformists 'to declare that they will not accept as a satisfactory representative any candidate for a seat in the House of Com-

mons who will not pledge himself to the amendment of the Education Act, in the sense and to the extent of the propositions adopted by the conference'. But J. Guinness Rogers complained that this was not strong enough and moved an amendment to replace the words 'will not accept as a satisfactory representative' by 'will not vote for'. This was necessary in order to make their position absolutely clear. Thomas Snape of Liverpool objected to the amendment, arguing that Nonconformist voters would soon find themselves in an impossible position because of the number of sections which appealed to them and were asking them to pledge themselves to vote only for a certain type of candidate. He objected to pledges for general elections. These were often dominated by major questions of 'imperial interest' and voters must be left free to subordinate their special concerns to such questions. R. W. Dale then spoke and indicated that he agreed with both Rogers and Snape. The resolution was intended to have the same meaning as the amendment, but he also recognised that 'great national exigencies' might arise, such as the issue of war and peace, when all else would have to be sacrificed to the need to elect a Liberal government. He then announced that Rogers had agreed to withdraw his amendment in favour of the following rider which would be added to the resolution: 'And further to make it clearly understood that, except under the pressure of great national exigencies, we cannot give such a candidate our support.' However, when he read this new wording a second time, there were loud shouts of 'Will not' and he agreed to make this further alteration. What he had done, nevertheless, was to build in to the electoral strategy an escape clause of the kind which was to be made increasing use of in the future by both politicians and supporters of particular causes.

The Manchester conference was followed by a series of conferences of Nonconformists in various parts of the country to consider the resolutions passed there. These mostly endorsed the electoral strategy there outlined, but there were some significant variations. Thus a resolution passed at the inaugural meeting of the Eccles District Nonconformist Association took a positive form as compared to the negativeness of the Manchester resolution. It pledged the Association to 'use all its electoral influence to secure the return to Parliament of such men as will pledge themselves to the amendment of the Education Act'. This left options open in case such a candidate did not appear.[9] There was dissension at a Nonconformist conference at Ipswich even although it was attended by both Chamberlain and

Rogers and the latter 'counselled a strict unwavering electoral policy as to the future'. A resolution was proposed entirely approving of the Manchester conference's electoral resolutions, but in the end only a modified form of this was carried and then not unanimously.[10] There was a lengthy correspondence on the subject in the *Nonconformist*. This also revealed considerable divergence of opinion among Nonconformists. Ignoring all that Dale had said about relating the strategy to the local strength of Dissenters, one correspondent, 'G.E.', argued that the Manchester 'test' would be pointless in most county seats where Dissenters were in too small a minority to make it worth a candidate's while to conciliate them by subscribing to the 'test'. The Dissenters in his own county

feel it would be their first duty to their fellow-Liberals and to the country at large to band together as one man and use the most strenuous efforts to deliver the county out of the hands of the Tories. To do more than that—to attempt to impose a test sure to be rejected, and then to withdraw themselves—the Dissenters of my county, I am persuaded, would feel to be most ill-advised, unpatriotic, and therefore criminal.[11]

This question of whether or not to countenance a strategy that might result in 'letting the Tories in' clearly deeply divided Nonconformists. Charles Croft of Shrewsbury wrote a reply to 'G.E.' which, although he himself strongly believed that this ultimate sanction was essential for an effective strategy, indicated the difficulties that implementing it was likely to encounter among Nonconformists at the constituency level. He recounted what had happened in the 1870 Shrewsbury by-election. He discovered that local Nonconformists were pledging their votes to a very weak Liberal candidate and not even bothering to ask him what his views were on the education question. Croft then persuaded some of them to send a deputation to the candidate, C. C. Cotes, but when he refused to give any pledge as to amending the Education Act, the other Nonconformists 'refused to see with me that this was a case for prompt and energetic action, and brought forward the old argument that "half a loaf is better than none"—that a weak-kneed Liberal is better than a Tory'. Croft then tried two more expedients. First of all, he persuaded Dale to come over from Birmingham and address a meeting which Croft had to chair himself, 'so nearly was I alone in my sentiments'. 'We had a stormy meeting, and though the force of Mr. Dale's arguments could not be disputed, their practical hearing was evaded. They would do very well for Birmingham, but *not for Shrewsbury*.' Then, secondly, he promoted an independent candi-

date and then withdrew him after Cotes gave 'some kind of undertaking' which 'he refused to call a pledge'. After all this, Cotes was
defeated and the Tories gained a seat.[12]

The dilemma for the Liberal party managers was that the interpretation of such election results was not nearly as clear-cut as the
militants tried to make out. Their thesis was always that Liberals
lost by-elections because of Nonconformist abstentions in protest
against the Education Act. But the indications are that there were
still very large numbers of Nonconformists such as 'G.E.' and the
people at Shrewsbury who did believe in the 'half a loaf' theory and
found deeply abhorrent the idea of deliberately abstaining and
thereby letting in the Tories, 'our unplacable foes', whose creed was
'reaction and repression'.[13] There was an alternative interpretation
of Liberal by-election losses, and this was that they were caused
principally by the desertion of the Liberals by Churchmen who were
alienated by the growing Nonconformist Radicalism in the party.
After all, as Truro demonstrated, acceptance of the National Education League's principles by a candidate did not render him immune
from the movement of votes away from the Liberals. Then there was
the case of Plymouth. The last time that a Conservative had been
elected for Plymouth was in 1859, yet a Conservative won the by-
election there in November 1871 by a majority of 242 and this was
widely attributed to the defection of Liberal Churchmen owing to
the Liberal candidate's disestablishment sympathies.[14] Then there
was the by-election in February 1872 for the Northern Division of
the West Riding of Yorkshire. Two Liberals had been elected unopposed for this constituency in both 1865 and 1868, yet in the by-
election a Conservative won after reports of Liberal Churchmen
having pledged themselves to support him because of the Liberal
candidate's support for disestablishment.[15] One can sympathise with
the hesitancies of candidates such as Cotes. They had every reason
to believe that any accession of Nonconformist support which might
result from a commitment to extremist points of view on ecclesiastical
questions would be considerably more than offset by a loss of votes
from Liberal Churchmen, especially as so many Nonconformist
voters seemed so little disposed to be alienated by 'moderation' on
these questions.

Such considerations did not, however, deter the militants of the
National Education League whose electoral machine was now being
made ready for the next general election. More and more of the
work of its agents was now electoral, and, like the Liberation Society

before it, the League decided to compile 'a Parliamentary register, containing a record of facts respecting different constituencies'.[16] The agents were set to work collecting information for this, and in addition the League's Central Office built up a network of correspondents to keep it supplied with news of changing circumstances in constituencies, early warnings of by-elections, and so forth. Agents were instructed to make contact with local Liberal leaders in order to advise them of the seriousness of the League's threats of withholding of Nonconformist electoral support. Chamberlain paid particularly close attention to this side of the League's work, filling his note books with detailed entries on situations in the constituencies.[17]

A start was made to implement the plan formulated by Dale and Chamberlain for Nonconformist Committees in the main centres to co-ordinate local Nonconformist organisations and try to get them to agree on a common electoral strategy. On 13 June 1872 representatives of these Committees in London, Liverpool, Manchester, and Birmingham met at Crewe and expressed the strong opinion 'that a considerable number of candidates should contest seats now held by Conservatives or nominal Liberals, on whose support the friends of religious equality are unable to rely'.[18] Chamberlain led a campaign to carry the war right into the constituencies of Liberals who were 'unsatisfactory' on the education question and whose forced surrender or electoral defeat might have a particularly dramatic or symbolic significance. H. S. Winterbotham, who was a Nonconformist, had made himself widely respected as a very able up-and-coming young politician. But he first of all declined to vote for Miall's disestablishment motion and then urged Dissenters to accept the Education Act and make the best of it and not co-operate in action which might have the effect of handing power to the Tories. Chamberlain went down to Winterbotham's own constituency of Stroud and made an attack on him which had a clear personal electoral warning.[19] The defeat of a Gladstone would also have immense publicity value and so Chamberlain concentrated on the constituency of Whitby which was held by W. H. Gladstone, son of the Prime Minister. In July 1870 he had gone there to try to form a branch that would 'give the Prime Minister's son some trouble at the next election'. On 23 August 1872 he fulfilled this promise when he addressed this branch and explained the League's electoral policy. The meeting then appointed a deputation which waited on Gladstone and threatened to withhold support from him unless he endorsed League policy on the education question.[20] Another constituency which attracted much attention was Pontefract where H. C. E. Childers had to stand for re-election following his appointment to the Chancellorship of the Duchy of Lancaster. A League deputation waited on Childers but he refused to support the League's policies. He won comfortably in spite of claims of numerous abstentions by Nonconformists and supporters of the League.[21] Much of this intervention in by-elections was organised by the League's agents. F. Adams, senior, was active at Preston in September 1872 and H. B. S. Thompson at Richmond two months later. Thompson and T. Paynter Allen were now engaged full-time on this work in the English constituencies, and the Rev. David Evans spent the summer of 1872 visiting constituencies in Wales on behalf of the League.

What was emphasised again and again was that the purpose of the League's electoral strategy was not to promote the League or Nonconformity as a separate political movement nor to disrupt and destroy the Liberal party but, on the contrary, to bring about the reorganisation and revival of that party. Given the strong attachment that the great majority of Nonconformists clearly felt towards the Liberal party, the League had to make its attitude to the Liberals appear very positive if it was to have any hope of being able to claim plausibly that it represented the feelings and interests of Nonconformists in general. Such an emphasis, moreover, chimed in very well with the aspirations of ambitious Radicals such as Chamberlain who associated themselves with the militant Nonconformist movement in the hope that it would transform the Liberal party so that their ambitions could be more adequately fulfilled in it than seemed possible in the party as it was then organised and led.

The Executive Committee's Annual Report, presented at the annual meeting on 5 November 1872, was at great pains to point out that the Committee had taken the utmost care, in pursuing its special electoral work, 'to do so in conjunction with, and by the aid of, the leaders of the Liberal party in the several districts'. Officers and Committee members had attended 'conferences of leading Liberals in those constituencies where it is thought the aims of the League can be advanced'. This was clearly the message which many of the delegates, who hated being torn by conflicting loyalties, wanted to hear. Isaac Holden, Liberal Nonconformist leader in the West Riding of Yorkshire, complained that the League's 'new programme' had 'interfered very much with the smooth current of political matters in Yorkshire'; but Edward Jenkins argued that all that they were trying to do was to bring 'the true Liberal party', namely the Nonconformists, '*en rapport* with the Government and the House of Commons'.[22] In all this, the fate of the Liberal Church-men was obviously critical. The Radicals welcomed their defection because it would hasten on the kind of polarisation which they favoured and which would enhance their own leadership. But many Nonconformists valued their alliance with Liberal Churchmen—of whom Gladstone was, after all, the most notable example—both because of what it had secured for them in the past and because it symbolised their own acceptance into public life from which they had been 'excluded' for so long. And to many the price of this Non-conformist take-over of the Liberal party would be unacceptably high if it involved the replacement of a government led by Gladstone by one of Tories who would now be much more likely to seek militantly to promote Anglican interests.

The Liberal government was now rapidly weakening, and a dis-solution of Parliament could come at any time. Candidates were being selected in anticipation of this. Consequently a new round of Nonconformist conferences was held to warn that candidates who did not promise to vote for the repeal of the twenty-fifth clause would lose many Nonconformist votes. But many Nonconformists were still far from clear whether they really could bring themselves to carry out these threats. This was revealed by the debates at a special conference in London on 11 February convened by the Liberation Society and the London Nonconformist Committee.[23] This was notable particularly for a speech by Edward Miall in which he condemned the more extreme kinds of electoral strategy. He pointed out that

There are two ways of going to work, in order to give what I may call 'electoral importance and significance' to our question. We could do it by making it unpleasant, such a disturbing element at elections as that, unless we won the first election, we shall be very little better off at the next one. I will not do such an invidious thing as to point out movements which I think are going in that direction, but we can do it in another way.

This was to start from the basis that Dissenters were a large section of the Liberal party and wanted to carry it, not break away from 'their old lines'. It meant then asking for as much recognition of their principles as their position in the party warranted and making as much advance as the Liberal party was prepared to concede but not fixing a rigid line and repudiating the Liberals unless they agreed to come right up to it at once. He did not agree with the notion that one election would suffice for an aggressive electoral strategy to produce the desired effect on the Liberals. The irritation and alienation would have their impact for an election or two beyond that one and so 'we shall find ourselves deprived of very much of that strength that we might have had if we had gone to work with a little more caution and consultation'. Nonconformists should try to keep with them 'those who have hitherto fought the battle with us of civil and religious liberty'.

In accordance with this moderate approach a resolution was proposed which referred only to the amendments which were desired in the Education Act and made no mention of electoral sanctions. Mason Jones, the well-known Liberationist lecturer, then proposed an addition to this calling for disestablishment, the repeal of the twenty-fifth clause, and the withdrawal of State aid to denominational education all to be made test questions at the next general election. He completely repudiated Miall's philosophy. They would, he claimed, get nothing from the government until they 'struck terror' into it. This was too extreme for most of the delegates. J. Guinness Rogers condemned the bringing in of disestablishment as 'reckless extravagance and a unwise policy'. Alfred Illingworth thought that it was too soon to make disestablishment a test question although they might be able to go so far as to refuse to vote for a Liberal candidate who would not at least promise to abstain on Miall's disestablishment motion. Miall pointed out that it was no use passing such dramatic resolutions in a state of great excitement if in fact they were not able to have them acted on. Mason Jones finally withdrew his amendment 'on the understanding that he was to be at liberty to propose it at any public meeting whenever he thought proper'. He was as good as his word. Speaking at the Exeter Hall on disestablishment after the conference, he uttered very strong threats against those Liberal MPs who had voted against Miall's motion.

The most spectacular episode in the electoral history of the National Education League was the Bath by-election of June 1873—to be precise, the second Bath by-election of 1873, for the long-suffering voters of that borough had to go to the polls three times during the course of that year and endure the bombardment of pressure-group propaganda on each occasion. Bath had returned two Liberal members in 1868, but at the first of the 1873 by-elections the Conservatives gained one of these seats. However, the Conservative victor almost immediately succeeded to the peerage and a second by-election had to be held. The polling was certain to be close. It was just at this time that W. E. Forster had produced a Bill amending the 1870 Education Act. This did not satisfy the League whose different ideas as to how the Act should be amended were embodied in a Bill being promoted by George Dixon, MP for Birmingham and Chairman of the Council of the League. Bath was therefore likely to be a crucial test of whether Forster's amendments had appeased Nonconformist opinion and checked their electoral alienation from the Liberal party. The circumstances made it in effect a trial of strength between Forster and the League.[24]

The League's Executive at once grasped the significance of the Bath vacancy and dispatched one of the agents, T. Paynter Allen, to Bath to investigate the situation. He tried to obtain an interview with the Liberal candidate, Captain A. D. Hayter, in order to ascertain his views on Forster's Bill and seek his support for Dixon's. Hayter refused to grant this interview. The Executive now decided to throw all its resources into the contest. J. C. Cox, a member of the Executive, agreed to hold himself ready to stand as a League candidate, and two more agents, Adams and Thompson, were sent to Bath. On 18 June they held a meeting with Hayter's committee which refused to allow them to discuss the matter directly with Hayter. The line which they took is one which is often to be found in the history of dealings between Liberal Associations and pressure groups—an insistence that the matter of a candidate's policy could be dealt with only within the regular local Liberal party machinery and that no pressure group from outside the constituency and the party had any right to make a 'requisition on the subject of their candidate's opinions'.

Upon receiving this rebuff, the agents then played their trump card and informed Hayter's committee that a third candidate was to be brought forward. There can be no doubt that the significance of Cox's intended candidature was seen entirely in relation to pre-election bargaining and manoeuvring, as a device to extort concessions from the official Liberal candidate. It was a strategy which had already been deployed with some success—at Shrewsbury. If Cox actually had to go to the polls, his candidature would, paradoxically, have been a failure. It is interesting to find the League resorting to this device rather than to the organisation of pledges to abstain. This indicates that it had neither the resources to mount an abstention strategy nor the confidence that an adequate number of Nonconformists would be prepared to co-operate in one.

The announcement of Cox's proposed candidature brought an immediate response. The committee agreed that Adams could put in writing the questions which he wished to submit to Hayter. Adams did so, but at 10 a.m. on 19 June two members of the committee met the League representatives and told them that Hayter declined to give any answer to the questions or express any opinion on the subject. Once again they argued 'that the League had no right to make any enquiry or to take any action in reference to the matter'. A suggestion that all that was required from them was a private assurance that Hayter was favourable to Dixon's Bill was flatly rejected.

There seemed nothing for it but to proceed with Cox's candidature. His address was issued and a canvass was commenced. On 20 June Cox himself arrived in Bath. He was at once waited on by a deputation from Hayter's committee who represented to him that his candidature would divide the party and so enable the Conservative to win. Hayter was, they believed, 'a candidate who would obtain the suffrages of all parties—Protestant, Nonconformists and Roman Catholics, Good Templars and publicans'. They therefore asked him to withdraw. But they still refused to say anything concerning Hayter's views on the education question, and so Cox declined the request. The atmosphere now rapidly deteriorated. Two of the eight signatories to Cox's nomination paper were found to be Conservatives, and so Hayter's supporters put it about that his candidature was a Tory plot to split the Liberal vote. A meeting which Cox tried to hold in the Guildhall was disrupted, allegedly at the instigation of Hayter's committee. Finally, seeing that Cox was determined to see it through, Hayter's committee decided to make concessions. In answer to a question at a public meeting Hayter indicated that he was in favour of the repeal of clause 25, and in a letter to the Rev. J. W. Caldicott, which was published, he pledged himself to support compulsion and universal School Boards and to oppose transferring the power of paying fees from School Boards to Boards of Guardians. Cox then announced his withdrawal. The League had achieved its objective, but Hayter still failed to win. The Conservative majority was 51, but Hayter could take consolation from the fact that in the first by-election only seven weeks earlier it had been 260.

Similar by-election interventions followed. At Dundee Edward Jenkins, another member of the League's Executive, although unsuccessful, polled 4,010, nearly four times as many votes as were obtained by James Fitzjames Stephen who stood explicitly as a supporter of the government's educational policy. All this was extremely controversial. The *Nonconformist* roundly condemned the League's electoral policy: 'To oppose every candidate who will not go the whole way with us, is to act in the very spirit we complain of in the Government. The policy of everywhere dividing the party appears to us to be suicidal.' Indeed, the *Nonconformist* took almost exactly the same line as that taken by the Liberal Party in Bath: Nonconformists should exert their power within the domestic arrangements of the Liberal Party and in the processes which lead up to the selection of candidates.[25] But the Executive Committee of the League issued a lengthy statement defending what had been done at Bath. The methods were the same as had been employed by the Anti-Corn Law League and were 'the one means by which the Government of this country may yet be convinced that we are in earnest in defence of our principles'.[26]

It seemed to begin with as if Bath was to be the commencement of a strategy of intervention in by-elections on a scale not witnessed since the days of the Anti-Corn Law League. Dale suggested this when addressing the Central Nonconformist Committee in Birmingham on the significance of what had happened in Bath. Such action, he said,

would have to recur again and again, in constituency after constituency, until the Liberal Party had learned to apprehend more distinctly and intelligently what those principles were which alone would secure for it the confidence of the great mass of the Nonconformists of the country. He felt that it was their duty to encourage their friends in every constituency in the kingdom whenever a mere Ministerialist invited their suffrages, to run another man, who, whether he won or lost, should stand on the principles of religious equality. They had a hard lesson to learn. It would be very hard for them to learn that the triumph of the so-called Liberal candidate did not always mean their triumph. It would be very hard for them to learn that the defeat of the so-called Liberal candidate ought not to awaken, in very many cases, any distress in their minds, as his success would have given them no satisfaction. It was necessary to break old political ties, and to escape from the influence of the old political traditions; but they had absolutely no choice.[27]

Accordingly, in phraseology highly reminiscent of the Anti-Corn Law League, the Executive Committee of the National Education League announced that it felt itself bound to give the electors in every borough constituency the opportunity of recording their votes in favour of League principles and would put 'gentlemen of position, character, and ability' in communication with constituencies as suitable candidates for this purpose if no acceptable local man could be found. Chamberlain himself entered into this new strategy with characteristic vigour and was soon doing all he could to persuade Radical associates to stand against unsatisfactory Liberals. One of his projects was 'the starting of candidates to lose'. For example, he asked John Morley to stand against Ughtred Kay Shuttleworth at Hastings: 'if you run *prepared to lose*, you will certainly throw S. out, even if you do not take his place'.[28]

But all was not as well as these bold words might suggest. Now that the League was for the first time preparing to wage full-scale electoral war, would its resources prove adequate or was there a danger of extending them too far and thus risking a humiliating débâcle? An awareness of problems is already evident in the Executive Committee's statement announcing the new policy, above all the question of whether appropriate candidates could be found. For on candidates the League had chosen to base its entire strategy. They must preferably be local men but, if not, men of sufficient reputation and ability to overcome local resentment at external interference. It did not take Chamberlain long to discover that here was the potentially fatal flaw in the entire scheme. Men of local standing were likely to be enmeshed in their local political worlds and would find difficulty in disengaging themselves in response to a strategy dictated by an external organisation, especially if the candidature was to be of the kind which Morley was invited to undertake. This meant that the candidates would in most cases have to be found by the League, and here Chamberlain found the same difficulties as did other pressure groups which attempted a similar strategy. 'I am sometimes almost disheartened,' he wrote to Morley on 19 July 1873.

There's no lack of men who approve, and there are a fair number who will find money, but I cannot get a positive pledge to fight, if necessary in person, from the majority of those to whom I have spoken. And yet without this we can do nothing. Unless I can make up a list of a dozen, it seems to me the responsibility and work will be too serious to undertake.[29]

The Liberal loss of East Staffordshire early in August in an election in which the drink question played a major part and the Liberal candidate, Jaffray, was treasurer of the National Education League, shocked Chamberlain and led him to conclude 'that hardly any constituency is safe for a radical at the present time'.[30] In other words, the time was extremely unpropitious for the launching of a massive campaign of independent Radical candidatures.

That a plausible excuse for abandoning this clearly over-ambitious and risky strategy would have been welcome at this stage is obvious, and suddenly one was provided. In a move which was in fact explicitly intended by Gladstone as a gesture of conciliation to the Nonconformists it was announced that John Bright was rejoining the Cabinet as Chancellor of the Duchy of Lancaster. The promptness of the response of the League's Executive Committee was remarkable. It met on 21 August and resolved to suspend all further electoral action 'until the precise meaning of the changes in the Cabinet is made known by the official declarations of Ministers'. It was announced that in the hope of important concessions arising out of Bright's re-entry to the Cabinet the League had abandoned for the present the attitude of direct hostility to the government. Much was made of Bright's own lack of responsibility for the 1870 Education Act (he was not in the Cabinet at the time) and statements which he had recently made in criticism of that measure.[31]

Undoubtedly the League would have found it even more difficult now to persuade Nonconformists to assist in a militant anti-government electoral strategy, for many were, as Gladstone intended, very impressed by Bright's appointment and confident that this meant that the government would henceforward be much more strongly influenced by Nonconformist concerns.[32] Probably, therefore, there was no option but to call off the electoral war. The real feelings of Chamberlain and his associates may have been more accurately expressed by John Morley when he wrote to Frederic Harrison on 'how little Bright's appointment really means. It is only meant to lull the Dissenting storm for the elections—and Gladstone will give the League not a jot: see if he does.'[33] But the occasion did bring certain advantages to the League. It enabled it to justify calling off a campaign which was threatening soon to involve it in great embarrassment and possible destruction of the League's credibility. As yet, however, the strategy remained largely untested. Furthermore, the League was able to claim that its electoral actions had had a good deal to do with the government's decision to appease the Nonconformists by appointing Bright to the Cabinet.

Critics such as the *Nonconformist* were delighted at the League's decision.[34] Militants in the constituencies were sometimes less pleased. Thus on 16 September the League's branch at Oxenhope passed a resolution condemning the suspension of the electoral policy.[35] Critical letters were written to the *Liberator*.[36] But from now on any local Nonconformists who wished to engage in a militant electoral campaign were on their own. A speech by Bright at Birmingham in October was regarded by the League's Executive as sufficiently satisfactory to justify an extension of the truce until the next session of Parliament, and the annual meeting which was due in October was replaced by a purely business meeting which received the report, re-elected the officers, and authorised them to call a general meeting at any subsequent time should they consider this desirable. Passages in Bright's speech were printed for distribution among the members.[37] Only in a few places did the desire for militancy appear to remain. Most notable of these was North Devon where Sir Thomas Acland seemed to be threatened for a time by a campaign to withhold Nonconformist votes from him in protest at his conduct as a member of the Endowed Schools Committee. But, in the event, he was re-elected unopposed.[38]

The sudden dissolution of Parliament at the beginning of 1874 found the Nonconformist politicians in a state of great confusion. A meeting of representatives of the Nonconformist Committees was hastily convened to condemn Gladstone's evasion of the educational question and indeed all other issues of religious equality in his manifesto and resolved to recommend Nonconformists to give no aid to candidates who declined to pledge themselves to vote for the abolition of the twenty-fifth clause and against parliamentary grants to new denominational schools. The London Nonconformist Committee issued a list of questions which should be put to candidates and advised them, 'in cases where the answers to their questions are unsatisfactory, to look out for candidates favourable to their views, and not to allow the suddenness with which the appeal of the Prime Minister has come upon the country to disconcert them, or divert them from this important and paramount duty'.[39] But effective electoral strategies cannot be hastily improvised on the eve of an election. They have to be prepared long in advance. The *Nonconformist* acknowledged this when it declined to give readers any advice as to the line of action which they should adopt in the election. This would be 'too late to be of any practical value'. There was 'neither time nor opportunity for that deliberation which ought to precede decisive action'.[40]

In view of this disarray and the fact, often overlooked, that the National Education League had called off its campaign of electoral opposition to the government six months before the election took place, the role of Nonconformist abstention in the defeat of the Liberal party is highly debatable. Guinness Rogers later claimed that Nonconformists did rally strongly to Gladstone at the end.[41] Correspondents of the *Liberator* suggested that the much more signifi- cant defections were on the 'right' of the party, from Liberals frightened by the radicalism of the disestablishment and temperance agitations.[42]

The National Education League ceased to be of any electoral significance after August 1873 and its electoral experience was transmitted, via Chamberlain and Schnadhorst, to the National Liberal Federation which was recognised as its successor when it was formally dissolved in 1877. Dale and Rogers became fervent advocates of the strategy of working within the Liberal party, and the militant strategy of 1873 rapidly became for them and other Nonconformists a bad memory of something that must not be allowed to happen again.

CHAPTER VIII

The Liberation Society, 1874–1900

The history of Nonconformist electoral policy after 1874 belongs
almost entirely to the Liberation Society which had been so overshadowed during the period 1868 to 1874. But there are no longer
any large-scale and heroic electoral strategies to be devised. Instead
the process is one of increasing integration of Nonconformist politics
within the structure of a 'democratised' Liberal party, with plans
for independent or coercive electoral action being seen as less and
less necessary. Indeed, one of the Nonconformists' principal strategies
now becomes to seek to exploit the gratitude of Liberals for the
absence of coercive electoral tactics in their relations with the Nonconformists. In this respect the contrast between the Nonconformists
and the Temperance movement is striking—and Nonconformist
leaders try frequently to bring it to the attention of the Liberal
leaders. The high point of this strategy of encouraging gratitude for
the non-employment of coercive tactics is the general election of
1880. With the return of the Liberals to office after six years in
opposition Nonconformists await their reward.

The demoralised condition of the Liberal party after its defeat in
1874 and the widespread belief that it would now have to undergo
a thorough process of reconstruction left the Liberationists in something of a quandary as to the proper tactics to pursue. There were
those who advocated seizing the opportunity to insist that disestablishment must be part of the programme of any re-organised Liberal
party and that Nonconformists would not co-operate with that party
unless it was. The idea was cultivated that the principal cause of the
1874 defeat was the discontent of Nonconformists and that therefore
Liberal revival and restoration to office were possible only through
the adoption of a programme which embodied the Nonconformists'

principal demands. Since it was an election which had revealed to the Liberal party how far the Nonconformists were prepared to take their 'revolt', it seemed only logical that the electoral threat should continue to be held over the party until it decided to bring its policy into line with what the Nonconformists were asking.

The role of electoral pressure in this new situation was debated at a conference of Liberationists from the northern and midland counties at Manchester on 4 November 1874.[1] This conference was chaired by Hugh Mason who began by urging that disestablishment be now made a test question at elections. The main resolution, however, which was moved by the Rev. George Reaney of Warrington was more cautiously worded. It declared that it was the view of the conference that disestablishment must, 'at an early period, become of paramount importance in the election of parliamentary representatives' and then went on to advise supporters that they should therefore persistently press the question 'upon the attention of the electors in every constituency (so) as to secure their intelligent concurrence and their unflinching support'. In other words, the turning of disestablishment into an electoral test question would have to be preceded by the education of the electors themselves. But Reaney's moderation did not extend to his view of what should be done about the Liberal party. He condemned as 'grossly immoral' the idea that they should be influenced by gratitude for what the Liberal party had already done for them instead of annoyance over what it had failed to do. He warned that in the end, once the electors had been educated, the party might still remain obdurate and 'they would have to be prepared to do some things in regard to local elections which must be very unpleasant'.

The ensuing debate revealed the delegates as divided on either side of the motion between the moderates who felt it went too far and the extremists who wanted it made more rigid. On the one hand, the Rev. R. Bruce of Huddersfield insisted on the importance of showing gratitude to the Liberal party if further advances were to be made, and an Eccles delegate, Caldwell, said that he would refuse to 'bind himself in every position to vote for any gentleman simply because he might happen to adopt the Liberation programme':

In certain circumstances he would do his best to oppose even one who professed Liberation principles. There were other matters on which a candidate who was in favour of disestablishment might be entirely opposed to his views, and he should not like to be coerced into voting for him under such circumstances.

This recognition of both the wrongness and the impracticability of trying to isolate a 'Liberationist vote' and keep it completely un-contaminated by all other political issues was to grow among the disestablishers and do much to establish the ascendancy of those who wanted to integrate their efforts within the broader context of Liberal politics.

The extremists replied in the form of an amendment proposed by Dr. Stock of Huddersfield to change 'must, at an early period, be-come' to 'has already become'. Alfred Illingworth, who had become much more moderate since the heady days of 1871, opposed this as decidedly inaccurate and premature.

They were not in a majority in many places, and those who could not claim to be a majority ought not to take the position of calling upon those who were in greater numbers than themselves to bow to them in every case. Every man was free to act according to his own convictions: but when they pro-posed to take organised action in the constituencies, they must be sure that they carried with them the feeling of the community. There was a great deal to do in the way of education before they could recommend such a policy as that throughout the whole country.

The delegates seemed on the whole well satisfied with a resolution which meant, as W. Crossfield, jun., of Liverpool put it, that 'they were to press their views upon the constituency, but they were not urged to ask for any pledges of those who sought their suffrages'; and Stock's amendment was heavily defeated.

Although the Society continued to keep a vigilant eye on by-elections, the emphasis throughout the next few years was on eschew-ing electoral action and concentrating on influencing public opinion. Very large sums of money were spent on advertising. The Society's lecturing efforts were greatly intensified, and special lecturers such as Frederic Harrison were engaged. The high point of this activity was the great lecturing tour of the main English centres in 1875–6 by Rogers and Dale (which they repeated in Wales the following year). This attracted very wide publicity. The Society's income was now very considerable.[2]

Every possible effort was made to play down electoral policy. The official resolutions proposed at conferences usually avoided any reference to the possibility of electoral action. This was not always popular. For example, at a conference at Birmingham on 9 February 1875 Jesse Collings moved an amendment to add to the resolution the following words: 'And this conference is of opinion that candi-dates for Parliamentary honours should be required to pledge themselves to vote for the disestablishment and disendowment of the English church.' He explained that the resolution, as it stood, 'resembled a Queen's speech, and was almost as meaningless. It required some indication of what should be done.' Illingworth opposed this as totally unsuited to constituencies where supporters of disestablishment were not in a majority. Collings, feeling that there ought to be some reference to electoral action, amended his rider to: 'And, in the opinion of this meeting, the friends of religious equality should enter upon political action, and seek every opportunity to secure the return of Parliamentary candidates favourable to their principles.' This replacement of the coercive by the positive approach seemed to suit the mood of the delegates much better, and the amendment was carried.[3]

The Nonconformist politicians recognised that there was at this time danger as well as opportunity in the re-organisation of Liberal associations and programmes which was going on in many centres. The opportunity was to insert into these new organisations, which aimed to be comprehensive and representative, a commitment to those reforms which were desired by the Dissenting section of the party. The danger was that, in order to secure harmony and integrate the Nonconformists whose disruptiveness was seen as largely responsible for the electoral disaster of 1874, there would be an excessive readiness to incorporate disestablishment into the new programmes without adequate consideration as to whether public opinion was yet ready to accept it as part of the policy of a party which periodically formed the government of the country. Great care was therefore needed, and above all they must concentrate on maturing public opinion.[4] During their lecture tours Dale and Rogers were very careful to deprecate any attempt 'to force any premature movement upon the Liberal party' and to discountenance electoral aggression. 'We do not intend', said Rogers, 'to come as Marplots into the electoral struggle.'[5]

Electoral organisation was by no means neglected during this period, but the Society's officers were at pains to keep this side of their work as much behind the scenes as possible. The Society's increasing affluence enabled it to commission more District and Local Agents, and much of their work continued to be electoral. Where there was a strong local Liberal Association in which Radicals were accorded a fair share of influence—and such Associations proliferated in the mid-1870s—the Society remained on the sidelines, but in some places Radicalism remained disorganised and the Society felt obliged to take the initiative. Indeed, there was some advantage in doing so and gaining the primary influence in the emergence of local Liberal organisation. The most notorious of these areas of 'vacuum' in Liberal politics was London, always extremely difficult for Radicals to organise effectively, and Carvell Williams, who took a particular interest in London, was quick to see a chance for the Liberationists to assert themselves. London was electorally very important, and weak Radical organisation there might spell disaster for the political interests of Nonconformity. Accordingly, on 11 December 1876 Williams and Lyulph Stanley went as a deputation from the Executive Committee to a conference of friends of religious equality for the purpose of 'organising a borough council' to cover the parliamentary divisions of London. Williams outlined a detailed plan of electoral organisation and defined the policy which it would implement as one of 'vigilance, but not of isolation'. He added that 'he thought it would turn out to be a gain to the Liberal party'.[6] This conference was followed by another one the next year at which Williams presented a most impressive, detailed report on forms of electoral action that might be taken in London. He listed seats in which he believed pro-disestablishment candidates could win and urged the London Liberals to give the Liberationists a say in the selection of candidates. Factors which some thought made disestablishment an electoral liability in other places were absent in London: 'there was no great landlord influence to contend against, and the ballot was known to be a reality.'[7] Then on 28 November 1877 he attended a meeting at Islington to help reconstitute the Liberation Society council for the borough of Finsbury. He urged Liberationists to 'attend to electoral affairs while candidates were being chosen'.[8] This policy was clearly paying dividends by giving the Liberation Society the lead in the reorganisation of London Liberalism. Thus it was to this conference that J. F. B. Firth, who was to be elected as Liberal MP for Chelsea in 1880, reported on electoral prospects in that borough. At the same time it was reported that the Liberal Two Hundred at Southwark had held a ballot to select two candidates and this had rejected J. Locke, MP since 1857, because of the unsatisfactory nature of his views on disestablishment.[9]

All this activity culminated in a conference in December 1879 of members of the Liberation Society's Borough Councils, the Dissenting Deputies, and other London Nonconformists. At this Williams unveiled the next stage of his electoral strategy for London when he analysed the usually very unsatisfactory state of Liberal candidatures in the adjacent counties such as Middlesex, East Essex, and Mid-Surrey and advised on what could be done to improve matters. His vision of electoral strategy was now rather like that of the Anti-Corn Law League: 'When the Liberalism and Nonconformity of London have done all they ought to do for London proper, there is an abundant field for action round the metropolis; London ought, in fact, to regard itself as a political centre from which to operate upon these adjacent counties.' But Williams had to admit that there were worrying signs that Nonconformity in London was no longer the stuff out of which a Radical political movement could be fashioned. He referred to the growth of

that modern political evil which I may designate as suburbanism. That means in a large number of cases respectability, which is incompatible with enthusiasm, great apathy, and sometimes downright snobbishness— (Hear, hear)—and a recantation of principles firmly held in days gone by. (Hear, hear.) We have to operate upon a mass of this kind of thing all round London, as well as that which exists within the metropolis itself. . . .[10]

For three years after the general election of 1874 the Liberation Society concentrated on its campaign to increase public support for disestablishment. But by the beginning of 1877 the feeling was growing that thought should once again be given to electoral strategy so that Liberationists would not face the next election in quite as much confusion as had characterised them in 1874. The man who now took in hand this task of devising an electoral strategy appropriate to the altered political circumstances was Charles S. Miall, brother of Edward Miall who was himself now ill and infirm and had retired from Parliament in 1874. Charles Miall formulated this new policy in a series of editorials in the *Nonconformist* in the early part of 1877 and then presented it in a paper to the Society's triennial conference in May. Miall takes as his basic assumption the belief that it would be 'unwise and self-defeating' to adopt any strategy which would have the effect of 'forcing the question of disestablishment prematurely to the forefront'. The wise strategy for Liberationists to follow was to get into the Liberal committee-rooms and gain an influence over the choice of the candidate. Their aim should be to insist and to ensure that after the next general election 'every great popular constituency, where Dissenters and working-men who are like-minded greatly preponderate', is represented by a member who is in favour of disestablishment and that, in all two-member boroughs where Nonconformists are an influential section of the party, one member should be perfectly sound on the question.

Such action has to be taken well before an election is held at the stage when candidates are being chosen.[11] Such a strategy was undoubtedly the only practicable one now, for many of the new Liberal Associations were welcoming in all disestablishers who wished to join, giving them, as individuals, a democratic voice in the selection of candidates and programmes, and incorporating support for disestablishment in the latter. Any attempt in face of this to formulate an aggressive strategy, full of threats of coercive action if the Liberationists' demands were not fully met, would have been doomed to failure because very few Nonconformists would have been prepared to support it or regard it as anything but highly immoral and wrongheaded.

The emphasis was now on finding convincing electoral reasons why the Liberals should take up disestablishment rather than on the negative strategy of preparing to bully them and force them out of office if they did not. Thus George H. Baines wrote to the *Nonconformist* from Leicester that county members ought to be confronted with the question in a positive way. They should be shown what popular support it would bring them and this could be done by, for instance, describing the large audiences attracted by the Liberation Society's lecturers. Liberationists who sit on Liberal selection committees should be encouraged to compare notes at Liberation Society conferences and debate what is the best way of handling that kind of work.[12] Another correspondent suggested supplying such men with names of good men who would be available as candidates and whom they could propose to their committees.[13] What this debate added up to essentially was an attempt to re-think electoral strategy so as to reconcile the fact that 'sooner or later systematic and continuous electoral efforts will be necessary if disestablishment is to be carried in Parliament' with the need to ensure that such efforts are put forth 'so as not to interfere with the regular action of the Liberal party, or become the occasion of disunion'.[14] The cardinal point now was that any strategy which caused disunion amongst Liberals would also seriously divide Nonconformists because of the great increase in their integration into Liberal constituency politics.

At the triennial conference in May 1877 most delegates concentrated on finding positive reasons why the Liberals should go in for disestablishment.[15] Very few threats were made. Stanway Jackson of Manchester who moved the resolution calling for preparation for the next general election expressly said that he was not asking for disestablishment to be made a test question. It is significant that the seconder was F. Schnadhorst, about to become the great organising genius of the National Liberal Federation. His message was simple:

The best way to accomplish their object was to organise their party on a popular basis. They would then soon have a large number of disestablishment candidates. It was too late to talk of disestablishment after the candidate was selected, but the matter should be so decided upon beforehand that no candidate would venture to come forward who was not prepared to accept their programme. (Cheers.) . . . He concluded by impressing on each delegate the necessity of doing all he could in his own locality to get the Liberal party thoroughly organised. (Cheers.)

He was clearly preaching to the converted. Having established the N.L.F., Chamberlain too began preaching the same message to Liberationist audiences, carefully pointing out that it did imply also accepting the decision of the majority where they happened to find themselves in a minority.[16]

One of the earliest tests of Miall's new policy came in connection with Bradford, a two-member borough, where Alfred Illingworth was being proposed as one of the Liberal candidates and a section of Nonconformist opinion was strongly in favour of deposing W. E. Forster, the sitting Liberal member, by a second disestablishment candidate. Bradford had had a very long history of Liberal dissension, and the probability was that if this proposed strategy were carried out this dissension would continue. For Forster would insist on standing again nevertheless and would retain his seat owing to his appeal to Conservatives as well as to 'moderate' Nonconformists, while the second seat would, as in 1874, be won by a Conservative owing to the Liberal split. Thus a bid to get two disestablishment Liberals elected for Bradford would almost certainly result in the election of neither, whereas if Forster were accepted Illingworth would probably gain one of the seats.[17] In an editorial of 9 January 1878 the *Nonconformist* explained that the new policy meant that a transitional period would have to be gone through. Tried statesmen who were 'strongly Liberal in some directions' and were of 'distinguished personal merit' should still be accepted, even if they did not come up to the mark on disestablishment. But in all constituencies where Nonconformists were strongly represented on the register new candidates must always be required to be strongly pro-disestablishment.[18] This interpretation of the policy was subsequently confirmed in a circular sent to the Society's friends in the constituencies in July 1878 by the Executive Committee.[19]

There was one part of the country where the trend was towards greater electoral militancy—Scotland. Here too the Liberation Society had endeavoured to foster a moderate approach to unsatisfactory Liberal candidates. Its Scottish Council decided in July 1878 to make every effort to secure Liberal candidates favourable to disestablishment and to change the attitude of Liberal MPs who at present did not support it, but the only recommendation it gave for action when a member or candidate would not give a favourable pledge was that he should be asked at least to commit himself not to vote against.[20] But it soon became evident that there was a much more militant section of opinion in Scotland which wanted strong electoral action to be planned. At a conference of the Scottish Council on 7 November 1879 there was a clash between Duncan McLaren, MP, who did not want 'black-balling' taken too far and advocated broadly the same approach as Miall had promoted in England, and the Rev. Dr. Hutton who said that he would abstain if a Liberal candidate said that he would not vote for disestablishment.[21] The disestablishment which they were referring to was Scottish disestablishment, and there were signs that this campaign was developing a life of its own independent of the more general agitation and was becoming caught up in a struggle for ascendancy between Radicals and Whigs in the Scottish Liberal party.[22] However, prior to the 1880 general election the official policy remained one of electoral moderation. At the Scottish Council meeting in November 1879 the main resolution explicitly ruled out any attempt 'to prescribe a uniform course of action in regard to the choice or the support of candidates' and simply recommended that 'the utmost efforts should be made to secure candidates favourable to the early disestablishment of the Church of Scotland'. The mover, Ex-Bailie Hunter, admitted that 'questions would arise whether a candidate who did not fully understand the question, or was not very anxious to have the question placed in front of a Liberal programme, should be pushed aside, and a course pursued that would result in the return of a Conservative'. But he rejected this type of electoral strategy. Such men could often be persuaded to advance further in their direction and, if there was any hope at all of this, should be preferred to Tories with whom there was never any hope at all.[23]

The official Liberation Society policy throughout the country was to avoid all action that might embarrass the Liberal party or give rise to accusations of 'dividing the Liberal interest'. The major reason for this was undoubtedly the re-emergence of Gladstone from retirement during the 'Bulgarian agitation' of 1876.[24] Nonconformists were deeply involved in this agitation and, swayed by Gladstone's passionate denunciations of Beaconsfield's foreign and imperial policies, many of them came to regard Beaconsfield's government as the very incarnation of evil. In these circumstances no serious thought could possibly be given to any electoral action that might result in the retention of office by such a government. Every effort was made to avoid the public appearance of a disposition on the part of the Liberationists to press their 'crotchets' at the expense of this wider national interest. Thus, when the Leeds Nonconformist Union proposed to have a great public conference to consider the position of the Liberal party on disestablishment, the Executive Committee put very strong pressure on it and persuaded it to have a smaller and less public gathering.[25] When a conference was held at Manchester on 5 November 1878, the general feeling was that Liberals should not 'sacrifice their party at this critical juncture of affairs by insisting too closely on their particular crotchets.'[26] When electoral action was discussed at a conference at Sunderland on 12 November, 'particular reference' was made 'to the duty of Liberationists, having regard to the present state of foreign politics and the proceedings of the Government'.[27] The conference which was held at Leeds on 23 January 1879 was very low-key indeed. Its proceedings were private and no detailed report of them was published. Carvell Williams read a paper, which was not published either, 'on the attitude towards the Liberal party which, under existing circumstances, should be maintained by the advocates of religious equality, and especially on the policy to be adopted in view of a general election'. The Executive Committee acted with extreme caution. They prepared an apparently very moderate resolution on electoral policy to follow Williams's paper 'with the understanding that it was not to be pressed if a difference of opinion as to the policy of passing it existed', and then it was withdrawn. The only resolution which was passed was one which referred to Scottish disestablishment and suggested that its inclusion in the Liberal programme 'would prove advantageous, by promoting united action at the next general election'.[28] 'Crotchety' candidates who stood on behalf of particular 'individual prejudices' were now regarded with extreme disfavour: the correspondence columns of the *Nonconformist* were filled with angry letters condemning the electoral tactics of supporters of the Permissive Bill.[29]

At the annual meeting of the Council in May 1879 Henry Richard admitted that they were going to 'be placed in a position of some difficulty' with regard to the general election.

The principles avowed and acted upon by the present Government are so execrable, and the policy they pursue one so full of danger, in my opinion, to the best interests of the country, that we must be prepared to make every sacrifice to remove the incubus of their official presence and power from the heart of the people. (Hear, hear.) At the same time we must beware of being too ready to set aside our own distinct principles. Our Liberal leaders, so far as I can see, are doing what they can to minimise to the utmost possible extent the expectations which they are willing that their followers should cherish in regard to anything they mean to do if they come back again to power. . . . while we are as anxious as any section of the Liberal party in this country to get rid, at almost any cost, of the present Government, I say we must not consent to have our great question shunted aside altogether.

The electoral resolution was extremely mild and contained no reference to threats or sanctions. Again Schnadhorst seconded it and expressed pleasure that 'the Liberation Society would not, like some organisations, attempt to split the Liberal party at the poll'.[30]

The suspicion that the Liberal leaders might be deliberately exploiting the alleged overriding need for the unity of the party in order to evade commitment on any questions of domestic policy was not confined to Richard. It is expressed with increasing frequency in the editorials of the *Nonconformist* which began to think that the whole policy of suppression was being taken a good deal too far. On 22 October 1879 it made a strong attack on resolutions passed by the Congregational Union at Cardiff which deprecated in particularly extravagant terms any action that might disunite the party at this great national crisis. The danger was that, if no electoral action was undertaken, the new Liberal government would find this a reason for saying that disestablishment was not an issue in the election and therefore did not have to be dealt with at all in the lifetime of that Parliament. What the *Nonconformist* was obviously especially worried about was that other questions, notably the Permissive Bill, were being promoted and might therefore get in ahead of disestablishment on the new government's legislative programme. Some electoral action there must be.

By electoral action is not necessarily meant the injudicious multiplication, or selection, of candidates, the withholding of votes, or the display of a divisive spirit. Short of that, there is much that may be done in pressing principles and aims on candidates and electors, and in placing questions in a train for settlement hereafter, if not immediately.[31]

Carvell Williams too was uneasy and warned of the danger that 'there would be some Liberal members who would take advantage of the fact that these questions were never pressed upon their notice at the general election, and they would profess to believe that the nation cared nothing about them'.[32] By the end of 1879 the movement seemed to be polarising between those who saw 'a policy of silence' and suppression as a patriotic duty and those who believed it to be unnecessary, open to exploitation, and dangerous to the interests of the movement over the next five or six years. The latter mood was especially strong in Scotland.[33]

Electoral action was debated at the conference held in London on 10 December 1879. The main electoral resolution acknowledged that priority had to be given to displacing the Beaconsfield government and so Liberal divisions had to be avoided, but it called for efforts to secure candidates favourable to disestablishment. The seconder, Dr. Underhill, admitted that they would never be able to get a commitment out of the Liberal leaders until they issued a definite threat to abstain from voting. Unfortunately, the impending election was not one on which this kind of action could be taken because of the great moral issue which Gladstone had raised and which superseded all other questions. Samuel Morley then spoke out against negative electoral tactics in general and advocated voting for a Liberal who was reasonably sympathetic but not yet ready to vote for disestablishment in preference to a Tory. Politicians should be and indeed were influenced by changes of public opinion and therefore there was no need to use coercive methods on them. A delegate then asked what was the duty of Liberationists with regard to Sir Arthur Hobhouse, one of the Liberal candidates for Westminster, who was not prepared to commit himself to support disestablishment, and was told by the Rev. R. Harley and Henry Richard that he should vote for Hobhouse rather than let a Tory in.[34]

The Electoral Committee of the Liberation Society issued a paper of advice to its supporters on how they should act during the election campaign. On the one hand, they should not 'divide the Liberal party, of which they form an integral part'; on the other, they should make sure that ecclesiastical questions were at least discussed and should pay very close attention to the selection of candidates. A long list of questions on which pledges should be sought was given.[35] Efforts were made to put pressure on particularly weak Liberal candidates, for example through the organisation of deputations of electors.[36] But, when Parliament was dissolved, no aggressive action was carried out. The Society did not even issue an Address to Electors but limited itself to the circulation of pamphlets, tracts, and placards.[37] In all of this publicity the emphasis was on promoting the Liberal cause while implying that one reason for this was the close identification between it and Liberationism. Society speakers and other Nonconformists constantly preached Liberal unity but also made a great deal of the self-sacrifice which this represented.[38] The strategy was clearly now to contrast the Nonconformists with other sections of the party and hope that a reward for loyalty would duly follow. Nonconformist opinion was very flattered by Gladstone's much publicised statement at Marylebone in which he praised Liberationists for their patriotic readiness to put their own question 'in the shade'.[39] Commenting on this, the *Nonconformist* claimed that it meant that Gladstone was recognising that the Dissenters 'are establishing a claim to more consideration in the future than they have ever yet received'.[40] At the same time, the *Nonconformist* went out of its way to draw attention to and condemn the disruptive electoral tactics of the temperance party.[41] Much publicity was given to extremes of submissiveness and loyalty on the part of Nonconformists. Thus it was reported that although the great majority of the members of one Liberal county committee were in favour of disestablishment, 'out of respect to the wishes of the minority—or, as they express it, for fear of dividing the Liberal party—they are willing to continue to be represented by two members, both of whom are opposed to Disestablishment'.[42] The noble example which Nonconformists were setting, by contrast to other 'crotchet-mongers', was constantly referred to. In spite of the great urgency of the questions in which they were interested and their strong feelings about them, declared the *Nonconformist*, 'the whole Nonconformist body is prepared to sustain any Liberal candidate who will vote strongly against Lord Beaconsfield's policy, without asking the question whether he will support Disestablishment and Disendowment or no'.[43]

The Liberationists' strategy in 1880 was to boast very loudly and frequently of not having one. It was a bold effort to make the best of a situation in which an aggressive electoral strategy would not in fact have been practicable owing to the very strong feelings aroused in Nonconformists by Beaconsfield's imperial and foreign policies and sustained by Gladstone's powerful rhetoric. The investment was in loyalty. The question now was whether Liberal gratitude would yield the desired dividend.

F

For some time after the general election of 1880 the predominant mood on both the Liberal and Liberationist sides was to extend much further and perhaps even complete the interlocking of effort which had been so striking a feature of that election and which was widely seen as having made a major contribution to the Liberals' triumph. At the Liberation Society's triennial conference in June 1880 an amendment was passed calling on the committee which was to appoint the Executive Committee to make a special effort to draw in prominent members of Liberal Associations. The mover, who originally intended it to apply specifically to London because 'the metropolis was behind the rest of the country on the question of Liberation', said how impressive had been Liberal organisation during the election. The Liberation Society would advance its interests much more effectively if it could try to work from inside that organisation to the greatest extent possible. Schnadhorst responded by inviting the Liberationists to join the Birmingham Liberals in the groups which the latter intended to send out on Saturday afternoons to preach Liberal principles in the villages surrounding Birmingham, 'so that the Liberal platform might also be the Disestablishment platform'. One might have been forgiven for thinking that the Liberationist conference was really a Liberal party conference. The Leicester committee of the Society invited the local Liberal Association and Liberal Club to send delegates, 'and for the first time, not without some discussion on their part, both these political bodies sent their officers as delegates to a conference of this society'. The electoral co-operation of 1880 was obviously already producing one kind of political dividend. Not surprisingly, delegates seemed to vie with one another to express their devotion to Liberalism as well as Liberationism. The Rev. S. Pearson of Liverpool referred to a clause in the Society's new constitution which declared that it would operate 'apart from party and sectional lines':

while he supposed they would all agree to that, he hoped they would also agree to the fact that they belonged to the Liberal party, and that the success of the Liberal party was bound up with the success of the society and its principles. There could be no success for their principles apart from the unity of the Liberal party. . . .

E. Lyulph Stanley, MP for Oldham, sought to make a philosophical explanation of the relationship between being a Liberal and being a Liberationist to show that the two naturally went together. Stanley was particularly assiduous in telling Liberation Society audiences that they were not mere specialists or people with a crotchet but reformers who would best promote the success of their cause 'by identifying themselves heartily with the most thorough-going Liberalism'. For Liberationist sympathisers such as Stanley who were now MPs and therefore had to balance a wide range of interests it was vital to get across this message.[44]

All the leading Liberationists were now strongly integrationist in their approach to Liberal politics. J. Guinness Rogers said in January 1882 that Nonconformists 'simply took their place in the ranks of Liberalism' and would be happy to do so again at the next election.[45] On 30 January 1882 Illingworth and Carvell Williams were entertained as a Liberation Society deputation at a meeting of the Liverpool Junior Reform Club. The meeting passed a resolution expressing appreciation of the Society's work. In reply Williams stressed the significance of the passing of such a resolution by a Liberal club. It symbolised 'the junction' of the religious equality party with the rest of the Liberal party'. 'The advocates of disestablishment had at length obtained the acknowledgement of the leaders of the Liberal party of the value of their section to the Liberal party as a whole, and an acknowledgement of the fact that the party could not exist without them.'[46] Williams now regularly addressed Liberal Associations and Clubs, endeavouring always to persuade them that it would be to the electoral benefit of Liberalism to take up disestablishment. Every effort was made to draw Liberals into the work of the Liberation Society. Thus at a Liberal meeting at York in April 1883 J. G. Rogers gave a lecture on disestablishment and then a resolution was carried appointing H. M. Cross, secretary to the North Riding Liberal Association, as a delegate to the Liberation Society's triennial conference.[47] At the conference itself the following month Carvell Williams pointed to the significance of the fact that

we have had in this conference a far greater number of representatives of Liberal associations, clubs, and Liberal organisations than we have ever had before. (Applause.) That, I take it, will be a sign, not merely that we are a growingly important portion of the Liberal party, but that we are fast becoming the Liberal party.[48]

Very little reference was now made to electoral policy. Williams argued that the Liberationists had done so well, 'not because they had coerced the Liberal party, but because they had done what was far better—convinced them of the justice of their cause, and satisfied them that what was right in the abstract was also politically practical and safe'.[49] In England electoral militancy was seldom expressed and, when it was, was easily suppressed. For example, at the annual meeting of the Manchester and District branch of the Society on 23 October 1883 J. H. Crosfield, chairman of the Committee, suggested that they ought to get the question of disestablishment pressed in Parliament by exploiting the fact that 'there was not a constituency in the whole of England or Wales which could return a Liberal member without the vote of Nonconformists', and Alfred Reyner moved a resolution which concluded by urging supporters to tell their MPs that their support for the three disestablishment motions in Parliament would be considered 'a test of their loyalty to Liberal principles'. But B. Armitage, MP for Salford, objected strenuously to this, and the mover and seconder acceded to his request to omit the offensive words.[50]

In Scotland, however, matters were very different. There the United Presbyterian Synod's Committee on Disestablishment, under Dr. Hutton's leadership, largely supplanted the Liberation Society and began to prepare a very radical election policy. Scottish disestablishment became a test question at by-elections, and Liberal candidates who failed to satisfy the test were subjected to extreme pressure.[51]

The interest of the Liberation Society itself in electoral policy revived only at the very end of 1884, as preparations began for the general election that was certain to follow the passage of the Third Reform Bill. The Executive Committee met and passed resolutions reminding supporters of the vital importance of seeing to the selection of Liberal candidates who were favourable to their aims. They should continue to work through Liberal organisations but should appreciate that the electoral reforms made it possible to adopt 'with a hope of success a bold and decisive electoral policy in many places in which formerly it would have been altogether impracticable, and more especially in the new county constituencies'. One point on which very great stress was laid was that this time there must be no suppression of the disestablishment question. The advocates of every other cause would be very active, and Liberationists would therefore have to make sure that they were too. But this does not mean that they had to insist on having a Liberationist candidate in every constituency or refuse to support Liberals who in all other respects were worthy of support. Their action must be largely determined by their strength in the particular constituency. In other words, the policy was 'strictly opportunist', recognising that the time had not yet come when they could attempt to coerce the Liberal party *as a whole* by threatening it with defeat unless it took up disestablishment.[52]

During January 1885 the Society concentrated on thinking of ways in which it could influence the Liberal party from within at this critical point when candidates were being selected and policies formulated. The Agency Sub-Committee produced a plan for employing the agents on this work. They should find out as much as possible about local Liberal Associations and consult with local friends as to how best to get an influence over the choice of candidates. They should make sure that persons favourable to the Society's policy became members of these Associations. The Parliamentary Committee recommended that local friends be asked to use their influence to get resolutions in favour of disestablishment passed by the Liberal Associations with which they were connected and also to induce these Associations to take steps to get that policy included in the programme of the National Liberal Federation.[53]

The biggest electoral challenge for the Liberationists in 1885 was the new voters. Politics were entering a new era and there would be 'a very nearly clean slate'. How could the Society influence the new voters so as to be able to determine what was written on it?[54] There was a general feeling that this coming election was critical for the Society.[55] And yet there was also some uncertainty. One correspondent in the *Nonconformist* warned that the agricultural labourers were very uneducated on the question of disestablishment and might oppose it. It might be safer to concentrate only on Welsh and Scottish disestablishment for the time being.[56]

There was remarkably little support for independent or militant electoral action. At conferences speaker after speaker repudiated any idea of making disestablishment a test question and abstaining from voting for candidates who would not adopt it. The most that was sought was a fair share of influence in the arrangements of local Liberal organisations. The mood was such that any call for militancy would almost certainly have met with only a tepid response. At a London electoral conference in March the Rev. Marmaduke Miller asked: 'If all those in the country who were in favour of Disestablishment were to stay at home on the polling day at the forthcoming election, where would be the Liberal party?' To this Rogers replied that he could not feel the same confidence about the possible readiness of Nonconformists to behave in this way.[57]

There was much debate on how to handle the new electoral situation in the rural areas. A good example of this is a conference

held at Northampton on 5 May to consider how to advance the
Society's aims in view of the approaching elections. Ashworth
Briggs, the chairman of the South Northamptonshire Liberal Asso-
ciation, provided a most interesting analysis of the new situation.
The leaders of the newly enfranchised class were, he said, mostly
Nonconformists, often indeed lay preachers, and so there could be
little doubt in which direction they would exert their influence:

On the other hand, the influence of the parson and the squire, though much
shaken, was by no means destroyed, and if the proposal for Disestablishment took a practical form, they would have arrayed against them an active
electioneering agent in almost every village. For almost the first time in the
history of the country districts, candidates on the Liberal side had been
chosen by representative delegates, and not by great county magnates. In
these associations the advanced element was generally predominant, and
their management was, to a large extent, in the hands of staunch Liberationists. But, at the same time, it might not be well in every case to put
Disestablishment in a prominent position, and so endanger the success of
gallant efforts to rescue county divisions from the grip of the Tories. That
must be left to the discretion of the local men, and in any case, since
Liberationists were the only Liberals who were in earnest, and Liberationism
was the legitimate and logical development of Liberalism, they were, in
teaching the principles of the latter, paving the way for the acceptance of
the former. (Cheers.) In districts where they were strong the case was, of
course, different.[58]

The Liberationists seemed aware that they might well now be
being confronted with an opportunity which would never recur and
which they must somehow take advantage of. Like all pressure
groups, they were very interested in the possibility of recruiting new
voters who had not yet been captured by the regular parties. Illingworth argued that the new voters' enthusiasm 'would count for
much'. They 'would listen more readily to their appeal than when
they had become used to the exercise of political power'.[59] The Rev.
Joseph Wood declared: 'If Disestablishment was to come within the
next thirty years it must come within the next five, for history and
experience showed that so great a measure could only be carried in
the full tide of Liberal feeling and reforming zeal which always
followed an enlargement of the constituencies.'[60] Yet there was uncertainty also. Difficulty was reported in getting farm labourers to
come to meetings.[61] Liberationist leaders constantly delivered
addresses exhorting Nonconformists to live up to their political responsibilities, thereby betraying much fear as to whether they could
any longer be relied on to support an advanced political agitation.
Illingworth warned that many politicians on the Liberal side were

Churchmen and that in some parts of the country the great majority of Liberal electors were opposed to disestablishment. There was need therefore for proceeding discreetly and perhaps asking for commitment for the time being to Scottish and Welsh disestablishment only.[62] Speeches by prominent Nonconformist MPs,[63] editorials in the *Nonconformist*, letters in its correspondence columns, all strongly opposed any independent or aggressive electoral tactics, stressing the need for Liberal unity behind Gladstone especially in face of the menace represented by the Irish Nationalists.

And yet disestablishment did become a prominent issue in the 1885 election campaign. The irony of this is that it happened without a militant agitation or use of aggressive electoral tactics by the Liberation Society and, indeed, against the wishes of that body.[64] It was the result of the promotion of the issue by three agencies outside the control of the Society—the Scottish disestablishers who made their agitation a very embarrassing factor in the Scottish Liberal electoral situation; Joseph Chamberlain who took up the broader issue in his own radical campaign; and the Tories who exploited both these demands for attention to disestablishment in order to promote general fears among Anglicans and rally their support. Once again, as with temperance in the 1870s or indeed Irish self-government in 1885, Chamberlain went ahead and promoted his own ideas with an ostentatious and undoubtedly deliberate lack of reference to the major pressure group operating in the area.

Chamberlain neither sought nor was given any specific electoral backing by the Liberation Society. Some Liberationists thought that as a result they had had to sit on the sidelines and watch disestablishment being made into a major election issue and then appear to be rejected by the electorate without anything being done to mobilise systematically the Society's resources as a strong electoral influence in support of disestablishment. But, they argued, the Liberal party had suffered also because it had been obliged to endure the hostility of the opponents of disestablishment without receiving the compensating advantage of that full-hearted support by Liberationists that could only have come from a definite Liberal commitment to the cause. At a conference of MPs and leading Liberationists held in London after the election much reference was made to the fact that all Liberal candidates, irrespective of whether or not they advocated disestablishment, were subjected to strong Anglican hostility. Henry Spicer, MP, argued that disestablishment now had to be made a formal part of the Liberal programme: 'He believed that the position the question got into at the last moment gave the Liberal party in London all the possible disadvantages with none of its advantages.'[65] At a conference at Leicester on 1 March 1886 J. Fisher, one of the Society's secretaries, gave similar reasons why the Liberal party would soon have to commit itself to disestablishment: 'Nothing was more apparent than that the Church of England was a party institution. It had become allied to the Tory party . . . The Church's electoral power was used almost exclusively on the side of obstruction, and Disestablishment had thus become necessary in the interests of Liberalism.'[66]

Any need for the Liberal party to make up its mind on this matter was, however, very soon obviated—or, at least, postponed—by the emergence of the Irish Home Rule issue which polarised politics in precisely the fundamental way that Liberationists had imagined was now about to occur in the case of disestablishment. This development also threw the Liberation Society even more back on to the defensive. It had to turn inwards to preserve its own unity as much as possible from the internal divisions which the Home Rule issue caused in all pressure groups.[67] Electoral aggression was in these circumstances even less likely than it had been in 1885. The Liberation Society, now running desperately short of funds and therefore having to make frequent retrenchments in its organisation,[68] subsided into a subordinate role of total dependence on a much weakened Liberal party, a party which was to hold office for only three years between 1886 and 1905—and then to be dependent on the Irish for its majority.

Only very occasionally was any voice raised in support of a renewal of vigorous electoral activity, and these aroused little response. There seemed to be little need for such action. In September 1890 the Executive Committee received a report that of the 362 Liberal candidates already selected in England and Wales 199 were in favour of disestablishment in general, 82 favoured it for Scotland and Wales, and only 13 were totally opposed. The views of the rest were still not certain.[69] This looked quite encouraging, and there were those in the Liberation Society who now began advocating leaving the entire matter in the hands of the Liberal party and abandoning thought of further separate political action.[70] But Carvell Williams and other Liberationist leaders strongly opposed this idea. The margin of hesitation and wavering among Liberal candidates was still very considerable and could only be reduced by constant effort on the part of Liberationists to make sure that their candidates became or remained sound on the question. And that effort could not be confined to the candidates themselves: 'it is not enough to secure disestablishment candidates, seeing that they cannot be carried without the votes of electors, and that these votes cannot be reckoned upon without much previous hard work in the constituencies.'[71] Counts of 'committed' MPs were very dangerous for pressure groups. They lulled them into a sense of false security and encouraged them to relax those efforts which were always necessary if an MP's commitment was to prove an electoral advantage for him and not a liability. The very success of the movement in 'converting' Liberal candidates and indeed the party itself proved to have its drawbacks, not least of which was the drying up of funds once potential or former subscribers concluded that everything was now being taken care of by the Liberal party. In March 1891 the *Liberator* issued an urgent appeal for extra funds: 'while the Liberal party has put Welsh and Scotch disestablishment into its electoral programme, it is still left to the Liberation Society to carry on the required propaganda in the constituencies. That is a business of great magnitude, and men and money are absolutely needful to sustain it.'[72] The Liberation Society's annual report for 1890-1 stressed that 'the mere insertion of items in a party programme will avail but little without the conviction, the enthusiasm and the energetic work, needed to secure a decisive vote of the electorate.'[73]

By the beginning of 1892 another general election was clearly imminent, and the Liberationists debated their tactics. One method that was favoured was to draw to the Liberals' attention the electoral advantages to be derived from putting forward disestablishment prominently, for example the recovery of the farm labourers' votes.[74] But should the Liberation Society itself put the question forward? On 13 February 1892 a conference was held at Sheffield to debate whether the local Liberationists 'should still pursue a waiting policy or one of a more aggressive character'. The unanimous decision was to try to make disestablishment, especially in Wales and Scotland, an election issue. 'The policy of winning elections by the suppression of opinions', was, declared F. P. Rawson, 'essentially a Tory policy and repugnant to all true Liberals.'[75] The annual report also pointed out that electoral inaction would provide politicians with their usual excuse for doing nothing after the elections, that it had not been an election issue.[76] At the triennial conference in May several delegates said that friends of religious equality should refuse to support candi-

dates who would not pledge themselves on at least Welsh and
Scottish disestablishment. The whole question of candidates' pledges
needed careful watching, it seemed. According to Carvell Williams,
the problem was now not the failure of candidates to give disestablishment pledges but rather the lack of prominence which some of
them gave the question in their campaigns. In this way, he feared,
they were hoping to be able subsequently to wriggle out of their
commitments by pointing to the absence of discussion of the question
during the elections. However, the best method of handling a candidate was the positive one of overcoming any fear that he might have
about giving the question prominence by showing him what voting
support he might expect to receive if he did so. But, although there
was much talk about the undesirability of any longer suppressing
the question, no general electoral strategy was put forward. It was
too long since the Liberationists had had one, and funds were now
too scarce for electoral organisation to be practicable on any large
scale.[77]

And, even if an aggressive electoral policy had been decided on,
it was very doubtful whether many Nonconformists were now militant enough to be prepared to support it. Here, as Evan Spicer
pointed out, was their real weakness. They had gone far towards
converting the Liberal party, but in the meantime, and perhaps
partly as a consequence of this concentration on external political
activity, there had been a steady falling away of that Nonconformist
enthusiasm which alone could make that political success anything
more than a transient, fragile and highly vulnerable phenomenon.

A last flicker of electoral aggressiveness came in connection with
a by-election at Horncastle at the beginning of 1894. The Liberal
candidate, H. J. Torr, was a prominent figure in the Liberal Churchmen's Union, a body suspected by the Liberationists of working to
get all proposals for disestablishment deleted from the Liberal programme. Of all these proposals the one that had advanced furthest
and was now actually in the Liberal government's programme of
legislation was Welsh disestablishment, and it was David Lloyd
George, at this stage one of the most militant of the Welsh radical
MPs and for some years a prominent speaker at Liberation Society
meetings, who drew the Society's attention to the unsatisfactory
nature of Torr's views on disestablishment. The Executive Committee
sent J. Fisher to Horncastle to extract from Torr a pledge of support
for the proposed Welsh and Scottish Disestablishment Bills. Torr
refused to give such a pledge, saying that he could not support any

disestablishment measure which did not continue the appropriation of tithes to religious purposes. On hearing of this, the Executive passed a resolution condemning him and advising supporters of the two Bills not to vote for him. This resolution was then printed and a copy was sent to every voter in Horncastle. The cost was borne by Lloyd George. This highly unusual display of electoral independence by the Society was very controversial. The Liberal leaders were very annoyed, and Carvell Williams had an interview with Gladstone on the matter. The Executive received a number of letters from supporters of the Society expressing their disapproval of what had been done. D. A. Thomas, on the other hand, wrote expressing the concurrence of Welsh MPs and electors.

The *Liberator* quoted much Nonconformist opinion in favour of the Horncastle intervention as the only way to check the incipient reaction against identification with disestablishment in the Liberal party. The *Freeman* argued that a victory for Torr in what was a Conservative seat might have caused other Liberals to feel that it was electorally expedient to repudiate the government's policy on disestablishment. The *Liberator* agreed. Horncastle was a test case. If the Liberation Society let it go, that would demonstrate that it had no independence left and that a candidate need henceforth have no fear of adverse electoral consequences if he came out in favour of dropping Welsh and Scottish disestablishment from the Liberal programme. Thus the whole situation would from that point on have deteriorated very rapidly. The action taken at Horncastle was aimed primarily at warning Liberal Associations not to choose candidates such as Torr and Liberal headquarters not to connive at any opposition to the disestablishment measures.[78]

Whether the advice to electors had much effect was very difficult to discern. Torr was defeated, but the voting figures were virtually identical with those recorded at the 1892 general election. Torr himself thought that only about 40 or 50 votes were affected, but the *Manchester Guardian* put the figure much higher than that. The deterrent effect of the intervention was also very doubtful. The Society quite visibly no longer had the resources to put such a strategy into effect on any substantial scale. In 1891 its leaders had had to go cap in hand to the National Liberal Federation to beg for financial assistance and had been rebuffed,[79] and now they could mount an absolutely minimal form of electoral action—one leaflet sent to electors—only because it was paid for by a source other than Society funds. And the fact that the action had been taken at all revealed another weakness in the Society's position. Since the 1860s the predominant strategy had been to work within local Liberal organisations to secure an influence over the choice of candidates and so avoid the need for coercive electoral action at the later stage when the candidate had already been selected. Suddenly to reverse that policy now or at least to have to intervene at that later stage in electoral proceedings was virtually to admit that the Society's electoral foundations were now disintegrating, in other words that it could no longer rely on local supporters who were numerous or vigilant or interested enough to exert themselves at the point when the candidate was being chosen. The Society's local roots were withering. After Horncastle, the Society had to issue a desperate appeal to its friends to try to ensure that this sort of thing did not happen again. It entreated them 'to do two things—one, that they will act wisely and energetically at the very beginning of an electoral movement in any constituency; the other, that they will keep the Society's Executive well informed of their proceedings.'[80] For a succession of Horncastles was bound to be disastrous. Thirty years of striving to integrate Liberationism and Liberalism and of promoting only pro-Liberal electoral activity had left their mark, and any anti-Liberal action would seriously divide the Liberationists and be rendered ineffective by the large number of them who would now discover that they were more Liberal than Liberationist and act accordingly.

The Liberals lost office in 1895 after failing to get Welsh disestablishment on to the statute book, and in the ensuing election disestablishment played a very minor role—except in Wales itself. Nonconformist political enthusiasm was diverted into a large number of alternative channels as more immediate issues such as the 1902 Education Act emerged to preoccupy them. The Liberation Society tried to use each of these as the basis for a revival of the campaign for disestablishment, but with little success. In 1899–1900 there was a brief revival of interest in electoral action. At the annual meeting of the Council on 3 May 1899 a resolution was passed that disestablishment be now given a prominent place in the Liberal programme. The mover, the Rev. J. E. Flower, said: 'They must assert themselves, and, if need be, make themselves extremely disagreeable.'[81] A deputation visited Sir Henry Campbell-Bannerman, the new Liberal leader, and presented various electoral arguments to him. If the Liberal party went in for the whole disestablishment policy, it was argued, 'no increase in the forces opposed to them would result, since they had the entire State Church party against them now.' That being so, it would be to the Liberals' advantage to adopt a policy that would array behind them the full enthusiasm of Nonconformists. But Campbell-Bannerman returned only evasive answers and was later advised by his Chief Whip, Herbert Gladstone, that the Liberals would be most unwise to make disestablishment a major election issue.[82]

The annual meeting of the Council in May 1900 showed the Liberationists' inability now to find a way of making themselves electorally 'assertive'. Guinness Rogers moved a resolution calling for steps to be taken to secure a distinct and prominent place for disestablishment among the measures to be advocated by the Liberals at the next general election. His language certainly was assertive: Nonconformists 'had been hewers of wood and drawers of water for the Liberal Party for many a long day' and 'had allowed their claim to be put off quite long enough'. But since 1874 Rogers had been one of the foremost preachers of Liberal unity and an- tagonists of 'sectionalist' conduct, and so now not surprisingly he was almost bereft of suggestions as to what could be done about this state of affairs. Of the possibility of independent electoral action he made no mention. John Kempster did refer to it, but his language was couched in so conditional a form as to make it clear that his ideas had no foundation in present reality:

if they had the votes and meant to use them they had the power in their own hands. They ought to be able to impress the Liberal leaders and the Liberal followers throughout the land that the question they had in hand was the one which obstructed all Liberal legislation. He agreed with Dr. Rogers that they had been hewers of wood and drawers of water long enough, but when were they going to give up the job? The time had come when there should be an organised section of the Liberal Party determined to pin their votes to this question and say, 'Give us this Bill of disestablish- ment, or we strike against the Liberal Party.'

A similar contrast between aggressive language and awareness of actual electoral weakness can be found in a speech by the Rev. J. Morgan Gibbon. On the one hand, he argued that Nonconformists had been 'postponed and deferred too often' and should refuse to wait any longer: 'as Nonconformists we should stand out and say we will not work for any Liberal candidate who is not sound on the question.' And yet he prefaced his remarks with the following admission: 'A large portion of the Nonconformists of our suburbs have only a washy decoction of Nonconformity which . . . is not sufficient to carry forward a great earnest aggressive movement such as this.'[83]

Nevertheless, Carvell Williams in 1900 made one last attempt to devise a coherent Liberationist electoral strategy. He started this with an article in the *Examiner* on 7 June in which he argued that, since the Liberals were certain to lose, it might be better to think of returning a smaller number of Liberal candidates 'who are sound on our questions than a larger number who are unsound or unreliable'. The *Liberator* took this up in its July issue by arguing that it would for this reason not be necessary at the coming election for Nonconformists to follow their traditional policy of preserving Liberal unity by keeping silence on embarrassing subjects and supporting candidates with doubtful or unsound opinions on ecclesiastical questions. It recognised that there would be many Liberals who would not approve of this notion. It was clearly the prospect of serious divisions within the Liberationists' ranks which persuaded the Executive Committee in the end not to proceed with formulating a strategy of the kind proposed by Williams. On 9 July he submitted to it a memorandum which argued that, according to present appearances, 'whatever may be the strength of Liberationists, the Liberal Party will be in a minority in the next Parliament, as in this; and that, therefore, there will be but little opportunity for directly advancing our object in Parliament'. This meant that, 'under such circumstances, there is no inducement to Liberationists to refrain from advocating their principles in order to secure the return of Liberal candidates whose views on ecclesiastical questions may be unsound or doubtful'. The Executive Committee debated this memorandum at length and finally decided not to proceed with it. Two weeks later a new draft of an appeal to electors was produced—and the passages just quoted were not included.[84] The South African War aroused very strong feelings among Nonconformists, and it was obvious that yet again the electoral assertion of the disestablishment question would have to be postponed. Never again was the subject to be debated. As an electoral organisation the Liberation Society had come to the end of the road.

CHAPTER IX

The United Kingdom Alliance, 1859–1874

By far the most systematic attempt made by any nineteenth-century reform movement to mobilise and employ electoral pressure in pursuit of its goals was that made by the temperance movement and particularly by the United Kingdom Alliance. The Alliance, founded in 1853, was dedicated to the achievement of a legislative remedy for the evils of intemperance—the prohibition by law of the sale and production of intoxicating liquors.[1] As its favoured political methods for accomplishing this—variously known as the Permissive Bill, Local Option, and the Direct or Popular Veto[2]—all involved referenda or polls of ratepayers, it is not surprising that it was very interested also in using the democratic machinery that already existed to enable the enactment of the measures that would institute these procedures. The temperance movement in mid-century was deeply divided between those who wanted to concentrate on 'moral suasion', that is persuading people to give up drinking by preaching, propaganda, and education in the evils of drink, and those who believed that legislative action was imperative to relieve people from the enormous social pressure constantly exerted by the easy accessibility of facilities for the purchase and consumption of alcohol.[3] The United Kingdom Alliance became the major organisation representing those who favoured the political solution. Its aim was to induce Parliament to pass a law enabling people in local districts to have the power, through periodic polls, of closing down the public houses in their areas. This being so, the Alliance had to win over a majority of MPs, and so from a very early stage it became interested in using electoral pressure to achieve this end.

The first instance of electoral action by the Alliance seems to be a by-election at Marylebone in 1854 when placards were issued urging voters to oppose any candidate who refused to pledge himself to independence of the publicans. By-election interventions of this kind were valued for the publicity which they afforded, and little serious thought was given at first to trying to get their own candidates elected. Early temperance candidatures, like that of Samuel Pope, the Honorary Secretary of the Alliance, at Stoke in 1857 were similar to those often indulged in by the Chartists, that is, they were withdrawn before the actual polling took place. Action at general elections began modestly with a test question which supporters were asked to submit to candidates in 1857. In 1859 there was considerably greater evidence of electoral activity, and several candidates stood as supporters of the Alliance programme. An important development in that year was the Alliance's decision to promote the formation of Electoral Permissive Bill Associations, separate from the local Auxiliaries or branches of the Alliance and intended to consist specifically of electors and for the purpose of urging the Permissive Bill on local candidates and MPs.[4]

Gradually also the Alliance built up a network of agents throughout the country.[5] Electoral work was always one of their principal duties. They were instructed to organise local temperance committees at election time, ensure that candidates were thoroughly tested as to their views on the Alliance programme, make themselves fully acquainted with local political conditions, and maintain a steady flow of this information back to Alliance headquarters. Any attempt to develop a general electoral strategy throughout the country depended very heavily on these men who then needed to compensate for deficiencies in purely local temperance organisation in particular areas or try to prod local people into making an effort to put the strategy into effect.

Before 1872 there was no secret ballot. This meant that blocs of voters who were determined to vote only in a certain way and on certain conditions could be made visible and held in reserve as a constant temptation to candidates to capture them by granting these conditions. This cliffhanging could be continued right through polling day almost until the polls closed because the tally of votes was kept and periodically announced as voting went on, and so with many very small electorates and margins between candidates often being very narrow the attraction of a bloc of votes that had not yet been cast could become very great.[6] The Alliance set to work systematically to exploit this aspect of the electoral system. When local people asked for advice as to what they should do when there was no candidate standing who supported the Permissive Bill, the answer always was that they should make no promises to any of the candidates who were standing but reserve their votes in a body until an hour or two before the closing of the poll.[7] In those days voters' pledges to candidates were actively canvassed, often paid for, and difficult subsequently to evade because it was known how in fact a voter did cast his vote. The difference made by the ballot can be illustrated by the complaint of one former MP quoted in the *Liberator* after the 1874 elections: 'The Ballot has given the power to men to pass as our allies, and to act as our foes at the critical moment.'[8] It was therefore vitally important to persuade supporters not to make any promises to candidates until such time as a decision had been made, perhaps by a meeting or a committee, as to how, in the interests of temperance, their votes should be cast. At election time the *Alliance News* would issue its readers with constant reminders of the importance of avoiding giving pledges to candidates until they knew their views and intentions with regard to the Permissive Bill.[9] Pressure to reserve votes was a major feature of Alliance intervention in elections. For example, when at Birkenhead in June 1865 neither candidate proved to be satisfactory, the Alliance commenced a vigorous campaign—through placards and other forms of publicity —to persuade its supporters to withhold their votes until one of the candidates pledged himself to the Permissive Bill.[10] At Liverpool a month later the local temperance electors met to discuss what they should do about a similar situation. There was a general feeling in favour of withholding votes. According to A. Dobbin, 'they knew not what power they might be able to exercise at the last minute or the last hour'. J. H. Plancke pointed out that 'it was thought there would be a neck-and-neck vote, and if the teetotallers could muster 300 or 400 votes, or even 100 or 200 votes, at three o'clock in the afternoon of the day of election, and one party was 50 ahead, the candidate who was in the minority might be suddenly converted to their views, in order to gain a majority'. J. H. Raper agreed. It was now too late to put up a candidate of their own, and so they should band together and vote for the candidate who would concede what they were asking.[11] With only a day or two left before polling and party feeling running very high, such pressure was often very hard to make effective or credible in practice. But there were occasions when it quite definitely did seem to work. One of these was the Devonport by-election in May 1866. Devonport was a two-member borough which was normally controlled by the Liberals. But in 1865 the Conservatives gained both seats, only to have the successful candidates unseated on petition. The stage was set for a very tense by-election, especially as very few votes had separated the first- and fourth-placed candidates in 1865. About 70 or 80 temperance voters decided to vote together after hearing the result of an interview with the Liberal candidates by a deputation from the local Alliance Auxiliary. The deputation advised them to vote for the Liberals and they did so *en bloc* between one and two o'clock in the afternoon. The Conservatives were then in the lead, but as the Liberals finally won with 1,275 and 1,269 votes to 1,216 and 1,215 for the Conservatives the Alliance could plausibly claim on this occasion to have turned the scales by its policy of withholding votes until satisfactory assurances were given.[12]

Indeed, one of the basic aims of Alliance electoral strategy came to be to hold the balance of power in constituencies. For this only a small number of voters was needed. What mattered was not their size so much as the fact that they were a bloc of voters available to any candidate who was prepared to give certain pledges. The attraction of this strategy was that it did in fact compensate for numerical weakness, such as was often demonstrated when actual temperance candidates stood, and gave temperance voters an importance out of all proportion to their numbers. This point was often emphasised. Thus at the Council meeting in October 1864 J. G. Thornton of Bristol urged delegates not to

be discouraged by our supposed electoral weakness in the various constituencies. He believed there was far more danger of our underrating than overrating our political importance. They had proved at the last general election at Bristol that although they had a constituency of something like 13,000 voters, with less than 200 united men they had turned the scale. . . .

Sir Robert Brisco echoed this. 'What large town was there,' he asked, 'that did not contain 200 temperance voters? And that number was nearly enough to win an election in most places.' This was because majorities were usually small and parties very 'nicely balanced'. A Deptford delegate reported that he had persuaded twenty-five voters to 'promise to vote together on this question, and he meant to test each candidate at the next election with these 25 at his back'.[13] The closeness of competition between the parties seemed to be the ideal opportunity for a pressure group organised as was temperance in the 1860s—or the Irish Nationalists in the 1880s. E. Vivian told the Devon Temperance League in December 1864 that 'he believed the temperance party was quite large enough to turn the scale in favour of any candidate for a seat in Parliament, and so evenly balanced were parties in the House of Commons that the temperance cause could make itself felt there'.[14] F. W. Newman argued that the very even balance of parties meant that their leaders 'cannot afford to treat us as enemies'.[15]

What was needed above all if this strategy was to work was discipline. The candidate had to feel sure that, if he made the commitment asked of him usually in face of considerable pressure from the drink interest, he would in return receive the votes which had been promised to him and, on the other hand, if he refused to make the required pledge, he would certainly be deprived of every one of these votes. This was why J. H. Raper 'attached more importance to a small, compact, and united party, who would not move except in a body, than he did to greater numbers of those who were not so single-minded'.[16] For there was a great danger that the promise of a temperance vote based on the latter larger and more amorphous body of 'temperance supporters' could not be fulfilled with consequent severe damage to the credibility of a strategy founded on the assumption that such a vote was always available for delivery. The only temperance electors who were worth anything as far as influence on candidates was concerned were those who agreed to act together and to abide by a decision reached by some procedure agreed on beforehand as to how their votes should be cast. The Alliance leaders knew this and devoted their efforts more and more to the organising of such electors through Electoral Associations and electoral pledges. The important thing was not so much what electoral action was taken as the fact that whatever action was decided on was accepted loyally even by those who might have favoured a different course. This was what impressed candidates most.

Experience soon showed that in the heat of an election contest, particularly the intensely local kind of contest which was characteristic of early and mid-Victorian Britain, voters were all too ready to give promises to candidates before obtaining what the Alliance recognised as satisfactory pledges from them in return. To combat this, and to make completely clear the existence of a withholdable temperance vote, the Alliance developed the idea of committing voters well in advance of an election to vote only for candidates who gave a particular form of pledge. The usual method of doing this was to canvass electors to subscribe their signatures to a pledge. The nature of this pledge may be illustrated by one to which signatures were being sought at Newcastle-on-Tyne in the early part of 1864:

We, the undersigned electors of Newcastle-on-Tyne, deeming it desirable to secure united action among those who are interested in the moral and social elevation of the community, hereby agree not to pledge ourselves to vote for any candidate to represent this borough in Parliament, until we have had an opportunity of meeting together to ascertain and discuss the views of such candidate on questions affecting the sobriety and social well-being of the people—the said meeting to be convened by the committee of the Newcastle-on-Tyne Temperance Union.

A less precise form was an Electors' Declaration being canvassed in London at this time in which the signatory declared his intention of making support of the Permissive Bill 'a question of the first importance in deciding how my vote and influence shall be applied'.[17] There was also the positive pledge to vote for candidates who supported the Bill. This left open the question of what action would be taken if there were no such candidates.

In June 1865 the Sunderland Auxiliary of the Alliance was seeking signatures to an electors' undertaking 'not to pledge ourselves to the support of any candidate at the next borough election unless he will distinctly promise to vote for the Sunday Closing and Permissive Bills, until we have had a meeting on the eve of the election, after the views of the several candidates on those important questions have been ascertained'.[18] This formula allowed the maximum scope for candidates to change their opinions even at quite a late stage and still gain the temperance votes.

Canvassing was also often done in order to ascertain how many of the local electors were in favour of the Permissive Bill. Where this was done, the names were then usually placed on a register which was kept up to date by further canvassing from time to time and used during elections to bring out the 'temperance vote'. A massive canvassing campaign in London, organised by the London Auxiliary of the Alliance in 1864–6, combined the two forms of canvass. Committees were set up in all the metropolitan constituencies to compile a register of the names and addresses of supporters of the Permissive Bill and to seek signatures from electors to a pledge to use their influence at elections in its favour. One aim of the London canvass was to get electors to influence one another. A draft of an 'Address to Electors' was circulated privately among known supporters of the movement and then, when 200–300 had signed it, issued in their names as an address to their fellow-electors. Really effective canvassing in the metropolitan constituencies was very expensive and work proceeded only very slowly. The aim was, however, eventually to canvass every one of the estimated 120,000 electors in them.[19]

There was an increasing tendency to try to organise the electors, once they had signed their pledges, into special associations or to create organisations which one could join by subscribing to a political pledge. This became one of the principal functions of Electoral Permissive Bill Associations. It gave a collective reality to the 'temperance vote' and made it likely that voters' pledges would be taken much more seriously by both candidates and voters. In August 1870, for example, a special Alliance Electoral Organisation was set up in Birmingham. Every member had to sign a pledge 'to reserve my vote and influence at Parliamentary elections until the Alliance Electoral Committee shall decide upon the course to be pursued, and to support such decision by my vote and influence'.[20] Early in 1871 an E.P.B.A. was formed for South Derbyshire. It was to consist of persons who had taken a pledge not to promise their votes to any candidate until he had been tested and recommended by the Association.[21]

Much importance was attached to furnishing solid evidence of this kind as to the existence of a temperance vote on which a candidate could rely if he did decide to come out in support of the Permissive Bill. The negative and coercive aspect of a strategy of withholding votes was often emphasised, but so too was the positive side, the recognition that without the assurance of gaining a substantial or election-swaying number of votes, a candidate could hardly be expected to brave the anger of the licensed victuallers, a most formidable electoral force, and throw in his lot with the prohibitionists. Thus Dr. P. P. Carpenter advised Permissive Bill supporters in Sheffield in 1864 to act together so as to 'give confidence to members to act according to their own convictions, many of whom could not at present do so on account of the strength' of the drink interest.[22] As well as maximising their own strength, the temperance reformers tried their hardest to demonstrate that the 'publican interest' was not nearly as electorally powerful as it was often claimed to be and that therefore candidates did not need to be paralysed in their approach to the question of licensing reform by their fear of it. This was one of the motivations behind the canvassing of electors. Candidates needed to be encouraged to stand up to public-house opposition. Thomas Judge of Brackley wrote to the *Alliance News* in January 1865: 'The power of the publicans in reference to the opposition they can make to a candidate willing to vote for the Permissive Bill is a bugbear afflicting would-be MPs. Let us who fear not enlighten them, and their support is gained.'[23] One who did undertake this task of enlightenment was George Tatham of Leeds who gave the following statistical analysis to a gathering of friends of the Permissive Bill:

> There were in the borough 779 publicans and beersellers, and at a parliamentary election only about 300 voted. When they analysed the votes of these and the influence they exercised, they found that not more than 75, perhaps less, would be likely to support a Liberal candidate unfavourable to the Permissive Bill. The political power of the publicans, he felt, was vastly overrated.[24]

It was not just candidates, of course, who needed such reassurance. Voters who were being asked to subordinate all other political considerations to this one question and even contemplate refraining from voting for the candidates of their own party had to be inspired to feel that it was all worth it and that the obstacles were not insurmountable.

J. H. Raper recommended the general adoption of Tatham's practice of scrutinising the electoral register in order to prove how exaggerated were the usual estimates of the strength of the publicans. Such work, he said in April 1865, was essential 'in order that a great bubble might be effectually burst, and the candidates and committees relieved from a fatal nightmare'.[25] The whole matter was debated at the Council meeting in October 1865. Thomas Whittaker argued that nine out of ten candidates would declare for the Permissive Bill 'if they did not fear that the advocacy would be fatal to their expectations'. Therefore the most important task facing the temperance movement was to make candidates feel safe in taking up the cause. Samuel Pope agreed about the problem. The real reason, he felt, why parties hesitated to adopt Permissive Bill candidates was their belief that they would be difficult to carry against the opposition of the publicans. The remedy was to entrust political power to the 'intelligent working men'. Then the influence of the publican in elections would be gone.[26] In 1866 Benjamin Whitworth said that he had been told by an MP 'that in every borough of less than 2000 electors the publicans had the power of returning almost any man they liked'. For this there were two remedies: 'an infusion of other electors to dilute this poison', and the secret ballot to enable voters to escape from the publicans' influence.[27]

During 1864 pressure steadily grew among Alliance supporters for the organisation of a general election strategy. But there was no clear consensus as to what form this should take. Some called for the promotion of a dozen candidates in specially selected constituencies, others for something more like the old Chartist practice of nominating candidates at the hustings for the sake of the publicity this provided.[28]

The critical question was how far temperance voters were prepared to go in withholding their votes altogether when there was no candidate who completely satisfied their demands. Such a strategy meant that one might have to abstain and so enable a Tory candidate who was totally opposed to temperance legislation to win over a Liberal who was partially, but only partially, in favour. The choice had to be between voting for the better man and refusing to vote for anyone who did not measure up completely to one's standards. There was a never-ending debate in the temperance movement over what to do in the classic case of a contest between a total opponent and a 'fifty per cent.' supporter.

There can be no doubt that for much of the period between 1864 and 1871 the 'better man' strategy was predominant. At the Exeter by-election of August 1864, when local Nonconformists were enforcing an abstention strategy on Coleridge, the Liberal candidate, because of his refusal to support the unconditional abolition of Church rates, the local supporters of the Permissive Bill nevertheless decided to give him their cordial support, even though he also refused to give them a pledge. The reason was that he did express general sympathy with their cause, whereas his Tory opponent was totally against it.[29] The same issue came up at the annual meeting of the North of England Temperance League at West Hartlepool on 28 September 1864. A motion was proposed calling on the elector to 'be guided by the rule of giving his support to no candidate who is not prepared to support the principles of suppressive legislation of the liquor traffic'. But an amendment was carried to change this 'rule' from the negative to the positive. The advice was now to support that candidate 'who is prepared to go furthest in support of the principle . . .'.[30] This policy was, on the whole, the one which was put into practice at the 1865 elections. The Leeds Permissive Bill Association gave its endorsement to two 'neutral' Liberals, Baines and Amberley, on the grounds that neutrality was a step in the right direction. At Nottingham Samuel Morley expressed strong sympathy with the temperance movement but refused to support the Permissive Bill. Nevertheless, the local temperance 'party' were unanimous in supporting him, 'not only because we believe he is very nearly right, but we also know that our electors are not prepared for a Permissive Bill policy'.[31] For all the fighting words at temperance meetings the policy of voting for the better man seemed usually to prevail at general elections. G. Charlton, President of the Newcastle Temperance Union, commented in January 1866 on how often

their leading men, who made motions at meetings for united action on the Permissive Bill question, were the first men to fall away and draw up documents thoroughly abnegating the thing they were trying for, and to take a man who would not vote either for a Maine Law or a Permissive Bill, though he was undoubtedly a better man than the one they put out.[32]

This question caused some embarrassment at the Manchester by-election in November 1867. The Liberal candidate was Jacob Bright. He had stood in 1865 but lost after, and some claimed as a result of, opposition by the Alliance. Since then he had moved somewhat closer to the Alliance position but he still refused to support the Permissive Bill. This put the Alliance in something of a dilemma. They wanted to show that candidates who moved in their direction were rewarded for doing so, and they needed very much at this time to give a dramatic display of their ability to get a candidate elected. Therefore, the Executive decided to throw all its resources behind Bright's candidature, even if this entailed adoption of the 'better man' policy. Benjamin Whitworth presided at a conference of temperance reformers and advised them to 'support the one who came nearest to their policy'.[33]

The advantage of the 'better man' policy was that it normally checked the emergence of what could be one of the most divisive forces in temperance politics—the conflict of loyalties between temperance and the Liberal party. Temperance reformers spent a great deal of time debating how to combat party feeling and persuade their supporters to be prepared, if necessary, to abstain from voting for the candidate of the party which they normally supported if he was not up to the mark on temperance questions. This was not at all easy and explains in part the attraction for this and other such movements of the new voter who had not yet been drawn into party politics. At the Alliance Council meeting in 1864 E. O. Greening made a special appeal to young men who were voting for the first time to break with voting habits inherited from their parents.[34] J. H. Raper saw the problem as stemming from the fact that many supporters of the Permissive Bill were by nature political activists, 'well defined in their convictions on other points' as well and therefore very likely in the heat of an election contest to go with their party 'to the sacrifice of the cause of public sobriety'.[35] These men defended their continued involvement in party politics by arguing that it was desirable to per-

meate parties with the Alliance's principles; but there was a danger
that in the process the reverse might happen and their own adherence
to the Alliance's policy become 'permeated' by a desire to compromise
in the interests of the party. Samuel Pope admitted that 'it was a
difficult thing—he was not quite sure that it would be a good thing—
to shake oneself entirely free from the party one had been accustomed
to work with. One was reluctant to break old ties, and he looked very
leniently on the man who found himself unable to do it.'[36] Consequently, as Charlton pointed out, radical election strategies more
often than not broke down in practice. Men who had said that they
were 'all in favour of a Permissive Bill', when faced with a choice
between Tory and Whig, 'could not find it in their hearts to change
sides for the sake of a Permissive Bill'.[37] At election time local temperance 'parties' were often divided on this point of readiness to
'sacrifice' Liberalism. This usually led to a great deal of local 'softness' at elections in the implementation of theoretically tough election policies. It became customary when drawing up estimates of the
local electoral strength of friends of the Alliance to distinguish three
categories amongst them: 'those who would vote on the Permissive
Bill out-and-out, independent of party or politics, those who would
support the measure in connection with Liberal principles—those
with Conservative principles'.[38]

It is not surprising, in the light of all these constraints on an
independent and coercive electoral strategy, that the electoral
tactics of temperance reformers in the 1865 elections were highly
flexible and even opportunistic. Thus when the North of England
Temperance League held a special electoral conference prior to the
election, and there was talk of getting candidates to give pledges in
writing, there was a general feeling that in some cases

even an opposite course might be preferable. In cases where confidence was
felt in the general sentiments and conduct of a candidate, it might be policy
not to commit him to an explicit declaration, if such declaration might tend
to damage his interest, and provided that the success of his election would
result in the rejection or ousting [of] a decided opponent to the measure.[39]

The Sunderland Auxiliary had drawn up a strongly worded electors'
declaration, but when the electors actually met on the eve of the
election and discovered that none of the borough candidates
favoured the Permissive Bill, they nevertheless decided to formulate
no collective recommendation as to voting and simply referred the
candidates' replies 'to the judgment of the subscribers to the declara-

tion'.⁴⁰ In fact, most activity in this election did confine itself to the questioning of candidates.

The disorganised, unsystematic nature of temperance electoral work in 1865 led to demands for a reconsideration of the entire question. Counties were felt to be particularly unsatisfactory, being unsuited to Permissive Bill Associations on account of their size and requiring instead some more appropriate form of organisation such as a central committee of representatives of local associations and temperance societies.⁴¹ At the annual Council meeting of the Alliance in October a resolution was passed calling for the promotion of 'county alliance auxiliary associations' 'for the purpose of more completely organising and registering the temperance and prohibitory sentiment of the county constituencies'.⁴² In some counties temperance feeling ran very high and immediate steps were taken to give effect to this resolution. A notable example of this vigour was Denbighshire.⁴³ Some boroughs also wanted to improve their electoral organisation but hesitated because of the expense that would have to be incurred in engaging agents.⁴⁴ One area where there was immense temperance electoral enthusiasm was Scotland. The Scottish Permissive Bill and Temperance Association began a systematic policy of interference in Glasgow municipal elections and of canvassing of parliamentary constituencies. In 1866 it decided to extend its electoral work beyond the Glasgow area and appointed the Rev. J. R. Gray as superintendent of the east and south of Scotland. The extent of their enthusiasm for electoral work can be gauged from remarks made by Thomas Knox at a reception held in Edinburgh on Gray's arrival:

He was greatly impressed with the importance of carrying out the electoral idea, and sending men to Parliament who would, instead of being responsive to the publicans, be responsive to the public. (Applause.) He would also carry the electoral idea into the municipal elections, and make the power of temperance men and temperance principles felt at every municipal election. (Applause.) He would also like to see temperance men carry the electoral idea into the church, and prevent, by their votes, the election of brewers or publichouse keepers as office-bearers in the church. (Applause.) If they worked their electoral power rightly, they would find that the power of a vote would turn the stupidest member of Parliament right round, just as the helm turned round the Great Eastern. (Applause.) The working of the electoral power would give a fresh impulse to the movement. The publicans were always found voting together as one man, and if they put their temperance votes in one scale and the publican votes in the another [sic], they would soon find that the temperance men would kick the beam, and the publican interest would be fairly crushed.⁴⁵

This militant 'missionary' attitude in Scotland towards temperance electoral work was eventually to have important repercussions in England as well.[46]

In England efforts were concentrated during 1866 and 1867 on the improvement of county electoral organisation. In October 1866 the Alliance Council passed a further resolution calling for the setting up of County Electoral Committees.[47] On 29 January 1867 the friends of the Alliance in the West Riding held a conference at Leeds and appointed such a committee for their own area. The aim of the committee was defined as being to register the 'voting power' of temperance and use it to secure the election of MPs who supported the principles of the Permissive Bill. In this, as in so much temperance electoral activity in Leeds and the West Riding, the prime mover was George Tatham.[48] The Leeds Permissive Bill Association was itself electorally very aggressive at this time. An active campaign was begun to get all friends of temperance on to the electoral rolls; and at the annual meeting in May 1867 John Iredale set a target of 1,500 electors available within three years of the passing of the Reform Bill to vote only for 'the candidate who would put down the public-house interest'. One recalls that it was in the West Riding that the Anti-Corn Law League's practice of accepting and implementing targets for the registration of voters was most enthusiastically adopted. There was action in other parts of Yorkshire as well. A conference at Batley on 17 September 1867 set up a South-West York and District Permissive Electoral Union.[49]

But how precisely was all this 'electoral power' to be used? The time was coming when what was needed was a demonstration of how much difference it really could make in an election. That was the only way to ensure that it was taken seriously by candidates. Joseph Malloy suggested in a letter to the *Alliance News* that such a demonstration should be organised against what seemed to be an attempt by candidates of all parties to close ranks and present very similar views on the Alliance policy. His idea was that in such cases 'we throw overboard all differences in opinion, unite ourselves together, and vote against one man, so that we may show these gentlemen that we are a power that is neither to be trifled with, slighted, nor despised'.[50] But a much more practical opportunity for an effective demonstration of ability to help or hinder a candidate came in connection with the Manchester by-election of November 1867. The fact that Bright had moved considerably nearer the Alliance position since 1865 provided the Alliance with a good oppor-

tunity to show that there was an electoral reward available for
candidates who did this. Furthermore, there was reputed to be a
large Conservative temperance vote at Manchester. If Bright won,
the Alliance could claim that it did command a temperance vote
which transcended party political allegiances, and Liberal candidates would see before them the enticing prospect of Tory votes to
be won if they adopted the Alliance programme. Therefore, the
Alliance decided to exert itself to the utmost to secure Bright's
election. It was a pure demonstration of electoral power, rather akin
to what Malloy proposed, since Bright did not actually support the
Permissive Bill which was supposed to be the Alliance's electoral
test. The exemplary nature of the contest was stressed. 'The candidates had been plainly told', said Charles Thompson, 'that temperance electors of all shades of opinion would be united in supporting the man of their choice'. The Rev. S. A. Steinthal spoke of 'the
duty of temperance men to march to the poll together'. 'The result,
if they were successful in returning the right man, would,' he added,
'be of great value in future contests.' Radicals swore that, if the best
candidate on the temperance question happened to be a Conservative, he would get their vote. Some Conservatives grumbled at
having to vote for so radical a candidate and accused the Alliance
of bias because it was prepared to lower its standards for him. But
others said that they would vote for Bright solely on account of his
being the best candidate from the temperance point of view. In the
event, Bright did win, and the Alliance claimed a large measure of
the credit for this.[51] The operation was repeated at Huddersfield in
March 1868 and similar reasons were adduced for the reversal of
E. A. Leatham's 1865 defeat in that constituency.[52]

The Alliance made little impact, however, at the 1868 general
elections. In April Samuel Morley was narrowly defeated at a by-
election at Bristol, and the temperance opposition to him on this
occasion provoked a flood of criticism of the Alliance's aggressive
electoral tactics. George Howell of the Reform League wrote letters
of remonstrance to the Alliance leaders,[53] and there were many calls
from Nonconformists for a cessation of such action while the dominant issue remained that of 'religious equality'. In June and July
there was an extensive correspondence on the subject in the *Nonconformist* which indicated that there were many Nonconformist
teetotallers who under the circumstances strongly deprecated and
would refuse to support independent temperance electoral action.[54]
The Annual Report of the Alliance Executive for 1868–9 had to

admit that the Alliance's question had been completely over-shadowed at the general election:

> Never probably during the last fifty years has an election taken place in which parties ranged themselves so decisively upon a single issue, as in the last. . . . in an election so warm, involving interests so large and questions so exciting, the full strength of the Alliance could not be put forth. On the one hand, many who felt it their duty to stand by their church, which they deemed to be the subject of unjust attack, held their temperance sympathies in abeyance; while, on the other, the strong desire on the part of the sup-porters of the present Government, to secure by a decisive majority, a measure which appeared to them to be just and righteous, doubtless silenced many ardent friends of prohibition.[55]

The confusion among supporters of the Permissive Bill as to the proper electoral tactics to pursue under such circumstances can be seen from this report of a debate which occurred amongst some of them at Plymouth:

> Some declared themselves willing to vote for the candidate, Liberal or Conservative, who would give a pledge to support the Permissive Bill and kindred legislation. . . . Others thought that no Permissive men ought to vote for any man who would not support that bill; others that the man who would go furthest towards it ought to have their suffrages. Some thought that as the Irish Church was the question on which the verdict of the country was asked, and would be distinctly given, it was useless to attempt to direct public opinion from that point, and that general politics should this once have an exclusive influence; others, again, would split their votes, on an understanding being arrived at between a Conservative and a Per-missive man, if the latter were a man of such weight in social matters as to be worth carrying in at any cost; others thought this impracticable, and believed that from the Liberals only could temperance men hope for per-manent help.

The Plymouth people could not make up their minds. They adjourned their meeting, and a week later they were still incon-clusively debating 'the extent to which the holding of Permissive Bill views should influence the support given to a candidate on general politics'.[56]

It was not until 1870, once the Irish Church question had been cleared out of the way, that electoral work showed signs of reviving. In that year new Temperance or Permissive Bill Electoral Asso-ciations were formed at Birmingham, Dudley, Cleveland, and Brad-ford (for the Northern Division of the West Riding).[57] In 1871 such organisations were set up at Derby (for South Derbyshire), the borough of Lynemouth, North Durham, Salford, and Dover.[58] In

Birmingham the new Alliance Electoral Organisation had come under very heavy attack from the Liberal Association, the *Birmingham Daily Post*, and the Radicals of the National Education League, who resented its potential for dividing the Liberal interest.[59] All the debating at Plymouth finally seemed to bear fruit when a by-election was held there towards the end of 1871. J. H. Raper visited Plymouth to test the candidates. Rooker, the Liberal, promised to vote for the second reading of the Permissive Bill, and so friends of the Bill were recommended to work with the Liberal party to secure his return. The Conservative temperance voters seemed finally to make their minds up. Many were reported to be giving Rooker their support. But the Conservative candidate received the solid support of the licensed victuallers. He won, giving the Conservatives possession of a Plymouth seat for the first time since 1861.[60]

Even in 1872 disestablishment feeling among teetotallers seems to have remained strong enough for many of them to be content to be lenient with strongly Nonconformist candidates who refused to go further than neutrality on the Permissive Bill. One such was Isaac Holden, candidate for the Northern Division of the West Riding.[61] 'Softness' at the local level was a perpetual source of dissatisfaction at Alliance headquarters. Much of it seemed to stem from this excessive readiness to endorse the Liberal. Friends at Oldham were chided for this in connection with a by-election there in June 1872. On that occasion the Liberal candidate, E. Lyulph Stanley, was a strong Liberationist. Local friends were warned that they would have to take a tougher attitude to politicians.[62] On 13 July 1872 'T.H.'—probably Thomas Hardy—published an article in the *Alliance News* advocating an aggressive electoral policy of abstention from voting for Liberals to force that party to take up the Permissive Bill. This might 'create temporary disorder' and lead to Liberal defeats, but that was necessary 'to prepare the way for future victory'.[63] At the same time Sir Wilfrid Lawson came out in favour of a policy of electoral militancy directed at the Liberals.[64] It was now becoming clear that a new electoral strategy was being planned. On 31 July the Executive Committee asked the Secretary 'to instruct the Agents to provide themselves with copies of the Parliamentary Registers for all the Boroughs in their districts with a view to Electoral action and organization'.[65]

The question was whether the constituencies were ready to co-operate in such a strategy. The evidence was conflicting. At the Pontefract by-election Childers was getting temperance support because he had always abstained on the Permissive Bill.[66] At Norwich, on the other hand, George White, honorary secretary of the Alliance and a leading local Nonconformist politician, said that he was now ready to make it 'a test question'.[67] But the real problem by the early part of September 1872, and the event which proved the catalyst that precipitated the new strategy, was a by-election at Preston. From the start Lawson seems to have been determined to make Preston a test case. The Liberal candidate, Major German, refused to promise to support the Permissive Bill, and Lawson advocated running an Alliance candidate against him or advising Alliance supporters to abstain. It was claimed that there were 1,000 to 1,500 temperance votes at Preston and that these could decide the result, especially as many of them were Conservatives. Raper and an Alliance deputation went to Preston, interviewed German several times, and set up a Preston Temperance Electoral Association. There was much talk of running a special Permissive Bill candidate, but in the end none was produced and, in spite of Lawson's continued calls for a policy of abstention, the new Association decided to support German even though he refused to give an unqualified pledge to vote for the Bill.[68] One lesson stood out very clearly from the Preston by-election: it was futile to try to work out and implement any coherent election strategy in a rush in the ten days or so before polling took place. A clear understanding must be reached long in advance as to how such complicated situations were to be handled. This was the theme of a South-East Lancashire Electoral Conference held at Manchester on 3 September. This conference decided to set up an Electoral Committee for South-East Lancashire to prepare a register of temperance electors and appoint an honorary temperance registrar in each polling district. William Hoyle was appointed convenor of this Committee. The aim was to organise temperance electors to take combined action at elections.[69]

Lawson was very indignant over what had occurred at Preston and told the Executive that it should formulate 'a more decided and definite policy in respect to Alliance action at future contested Elections'.[70] Accordingly, on 30 September 1872 a resolution was agreed to embodying such a policy, and Lawson moved this at the Council meeting on 15 October. It went as follows:

That whenever a vacancy occurs in the representation of any constituency the electors will be recommended to put a candidate favourable to the Permissive Bill in nomination, and the Council of the United Kingdom Alliance pledges itself to give such candidate every possible support, by deputation, lectures, and the distribution of publications. In the event of any constituency being unable to procure a suitable candidate, the Council pledges itself to find candidates, so as to afford every elector an opportunity of recording his vote in favour of the Permissive Bill until the question is decided.

As Lawson pointed out, this was copied almost word for word from the Anti-Corn Law League's 1843 resolution. It was a clear commitment to a strategy based on independent candidatures rather than on abstention of voters, in spite of the fact that the record of Alliance candidates had hitherto been poor. Recent elections had, however, indicated that it was very difficult to organise effective abstentions. In his speech Lawson dwelt on this problem. Abstaining from voting was, he admitted, often very distasteful to people keenly interested in politics. Yet it was the strategy which he had urged at Preston, and in his speech he retreated somewhat from the resolution's apparently rigid commitment to Permissive Bill candidates in every constituency by saying that sometimes abstention might be a wiser course of action. Like that passed by the Anti-Corn Law League, the resolution was ambiguous: was the Council obliged to find a candidate in all circumstances or only when they were requested to do so by the people in the constituency?

Delegate after delegate arose to utter militant expressions of support for the policy. The ambiguities and the practical difficulties were not noticed until Samuel Pope stood up and administered a very stern dose of realism: 'he was a little doubtful whether enthusiasm and popular discussion, and calling out our political principles, and professing our readiness to sacrifice them, was precisely the sort of thing which this resolution demanded. . . . One or two ardent and enthusiastic friends rising and saying they were prepared to sacrifice their political principles, was not enough.' He admitted that he himself had had the greatest difficulty at first in accepting the resolution and had done so in the end with 'serious misgivings'. He explained what these were:

Looking at this question as practical politicians, we must remember that if we adopted the resolution in such a way as to make it worth the paper it was written on—namely, by acting upon it—this would involve us in a contest with all our accustomed political associations, and it would require a very great amount of stamina to stand that when it came to the point. . . . Far better to pass no such resolution than, having passed it, to allow it to be laughed at by not acting upon it.

Theoretically, as a policy of agitation, it was a wise course to recommend: 'the moment we made ourselves sufficiently disagreeable or important to any one of the political parties, and were strong enough to make our support more valuable than that which they lost by it, the party would adopt our principle as a plank in their platform.' The history of the Anti-Corn Law League proved this. The practical problem was that the 'stress of this resolution' would affect mainly the Liberals and would indeed help the Conservatives. Conservative members should recognise this and be prepared to vote for Liberal candidates who did support the Permissive Bill. Pope also clearly disliked the policy of running candidates in every constituency: 'Many constituencies, and even the publicans, would be glad if the Alliance would bring forward candidates just to have an election flare-up.'

The critics joined Pope in doubting whether the resolution would work. Thomas Whittaker said that 'there were thousands of friends of the Permissive Bill agitation who would stumble' at it and moved an amendment to defer it until the next annual meeting. But Lawson disarmed such opposition by admitting that there was much truth in it: 'Mr. Whittaker thought the temperance men would not stand true to their colours and vote. He (Sir Wilfrid) believed that in a great many places they would not, but then the responsibility would be theirs, not ours.' Whittaker then withdrew his amendment, and the resolution was carried with only three votes against. Lawson's retreat continued at the public meeting in the evening when he produced a further re-definition of the policy by indicating that abstention should be the practice to follow unless the local people actually approached Alliance headquarters and asked for a candidate. Thus during the course of one day he had shifted from an apparently rigid and universal strategy to one resting largely on local initiative.[71]

The reception of the new policy in the constituencies indicated that the fears expressed were well-founded. Hugh Mason spoke out against it at Ashton on 14 October, for instance.[72] Accordingly, the Executive began sending out deputations to the Auxiliaries to explain it to them and persuade them to endorse it. Lawson toured the country promoting the policy while warning that it would not be easy to put into effect.[73]

There was now a considerable expansion in the Alliance's electoral organisation. J. W. Owen was appointed full-time electoral organising secretary and Robert Swan electoral agent for the northern counties. The Committee of the Liverpool P.B.A. engaged N. Smyth as their electoral and registration agent, and the friends of the

G

Alliance in South-East Lancashire appointed Spencer Huggins as electoral agent for that area.[74]

Gradually signs began to appear that the threat to implement the policy and thereby disrupt local Liberal politics might be all that was needed to bring about the requisite change in Liberal attitudes. On 20 November the Executive Committee had before it a request from the leaders of the Liberal party in Liverpool to help them find a candidate in favour of the Permissive Bill to run alongside W. Rathbone at the next general election. When W. S. Caine decided that he would accept nomination, the Alliance guaranteed its full support for him. This obviously mattered very much to the Liverpool Liberals, for the Liverpool Permissive Bill Association claimed to have a voting strength of nearly 6,000, including about 2,000 Conservatives.[75]

In other constituencies where Liberal Associations were less ready to forestall trouble by coming to terms with the local temperance party coercive action began to be prepared. One such place was Bath where the question of the Permissive Bill had long caused dissension among the Liberals. In 1868 the Workingmen's Association there—which co-operated with the middle-class Liberal Association on a joint Election Committee—was deeply divided. The secretary, Withy, a teetotaller, and most of its committee were in favour of the Bill, but the bulk of the members were against it, and meetings could not be held on account of the discord. Efforts were made to put pressure on Dr. Dalrymple, one of the Liberal candidates, to promise to vote for the Bill, but his agent was at that stage not inclined to worry about the implied threats.[76] In 1873 Withy and his teetotal associates decided to make another assault on Dalrymple, who had been elected in 1868, and to try to induce the Liberal Association to drop him. A meeting of about 150 electors favourable to the Permissive Bill was convened on 17 February and a resolution was passed refusing support to any candidate who would not support the Bill. The favoured strategy here was abstention. Indeed, Withy, who moved the resolution, stated that it was not their intention to bring forward a candidate of their own. The meeting then set up a Permissive Bill Electoral Association for Bath and took a pledge not to promise votes to any candidate until his views had been ascertained by the Association's committee and a meeting held not later than a fortnight before the election.[77]

In late April the new Association at Bath found itself faced with an unexpectedly early challenge to its policy of electoral militancy.

Dalrymple's Liberal colleague, Sir William Tite, died, and a by-election was necessary. The Liberal leaders were evidently worried over what had happened in February, for they let it be known that they were 'exceedingly anxious' for the co-operation of the temperance electors 'who ordinarily work with them'. Jerome Murch, whom they chose as their candidate, stated that 'unless he could obtain the united support of the Liberal party he should retire'. However, he would not promise to vote for or even stay neutral on the Permissive Bill. The dilemma for the temperance people was that his Conservative opponent, Lord Chelsea, was totally opposed to the Bill and was strongly backed by 'the trade'. This caused several of them to commit themselves to Murch without further ado, and at the promised meeting of supporters of the Bill on 24 April a resolution was moved that they do their utmost to secure his return because his views were 'most favourable to the objects of the association'. In other words, he was the 'better man'. To this an amendment was proposed, pledging them to withhold their support from both candidates. The resolution was carried, but only by a small majority. This upset one of the fundamental principles of temperance electoral action, that the temperance vote should be available as a bloc vote. Accordingly, a second meeting was called on 28 April and received a recommendation from the committee that because of 'the great desirability of unity of action' support should be withheld from both candidates. This was accepted without dissent. Murch now decided to yield. He issued a promise not to vote against the Bill and said that he supported its principle 'to some extent and in some form'. This was not very satisfactory, and yet Chelsea was an especially obnoxious candidate. On hearing of what had happened, the Alliance Executive had a telegram sent to the agent in Bath, A. Scholfield: 'Our opponent must be kept out. If you support the neutral keep on the pressure till you get him up to the mark.' Chelsea gained the seat for the Conservatives on a reduced poll, and this was held up as proof of the desirability of having Liberal candidates who would receive the full support of the temperance vote.[78]

The Gloucester by-election which was being held at the same time posed a similar dilemma. The Tory candidate was hostile but the Liberal was prepared to be neutral. J. H. Raper advised the local people to stay unpledged to either. Many of them had taken a pledge not to vote for a candidate who would not support the Permissive Bill, but in the end the local committee resolved to release them from their pledges and to advise them to support the Liberal 'as the better candidate for Alliance interests'. He, nevertheless, lost and the Conservatives gained a seat in a constituency where no Tory had won since 1857.[79]

Neutrality was a controversial stand-point, and much depended on the virulence of the Trade and Tory opposition. In Leeds where Edward Baines had been strongly supported in 1865 because he went at least as far as neutrality Tatham was now organising a campaign to withhold temperance votes from him because he would not go any further.[80]

In June occurred the year's second Bath by-election. This time the limelight was occupied by another pressure group and temperance could play only a secondary role. J. C. Cox was most anxious not to get mixed up in local temperance politics. The local people were again torn both ways. They passed a resolution refusing to support either candidate and yet they acknowledged that Captain Hayter was more favourable to temperance legislation and therefore had some claim on temperance electors. The only way out of the dilemma now seemed to be to return to Lawson's original proposal and look for a candidate of their own. The committee decided that, although it was too late to put one up at the by-election, they would find out what support there would be for one at the general election and whether anyone was willing to stand. The divided state of the temperance party at this by-election was no good advertisement for the new strategy, and Lawson was very angry, saying that action should have been taken at the outset to bring out an Alliance candidate in terms of his resolution.[81]

The Liberals' dilemma was also considerable. By now they wished, in most boroughs at least, to conciliate and retain the temperance vote, but they were averse from having candidates who were too explicitly identified with temperance as this dangerously provoked the liquor interest. The answer was to have candidates of broad Liberal appeal who included among their Radical qualifications support for the Permissive Bill. The Alliance soon had a list of such men on whom it could reach agreement with local Liberal Associations. Thus there was satisfaction when the Barnstaple Liberals decided to adopt S. D. Waddy, a well-known Nonconformist lawyer and supporter of the Bill. At Liskeard, on the other hand, E. Horsman, the sitting Liberal member, was wavering most uneasily between opposition and neutrality, not wishing to offend either party, and the local agent wrote to the Executive expressing the hope 'that another candidate may be found to take the field in opposition to Mr. Horsman, without being ostensibly the candidate of the Temperance party'.[82]

The next by-election challenge came at East Staffordshire in early August. This area was a stronghold of the brewing industry, and both candidates were opposed to the Permissive Bill. The Alliance advised its adherents to abstain from voting. The Liberal then lost, and several letters of protest were received by the Executive. The evidence is that the local Liberal party was deeply divided between the Bass brewing interests and the supporters of the Permissive Bill.[83]

Constituencies where Liberal Associations were already well established presented great complexities for the pressure-group strategists, and it is not surprising that they took a particular interest in areas which were still completely unorganised on the Liberal side. For example, Stamford was a tiny borough, sunk in corruption and political torpor, where there was no Liberal organisation and no contest had been held since 1847. On 5 August 1873 Owen and William Mart, the local Alliance agent, arrived in town to preside over a conference of about 50 electors which they had convened by private circular. Mart urged them to collect about 100 votes and 'hold the balance of power'. Detailed advice was given on how to organise the temperance vote and what to do in the various permutations of candidates' attitudes to the Permissive Bill.[84] It is seldom that one can so precisely pin-point the day on which sophisticated modern politics arrived in the life of a community. In 1874 Stamford enjoyed the novelty of a contested election, and in 1880 the Liberals gained the seat.

In September the electors of Bath were subjected to their third by-election of the year when Dr. Dalrymple died. Once again the supporters of the Permissive Bill were thrown into a state of turmoil. On 19 September they held a meeting at which they resolved, after three hours of animated discussion and much divergence of opinion, that they could not support any candidate who would not pledge himself to the Bill. Owen and Scholfield attended and urged strict compliance with the Alliance's electoral policy. Owen told them that the Alliance Executive

considered that the Permissive Bill was of such importance that if candidates who came forward to represent places where supporters of the bill held a material portion of the political influence would not make it a plank in their platform, they must take the results. They must recollect that the same charges as to the breaking up of parties had been brought against the promoters of the Corn Law Abolition agitation. . . .

The decision was made, therefore, to run their own candidate this time, and an invitation was issued to Charles Thompson. The Alliance Executive, on hearing of this, fully approved of it and instructed Owen and Scholfield to give the friends in Bath all possible aid in thus carrying out Alliance electoral policy. The local people justified their action by claiming that at the time of the last by-election they had been about to nominate William Hoyle when Hayter's committee had given them an assurance 'that if they would not oppose on that occasion, when there was another election their views should be taken into consideration in the election of a candidate'. This promise had not been fulfilled. Thompson's candidature turned out to be a disaster and undoubtedly did much to discredit the Alliance's policy of temperance candidates. It was hotly opposed by many of the temperance Liberals in Bath since the Liberals had held a ballot to choose their candidate and they considered that the temperance party ought to have abided by the result of this. Thompson gained only 57 votes, and Hayter won by a margin of 139, thus denying the temperance enthusiasts the consolation of even having held the balance of power.[85]

The efforts of Owen and Scholfield to promote the electoral policy in the West of England now became very controversial. They held meetings at Bristol and Malmesbury which passed resolutions endorsing the policy and pledging not to vote for any candidate who would not promise to vote for the Permissive Bill. The Bristol resolution was vehemently denounced by Handel Cossham, one of the leading Nonconformist politicians in that part of the country. He wrote: 'How a policy that will place the representation of the country in the hands of our opponents, instead of those who, at any rate, partially support our views, can be wise I am at a loss to understand.' He particularly condemned the analogy with the Anti-Corn Law League, arguing that the Alliance was not yet within a hundred miles of having the popular support which entitled the League to take action to compel the Liberal party to adopt its policy. He opposed the use of small minorities to coerce parties into going so far in advance of public opinion.[86]

When the Alliance Council met again in October 1873, a year after the adoption of the new electoral strategy, enthusiasm for it among the delegates was far from universal. Pope admitted that he still found it a 'disagreeable operation' which he was not enjoying at all. He was only carrying it out because he was a Liberal, indeed 'a Radical of Radicals', who wanted 'to see a permanent and strong Liberal association in the community' and therefore had to act 'to prevent the Liberal party from ever becoming the party of the publicans'. Several delegates expressed scepticism as to whether temperance people would actually carry out the strategy at election time. The Rev. M. Morgan condemned the running of candidates where the local party, as at Bath, was not united. This only exposed their weakness to the enemy. A delegate from Barrhead asked for clarification as to how they should deal with 'neutral' candidates and whether they were obliged to vote in all circumstances *only* for Permissive Bill supporters. Thomas Whittaker opposed this policy and condemned the 1872 resolution as impractical. J. H. Raper advised delegates to judge for themselves in their own local contests how best to deal with 'neutrals'. There was much debate on what had happened in East Staffordshire when abstention from voting for a Liberal had let a Conservative brewer into the House of Commons. William Malins defended such action: 'If we are to be ruled by the liquor interest the sooner the House of Commons is saturated with brewers the better. (Cheers.) Then the country will realise the case, and rise up in indignation against the rule of the beer barrel.'[87]

The next controversial by-election was that at Hull in late October. The two seats at Hull had been won by the Liberals in 1868, but the supporters of the Permissive Bill had given their votes to the Conservative candidates who appeared to be more sympathetic to temperance legislation—a rare instance of this.[88] On this occasion the Tory and Liberal candidates were equally hostile to the Bill, and so the friends of the Alliance decided on a policy of abstention. However, William Hoyle went to Hull and persuaded them to adopt the full electoral policy by running their own candidate. He found one for them, Lieutenant-Colonel Langley, and they pledged him their support. This support proved not to be unanimous, and Langley retired from the contest. The Liberals' subsequent loss of the seat was attributed to temperance abstentions.[89] Hull virtually completed the discrediting of Lawson's 1872 strategy of independent candidatures. Abstention was now the predominant method.

In some constituencies, however, co-operation between the Alliance and the Liberals was now the order of the day. For example, Hoyle visited Woodstock and conferred both with the friends of the Alliance and with the Chairman of the local Liberal party who was a supporter of the Permissive Bill. They agreed that J. S. Wright, the prominent Birmingham Liberal, should be approached as a possible candidate who would be acceptable to both sides. Strenuous efforts were also made to find a candidate who would bridge the gulf at Hull.[90]

The minute books of the United Kingdom Alliance provide, in their coverage of the 1874 general election, an almost unique opportunity to see and study the electoral operations of a pressure group. The Executive Committee met sometimes two or three times a day, and the minute books give an almost hour-by-hour record of the flow of information and advice in and out of the Alliance headquarters. They reveal the remarkably extensive but also largely behind-the-scenes activity of the Alliance in this election.[91]

The existence of a large number of two-member constituencies meant that the Alliance had to tolerate a good deal of neutrality on the Permissive Bill in order to protect the position of Liberals who were supporters of it. The normal practice in such constituencies was to advise voting for a 'neutral' Liberal if his colleague was a supporter of the Bill. This was done partly to ensure the reciprocity which was involved in a joint candidature and would secure Liberal votes for a Permissive Bill candidate even from Liberals who did not favour it in return for temperance votes for the 'neutral'; and partly to keep out Tories who were usually definitely opposed. This advice was given in connection with the contest at Liverpool where Caine was a supporter and Rathbone a neutral and at Northampton where the running mate of Gilpin, who favoured the Bill, was Henley, who promised not to vote against it. The friends at Stroud were advised that if W. J. Stanton would promise to be neutral his joint candidature with S. A. Dickinson, a supporter, should be endorsed. At Lambeth the local Permissive Bill Association, after taking the advice of the London Auxiliary, instructed its friends to vote for only one of the two Liberal candidates, W. McArthur. The other candidate, Sir James Lawrence, was said to be neutral, and so the Executive sent telegrams to Lambeth urging them to vote for him as well and so 'keep out an enemy', the single Tory candidate.

Where all candidates were opposed to the Bill, the recommendation was usually that friends should abstain from voting for any of them—or at least announce that they would follow this course unless at least one changed his mind. This was the policy decided on at Bath, where the independent-candidate alternative had proved such a failure, at Oxford, where Harcourt and Cardwell were both opposed, at Northallerton, and at South Derbyshire where the Executive assisted the local Temperance Electoral Association by printing and sending to it placards and leaflets publicising the decision. On hearing that both or all candidates in other places were hostile, the Executive sent messages urging abstention unless a change occurred in their attitude.

Where one Liberal was opposed and the other in favour, as was the case at Newcastle-upon-Tyne with Headlam and Cowen respectively, the advice was to do everything possible to get the opponent up to neutrality and then to support both. Headlam refused to budge, however, and this left the local friends in a quandary.

Very occasionally support was given to Conservatives in preference to Liberals. This happened at Grimsby where an estimated 400 Alliance voters were recommended to cast their votes for John Chapman, the Conservative, and not Edward Heneage, the Liberal opponent of the Permissive Bill. Chapman duly won, converting a Liberal majority of 219 in 1868 to a Tory majority of 59. When he died in 1877 the Liberals regained it with a majority of 484.

Sometimes Liberal candidates were prepared to pledge their support to the Bill as long as the fact that they had done so was not widely publicised. They were afraid of provoking the drink interest into damaging counter-activity. The Alliance was usually ready to comply with such requests. A letter came in from Cricklade stating that the two Liberal candidates, F. W. Cadogan and H. Tucker, supported the Bill '& are being helped by our friends without bringing the question prominently forward'. A telegram was sent back signifying approval of this course. Discretion was taken further at Frome where W. H. Willans would give only a private assurance of neutrality and at Ayrshire where 'Mr. John Paton reports temperance party have but little political power and are afraid to make any demonstration lest they rouse the enemy's activities'.

Neutrality on the Permissive Bill became the acceptable minimum which qualified a candidate for temperance votes. Such a standard was substantially lower than that advocated by the Alliance in its official electoral resolutions and embodied in large numbers of voters' pledges and declarations. But to most temperance electors it seemed a considerable advance to persuade a candidate to abandon complete opposition, and as they were often also Liberals and anxious to reconcile their two 'loyalties' it appealed very much as a compromise which could be agreed on in the course of the bargaining which went on at interviews with Liberal candidates. It would have been impossible to have induced temperance Liberals to oppose neutral Liberals in the many cases where the other candidate was a hostile Tory, strongly supported by the drink interest.

The trend was clear at the start. In the Stroud by-election in January the temperance party gave their full support to Sir Henry Havelock, a neutral, against a totally antagonistic Tory.[92] In the general election neutrals were usually supported. At Bristol three candidates were hostile to the Bill but Samuel Morley said that he would not vote against it. The local people were reported to be divided as to what to do, and so the Secretary was instructed 'to write them encouraging support of Morley as against decided opponents'. A similar reason was given for supporting the neutral George Leeman at York. When a report arrived from the Isle of Wight that Evelyn Ashley had said that he would not vote against the Permissive Bill and would vote for Sunday Closing, a telegram was at once sent back: 'better support a friend to keep out an enemy'. In fact, probably the main electoral activity in which Alliance supporters engaged in 1874 was 'getting' or 'screwing' the candidate 'up to neutrality'. This was the burden of a large proportion of the advice poured out from Alliance headquarters. Friends were told to support hostile candidates only if they could be persuaded to shift so far as to promise to abstain from voting on the Permissive Bill. For example, a report that neither candidate at Evesham was favourable at once produced a telegram 'urging friends to get promises of neutrality at least'. The process of coaxing some candidates in this direction was very drawn out and tortuous. Backsliding had constantly to be watched out for. This happened at Denbigh where Watkin Williams first promised neutrality and then announced that he would vote against the Bill. This threw into great confusion the local temperance Liberals who had started to campaign for him and were most reluctant to have to give up doing so. Eventually, after many anxious conferences the following report was dispatched to headquarters: 'Friends now supporting Watkin Williams being quite satisfied that if returned he will not vote against Sir Wilfrid [Lawson].'[93]

Through the minutes one can trace the process by which some candidates were slowly and painfully moved by such methods closer to the Alliance's policy. At Bath, for instance, Captain Hayter was by now understandably in a state of some nervousness. On 30 January appears this item: 'Mr. Scholfield reports friends resolved on abstention. Hayter anxious for some compromise.' On 2 February came a further report from Bath: 'Hayter promises to go in for a Licensing Board. Feels his position a little shaky.' The Executive debated this and decided to send back a telegram 'urging firmness to abstention policy unless Mr. Hayter will make some decided concession, in which case our friends to support him.' In the end it was all to no avail. Hayter made no substantial concessions but nevertheless held his seat at the top of the poll. 'Our misfortune,' commented Scholfield, 'is that the majority of our friends are such ardent Liberals that temperance politics must bend to circumstances.' At Halifax efforts persisted almost to polling day to coax James Stansfeld into joining his colleague, John Crossley, in a pledge of neutrality. At Berwick-on-Tweed all four candidates were at first opposed to the Permissive Bill. A group of temperance voters announced that they would vote preferably for candidates who supported it but, if there were none, for candidates who would at least promise not to vote against it. Eventually one of the Conservatives, Captain D. M. Home, agreed to make this latter pledge, and several of the temperance voters promptly 'plumped' for him. He was elected, although Berwick-on-Tweed had returned two Liberals in both 1865 and 1868.[94]

Very few attempts were made to give effect to the election strategy which the Alliance had actually adopted as its official policy in 1872 —the commitment to making sure that every voter had the opportunity to vote for a Permissive Bill candidate. There were not many independent candidatures. A half-hearted attempt was made to find one for Southampton when all four candidates there were reported to be against the Bill. The problem was that independent candidatures were likely to be very expensive if they were to be anything more than token gestures. Thus at Berwick, when all candidates were reported as hostile, the initial suggestion of the local agents was that an Alliance candidate be nominated, and this was approved at headquarters. But, when the next day a telegram came in advising that this would yield 150 votes at a cost of about £100, the agents were urged to have another try at changing the positions of the existing candidates. At Mid Somerset any attempt to run a candidate was abandoned, when it was estimated that at least £500 would be needed to make any kind of a fight and at least £1,500 if the candidate was to have any chance of winning.

Far more successful—and arguably an alternative way of giving effect to the 1872 resolution, i.e. making sure that voters had a Per-

missive Bill candidate to vote for—was the work done by the
Alliance in placing men sympathetic to their cause in Liberal and
Radical candidatures. The Alliance became in effect a great candi-
date-finding and candidate-placing agency, using its almost unique
network of contacts throughout the country to help aspiring Radical
politicians who needed to be introduced to good Radical constituencies and also Liberal associations which wished to know of
good candidates who would be willing to stand for them and could
unify the party by being acceptable to the local temperance enthusiasts. Some examples from the minutes will illustrate the range
of these activities. On 26 January messages were sent to Joseph
Chamberlain and Sir Charles Bazley urging them to stand for
Leicester and Manchester respectively and promising Alliance support. A telegram was sent to the 'York friends' suggesting names for
the Liberal nomination, including Arthur Pease and George Tatham.
On 27 January efforts were made to get a Permissive Bill candidate
selected by the Liberals at Walsall. On the 29th constituencies are
being sought for Handel Cossham and Alfred Illingworth. Henry
Hibbert, the Alliance agent in Bradford, interviewed the latter and
reported that he was 'not anxious to go to Parliament but wishes to
know what constituency is open'. A list of such constituencies was
immediately sent back. The Alliance did not confine itself to candidates whose sole interest was the Permissive Bill but was sensitive to
the need to find men whose standpoint, while including that measure,
was much more generally Radical. Thus, when a report was received
from Falkirk 'that a Radical disestablishment candidate would have
a chance', the names of F. R. Lees, Cossham, and Illingworth were
immediately dispatched.

Great stress was laid on temperance unity as regards electoral
action. The temperance vote must be seen as a *bloc* vote available to
any candidate who was prepared to cultivate it. Where disunity was
reported, as at Walsall, the Alliance did its best to remedy this state
of affairs. But sometimes the local temperance people were so
divided that no effective electoral action on behalf of temperance
was possible. For example, on 3 February came the following report
from Gloucester: 'All 4 candidates declared against Permissive Bill.
Our friends not united and firm for abstention so that nothing can
be done re the screwing policy.' An abstention policy was particularly hard to enforce, especially when many of the temperance voters
were also keen Liberals, and some serious divisions resulted when
abstention was recommended. Worst affected in this respect was

Oxford where the Chairman and four others dissented when the local auxiliary decided on abstention. On 30 January the local agent sent a report that a 'small section of temperance party [was] endeavouring to counteract our policy'. At Lewes an ingenious compromise was proposed. The temperance voters held a meeting at which '12 gave their pledge not to vote for either candidate, provided that at least 20 would agree to the same policy of abstention'. But this did not work and on 4 February the agent had to report that at Lewes 'the policy of abstention could not be carried out, so few would agree to stand firm'.

Complications sometimes arose, as at Bath the previous year, when supporters of other causes were already on the scene and threatening militant electoral action. This happened at Whitby where neither candidate would support the Permissive Bill but the opponents of the Contagious Diseases Acts were talking of running their own candidate against W. H. Gladstone. The Alliance did its best to sort out local tangles. At Blackburn 'some temperance friends' were reported by the agent to be 'embarrassing Mr. Shackleton', one of the Liberal candidates, and a message was sent 'asking friends to support him'. When at Sheffield a ballot favoured Chamberlain over J. Allott as one of the Liberal candidates, efforts were made to find an alternative constituency for Allott. Unavailing attempts were made to eliminate one of the three Liberals, all supporters of the Permissive Bill, who were standing for the two seats at Stoke.

Three examples will show how difficult it was to make complicated local political situations fit into general electoral strategies. The incomplete nature both of the development of representative Liberal associations and of the integration of temperance workers into them was sometimes responsible for immense electoral confusion and complexity. At Peterborough there had been three separate Liberal organisations until just a few months before the election. Then the members of these bodies held a mass meeting and agreed on a joint programme. This included the Permissive Bill, as the temperance 'party' was strong in Peterborough Liberalism. A committee of fifteen—five from each organisation—was set up to choose the candidates, but their choice was not generally accepted, and Peterborough ended up with five Liberal candidates and one Conservative for its five seats. One of the Liberals, Thomson Hankey, was supported by the publicans. The two chosen by the committee, G. Potter and N. Goodman, were endorsed by the new combined

Association, but the temperance electors, after hearing reports on interviews with all candidates, decided to support two other Liberals, G. Whalley and R. Kerr. Then just before polling Potter told some of them that he would vote for the second reading of the Permissive Bill, and so some temperance votes went to him. Much of the trouble in Peterborough clearly arose because a new Liberal Association was hastily organised for election purposes and then failed to secure candidates who endorsed its full programme which included the Permissive Bill. This gave the temperance people their justification for breaking away and supporting alternative candidates who were refusing to accept the new Association's selection of candidates. Conservatism in Peterborough was very weak: the Conservative candidate could not win even with the Liberals so divided. And so the election became in effect a struggle amongst the various sections of the Liberal party, one of which was temperance.[95]

Another very tangled situation was that which developed at Leeds where Dr. F. R. Lees stood as an independent Radical and Temperance candidate and took 5,994 votes, enough, it was claimed, to deprive Edward Baines of a seat which he had held since 1859 and hand it over to a Conservative. This candidature caused intense bitterness in Liberal circles in Leeds where the Baines family had held a dominant position for many years, and much of this bitterness was directed against the Alliance, for Lees was a celebrated temperance lecturer and propagandist whose best known work was his *Alliance Prize Essays*. But, in fact, although temperance—particularly in the person of Alderman George Tatham—did play an important role in the promotion of Lees's candidature, it was the product of a far broader Radical protest against the Leeds Liberal establishment. It was not the first time that Lees had stood as a Radical, and not merely a temperance, candidate, and on this occasion he received much support from workingmen, for instance. The Alliance refused to endorse Lees's candidature which greatly embarrassed it as it did, after all, look like a fulfilment of the 1872 commitment to put Permissive Bill candidates before every constituency. But there was one already for Leeds, R. M. Carter, the sitting member along with Baines, and many temperance people did not want to claim both nominations and thus break the compromise and perhaps as a result end up with neither. They were very divided over how to handle Lees's candidature. T. H. Barker sent a message from Alliance headquarters a day or two before polling urging them to persuade Lees to withdraw. After Baines's defeat a deputation of friends of temperance called on him to apologise. A. W. Scarr told Baines that he thought that nine-tenths of the temperance electors really did vote for him and that Lees was supported mainly by workingmen and Home Rulers. Baines retorted that 'he understood one of the leading officers of the Alliance in Leeds took a very active part in promoting the candidature of Dr. Lees'. Scarr then explained that this was Hector Davidson who 'was only the working agent of the Alliance in Leeds, and must not be regarded as having great influence over the temperance friends in town, nor as by any means representing the power of the temperance movement'. Baines read out a resolution which he claimed had been adopted on 24 January at a special meeting of the Leeds P.B.A. and Alliance Auxiliary saying that support would be given only to candidates who were pledged to vote for the Permissive Bill. The officers explained that such a resolution had been discussed but not passed and that the subsequent publication of it in their name had not been authorised by them. Indeed, upon receiving Barker's letter, they had done all that they could to induce Lees to withdraw.[96]

The third tangled local situation was at Birmingham. Here there was a history of tension between the more militant temperance 'party' and the equally militant Liberal Association which aggressively preached a doctrine of democratic representativeness but was also dominated by the organisers of the National Education League who had on numerous occasions, most especially in the recent East Staffordshire by-election, made no secret of their intense dislike of electoral action by other pressure groups. At the general election in 1874 the Liberal candidates looked like being returned unopposed. But there were threats that a 'working man's candidate', nominated by the Trades Council, named Gilliver, would run, thus causing a contest and probably inciting the Conservatives to change their mind and run a candidate of their own to take advantage of this rift in their opponents' ranks. What gave Gilliver's candidature real seriousness was the decision of the committee of the Alliance Auxiliary to support it. Gilliver had told them that he would vote for the Permissive Bill whereas P. H. Muntz, one of the Liberal candidates, had said that he would vote against it. From this point on Gilliver's candidature became more and more oriented towards the temperance cause. The temperance people began organising ward committees for him, and then on the morning of nomination day the Trades Council announced that they were so short of funds that they could not afford to carry on the candidature and would have to

hand over full responsibility for it to the Alliance. At this news the
Auxiliary was thrown into confusion. Some of them refused to take
Gilliver's candidature any further, but when he drew up a statement
announcing his retirement and sent it over to the Alliance offices for
approval, it was intercepted by some of the more militant temperance
men who, without submitting it to their committee, 'ran over to Mr.
Gilliver's committee, urged them to reconsider the suggested withdrawal and go to the poll, personally offering them all the money
requisite for the nomination, and many pounds over'. In the meantime the Liberals were becoming worried and invited the Auxiliary
to send a deputation to meet the leaders of the Liberal Association.
According to Joseph Malins, Muntz was in the room when the
Alliance deputation arrived but was asked to withdraw by R. W.
Dale who acted as spokesman for the Liberals. This withdrawal
from the room was later to assume critical significance and was
probably intended to do so by Dale who was a notably crafty politician.

The Liberals then 'asked the temperance deputation what they
could do to induce them to withdraw their support from Mr.
Gilliver, and thus save the town the bitterness and expense of a
contest in which Mr. Bright's seat would be imperilled, and the
Conservative probably returned'. The stress on Bright was an
obvious appeal to Nonconformist sympathies with the Liberal cause.
The answer was that Muntz would have to withdraw his threat to
vote against the Permissive Bill. Dale then, according to the report
of the Alliance's post-election committee of inquiry, replied that, 'if
the temperance men would withdraw, Mr. Muntz should not be in
the House when the bill came on—he (Mr. Dale) would "invite
him to tea," or they would keep him away somehow. The deputation
could rely upon their pledge that Mr. Muntz should not vote
against the Permissive Bill.' This was a very unsatisfactory 'pledge'
for it was given privately and orally and in Muntz's absence and
seemed to depend on Dale's being able to inveigle Muntz away
from the House of Commons on the day of the division without
Muntz being aware of what was going on or being required to
change his opinion as to the Bill. Nevertheless, the deputation
reported back to the temperance men that Muntz would now
abstain from voting on the Bill and they decided to accept the
'compromise'. Gilliver did not turn up to be nominated, the candidate whom the Tories had ready to bring forward withdrew, and
Bright, Dixon, and Muntz were returned unopposed. A few days

later Muntz issued a statement saying truthfully that he himself had not seen or met any deputation from the Alliance (although Malins claimed that he did 'see' them since he was in the room when they arrived) and that he had not altered his views on the Permissive Bill. In June 1874 Muntz voted against the second reading of the Permissive Bill. Dale had not taken him to tea.

The Birmingham Auxiliary had been hopelessly outmanoeuvred on this occasion. Their fatal mistake was not to insist on Muntz being present at the interview and thus a party to the 'pledge'. But instead they succumbed to an invitation by the wily Dale to participate in a secret plan to deceive Muntz, a plan which required for its success that he should not be in the room and not know what was said. They did this all the more readily, no doubt, because of a belief held in the Alliance that Muntz had not originally been wanted by the Liberals as a candidate but had 'thrust himself upon them', threatening that if not adopted he would split the party by standing as an independent. This belief made it easy to connive with Dale at an apparent attempt to do a deal behind Muntz's back. One suspects that in fact Muntz's withdrawal from the room was agreed to by Muntz precisely so that a manoeuvre of this kind could take place and he could be left entirely free subsequently to take his own line and say that he had nothing to do with it. The Alliance's gullibility is, however, entirely understandable. The affair illustrates vividly how difficult it was to maintain a coherent strategy during the intense pressures of an election contest in a particular constituency—and especially those pressures which resulted from the involvement of so many temperance people in local Liberal politics and the consequent incessant tug of loyalties.[97]

CHAPTER X

The United Kingdom Alliance, 1874–1880

During the general election of 1874 many Liberal candidates who did not promise to vote for the second reading of the Permissive Bill nevertheless received endorsement and support from the Alliance and from local temperance 'parties'—as long as they were prepared to pledge themselves to take no part in the division at all. This moderate approach continued after the election. When Cardwell accepted a peerage after having won one of the seats at Oxford for the Liberals, a by-election was held in March. The Liberal candidate, J. D. Lewis, first promised to support the Bill and then retracted this promise, but the local Alliance people decided not to bring out a candidate against him on the understanding that he would at least observe neutrality. The Oxford Auxiliary had been very divided over the abstention policy adopted at the general election, and then it had not worked, as Harcourt and Cardwell who were elected remained adamantly opposed to the Bill. Nobody seemed anxious to renew these divisions when it was very doubtful if a militant strategy would get support.[1]

One result of the 1874 elections was to identify the Tory party much more explicitly as the party of the liquor interest. This meant that temperance people henceforth felt a considerably stronger dislike for Tory candidates and a correspondingly greater readiness to vote Liberal in order to keep them out, even if the Liberals themselves were not completely satisfactory on the Permissive Bill. Thus at the Norwich by-election in March 1875 they decided to support J. H. Tillett and work hard for him, even though he would not give a pledge on the Bill and would go no further than to promise to support Sunday Closing. His Tory opponent was totally against the Bill and received the endorsement of the Licensed Victuallers'

Association. 'The Temperance party were driven to a more determined effort by this action of the publicans.'[2] In July 1875 the
Alliance's friends at Hartlepool made a similar decision when confronted with a choice between a hostile Tory and a Liberal, I.
Lowthian Bell, who said that he supported the principles of the Bill
but could not say definitely that he would vote for the second
reading.[3] Bell duly held the seat for the Liberals. However, by 1876
there were signs of a hardening attitude to 'neutrals'. At East
Retford in February the unsuccessful Liberal candidate, H. F.
Bristowe, promised not to vote against the Bill but failed to receive
strong support from the temperance party.[4] There was a considerable amount of controversy over the East Cumberland by-election in
April where the Liberals saw a chance of a gain from the Tories and
the Alliance decided to support a neutral Liberal, E. S. Howard,
against a hostile Tory. Sir Wilfrid Lawson himself campaigned
vigorously on Howard's behalf and defended his action thus:

You may say, why do I support Mr. Stafford Howard when he has not
made up his mind? Well, half a loaf is better than no bread. (Laughter.)
And I support him because if we win this election our candidate has
declared he will not oppose the bill, while the other candidate has declared
his opposition to it, and it will be—if not a thorough—a satisfactory triumph
over the monopoly of the people who are opposed to the bill.[5]

Howard won by 156 votes, a Liberal gain. In November 1876, by
contrast, when there was a by-election at Frome, another seat won
by the Conservatives in 1874, and the temperance people decided to
give hearty support to the neutral H. B. Samuelson against a hostile
Tory, the Alliance Executive was not happy about this and instructed the agent to 'pay another visit to Frome and urge the
friends to put all possible pressure upon Mr. Samuelson to induce
him to promise his support to Sir Wilfrid Lawson's Bill, etc.'.[6] The
dilemma was always to decide which course of action better advanced the interests of that Bill: keeping out of the Commons men
whose votes would definitely be against it, and taking action that
might force the Liberals to come down off the fence and adopt
candidates whose votes would definitely be for it. The following
report on the North-East Lancashire election in 1880 illustrates the
perplexity which this caused for many local temperance 'parties':

None of the candidates come up to the requirements of the N.E. Lanc. Per.
Bill Association. Messrs. Starkie and Ecroyd [Conservative] are entirely
and completely opposed. Lord Hartington and Mr. Grafton [Liberal] fall

short of the said standard but the latter are prepared to travel some little distance in the right direction. The Executive of the Per. Bill Ass\n. held several meetings before their course of action could be agreed upon, but finally they agreed to favour the candidature of Lord Hartington and F. W. Grafton, Esq., who were to some extent favourable, and feeling convinced that an opposite course, in the peculiar circumstances of the situation, would only have been playing into the hands of the avowed enemies of the principle of Local Control upon which the North East Lancashire Permissive Bill Association is based.[7]

On the other hand, abstention continued to be advised where the Liberal candidate was opposed to the Permissive Bill. An example of this is the Hackney by-election in March 1874.[8] But abstention was now much more of an emotional and divisive issue, largely owing to the belief that it had had a great deal to do with the defeat of the Liberals who had at least produced Licensing Bills and the handing over of power for six years to the party of the brewers and the publicans. It was hotly debated at the Council meeting in October 1874. Hewins of Birmingham said that 'he differed from others in thinking we ought to vote for the man who went furthest with us, and not abstain from supporting him because he did not go further'. But others argued that such tactics were necessary in order to force the Liberals to bring forward supporters of the Permissive Bill. G. Charlton of Gateshead 'recommended friends like Mr. Hewins to have the courage to be willing to be beaten at an election for once. We had to stoop to conquer.'[9] Whether advice to abstain was now followed by any considerable number of temperance electors is very doubtful. At Kirkcaldy in April 1875 a half-hearted attempt was made to organise abstention in the case of a neutral Liberal, but a report admitted that some temperance people did not go along with this because they 'felt they must vote'.[10] Abstention even in the case of hostile Liberals tended to divide temperance people more and more. This was so at Liskeard in December 1876 where there were two Liberal candidates, both opposed to the Bill, and the Alliance tried to encourage voters to abstain. Most of the temperance electors nevertheless supported one of them, Leonard Courtney. One local man, Daniel Sergent, estimated that at the most only 15 out of 150 temperance electors abstained in spite of the fact that they had previously held meetings which had carried resolutions pledging them to carry out the Alliance's electoral policy.[11]

There was one man who came to believe that that policy—not voting for any candidate who would not vote for the Permissive

Bill—was now complete humbug and ought to be replaced by some more realistic strategy. He was Thomas Whittaker of Scarborough, the veteran temperance lecturer. At the Council meeting in October 1877 he attacked the policy as meaning the sacrificing of 'many men who were good all round excepting in this particular'. He said that he himself had decided to follow it out,

and what had he gained? A worse man by half, a thing belonging to the publicans, a man who did the publicans' work hip and thigh, all round, who opposed every effort at temperance legislation. . . . In his judgment they had been for some time playing into the hands of what he called the opposite party, and he did not feel free to do that.[12]

At temperance conferences these issues now began to be debated, as Whittaker pleaded that they should. For example, at a North of England Temperance League conference in September 1878 there was considerable disagreement as to whether they should refuse to vote for any candidate who would not promise to vote for the Bill. On the one hand, these were the extremists like John Howie who 'would not vote under any circumstances for a man who did not vote for the Permissive Bill' and Clarke of Whitby who 'advised shutting up their votes for ten years if need be, if they could not use them in support of the Permissive Bill'. But others insisted that questions other than temperance had to be taken into account.[13] The Council meeting in October 1878 reached a compromise between these two viewpoints. The main electoral resolution, moved by W. Farish, called on the friends of temperance 'to lose no time in extending and strengthening their electoral organisations, so as to be prepared to use their influence, by combined and energetic action, to secure the selection and return of candidates pledged to vote for the second reading of Sir Wilfrid Lawson's Permissive Prohibitory Liquor Bill, or an equivalent measure'. This is significant in that it makes no reference to what should be done by them if such candidates are not selected. John Kempster of London perceived this and moved an amendment seeking to mobilise electors to vote 'only' for such candidates. But this was rejected and the main resolution carried.[14]

In North-East Lancashire the Permissive Bill Association held a series of meetings to mobilise support for a rigid abstention policy— only, as we have seen, to abandon this at the general election. A good example of a debate on the issue is one which took place at Hippings on 31 October 1878. The resolution that was proposed pledged those present to vote solely for Permissive Bill candidates and to use their influence to induce others to do likewise. The following is a report of the debate which ensued:

It was thought by some present that it would not be right to pledge themselves to refrain from voting altogether in places where no Permissive Bill candidates were brought forward. In that case it was contended that they should be at liberty to vote as they thought proper. It was pointed out by some Liberals present that if they refrained from voting when no Permissive Bill candidates were brought forward it would injure their own party by taking away a large number of voters, and would allow men to get in who were more strongly opposed to the bill than perhaps those from whom they withheld their votes. In favour of the resolution it was contended that the course pointed out was the only one to take in order to get the bill passed, for it would induce those candidates who lost the elections through the action of the Permissive Bill voters to pledge themselves at future elections to vote for the bill.

An amendment which sought to have them at liberty to vote as they thought best where there were no Permissive Bill candidates was heavily defeated.[15]

The opponents of abstention were out in greater force at another North-East Lancashire conference at Bacup three weeks later. The main resolution pledged the meeting to work and vote only for candidates who promised to vote for the Bill. H. Mottram opposed this, advocating the alternative of voting for the man or men 'most favourable to the temperance cause, even if they would not vote for the Permissive Bill'. The Rev. J. S. Hughes, a Baptist minister, agreed: 'Although he was a temperance man, he was a citizen first, and he should not sacrifice twenty principles to secure one.' Another clergyman advocated voting for the Liberals because as a party they were more in favour of temperance reform than the Conservatives. Abstention clearly repelled Nonconformists because it represented a 'giving up of citizenship', and to counter this James Whyte from Alliance headquarters argued that 'Mr. John Bright, in urging his followers to vote for no one who would not promise to support the repeal of the Corn Laws, had virtually urged them to "give up their citizenship"'. Finally an amendment was moved, and carried by 27 to 23, replacing the negative pledge in the motion by a positive one to work and vote for candidates who did promise to vote for the Bill.[16]

At the Council meeting in October 1879 the main electoral resolution was similarly positive. This aroused some complaints, but the mood of the meeting was clearly such that no attempt to turn this into a negative pledge could have succeeded. John Kempster hoped that a stronger resolution might be moved the following year. In his opinion, they ought also to decide 'to oppose the candidates who opposed them and oppose the candidates who were neutral upon this question'. 'To talk of voting for the party that seemed most likely to give them what they desired was nonsense.' They should, he maintained, 'have no part in sending any man to power who would not give them the power of prohibition'. But he was passionately opposed by Thomas Hardy who 'believed that there was a clear course before them—to take as candidates for Parliament those who were the nearest to them and the most advanced as regarded Alliance principles. Taking such men and using them they would get to the goal they sought to gain.'[17] It is significant that numerous conferences which were held after the Council—the last before the general election—adopted its electoral resolution. The only one which adopted a strongly worded negative resolution calling for the withholding of votes was at Middlesbrough.[18]

The debate between the advocates of abstention and of voting for 'the best man' reflected the fact that there were now two sharply contrasting and diverging trends in temperance politics.

On the one hand, there was the by now extremely powerful trend towards integration into Liberal party politics—powerful because it is this period that sees the climax of the development of new-model representative Liberal Associations. The Liberal party in the constituencies amends its structure to accommodate the sections, and many of the temperance enthusiasts respond to the invitation. The result is that they can no longer be regarded as available to participate in independent temperance electoral action. Typical of the new situation is this item in the Alliance minutes: 'Mr. Owen reported visit to Nottingham where he was not able to get any of the Temperance voters to promise to act in unison and irrespective of party ties.'[19]

Many in the Alliance believed that the existence of this state of affairs had to be accepted and strategy adapted to take account of it. This realism began to move the Alliance much closer to the kind of strategy that had long been favoured by the Liberation Society—working within the Liberal party to the greatest possible extent. An example of this is in connection with the Northampton by-election of October 1874. As soon as word of the vacancy was received, the Alliance Executive instructed the Secretary to write to the agent 'to urge that our friends unite and act together so as to induce the Liberal Party to select a Candidate who is in favour of the Permissive Bill'. Moreover, he was to suggest to the Northampton friends the name of J. S. Wright 'as a suitable Candidate for the Liberal party to invite'.[20] One of the most ardent advocates of this approach was Handel Cossham who called on the movement to accept combination with the Liberal party as the only possible way of achieving its goals.[21] A symbol of the new rapprochement which many Liberals and temperance workers strove to facilitate was the National Reform Union's agreement, when it held a conference at Manchester in December 1875 to adopt a new constitution, to add to that constitution 'popular control over licences for the sale of intoxicating liquors' as one of its objects. The motion to add this was proposed by W. S. Caine who argued that, since the Liberals had lost the licensed victuallers as a body 'and were never going to get them back again', 'he saw no reason why they should not secure the unanimous support of all temperance reformers'. A message was read out from Pope, the Honorary Secretary of the Alliance, saying that the proposed form of words satisfied him and he could work with such a body as the Reform Union if it adopted them. The move towards integration was indicated further by the fact that it was Caine at the evening meeting who moved the resolution calling on all Liberals 'to concentrate their energies in furtherance of those principles and objects which have been adopted as the basis of the future operations of the National Reform Union'.[22] Two months later the Manchester by-election gave the local temperance reformers the chance to show that they meant what they said. This they did by giving Jacob Bright a strong endorsement and advising their supporters that, instead of 'working on an independent basis in their respective organisations', they 'should join the various ward committees already formed for the purpose of securing' his return.[23] As for the Liberal party, its side of the bargain soon began to become apparent and first reports were received of action being taken by local Liberal parties—not local temperance organisations—against Liberal MPs who opposed the Permissive Bill. What this reflected, of course, was the great temperance strength in these Liberal Associations, for example in Denbighshire, the scene of some remarkably intensive temperance electoral canvassing in recent years.[24] In other places, however, the Liberals had decidedly the best of the bargain, as temperance people seemed ready to accept extremely weak Liberals just because they were Liberals. At North Norfolk in April 1876 they supported Sir Fowell Buxton even though he not only refused to vote for the Permissive Bill but was himself a brewer. At the last moment he said that he would vote for the Irish Sunday Closing Bill, and that seemed quite enough to satisfy the temperance workers.[25] Even at Leeds all was now harmony. A by-election in August 1876 found the Permissive Bill people all supporting the Liberal candidate, J. Barran, who had promised to vote for the Bill.[26]

Samuel Pope became an enthusiastic promoter of the new departure. 'He would not object', he said, 'to seeing the temperance question made a party question if they liked.'[27] A critical test of whether this reconciliation between temperance and party was really going to be possible was the Halifax by-election of February 1877. As soon as word was received of the vacancy at Halifax, James Whyte was sent to confer with Henry Hibbert, the district agent, about inducing the friends of the Alliance to take united action to secure a Liberal candidate favourable to the Permissive Bill. The temperance electors held a meeting which passed a resolution indicating that only such a candidate would be considered satisfactory to them, and a deputation was sent to the Liberal Association to notify them of this. The Liberals, however, chose a candidate, J. D. Hutchinson, who refused even to promise that he would not vote against the Permissive Bill, although he indicated that he would support certain other temperance measures. The initial reaction of the temperance leaders to this was to urge their friends not to pledge their votes to Hutchinson. But the connections between the Liberals and the temperance people in Halifax were already strong enough to render any united electoral action against Hutchinson out of the question. Charles Watson who led the deputation to Hutchinson expressed regret that the resolution passed by the temperance electors prevented him from signing Hutchinson's nomination papers but assured him that he would nevertheless vote for him and referred to his admiration for Hutchinson's work as a Poor Law Guardian. The temperance electors then met again and passed a remarkably feeble resolution—that, 'having heard Mr. Gamble [the Conservative candidate] express his opinions on the Permissive Bill, and considering them less satisfactory that those of Mr. Hutchinson we withdraw all opposition to the candidature of Mr. Hutchinson, in the hope that if he be returned to Parliament, he will ere long espouse our cause and advocate our claims'. A minority did, it was reported, abstain from voting, but on the whole it seemed as if Liberal candidates could now safely get away with any sort of vague statement on temperance reform.[28]

When local Liberal Associations took a firm line and refused to be conciliatory, the temperance people often did not know what to do, especially as so many of them had a foot in both camps. An example of this is a conference of temperance electors held at Hackney on 8 December 1877. The chairman, John Hughes, began by explaining

that the meeting had been convened to consider the attitude of the leaders of the Liberal party toward the temperance electors, and the position of the latter, most of whom were Liberals, with relation to the newly constructed Hackney Liberal Association, as Mr. Gowland, president of the Liberal Club and president of the Hackney ward committee of the Hackney Liberal Association, and other leaders of the Liberal party, had at the recent ward meetings (held to organise 'the party' on the basis of the Birmingham scheme) declined on its behalf to entertain the 'strong conscientious convictions' held by the temperance section, though the former professed to desire to unify their forces, which (Mr. Hughes urged) could only be done by conciliation.

Hughes argued therefore that the temperance section in Hackney must now 'stand out' and 'seek in their own way to make their power and influence felt in the borough'. After being told by John Hilton of the Alliance that 'the temperance people in the borough could and would command 2,500 electors at least, to pledge themselves to make it a test question, and withhold their votes' from candidates who were not favourable to the Permissive Bill, the meeting passed a resolution to institute a canvass for signatures to such a pledge. But it seems that in fact many present agreed with W. E. Corner who attended as a representative of the Political Council of the Hackney Liberal Club when he condemned this idea 'because, after all, temperance people had more to hope and expect from Liberal members of Parliament than from Conservatives, whom such a course would have the undesirable effect of returning'. For a month later one finds the temperance electors of Hackney meeting again and continuing their debate. Many feel that they cannot bring themselves to take action against Liberal members of the high quality of J. Holms and Henry Fawcett.[29]

At other places co-operation seemed to be becoming firmly established. In January 1878 the Liberal Association and the Temperance Association in Newcastle-upon-Tyne met to consider the choice of a second Liberal to run with Joseph Cowen.[30] In December an Alliance deputation met the Chairman and Secretary of the Manchester Liberal Association to discuss the question of Gladstone's proposed candidature there.[31] At Middlesbrough in July 1878 the Liberals produced a candidate, Isaac Wilson, who supported the

Permissive Bill.[32] This was in contrast to 1874 when Alliance support had been withheld from one of the Liberals, H. W. F. Bolckow, and given instead to the Labour candidate, John Kane. In October 1878 J. H. Raper himself stood at Peterborough but was scrupulous in following all the rules laid down by an unfortunately as yet very imperfectly organised representative Liberal 'hundred'. The Fitzwilliam family ignored this body altogether and the by-election was won easily by the Hon. J. W. Fitzwilliam.[33]

It is not surprising, however, in the light of the concessions which temperance people were often persuaded to make to demonstrate their loyalty to the Liberal party, that there were many critics of this strategy of working through the party. To some it seemed a trap in which loyalty to the temperance cause would be steadily sapped away. Electoral strength, it was argued, could be 'known' and therefore effective only if kept strictly separate from party politics. Hugh Mason argued that 'we must not hang our faith on either party, but work for ourselves'.[34]

Nobody illustrates this conflict within the temperance movement better than Thomas Hardy, for it was very often a conflict within individual temperance workers. In 1876 Hardy was in Birmingham and closely identified with the Temperance Electoral Union which was in revolt against the alleged excessive orientation towards the Liberal party of the Birmingham Alliance Auxiliary. And so at the Council meeting in October he declared that

he had been educated by the Alliance to stand outside of all political parties . . . the only way of settling this question was for temperance reformers to take their stand as a definite party, and to give their support only to the party of temperance on which ever side it might be. That was his political creed.[35]

But shortly afterwards he moved to Manchester where, as we have seen, there was a very different atmosphere, one of harmony and co-operation; and at the Council meeting in October 1879 he repudiated all his former opinions on the matter.

He believed that a policy of isolation had been carried out by some of them to an extent that had positively put back their work—('No')—and they were not so far advanced to-day as they would have been if that policy had not been adopted. The question with him as a politician was, which of the two great parties in the State—(cries of 'No'). Well, he would turn off that line—(laughter and cheers)—because he was confident that although they did not talk politics there yet they talked politics when they got away, and that was the mischief. . . . The liquor traffic was the greatest curse in the country, and it ought to be prohibited. How could it best be done; and what were the means to be employed? He had been operating outside parties for a long time; he now believed in operating inside parties. (Hear, hear.)[36]

The varying reactions of the audience show the range of opinion in the movement on this question of relations with the Liberal party.

The alternative to working inside the Liberal party was to mobilise the temperance vote as a separate and independent factor in politics and some temperance people begin in this period to work very hard indeed to do this. If one worked within a party, one had to accept its rules which included abiding by the decision of the majority. This was not tolerable to the electoral militants who wished there to be a temperance vote which could be withheld from any candidate who opposed the Permissive Bill, even one who had received the endorsement of a Liberal Association after deliberations in which temperance supporters had participated. Only the knowledge of the existence of this ultimate sanction could persuade politicians to take the subject seriously.

The proponents of this point of view now began talking in terms of a separate temperance party. Indeed Lawson said in December 1875: 'We must form an umpire party. We have not much at the present moment to expect from either political party.'[37] The great argument that was used against this was that it was neither possible nor desirable so to isolate and insulate the 'temperance vote'. But there now appeared within the temperance movement a militant section which maintained that such isolation could be achieved and that they had evolved a method for carrying out this work.

Mention was made in the previous chapter of the electoral 'missionary' work which developed in Scotland in the 1860s.[38] This work had been proceeding steadily for some years, and then after the general election of 1874 its promoters decided to bring their techniques, their ideology, and their accomplishments to the attention of the Alliance membership in general. At the Council meeting in October 1874 Dr. J. Murray McCulloch of Dumfries explained their scheme. It was to visit electors individually in their own homes and ask them to sign a pledge to abstain from voting for all candidates except those who would promise to vote for the Permissive Bill. This was a new departure in that most previous pledging of voters had been done by resolutions at meetings and was therefore confined to those who bothered to come to meetings and lacked the same force as pledges signed by individuals contacted in their homes. McCulloch advocated concentrating on constituencies with very narrow majorities. In Scotland, he said, one seat with a majority of 2 was now controlled by 57 pledged temperance voters. J. H. Raper then strongly commended McCulloch's scheme and stressed the great advantage of being able to place before a candidate even a small list of names of pledged voters.[39]

The most celebrated temperance electoral canvasser was John Paton. His work which he carried out with the zeal almost of an evangelist was remembered in Scotland particularly for many years. At the Alliance Council meeting in 1897 one delegate, Thomas Robinson of Glasgow, said: 'Some 30 years ago he signed a pledge with John Paton—(applause)—that he would never give his vote to the party that would not give their vote to him. He had kept that pledge to that moment, and God helping him he would not vote for a man who would not vote for Local Veto.'[40] Paton worked systematically among the electors of the Scottish constituencies obtaining signatures to the pledge. In February 1875 the Alliance Executive were informed that he had secured 163 signatures to it at the Wigtown Burghs—the seat to which McCulloch had referred, where the Conservatives had a majority of 2 and the Liberals were to win in 1880 by a majority of 12.[41]

Soon such methods began to be used in England. In June 1875 the Bristol Auxiliary began a canvass of electors seeking signatures to a pledge not to vote for any candidate who would vote against Lawson's Bill.[42] The next month the *Alliance News* published a paper on 'The True Method of Political Temperance Electoral Organisation' which McCulloch had presented at a recent conference in Edinburgh. In this he gave further details of Paton's canvassing. More than one-fifth of the voters had signed in the Dumfries Burghs where the Liberal majority was 297 out of an electorate of 2,903. 725 had signed at Paisley and 400 at Renfrewshire (Liberal majority 88). He waxed very eloquent on the possible consequences of such action.

Think well what would be the result to the temperance reformation if from a fifth to a tenth of all the electors in every, or most, constituencies had signed this pledge; if the pledges were kept in the Permissive Bill and Alliance offices, and copies thereof in every constituency, with active committees to look after, organise, and, if I may use the expression, drill the recruits and raise new ones.

Petitions, public meetings, speeches, &c., are all very well, and all occasionally required, and, no doubt, many members of Parliament are conscientious men, and respectable, and may be influenced by such, but the ruck of them are influenced by votes and by votes alone, and the knowledge that there was a phalanx of pledged and inflexible temperance voters out-numbering the liquor traffic votes in their constituencies, would convince them of the excellence of the Permissive Bill with marvellous rapidity! The fact is, that the temperance party must adopt the system of exclusive voting, or otherwise consent to continual defeat. . . .

McCulloch advocated a ruthless exclusion of all other politics until the Permissive Bill was on the statute book. This would not be long if 'exclusive voting' were systematically practised.[43]

McCulloch's ideas became official Alliance policy at the Council meeting in October 1875 when a resolution was adopted which in-corporated them—in particular, the contacting of 'individual electors' and the stressing of their 'individual responsibilities' in connection with the temperance question, and then the preparation of 'lists of all electors who regard the claims of this movement to be of paramount importance to the national well-being, and who are prepared to act in unison at elections, so as to secure an efficient representation of temperance principles'.[44] The question now was how to give effect to this resolution, and the Alliance Executive asked Paton for a report. He informed them that in Glasgow nearly half the registered voters had now signed an Electoral Declaration and assured them that it was quite possible 'to organise a Permissive Bill party of voters in every constituency in Scotland sufficiently numerous to secure the votes of their representatives in the House of Commons'.[45] In order to demonstrate to them that this was also possible in England he came south and engaged in an electoral canvass at Chester where he found an ardent convert to his methods in the person of William Farish. By the beginning of February 1876 he was able to report that 209 voters there had signed the pledge.[46] Not surprisingly the idea was at once taken up by the enthusiasts at Wrexham who had already engaged in the more orthodox form of canvassing to find out how many voters were in favour of the Permissive Bill.[47]

The Alliance's agents and officers now began encouraging other areas to begin canvassing for subscriptions to the pledge. J. W. Owen and J. P. Uran attended a conference at Plymouth on 6 April 1876 to discuss the idea which was received with some caution, as the many Liberals present did not like the thought of having to vote for a Conservative if one did promise to vote for the Bill.[48] The next stage was the formation of special Electoral Associations of signa-tories to the pledge. This was done at Wakefield in June 1876 after

154 electors had signed. (Wakefield had a Conservative majority of 187.)[49] Paton now began helping with cavassing in the Midlands and concentrated on Coventry where in 1874 in an electorate of 8,393 only 195 votes had separated the first and the fourth of the candidates. By October 1876 he had 473 signatures there.[50] At the Council meeting William Jones of Birmingham reported on this canvass in which he was Paton's associate. They had selected Coventry 'because the two parties were pretty equally balanced'. They hoped eventually to have 1,000 signatures, and already the leader of the Coventry Liberals 'had been heard to say that it would be folly indeed to think of bringing forward a Liberal candidate there unless he were acceptable to those men who had signed that declaration'. In his opinion, the time had now come 'when the machinery of the Alliance should be chiefly directed to this most important work'.[51]

The existence of pledged voters was used as a weapon to put pressure on MPs. For instance, when M. E. Grant Duff, MP for the Elgin District, said that he was opposed to the Permissive Bill, the Alliance executive sent him a letter reminding him that 170 electors in his constituency were pledged not to vote for anyone who took this attitude.[52]

The next Midlands constituency to be canvassed for pledges was Dudley where 597 signatures had been obtained by late March 1877 and the signatories were organised into an Electoral Association.[53] A canvass was also begun at this time in Lincoln and, having been signed by 450, the electoral pledge was adopted in August as the basis of the political action of the Lincoln Permissive Bill Association.[54] The first real test of the reliability of these pledges came at the Oldham by-election in February 1877, and the result was to indicate that even they were not completely proof against the influence of Liberal political sympathies. The Liberal candidate, J. T. Hibbert, announced that he would probably remain neutral on the Permissive Bill but would vote for a Licensing Boards Bill which Cowen was promoting—and which was not recognised by the Alliance as an acceptable substitute. The electors who had recently signed a declaration not to vote for any candidate who would not support the Permissive Bill met and passed a resolution, with only two dissentients, that the principles of Lawson's Bill were embodied in Cowen's and that therefore Hibbert should be supported.[55]

Nevertheless, the Alliance was now committed to electoral pledging and indeed at its Council meeting in October 1877 it accepted an even stronger resolution on the subject, moved by McCulloch. This strongly recommended the Executive to 'prosecute the electoral canvass work, so as to form a solid party in each constituency' ready to support Permissive Bill candidates. McCulloch argued that 'the canvassed places render anti-Permissive Bill candidates either nearly or altogether hopeless, and, if exhaustively canvassed, entirely so'. It reached large numbers of sympathisers who did not attend meetings. William Farish said that at Chester the Liberal candidate, although a sympathiser, had hesitated to tell a deputation that he would vote for the Bill because they 'had no *bona fide* facts to lay before them as an encouragement for him to take up their cause, in opposition to the influence of the publicans'. But now the political power of temperance in Chester was no longer a 'rope of sand'. They had pledges which greatly exceeded the margin between the candidates. Paton himself then spoke and referred to the results of his electoral 'missions':

The fact was clearly demonstrated that there is in every English, Scotch, and Irish constituency a nucleus of a new political party which, when fairly organised, would reform the House of Commons in a higher sense than that in which it was reformed in 1832. . . . The Alliance was nothing if it was not a voting power, if it was not supremely respected in the House of Commons. . . . No great measure of reform had been put on the statute book except by special voting.

This vision of what an electoral strategy might achieve is reminiscent of Cobden and his forty-shilling freeholds. Even Samuel Pope was momentarily swept along. 'They must', he said, 'work upon what are called the political parties, and if they could not revivify the old parties they must and would necessarily in the end create a new party—call it Puritan, or whatever they pleased.' There were one or two sceptics, however. Tugwell of Scarborough—a stronghold of scepticism about electoral militancy—warned against relying on canvassing and pledges. Many people did not remain true to these pledges.[56]

At this stage there were not many doubters. Enthusiasm for pledging spread rapidly. In December 1877 the Hackney temperance electors resolved to start a canvass with a target of at least 2,500 set by John Hilton, a canvass was begun and an Electoral P.B.A. founded at Banbury, and a Temperance Electoral Association was formed at Holloway in London to carry out a canvass.[57] Paton carried out further canvasses at Warwick and Cheltenham, while by March 1878 500 electors were reported to have signed the pledge at Portsmouth.[58] Assisted by E. C. Brambley, an Alliance superintendent, who always took a keen interest in electoral work, Paton canvassed Bedford, one of England's most marginal constituencies, and in August 1878 formed 90 pledged electors into an Electoral Association.[59] Canvassing for pledges was not universally adopted, however. The North-East Lancashire P.B.A. instituted a very active pledging campaign, but these pledges were always the traditional kind of resolutions passed at meetings.[60]

Paton's next canvass was at Newport in the Monmouth constituency in October 1878. Here 450 signatures were obtained in three weeks. A month later this figure had reached nearly 600.[61] The London Auxiliary announced at this time that as a result of canvassing in the Metropolitan boroughs the names of more than 17,000 electors were marked on the registers as pledged to support Permissive Bill candidates. However, it revealed that, although it recommended that the pledge be to abstain from voting for any candidate who would not vote for the Bill, 'the forms of these promises have varied according to the judgment and choice of the local committees'—which meant that many of the promises did not commit the signatories to abstain if no Permissive Bill candidate was standing. Two examples may be given of these weaker pledges in London. In Marylebone, where the temperance societies were very anxious to find a course of action that everyone could agree on and would not interfere 'with any existing political organisation, Liberal or Conservative', the pledge was to abstain from voting for any candidate who himself refused to take a pledge 'to support by his vote such a measure, or measures, of temperance reform, or give such evidence of active sympathy with the temperance movement as may satisfy the representatives of the various temperance societies in the borough, assembled in conference'. This deliberately omitted reference to the Permissive Bill, Frank Debenham explaining that they must try to get what they wanted from Parliament piecemeal and work for something less than that measure for the time being. A second example is Finsbury where 1,600 signatures were given to a pledge not to promise votes 'before consulting with the friends of temperance in the borough'. Thus the 17,000 pledged electors in London were not nearly so formidable a force as the Auxiliary claimed.[62] It was not only in London that such weaker formulae were devised. At Bodmin the new East Cornwall Temperance Electoral Association adopted a voters' pledge which was virtually identical with that accepted at Marylebone—and for the same reason, viz. to

H

ensure united electoral action among all temperance organisations, which included many keen Liberals.[63]

Two constituencies were fated during this period to become battle-grounds between the advocates of working within the Liberal party and those who preferred independent electoral action.

The first of these was Birmingham. Here Muntz's post-election conduct shattered the compromise arrived at in late January 1874 and caused intense bitterness among some of the temperance advo-cates who regarded themselves as having been betrayed and cheated by the Liberal Association. So angry were George Cadbury and Joseph Malins that they went along to one of Muntz's meetings and moved an amendment censuring him, an action which in its turn greatly annoyed the Birmingham Liberals and divided the tem-perance people.[64] The temperance question was threatening to disrupt Birmingham Liberal politics, and so the Committee of 400 of the Liberal Association decided to hold a special meeting in order to agree on a policy which would heal the divisions. The local Alliance Auxiliary met beforehand and decided that, as there was no hope of getting the Permissive Bill itself adopted by this meeting, they would leave the members of the Liberal Association who also belonged to the Alliance to make up their own minds as to the proper course of action. These men then held their own meeting and decided to support a motion to be proposed by Hewins that control of the liquor traffic be in the hands of special licensing boards, elected by the ratepayers. However, when the Committee of 400 met on 13 May 1875 and Hewins moved along these lines, Chamberlain proposed an amendment, 'That this meeting is of opinion that the liquor traffic should be under the control of the ratepayers, and requests the officers of the association to take the matter into their consideration, to draw up resolutions, or prepare a scheme upon the subject, and to report to a future meeting of the association.' Several temperance speakers supported this amendment, for example J. Rutherford who seconded it, and the Rev. H. J. Heathcote who said that the temperance people 'were anxious to go with the association'. Jesse Collings reciprocated the sentiment. He

welcomed their Permissive Bill friends on that occasion, because he saw in their presence an advance in the direction of the principle of representative government. They were most anxious to go with them, and if they would come and accept the full representative principle, they would have all true Liberals on their side.

But both he and J. S. Wright stressed that the meaning of that principle was acceptance of the will of the majority, even if that will turned out to be for regulation and not the veto. Hewins sensed the mood of the meeting and withdrew his motion. Chamberlain's amendment was then carried.[65] A year passed and nothing happened. No report was issued. Finally Hewins raised the matter again at the annual meeting of the 400 in March 1876. J. S. Wright gave a variety of unsatisfactory excuses for the inaction. Chamberlain in the meantime was touring the country trying to test the extent of support for the Gothenburg scheme for the municipalisation of the liquor traffic—not a proposal which could be adopted by adherents to the Permissive Bill.[66]

By this time the patience of the more militant temperance enthusiasts in Birmingham was running out. Why, they asked, were Birmingham's three Liberal MPs all either neutral or hostile to the Permissive Bill? The answer was, they believed, 'to be found in the fact that the Liberal Association which has ruled all the politics of the town has absorbed most of the temperance men and neutralised their temperance political action, and although it has declared in favour of local control of the liquor traffic, has never in any way given effect to that declaration'. Accordingly, about 50 people attended a meeting on 8 March 1876 to inaugurate a Temperance Electoral Union. Among those who convened it were William Jones, the district superintendent of the Alliance, Joseph Malins, and Merryweather who was treasurer of the Alliance Auxiliary and was also elected treasurer of the new body to show that no hostility to the Auxiliary was intended. The meeting drew up a declaration which was to be signed by all members. This dealt separately with 'hostiles', who were on no account to be helped, and 'neutrals', who were covered by the following formula: 'irrespective of all other political parties, I will always vote for such candidate, or candidates, and for such only, as will vote in Parliament for [a prohibition bill], unless a majority of the committee of this union, in the absence of a prohibitory candidate, decide (in order to defeat an opponent) to support one who will be neutral.' Although about one-third of those present belonged to the Liberal Association, all signed this declaration.[67]

The Alliance Executive was now becoming very worried about the Birmingham situation and instituted an inquiry into complaints that the Auxiliary's conduct at recent municipal and Board of Guardians elections 'had not been free from a political partisan

bias'. The Executive then passed a resolution laying down guide-
lines for the future conduct of the Auxiliary. This was a compromise
between the two schools of thought. On the one hand, it recommended the Auxiliary, which admitted that it might have made
some mistakes, to be very careful to avoid any action other than
what clearly advanced the interests of the temperance movement.
On the other hand, it produced the following recommendation concerning relations with political parties:

whenever, without compromise of the primary principle of allegiance to
prohibition policy, members of the U.K.A. can obtain positions of influence
in the ranks of political parties, the Executive deem it of importance that
the opportunity should be made use of, and recommend their friends in this
manner to permeate the councils of the political organizations.[68]

This was a clear repudiation of the contention that such involvement could only have a negative effect on temperance interests.

The response of the Birmingham Auxiliary to this was to pass a
resolution at its annual meeting later in the year pledging members
'to adhere to the political platform of the United Kingdom Alliance,
i.e., to allow no party consideration to prevent them voting for any
candidate for parliamentary honours who will support, or against
any candidate who will oppose, the passing of the [Permissive]
bill through Parliament'.[69] Nevertheless, by 1879 the Birmingham
Auxiliary was once again very seriously divided over electoral policy.
The Liberals were determined to nominate Muntz again although
he still would not support the Permissive Bill, and the Auxiliary's
Committee was torn with dissension over how to deal with this
situation. Finally the Committee decided not to put forward a
candidate of their own, as some wanted, but to advise friends to vote
only for Chamberlain and Bright and to withhold votes from
Muntz.[70] This did not stop Muntz from coming top of the poll, nearly
3,000 votes ahead of Bright and nearly 3,500 ahead of Chamberlain.

It was in Hull that temperance electoral militancy created perhaps the most serious complications for Liberal politics and threatened indeed to tear apart the local Liberal Association which
contained many strong temperance enthusiasts.

Hull had two Liberal MPs. One, C. H. Wilson, was a supporter of
the Permissive Bill. The other, C. M. Norwood, was not. Repeated
visits by deputations from the Alliance Auxiliary failed to persuade
him to change his mind. Therefore, on 10 July 1878 the Auxiliary
met the executive of the Hull Liberal Association and asked whether

it was prepared to replace Norwood by a Permissive Bill candidate at the next election. Having heard this deputation, the executive decided to refer the matter to a special meeting of the Liberal Association on 24 July. The meeting adopted the following resolution on the recommendation of the executive: 'That the Association, in the selection of candidates, cannot bind itself to select only candidates pledged to the Permissive Bill; and it must leave the same an open question between the candidates and those interested in the measure.' It then proceeded to consider the adoption of candidates for the next election. C. H. Wilson was re-adopted without dissent, but when Norwood's name was submitted a vote of want of confidence in him was moved and seconded. When it became apparent that this was likely to receive considerable support, the debate was adjourned. Three days later the Alliance Auxiliary met and resolved to take steps to find 'a suitable candidate to contest the borough in favour of the Permissive Bill, in conjunction with Mr. C. H. Wilson, MP, at the next election'. A deputation was formed to wait upon N. B. Downing and Arthur Pease to find if either would be prepared to respond to a requisition to stand. Pease was not interested, but Downing was. On 16 September he came up to Hull from London and addressed an Alliance meeting which resolved to recommend him to the 'Liberal Two Hundred' as the second Liberal candidate in place of Norwood. On 2 October the committee of the Auxiliary resolved that, if the Liberals did select Norwood, they would run their own candidate.[71]

The Liberal Two Hundred held a public meeting on 1 November to resume the debate on the candidature. The Chairman, James Reckitt, was now inclining to the view that Norwood was too divisive a candidate. He said:

If only a section supported Mr. Norwood it was simply impossible, in his opinion, for him to be returned. . . . They had nothing to do with the Permissive Bill there, but there might be a difficulty with that section of the party, and that was a section of the party they must consider, because if they lost the Permissive Bill men and the temperance men and a considerable section of the Liberals upon the Eastern Question, where were they? . . . It was with the greatest difficulty that they could secure a majority in a town like Hull unless they were very much united.

Once again a motion was proposed that they adopt Norwood. But an amendment to this called for a further postponement of a decision and was carried by 82 votes to 81.

By this time, as Reckitt's remarks indicate, a more radical section of Hull Liberals—the Hull Reform Union—were willing to co-operate with the Alliance in a campaign against Norwood because of displeasure with other aspects of his politics. Nearly 300 voluntary canvassers set to work seeking signatures to a pledge to vote only for Permissive Bill candidates, and, in spite of appalling weather, nearly 1,000 signatures were obtained by the time of the annual meeting of the Auxiliary on 27 November. At this meeting the executive was criticised for having become too involved in Liberal politics. But the President pointed out that the Conservative Association had 'treated their communication with contempt and did not answer it until after two months'. This was of some significance, for Hull was one of the very few places where in recent times supporters of the Permissive Bill, including Liberals, had voted for Conservative candidates.[72]

A requisition signed by over 2,000 voters was now presented to Downing, but on 26 December 1878 he replied declining the invitation. The search now began for an alternative candidate. William Hoyle was interested and, after he had addressed meetings in Hull in June 1879, plans were made for a special Alliance meeting in September for the purpose of adopting him. However, the Alliance Executive intervened and, after considerable discussion and investigation, resolved at its meeting on 3 September to recommend that no Alliance supporter should stand against Norwood since 'such contest [was] likely to damage if not oust Mr. Wilson, a supporter of the [Local Option] resolution'. Hoyle then withdrew and the meeting was called off. Some of the militants at Hull were very angry about this. The Alliance minutes give this report of an interview between two of them, Hargreaves and Guy Hayler, and a deputation from the Alliance Executive:

Mr. Hargreaves complained that Mr. Hoyle had disappointed them at Hull in not becoming a candidate for fear of splitting the Liberal Party, and that the Executive had used its influence to prevent Mr. Hoyle becoming a candidate at Hull. Mr. Hargreaves read some of the correspondence he had had with Mr. Hoyle and the Secretary, from which it clearly appeared that the consideration that influenced Mr. Hoyle most was his fear of damaging Mr. Wilson and perhaps losing his seat which would be a disaster to the Temperance Cause. Mr. Hargreaves withdrew his imputation, it having been explained to him that Mr. Hoyle came to his conclusion not to contest Hull, before consulting the Alliance Executive.

The Executive, upon receiving this report, passed a resolution stressing 'the necessity of acting in such a case with reference to nothing but the interests of Temperance Legislation'.[73]

This did not satisfy the militants in Hull. At the annual meeting of the Auxiliary on 19 December 1879 it was announced that negotiations were going on to find yet another Permissive Bill candidate. The Alliance, said the President, 'had made up their minds, in conjunction with the Radicals, to oust Mr. Norwood from his seat'. Early in February 1880 E. S. Pryce, the well-known Liberationist, was announced as the man whom the Hull temperance people were now asking to stand. Accordingly on 18 February a motion of support for Pryce was proposed at a meeting of the Auxiliary. This was passed after the withdrawal of an amendment that they should support only Wilson and not have a candidate of their own. All this placed Wilson in a serious quandary for the Liberals had decided to re-adopt Norwood and a third candidate might split the Liberal vote and allow the Conservatives to take one of the seats, possibly his own. What the Alliance Auxiliary wanted was a Temperance-Radical slate of Wilson and Pryce, but Wilson decided that he would have to put his foot down. Immediately after the meeting endorsing Pryce's candidature, he asked the Alliance to send a deputation to confer with him. He told them that

in dealing with temperance legislation, naturally he should have to consider his position in connection with the Liberal party, and was afraid that it would involve some very decisive steps being taken by him to check, as far as able, the division in the party. The interests of the Liberal party, as far as he was able to uphold them, would have to take precedence over the temperance question, and his feeling and intention were to act in unison with Mr. Norwood. He should have to consider himself perfectly at liberty to take what action he thought wise and proper, and that might seriously affect his ability to assist the temperance party, and the result might be, in trying to get two temperance members in for Hull, they might lose both. That was what he was afraid it was drifting into. He hoped by some means or other some arrangement could be come to so that the candidature of Mr. Pryce could be done away with.

A long discussion of this followed, and finally Wilson made his position completely explicit:

if the temperance party and the extreme party, headed by our friend Mr. [H. F.] Smith, produce discord in the Liberal ranks, and think it their duty to do so, I feel myself that in all probability the result may be that I may not stand for Hull. . . . I tell you candidly I should not like the worry and excitement and trouble in every way it would cause of having to stand for Hull with a divided Liberal party.

Hargreaves replied that what he was saying could not shake their resolve to support Norwood 'under no consideration' at the election. If this was so, commented Wilson,

> it might make me say, 'I am not going to be a party in any way to a division of the Liberal party.' There you see the two things clash—the temperance question and the Liberal party. I should have nothing to do with the introduction of another candidate by the Liberal party.

In spite of Hargreaves's brave words, the Hull Auxiliary was forced by Wilson's virtual ultimatum to have second thoughts. Eventually, after a good deal of negotiation, Norwood gave a promise that he would vote for Sunday Closing and also for a ratepayers' vote on the issue and renewal of licenses—as long as publicans were compensated for loss of license. The Auxiliary accepted this, withdrew the Pryce candidature, and called on supporters to vote for Norwood and Wilson.[74]

In view of the intensive canvassing for pledges which had gone on in many areas since 1874, one might have expected that temperance electoral militancy would have been at its peak in the general election of 1880. But this was not so.

For the subdued role of the Alliance and of temperance politics generally in 1880 three main reasons may be adduced. First was the intense pressure of Nonconformist feeling in favour of subordinating all other considerations to the primary responsibility of supporting Gladstone and getting rid of the Beaconsfield government and its allegedly immoral foreign and imperial policies. This must have had a considerable effect on the many Nonconformists who belonged to the temperance movement and made them even less disposed to countenance aggressive anti-Liberal electoral action. It is certainly true that there was a revival in the *Nonconformist* and other Dissenting journals and in the speeches of prominent Nonconformist politicians of the kind of bitter attack on temperance sectionalism and disruptive electoral tactics which had characterised an earlier period of Gladstonian appeal to Nonconformity—1868.[75] Secondly, there was the fact that, as we have seen, many of the pledges given by voters were not quite as rigid in practice as superficial appearances tended to suggest. There were enough loopholes and possibilities for flexible interpretations of them to enable accommodations to be reached with Liberal candidates in quite a few constituencies on policy stand points which, as at Hull, fell some way short of the Alliance ideal which was supposed to be embodied in the pledges. This process was undoubtedly helped on by the desire of so many Alliance supporters to find a way of ending the conflict of loyalties in which the obduracy of Liberal candidates often threatened to involve and paralyse them. Furthermore, at a time like this reaching a compromise, even if it meant some sacrifice of principle, seemed almost a patriotic duty to the Nonconformists among them.

But thirdly and most important, there was a major change in Alliance tactics which immensely facilitated a rapprochement between the Liberal party and the temperance movement and abruptly undercut the entire basis of the electoral militancy which Paton and the canvassers had been preparing since 1874.

Since 1869 Lawson's Permissive Prohibitory Liquor Bill had been making little progress in the House of Commons. The number of MPs voting for it rose from 87 in 1869 to 124 in 1871 but then fell back and never once in the five divisions taken on it between 1873 and 1878 did it again reach even the point at which it had started in 1869. Only 84 voted for it in 1878. The majorities against were at first fairly low—only 31 in 1870—but this was owing to massive abstentions. Subsequently they ranged from 194 in 1878 to the high-point of 285 in 1875.

Following the 1878 defeat Lawson decided on a complete change of method. He gave up the attempt to promote a Bill and introduced instead the tactic employed by Miall and the Liberationists—a resolution calling on the government to introduce legislation to confer the right of 'local option' with regard to liquor licenses. This effected an immediate transformation in the Alliance's parliamentary situation, for many Liberal MPs were far happier to vote for a resolution than for an actual piece of legislation. The number voting for the Local Option Resolution when it was moved for the first time in 1879 was 164, an increase of 80 on the supporters of the Permissive Bill the previous year, and the majority against was 88, the lowest since 1871. There was a deterioration when the vote was taken again just before the 1880 elections—134 voted for, and the majority against was up by 26 to 114. But all was changed by the great Liberal election victory. When Lawson moved his resolution again in June 1880 the new House accepted it by 229 to 203. Significant of the transformation was the fact that, while the Scottish and Welsh Liberal MPs were strongly for it, even the English Liberals voted in favour of it by 133 to 35. Eighteen members of the government voted in the majority, including Harcourt, Chamberlain, and Bright, and, although Gladstone was not among them, he announced that he accepted the principle of popular control of licensing and promised government attention to the task of reforming the licensing laws 'as early as the pressure of business will allow'.[76]

At the Alliance's Council meeting in October 1879 electoral policy was adapted to suit the new circumstances. When one of the militants, Jonathan Hargrove of Liverpool, attacked the Local Option Resolution as too weak and moved an amendment to delete the reference to it in the main electoral resolution, he could not even find a seconder. Most speakers expressed strong support for the new approach. Some said that there was now considerable confusion as to whether candidates were to be asked to support the Resolution in place of the Permissive Bill and how this affected the system of pledges. But William Farish reported that the Chester people had promptly brought their canvass up to date. 520 electors had now 'signed a declaration pledging them to support only candidates who would not vote for the second reading of the Local Option Resolution, on the ground that it involved the Permissive Bill'.[77]

In numerous constituencies Liberal candidates announced that they were prepared to support the Local Option Resolution although they had previously not supported the Permissive Bill. The new harmony and reconciliation of old antagonists may be illustrated by reference to that much fought-over constituency, Bath. On 5 February 1880 E. Hill moved a resolution at a meeting convened by the committee of the Bath Auxiliary. This pledged support for candidates who would support the Local Option Resolution. Hill's arguments in favour of it indicate how far many Temperance Liberals were now willing to go to settle their differences with the Liberal party:

It was understood well by Sir Wilfrid and by the Executive of the Alliance in Manchester that any member of Parliament or candidate promising to vote for the local option resolution did not necessarily pledge himself to vote for the Permissive Bill. They accepted that in Bath who had been working for the Permissive Bill question for some years. For a long time there had been a division between a section of the temperance electors and the Liberal party.... the temperance electors of Bath, 19 out of 20 of them, were ardent Liberals. (Applause.) He was sure he could say it for those of them who had taken an attitude some of them had deprecated, that it had been a painful position for them to occupy. . . . Some of them would say they had hauled down their flag. He did not think they had. Circumstances had changed, the Permissive Bill was withdrawn, and Sir Wilfrid Lawson had brought in his local option resolution. A certain number of them said they would not vote for any candidate who would not pledge himself to vote for the Permissive Bill, and they insisted on neutrality—that if a member would not vote for the Permissive Bill he should not vote against it. There were great difficulties in the matter; they found that; but directly the local option resolution came before Parliament Sir Wilfrid Lawson withdrew the Permissive Bill, and it was therefore no use asking a member or candidate to vote for a bill that was not before Parliament. They found that the case throughout England, and that there had been, especially among Liberal candidates, a desire to meet them.

Hill then revealed what had happened when a deputation had interviewed the two Liberal candidates, Hayter and Wodehouse. They had said that they were prepared to support the Local Option Resolution as long as it was recognised that they interpreted it in a narrow sense as not covering the Permissive Bill. The deputation accepted this, considering 'that under the present circumstances they had no right to ask for more than that'. The flexibility of manoeuvre provided by the Local Option Resolution was abundantly clear. As Hill admitted, there were 'all varieties of interpretation put upon it'. Not all the Alliance people in Bath were convinced. One pointed out that, in their rush to bury the hatchet with the Liberal party, they were omitting to carry out the standard Alliance electoral procedure of seeking the views of the Conservative candidates as well. Hill's resolution was carried, but nearly half those present abstained, and there were four or five votes against.[78]

There was remarkably little temperance electoral militancy in the 1880 elections. In most cases Liberal candidates received support from their local temperance organisations. There were only a few isolated pockets of organised abstention. One of these was Southampton where in 1878 temperance opposition to H. M. Bompas, a strong Liberationist, had angered the Nonconformists and been blamed by them for the Conservative victory. In 1880 the signatories to the Temperance Electoral Declaration resolved once again not to support any of the candidates. This again annoyed the Nonconformists. Henry Lee, one of the Liberals, was a friend of the Rev. R. W. Dale who had warned him after the 1878 by-election that he could not count on the teetotallers having 'learnt a lesson': 'They are slow to learn and swift to forget.'[79] However, in 1880 the Liberals did win both seats—although only by an extremely narrow margin.

The more normal state of affairs in 1880 is illustrated by Dewsbury. The sitting Liberal member, Sergeant Simon, was a longstanding and notorious opponent of the Permissive Bill. But the Liberal Three Hundred at Dewsbury became a stronghold of temperance enthusiasts, and when they held a ballot to decide who should be their candidate Simon received only 19 votes as against 156 for William Hoyle, the prominent temperance advocate. Simon stood nevertheless and defeated Hoyle by a majority of 345.[80] More often than not, neutrals or Liberals who supported compensation were supported in preference to totally hostile Conservatives.[81]

CHAPTER XI

The United Kingdom Alliance, 1880–1885

For some years after 1880 interest in electoral action was at a very low ebb, largely owing, no doubt, to the spectacular success of the conversion to the Local Option Resolution. In 1883 it was passed by 288 to 141, and Gladstone himself voted for it for the first time. In these circumstances very few temperance supporters wished to rock the Liberal boat. At Alliance Council meetings there was virtually no discussion of electoral action. Interventions in by-elections usually took the form of enthusiastic support for Liberal candidates. And Liberal Associations were usually now most anxious to reciprocate and make sure that their candidates were acceptable to the temperance section. There were some who were worried that identification with Liberal politics was proceeding too rapidly. Alliance agents were sitting on Liberal selection committees,[1] and Conservatives complained that temperance deputations were not bothering any more even to seek the views of Conservative candidates.[2] At former trouble-spots harmony now prevailed. C. M. Norwood could even be found taking the chair at meetings of the Hull Auxiliary.[3] Liberal candidates, it seemed, no longer had any reason to fear temperance electoral action against them, and some, sensing this, began to reclaim their freedom from pledges. In December 1881 'An Alliance Man' wrote to the *Alliance News* complaining about the conduct of the Liberal candidate, George Howell, at the Stafford by-election. Howell, he reported,

would make us no public promise whatever although asked to do so, feeling sure that the temperance section in Stafford being Liberals first and Alliance men afterwards would give him their votes in any case. It is very lamentable that the temperance reformers of this town will not show a more independent spirit. Were they less slavish in their Gladstonism we might have got a public pledge from *either* of the candidates; whereas, in Mr. Howell's case, he would not promise, feeling assured of our votes; and Mr. Salt would promise nothing, knowing full well that with not more than half a dozen exceptions the temperance party would vote against him on political grounds, however much he might grant them.[4]

In fact, pledge-giving was now to go more and more out of fashion. What candidates were able to do instead was to say that they stood on the programme of their Liberal Association which very often in cluded local option. This allowed them to give the question much less prominence in their campaign than when they were forced to give a specific pledge, and this apparently is what quite a few of them, fearful of provoking opposition from 'the Trade', wanted. Typical of this new situation was the by-election of May 1882 in the North-West Riding of Yorkshire. The Liberal candidate, Isaac Holden, took pains to show the temperance people a draft of his address in which appeared a sentence declaring his intention to vote for Local Option. Yet when it was issued this had gone because his committee 'thought it better to avoid all reference to this vexed question'. During the campaign in some places temperance people were begged to maintain silence while in others the Liberals publicised the fact that Alliance representatives were to speak on Holden's behalf.[5] As far as some candidates and MPs were concerned, the matter was now in the hands of the government and they wanted to hear as little about it as possible.

Sometimes Liberals took their assumption of temperance acquiescence a little too far, and then there was trouble. Discontent with the Liberal party's temperance policies was never far below the surface at Birmingham, for example. There was an eruption in the later part of 1882 when the Birmingham Liberals nominated a brewer for a municipal election and the Alliance Auxiliary advised its supporters not to vote for him. His defeat led to very bitter recriminations between the Liberal Association and the Auxiliary.[6] There was by this stage evidence of a resumption of the work of organising pledged voters. E. C. Brambley was busy forming temperance Electoral Unions in East Anglia.[7] A canvass for signatures to an Electoral Declaration to vote only for Local Option candidates was begun in Aylesbury.[8] In May 1883 a new Alliance Electoral Association was reported at Batley.[9] Finally, at the Council meeting in October 1883 electoral militancy raised its head again for the first time since before the general election of 1880. When an innocuous motion was proposed calling on the Alliance to continue to demand for the people the power of direct veto in their localities, John Kempster moved to amend it by adding the words, 'And this council urges patriotic citizens everywhere to demand this power as a condition of their votes at all future elections'. He argued that 'a strong electoral policy' was essential. The only way to get the government to do anything about the Local Option Resolution was to threaten to overthrow their supporters in their constituencies. The mover and seconder of the resolution accepted this amendment, but when the seconder, G. Charlton, said that it simply expressed what they had been doing all along, there were shouts of dissent. What Kempster did in fact seem to be proposing was a new departure—abstaining from voting for MPs who supported the government, even if they themselves individually supported Local Option. Charlton thought that this was wrong. 'Out of thirteen members twelve go with us entirely; are we to abstain from voting for the twelve?' The mixed feelings of the delegates were reflected in their response to this which was negative from some and affirmative from others. What was needed, Charlton argued, was for them to send the same men back but for those men as MPs to do the abstaining and say to the government, 'Until you act upon principle we cannot support you.' Thomas Whittaker again strongly condemned electoral aggression. It would not be wise or prudent, he said, 'to hold out threats to Parliament'. He 'was not going to be a party to a similar action to that of '74'. But Henry Hibbert retorted that '1874 was a memorable year in the history of this grand movement'. 'They had first to smash the party to prove their authority, and then the party respected them. (Hear, hear, and "That's it.") . . . Dr. Lees convinced the Liberal party of Leeds that they could not win without the temperance vote.' After this resolution as amended was carried, Samuel Pope moved the official resolution which Kempster had attacked as 'of a very tame and milk-and-water description' and which simply said that temperance men would have to consider seriously whether they could support the government if it failed to introduce a Local Option measure next session. Joseph Malins thought that the previous resolution made nonsense of this but failed to carry an amendment to delete reference to 'serious consideration as to whether'.[10]

Many temperance people became seriously alarmed about all this talk of electoral war against the Liberal party. The implication that the movement would detach itself from that party and once again adopt an entirely external relationship to it threatened to destroy the very real advances that had been made through seeking a more organic and internal connection. The more practical-minded Alliance workers were sceptical of high-sounding resolutions. For example, when at the annual meeting of the Leicester Auxiliary in March 1884 a resolution was moved pledging them henceforth to prefer 'those candidates who are favourable to temperance legislation, irrespective of party', William Mart, the chairman and the Alliance district superintendent, caustically remarked that 'he hoped that whilst they were talking about sinking their political differences they would not sink the Alliance'. The Liberals were taking steps to find a new candidate, and they ought to be bringing their influence to bear on the Liberal Three Hundred to make sure that he was a man who would support the Alliance.[11]

The problem was that the Alliance was confronted with a new and very perplexing situation for which none of the old methods seemed appropriate. They had now attained the goal for which they had been striving—a majority of MPs in their favour. And yet nothing was happening. Commanding the votes of MPs was clearly not sufficient. Governments still possessed the critical power of being able to determine at what time and in what order of precedence and priority the reform measures which their party supported were actually placed before Parliament for legislative enactment. If governments dragged their feet over this, as the Liberal government was plainly doing over Local Option, what sanctions did pressure groups have to enable them to remedy this state of affairs? Perhaps it was not enough to consider whether candidates and MPs personally supported Local Option. That question had to be superseded by one relating to the policy and action of the government which they kept in office. Could an electoral strategy be devised which would coerce MPs into rebelling against their parliamentary leaders and themselves threatening to abstain unless a Local Option measure was produced? Serious thought was given to this possibility by the Alliance. The following resolution was drafted by the Executive for the Council meeting in October 1884 but in the end not proceeded with, largely owing, it seems, to Lawson's disapproval of it: 'That this Council commends the friends of the United Kingdom Alliance throughout the Constituencies to refuse support to any candidates proposing to support a Government which has failed to bring in its promised legislation based on the thrice adopted Local Option Resolution.'[12]

This question of precedence dominated the 1884 Council meeting. Many delegates wanted efforts to be made to get the government to be much more specific about the order in which it intended to take up the various reform measures to which it was committed.[13] Early in 1885 one of the Executive members, S. A. Steinthal, wrote to G. O. Trevelyan, a government minister, warning him of the very serious electoral consequences which could follow from the frustration of the temperance enthusiasts over the government's inaction. Temperance candidates might be brought forward and Liberal votes lost in large numbers in many places.[14] Correspondence cited in the Alliance minutes shows that the Alliance leaders were most undecided as to what action to take in these circumstances and how militant their supporters could really be relied upon to be.[15] The problem of a strategy that would enforce early action on their question continued to be debated. At a conference of the North of England Temperance League on 28 September 1885 the main resolution referred to voting only for candidates who would 'support early and thorough legislation'. One delegate tried unsuccessfully to amend this to 'support a Cabinet pledged to give early and thorough legislation':

If the members would promise to support only a Cabinet pledged to Local Option, he took it they would have a chance of getting Local Option pretty speedily; but if they preached Local Option on the platform, and supported a Cabinet that thought nothing of introducing Local Option into the House of Commons, where was Local Option to come from?[16]

To some it seemed that what had gone wrong was the movement's relationship to the Liberal party. That had become too close, with the result that the Liberals took their temperance support for granted and saw no need to do much to retain or reward it. Some degree of disengagement from Liberal politics was needed in order to show that support for the Liberals was conditional and not absolute.

During 1885 there was a marked revival of the old idea of organising a separate temperance vote. But the plan this time was considerably more ambitious. It involved attempting to create something very close to a separate temperance or prohibition party.

The principal promoter of this scheme was F. H. Smith of Salford, a member of the Alliance Executive. At the Executive meeting on 18 February 1885 he moved, and James McMaster of Manchester seconded, a resolution, 'That the Executive recommend to the electors the formation of Direct Veto Parties in every electoral district so that the question can be pressed more strongly on any government irrespective of political party'. An alternative proposal was made that they be called Direct Veto Electoral Associations—

which would have kept continuity with the old Permissive Bill Electoral Associations and avoided the clear rift with the Liberals implicit in the word 'party'. But a week later, after Lawson, Pope, Whitworth, and Raper had been consulted, Smith's resolution was adopted.[17] The demand for an emergency Council meeting at Easter had, however, been averted, and the unusual step taken of having the Executive itself decide a major change in electoral policy.

The terminology remained very inexact. Already steps had been taken to form what were called Temperance Electoral Organisations in the new constituencies created by the Redistribution Act. The Executive itself drew up a set of rules for Temperance Electoral Associations.[18] The Manchester people decided to clear up the question by leading the way and providing a model for other areas to adopt. Accordingly on 11 March McMaster convened a conference of temperance electors in Manchester 'to consider the expediency of forming a temperance political party for Manchester, Salford, and South-East Lancashire'. McMaster told the meeting that in his opinion the 'temperance party' both in Manchester and throughout the country was not only stronger than other sections such as disestablishment and land reform but also outnumbered the Liberal party itself. Consequently their support of either party in an election 'would more than turn the balance of power'. James Whyte admitted that they were well aware that many Liberal and Conservative temperance men would continue to vote for their own parties even if such an organisation were set up. But that did not matter. A small bloc of determined men would suffice. The meeting then resolved to constitute the Manchester, Salford, and District Temperance Electoral Association.[19]

Similar associations were set up in other places. On 7 March one was established at Skipton. It is very doubtful, however, whether it could be regarded as conforming to the type of organisation which Smith and McMaster had had in mind. At its inaugural meeting there was a long debate on 'what stand the association should take as a body in regard to Parliamentary candidates', and finally 'a motion was carried to the effect that moral suasion was the wisest course to pursue, seeing that many of those present had strong political opinions, and stated that they were not prepared to sacrifice them altogether for the temperance movement'.[20] Henry Hibbert busied himself helping to form Electoral Associations in the Bradford area. This was in conformity with the Alliance Executive's decision to leave the matter as much as possible to the discretion of the agents and not to give great publicity to the Smith resolution.[21]

In some places readiness to support independent temperance politics stemmed from disillusion with the working of representative Liberal Associations. At Shipley one man complained that temperance advocates were included in these only to find themselves swamped, no doubt deliberately. 'He supposed that the real fact of the matter was that they [the Liberals] did not want much of the temperance element amongst them, but if they formed themselves into an association, the political parties would have to consider them.'[22] Instead of joining other people's 'Hundreds', they should form their own. When a Temperance Electoral Association was formed at Dartford at the end of March, the chairman said that 'he had come to the conclusion now that the only practical way of showing their strength was by standing out as a separate political party and forming a Temperance 200 or 300, the same as the Liberals and Radicals were doing'. A Temperance Hundred was set up at Halifax.[23]

The term 'Temperance Electoral Association' was used in all these cases, as the Alliance Executive was very reluctant to publish the Smith resolution. Finally it did so and revealed that it was recommending 'the formation of a Direct Popular Veto Party in every electoral district'. This seems only to have added to the proliferation of variegated titles for what were presumably really much the same type of organisation. Liverpool, for instance, formed an Intoxicating Liquors Direct Veto League.[24]

The idea of ignoring the existing parties and forming their own instead was by no means generally accepted. At most conferences and meetings when it was proposed there was a substantial group, usually a minority, however, who refused to support it. For example, at the North of England Temperance League conference in September 1885 the Rev. J. F. Barnard asked: 'Were they to have a separate party, like the Parnellites? He hoped not. His conviction was that their hope was in the Liberal party. (Applause and "No.") . . . He was not prepared to throw over general politics, even to carry temperance legislation. (Applause.)' The motion to urge temperance reformers to set up their own party was carried by 134 votes to 39.[25]

Three principal reasons can be adduced for this revival of interest in militant and independent temperance electoral action. The first—frustration at the inaction of the Liberal government after the expectations built up by the spectacular success of the Local Option

Resolution—has already been referred to. The second is the challenge and the opportunity presented by the Third Reform Act and its accompanying Redistribution Act. The large number of new constituencies in any case necessitated the creation of new temperance electoral organisations, particularly in the large cities which were broken up into divisions and were no longer to constitute single constituencies. This necessity provided a stimulus for new thinking about the nature and function of such organisations. A large number of new constituency committees and associations sprang up and, because they were new, tended to reflect the ideas then current about the desirability of distinct 'temperance parties'. The reason why the Smith resolution was considered by the Alliance Executive in the first place was that the Executive was obliged to give guidance to its adherents in any case as to the appropriate type of organisation to adopt in the altered electoral circumstances. Quite apart from the new constituencies, there were the new voters many of whom could be assumed to have no existing party loyalty and therefore to be particularly open to 'capture' by alternative political movements which gave expression to the feelings which temperance lecturers, for instance, had been fostering throughout the country for many years. Such people could more than compensate for the large numbers of existing temperance voters who were now too deeply attached to the main parties. The Alliance declared when issuing its recommendation about Direct Veto Parties: 'Though many excellent temperance men may be averse from combined action outside their political party, it will be found that among the new electors thousands belong to no party, but the party of Sobriety.'[26] There was a feeling that the profound electoral changes had placed party politics in general in a state of flux from which a new party might well benefit if promoted vigorously enough.

The third reason was the Conservative temperance vote. The evidence about it which comes to the surface in 1883–5 suggests strongly that it normally was of significance, especially for a type of electoral politics which depended so much on the balancing effect of small minorities of voters, but that in this period it was under very heavy strain. By this time the great majority of candidates who supported Local Option were Liberals. But it was becoming less and less easy to persuade Conservatives to vote for Liberals—or even to abstain—for the sake of temperance because of the increasing identification of Liberalism with Chamberlainite Radicalism and the policy of disestablishment. These difficulties made temperance leaders concerned to make definite gestures of independence from Liberalism and to erect organisational structures which would enable temperance politics to *appear* more detached from Liberal politics.

Chamberlain's first round of radical speeches in 1883 seems to be the starting-point for this problem. It attracted much attention during and as a result of the York by-election in November of that year. The Alliance Auxiliary recommended its supporters to vote for the Liberal candidate, Frank Lockwood, who had said that he would vote for both the Local Option and Sunday Closing. Sir F. Milner, the Conservative candidate, refused to promise to vote for either. 'The friends thought it best to work independently—so that party susceptibilities might not be disturbed'—and they ran their own campaign on Lockwood's behalf. This, however, did not prevent some of the Conservative temperance people from working for Milner. The result was a Conservative gain—by 21 votes in a total poll of nearly 7,900. This was a setback to the Alliance for the former Liberal member, J. J. Leeman, had been a supporter of the Local Option Resolution.[27]

Occasionally a Conservative candidate did support Local Option. When this happened, as at Hackney in November 1884, the Alliance Executive had to be very vigilant to ensure that the Liberal was not nevertheless given temperance backing.[28] Where a Conservative was only slightly less favourable to temperance legislation than the Liberal, there was some divergence of opinion over what should be done. This happened at Rugby in August 1885. A. Scholfield, the Alliance agent, addressed the temperance workers and 'urged the necessity of united action apart from party considerations'. The meeting acknowledged this but decided to adopt a policy of allowing abstention by Conservatives and not forcing them to vote for the Liberal.[29]

When the Temperance Electoral Associations were promoted, they were constantly referred to as intended to secure temperance action that was 'irrespective of party'. But this did not convince all Conservatives. Thus E. Spafford said at the Manchester conference:

He was a Conservative. The effect of the resolution would be that Conservatives would be asked to vote for Liberal candidates in the majority of instances. At an ordinary time they might sacrifice all to their love of temperance, but hardly now, when such questions as those of disestablishment and religious education were in the front. These matters they put before temperance even.[30]

The following report on the situation at Cheltenham indicates the influence over the reorganisation of temperance electoral politics of the desire to retain the Conservative and Anglican temperance vote. The main theme is the ostentatious severing of links with the Liberal party.

Acting on the advice offered by the Church of England Temperance Society, the local auxiliary of the United Kingdom Alliance has determined to cut itself aloof from political parties, and to accord its support to the candidate who will pledge himself to vote for Local Option, to whichever political party he may belong. This step has, I believe, been resolved upon chiefly in consequence of the pressure brought to bear upon the Rev. H. McNeile Minton-Senhouse, to compel him to resign the office he had undertaken of chairman of the local branch of the U.K.A.; and the new chairman, Mr. E. Wethered, has given a practical impetus to the movement by withdrawing himself from all official connection with the party for which he has in the past done useful service.[31]

In fact, much of the new machinery which was created in 1885 continued to have its primary relationship with the Liberal party, being designed to represent temperance interests in the new constituencies in negotiations with Liberal Associations over the selection of a candidate. During these negotiations more threats to run their own candidates were made than had been customary in recent years, but nothing ever seemed to come of these. It is doubtful whether there was much substance in many of the bold resolutions passed by local temperance meetings. A correspondent of the *Alliance News* reported attending one such meeting at Blackburn in June 1885 when a resolution was passed that they should take 'independent action'. When he asked them what this meant, nobody seemed to know; and so he explained

that I understood it to mean that as the Liberals had always claimed to be our best friends in the past, the time had arrived when they should prove themselves so by placing our plank in their platform, failing this, that we should vote for the Conservatives. This brought out what I had more than suspected was the fact, that was, that the movers for the 'independent action' meant that under any circumstances we should vote for the Liberal candidate, whether he supported our principles or not, on the vague ground that the Liberals were more likely to support us than the Tories.[32]

There was trouble again at Hull which was now in three divisions. The temperance interest was well looked after in the East Division where William Saunders, the well-known Alliance personality, was adopted as Liberal candidate, and in the West Division where C. H. Wilson stood. Both had comfortable victories. But the candidate in the Central Division was C. M. Norwood and he was the target of a

renewed onslaught by the temperance militants. Guy Hayler complained that Norwood had not 'fulfilled his promises to the temperance voters during the last five years', having taken part in only
three out of the twenty-six temperance divisions in that period. A
Labour candidate, N. B. Billany, stood against Norwood and probably attracted some temperance votes as 'an out-and-out Local
Optionist'. He won 735 votes, while Norwood was defeated by a
Conservative by a margin of 166.[33]

Liberal brewers caused difficulties in some places. At Kingston, in
Surrey, the temperance party was thrown into great confusion by
the selection as Liberal candidate of C. D. Hodgson, a brewer who
supported Local Option. Some wanted them to vote against him
because he was a brewer, others to vote for him because of his attitude to Local Option. The Liberals' selection of S. Whitbread at
Bootle also caused some hard feelings.[34]

The temperance question occupied a very minor role indeed in
the 1885 general election. Other issues, notably disestablishment and
Ireland, were so dominant that there was no scope for the assertion
of Local Option and little support would have been forthcoming
for an aggressive electoral strategy. There was a somewhat unreal
atmosphere about the debates on electoral policy at the Alliance
Council meeting in October. The main electoral resolution moved
by Pope was very moderate, calling for support for candidates who
favoured a direct veto by ratepayers. This left open the question of
how one voted if there were no such candidates. But F. H. Smith
then proposed an amendment calling on people to vote 'only' for
such candidates. The comments of those who supported him indicated what was currently going wrong in the electorates. Dodds of
Newcastle admitted that temperance people in the North were
giving support to Liberals who were weak on their questions. Rev.
Prebendary Grier, a Conservative, said that in his area, Rugeley,
the temperance people had gone over to the policy of regulation by
local authorities in order to protect the prospects of the Liberal
party in a district where the drink interest was strong, and he was
left alone to fight for the Direct Veto. T. C. Rayner claimed that
many Liberals exploited resolutions such as Pope's to try to get
away with vague promises well short of the Direct Veto. Accepting
the better man now often meant accepting a weak man. Therefore
the threat to abstain must be made: 'There was as great a power in
abstaining from voting as in voting. . . .' Alderman Scarr of Leeds
agreed and attacked those temperance people in Yorkshire who were

now so anxious to maintain Liberal unity that they refrained from pressing for any definite pledges. The resolution was finally passed with Smith's amendment incorporated. It was, however, strongly opposed in this form by J. H. Raper who said that the resolution had been aimed at the broad mass of electors who were interested in other questions as well. To invite people to abstain from voting on one question opened the way 'for a great cessation of voting, not on this question, but upon all other questions'. It incited proponents of other questions to adopt similar tactics. W. S. Caine said that 'the first business of temperance reformers in a country which is governed by party is to secure a dominant influence on the organisations belonging to either of the respective parties'. He himself would refuse to give any pledges on the subject.[35]

Any effort to give effect to the Alliance's electoral policy as defined in this amended resolution created dissension in the temperance ranks. An example is Oldham where one of the Liberal candidates, J. T. Hibbert, supported the Local Option but the other, E. Lyulph Stanley, did not, although he favoured a considerable measure of temperance reform apart from it. The Alliance issued a statement of support only for Hibbert, and Stanley was subsequently defeated and a Conservative elected just ahead of him as Hibbert's colleague. It seemed that some temperance voters had followed the Alliance's advice, but others were very angry. 'It was all very well,' said one, 'to talk about rising above party, but by adopting this course they played into the hands of the Tories.' Stanley had been much more advanced than either of the Conservative candidates, especially the one whom they enabled to win the election to Parliament. The Alliance 'had made a great grievous mistake', said another. 'The Liberal party was the only party that was likely to prove useful to the temperance party.'[36]

But the real reason why militancy and abstentionism were so controversial in 1885 and why support for such action was so lacking can be illustrated by a statement made by another Oldham temperance supporter, a clergyman. 'If it [the Alliance's electoral policy] meant placing it in front of everything else he could not agree with it,' he said, 'as there was the Irish question, which might mean the dismemberment of the Empire, and other questions of similar import; and he could not agree to put these things in the background.'[37] Yet again 'other politics' had intruded and rendered futile any attempt to mobilise the temperance vote as an isolated and independent and completely detachable factor in a general election.

CHAPTER XII

The United Kingdom Alliance, 1886–1892

After the general election in July 1886 the Liberals were in opposition for six years. Without the frustration and provocation caused by the absence of Local Option legislation at the time of a Liberal government, the trend towards the integration of the temperance interest into the fabric of Liberal politics continued and reached its climax in the incorporation of popular control over the liquor traffic in the 1891 'Newcastle programme' of the National Liberal Federation. An identity of interests between the Liberal party and the Alliance was often assumed automatically at by-elections, and there was a tendency to overlook what was now felt to be the tedious formality of sending a deputation to interview the Conservative candidate. Agents and Auxiliaries sometimes needed reminding to do this before they announced publicly their support for the Liberal.[1] In September 1889 W. Mart reported that the temperance people at Sleaford were already hard at work for the Liberal candidate, F. Otter, and had to be told to get a more definite statement from him and have the Conservative interviewed.[2] But when agents tried to intervene in this way and observe some impartiality, they were sometimes met with resentment by the strongly Liberal temperance people in the area. For example, George Tomlinson went to Stamford at the beginning of March 1890 and found that the temperance men wanted to have nothing to do with him. Not only were they perfectly satisfied with a private assurance from the Liberal candidate, A. Priestley, that he was with them 'on all points' but they had in fact suggested to him that he should not 'mention our subject in his address as it would certainly damage his prospects'. Tomlinson ventured to inquire about the Conservative candidate, only to be met 'with the statement "The whole of the liquor traffickers are on his side", and they concluded that therefore he must be dead against us'. 'I am afraid,' commented Tomlinson, 'that most of the men in the Division are party men first and Temp. men afterwards.'[3] What this showed was that in some constituencies the temperance section had been all too successful in 'permeating' the Liberal party and now virtually was that party. After the sweeping redistribution of seats in 1885 and the equally drastic upheaval in Liberal politics over the Home Rule issue in 1886, Liberal organisation in many constituencies was extremely weak, and this gave some local temperance 'parties' the chance to find themselves the only effective political machine in existence on the Liberal side. In October 1890 William Canning, wishing to demonstrate how easy it would be to 'squeeze' the Liberals by a deployment of temperance strength, said: 'Temperance reformers, who worked outside political parties, did not adequately realise that the actual workers in any constituency were very few, and not so powerful as people were apt to imagine.'[4] The events and developments of 1885-6 had left a vacuum in Gladstonian Liberal politics in many constituencies which it was all too easy for temperance people to be drawn into. Some Alliance leaders became ardent advocates of welcoming this state of affairs and abandoning all pretence of non-partisanship. One such was the agent, E. C. Brambley, who vigorously defended himself when under criticism for his attendance as a delegate at National Liberal Federation and other Liberal conferences. He would tirelessly cheer every allusion to temperance legislation and button-hole other delegates to impress on them the need to select candidates who were sound on the Direct Veto.[5] Of course, so monotonous did the succession of Alliance endorsements for Liberal candidates at by-elections and general elections become that it was very hard to make out a case that the Alliance was a non-partisan organisation.

Some Liberals, having placed the 'Alliance question' on their programme, considered that the Alliance ought to need to take no further interest in elections and, sometimes with the connivance and approval of the local temperance Liberals, tried to suppress discussion of the question. But some of the more perceptive temperance politicians recognised that a new electoral battle must now begin—a battle to demonstrate that it was one's own question rather than somebody else's which did most electoral good for the Liberals and therefore deserved to be given a very prominent place in the party's programme. 'At every election', wrote one of them, Jonathan Hargrove, 'our voices should be louder than those of the Home Rulers or the supporters of any other question. . . . We should be an active, irrepressible, clamorous, importunate, omnipresent factor in every election.' Only then would the Direct Veto be 'first of all'.[6] This points the way to a new phase of temperance electoral politics which is to appear after 1892.

What has been said so far relates to the Gladstonian Liberals. Did the temperance movement succeed in maintaining an equally close relationship with that section of the Liberal party, the Liberal Unionists, which allied itself with the Conservatives in opposing Gladstone's proposals for Irish Home Rule? There were numerous temperance supporters among the Liberal Unionist politicians, and it was very unclear at first whether the Alliance could continue to rely on them for assistance. One of the most prominent of them was W. S. Caine who acted as Liberal Unionist Whip in the House of Commons. He remained as devoted as ever to the temperance cause and believed, like many of the Radical Unionists, that the preoccupation with Home Rule was temporarily essential but would not have to last long as Gladstone would soon retire upon appreciating the futility of persisting with his policy. He was anxious to have Local Option included in the programme of the National Radical Union which Chamberlain inaugurated in June 1886, but Chamberlain resisted this, not wishing to erect obstacles to co-operation with Whigs, right-wing Liberals, and Conservatives in the primary work of opposing Home Rule.[7]

The official Alliance policy was to recommend supporters to judge candidates, whether Gladstonian or Unionist, strictly according to their views on the temperance question. But this strategy was severely strained during the general election of 1886 when, as part of the alliance between the Conservatives and the Liberal Unionists, Liberal Unionists who were adherents to the Alliance spoke and worked on behalf of Conservative candidates who were hostile to the Local Option against Gladstonians who were strong supporters of it. The result was that many local temperance 'parties' were split down the middle, and a move developed to expel these Liberal Unionist 'traitors'. The controversy erupted at the Alliance Council meeting in October 1886 when William Canning moved that the name of T. C. Rayner of Manchester be deleted from the list of members of the Executive because, although at the 1885 Council he had advocated that they vote for no man who was not prepared to vote for the Direct Veto, he had now acted against this doctrine. Another delegate 'said they had suffered from the same disease in West Worcestershire, and he seconded the amendment with pleasure'. But hardly any other speakers supported them and they finally agreed to withdraw the motion. Alderman Clegg of Sheffield argued that Conservative members of the Alliance were as entitled to have opinions on other questions as were Radicals. 'If they were to carry this resolution to its logical effect they would have to form a Radical United Kingdom Alliance.'[8]

However, actual support for Conservatives who were well-known to be totally hostile to the Alliance and all its aims was bound to arouse very deep resentment. The man who became the principal target for this was W. S. Caine who bravely went on addressing Direct Veto meetings but found himself under mounting verbal and even physical attack from the Gladstonian Liberals in the movement.[9] On 13 March 1887 he published a letter explaining his position. This is significant as a repudiation of the basis of Alliance electoral policy, especially the assumption that temperance could be treated as a factor in politics completely independent and isolated from all other issues:

Many temperance men are able to divest themselves of all consideration of other political questions, and make what is known as 'Local Option' the sole basis for their support of candidates for Parliament.

To my mind such a position would be absurd, and quite untenable, for a member of Parliament.

I am chosen by a large constituency to take my share in the democratic government of a great empire. It does not rest with a humble member of Parliament to pick and choose those subjects which from time to time are made the burning questions at elections. They are brought to the front by great leaders of governments, in response to public agitation; and as these questions come forward into the range of practical settlement, each in its turn receives, *and ought to receive*, the prime consideration of members of Parliament, often to the exclusion of subjects which are still distant. . . . I have never in all my life bound myself to support 'Local Option' candidates to the exclusion of all other questions. . . .[10]

It was now clear that what was at issue was the electoral policy of the Alliance. Did it enforce on members an obligation to vote for candidates who favoured the Local Option, irrespective of what might be the views of either members or candidates on other questions? Caine denied that membership of the Alliance did entail such an obligation, and he wrote to the Executive asking for a ruling on the matter. The Executive debated this at much length and approved a draft of a reply to Caine reminding him of certain resolutions which defined the Alliance's position, for example the recommendation that members abstain from voting for candidates who refused to support the Direct Veto. The Alliance had never, however, made adhesion to such resolutions a test of membership. The draft concluded: 'Obviously it is desirable that we should present a united front to the enemy, and we are of course individually bound to consider carefully the effects of our example.' This was certainly a sting in the tail, for it implied a rebuke to those Liberal Unionists who were breaking the united front of opposition to the 'traffic'. Before the letter was sent, Benjamin Whitworth saw Caine informally and indicated to him what it would contain. Caine intimated that it was unacceptable and would lead to his resignation from the Alliance unless it was considerably toned down. Therefore a new draft was agreed to, omitting the final paragraph about the 'united front'. Whitworth recognised the acute dilemma in which the Alliance now found itself. It had either to condone the apparent flouting of its electoral policy by members who supported candidates who not merely were opposed to the Direct Veto but were also backed by the publicans, or else it had to appear to be a mere tool of the Gladstonian Liberals by driving out men because of their opposition to Irish Home Rule. 'I deeply regret that this question has turned up', he wrote. 'It must injure us whatever decision may be arrived at by the Executive.'[11]

The Liberal Unionist Vice-Presidents of the Alliance continued to be a particular source of embarrassment. For example, in November 1888 there were loud protests when one of them, Arthur Pease, supported the Liberal Unionist candidate at Dewsbury who was an opponent of the Local Option against M. Oldroyd, the Gladstonian, who supported it.[12] At the 1891 Council meeting an attempt was made to have Pease's name struck off the list of Vice-Presidents. Much was made of the discouraging effect on temperance voters of finding that their own leaders were not prepared to let the temperance question have the predominant influence over their use of the vote. But the weight of opinion was still against such a move.[13]

The emergence of the Home Rule issue had seriously undermined the integrity of the 'temperance vote'. To some it seemed that the only way for it to survive in these circumstances was for even more strenuous efforts to be made to withdraw and isolate it from the corrupting influence of party politics.

Even in 1886 energetic agents such as E. C. Brambley continued to found new Temperance Electoral Associations.[14] But something more than this was now thought to be needed, and in October the Alliance Council passed a resolution requesting the Executive 'to take all practical steps to organise a Prohibition Party in every constituency, pledged to vote only for candidates who will support the Direct Popular Veto on the Liquor Traffic'. The mover, the Rev. Prebendary Grier, had a vision of a party 'formed of men who had made up their minds on this question, and who did not want to drag in a whole lot of other questions, about which people were hopelessly divided', 'a great union of temperance reformers, who for the time would put aside all other issues and bend all their energies upon this great question'. Grier was an Anglican clergyman and a professed Conservative who fought for temperance reform in that stronghold of the brewing industry, West Staffordshire. He was therefore at one and the same time peculiarly sensitive to the nature and strength of 'the enemy' and aware of the great difficulties involved in securing a temperance vote independent of all other politics. First of all, in 1885 he had tried to get the local temperance people to follow a certain line but had been deserted by them because they gave greater priority to the Church question. Then in 1886, he admitted, he himself had spoken against the Liberal candidate in North Staffordshire because that candidate was a Home Ruler, even though he also supported Local Option. Grier was supported by F. H. Smith who recognised that previous pledging of voters had not proved adequate and needed to be reinforced by the formation of definite 'prohibition parties'.[15]

Grier now became something of an evangelist for his scheme which he envisaged as being on a very grand scale. He succeeded in getting a motion in favour of it passed at a temperance convention in London in February 1887.[16] This put the Executive under considerable pressure, and it decided that it would have to take steps to implement the policy. On 4 March it issued a circular to agents urging upon them 'the policy and necessity of pushing the formation of Electoral District Veto Societies and Committees in each constituency, and especially in the county constituencies'.[17] But, when Grier applied for financial assistance in connection with his proposed Staffordshire Temperance Electoral Union, he was told that none was available.[18] He went ahead anyway and it was inaugurated at a meeting at Rugeley. It was to consist of people pledged to vote only for 'Parliamentary candidates, who will above and before all things support the Direct Local Veto on the liquor traffic and similar prohibition measures'.[19]

The formation of new or revamped electoral organisations now proceeded apace. The proliferation of names for them was quite bewildering, although the word 'party', in spite of its having been used in the Alliance's resolution, was almost always avoided—in order, no doubt, not to alarm local temperance Liberals, who could be sure that in almost all cases now there would be no conflict between their loyalty to their party and a commitment to vote only for a Local Option candidate as long as they were not required to form themselves into what might look like a new party. The name most often used was Temperance Electoral Association, although Oxford acquired a Prohibition League.[20] This title was also subsequently adopted at Wigan and Hull.

There was some confusion as to whether it was to be a condition of membership of such organisations that one subscribed to an electoral pledge. When the temperance electors of Peterborough met on 22 March 1887 to consider setting up a T.E.U., several Liberals expressed unease about the pledging aspect. John Hilton, the Alliance's Parliamentary Agent, then 'explained that they could form a union which should exist for electoral purposes without the members pledging themselves; but if any member desired to give a pledge not to vote for any candidate but a supporter of the Direct Veto, they should keep a list of such pledges'. It appears that it was this weaker form of organisation which was set up at Peterborough.[21] An issue had been raised, however, which was soon to embroil the Alliance in one of the most fierce controversies of its history as an electoral organisation.

The trouble stemmed from the formation in Sheffield of a remarkably militant T.E.A. They were thoroughly dissatisfied with all the compromises in electoral policy which the Alliance had agreed to since 1885. They therefore informed the Alliance Executive that in order to force the Alliance to adopt 'a more forward policy' they would present two resolutions to the Council meeting in October. These involved adopting the electoral pledge as 'the future electoral policy' of the Alliance, having it used 'by all its Agents, Superintendents and Auxiliaries', and, most controversial of all, forbidding anyone not prepared to take the pledge from sitting on the Central Executive and the Executive of any of the Auxiliaries.[22] This would have virtually converted the Alliance into an organisation of pledged voters and compelled the withdrawal of all Liberal Unionists in particular.

When the Council met on 11 October, one of the first items of business was a resolution appointing the officers and Executive. Jonathan Hargrove of Liverpool, another of the militants, moved as an amendment the addition of the following words: 'It being understood that the members of the Executive shall accept the electoral policy as laid down in Number 6 resolution of 1886, which is that this Council requests the Executive to take all practical steps to organize a prohibition party pledged to vote only for candidates who will support the Direct Popular Veto on the liquor traffic, and will themselves act on it during their continuance in office.' Guy Hayler seconded this and attacked Liberal Unionists who were insisting on giving the Irish question priority: 'If they had a sober people they would be able to settle political questions much sooner than in the way they were tinkering at them to-day.' For the Executive the Rev. James Clark said that they would treat the amendment as a vote of censure. Samuel Pope said that he would resign if it was passed. Even F. H. Smith opposed it, while one of Hargrove's Liverpool colleagues repudiated it on behalf of most of the rest of the temperance people there and made a spirited defence of working from inside political parties. Against this weight of opinion Hargrove and Hayler had no option but to withdraw the amendment, and the name of Alderman Clegg of Sheffield was added to the list of Vice-Presidents in what was to prove a singularly unfortunate gesture to appease them. The Council then passed the other Sheffield resolution calling on the Executive to continue the formation of Direct Veto Parties and to take steps to have this work carried out by the agents, superintendents, and auxiliaries.[23]

At the Council there were complaints that the Executive had not been doing nearly enough to promote the formation of Electoral Associations. Everything was left to local initiative or to the work of particularly energetic agents such as E. C. Brambley. In the succeeding months there was little evidence of change in this state of affairs, apart from an authorisation to Brambley to spend up to £5 'in organising a Temperance electoral party in Worcester'.[24] In some areas vigorous activity was carried on in spite of the Executive's detached attitude. At Bury a Veto Electoral Association was formed and 396 pledge-signers reported.[25] In London a meeting between the London Auxiliary's Committee and many of the Committees of the Local Option Unions in the boroughs decided to circulate a pledge for signature in spite of the fears of some present that strong pledges were not practicable in London constituencies.[26] But the energy displayed at Sheffield was the most remarkable. They specialised in enrolling non-voters, especially women, and by late April 1888 their T.E.A. had 1,238 members, of whom more than half were non-voters. The Sheffield Liberals began to express concern.[27] One disturbing development as far as temperance politics were concerned was the multiplication of organisations in the same area. The role of Alliance Auxiliaries was now particularly unclear. The first sign of a backlash against this trend was at Ashton-under-Lyne where at a meeting of signatories to a pledge canvassed by John Paton a motion to set up a Direct Veto Association was amended in favour of a proposal to add the words 'and Direct Veto Association' to the title of the local Auxiliary.[28]

Where this was not done and separate Auxiliaries and Temperance Electoral Associations existed, it was very likely that tension and even conflict would develop, especially as the militants would gravitate to the latter organisations, leaving the more moderate and Liberal-oriented people even more in charge of the Auxiliaries. This is precisely what happened at Sheffield.

The peak of temperance electoral activity in Sheffield came in 1889. The Electoral Association held frequent meetings of a marked missionary flavour both in Sheffield and in neighbouring districts at which the electoral pledge was explained, signatures sought for it, and steps taken to organise local Electoral Associations.[29] Much of this work was done in conjunction with the Sheffield Auxiliary, and for a time relations appeared on the surface to be reasonably harmonious. But from early February the Alliance Executive was made aware that there were in fact two deeply antagonistic factions struggling for supremacy in Sheffield temperance politics and that the main area of contention between them was the interpretation of the Alliance's still very ambiguous policy on 'Direct Veto Parties'.

On 13 February 1889 the Alliance Executive received a letter from Alderman W. J. Clegg, long recognised as the leader of the temperance movement in Sheffield, warning of the trouble that was brewing there. 'I yield to no man in anxiety to get rid of the Liquor Traffic', he wrote. 'Some of the friends in Sheffield have got a craze on just now. It can only be done in their way; that is by everybody pledging themselves to vote for no candidate who will not pledge himself to vote for the Direct Veto.'[30] Six weeks later the Executive received another communication from Sheffield, this time a memorandum from certain members of the Sheffield Auxiliary. They outlined the course of events since Clegg had written his letter. On 15 February at a meeting of the General Committee of the Auxiliary the militants had moved that in future all agents and deputations of the Auxiliary who attended meetings for the purpose of setting up district organisations to be affiliated to it should ensure that these are formed on the basis of the Alliance electoral pledge. An amendment was proposed that the advice to be given at these meetings should be that members of the Alliance ought not to form such organisations but to 'join their various political parties with a view to having a voice in the selection of candidates for their divisions'. This extreme Liberal 'integrationist' viewpoint was rejected. After a second amendment, leaving deputations perfectly free at such meetings 'to recommend personally what course of political action they themselves think desirable', was also defeated, the original resolution was carried by 25 to 19. But the majority itself was then divided over whether this meant that anyone who opposed the formation of Direct Veto Associations and preferred working within the Liberal party—like Clegg himself, for instance—was debarred from being a member of such a deputation. Hence the memorandum—an appeal for guidance from Clegg and his supporters who wished to continue their practice of concentrating on influencing the Liberal party.

We desire the opinion of the General Executive Committee whether or not they approve or disapprove of members (who must necessarily be in favour of prohibition including the Direct Veto) advising such political action as they (judging from local circumstances) deem most likely to promote the objects of the Alliance, and whether any member is in any way disqualified from addressing Alliance Meetings & freely recommending the course he thinks best because he is not prepared on all occasions and under all circumstances to promote the formation of Direct Veto Associations involving the personal taking of the Direct Veto pledge.

The only answer that the Executive was prepared to give at this stage was to reiterate the Alliance principle that its support could be given only to candidates who promised to vote for the Direct Veto.[31] But the issue refused to die away. On 29 April Clegg was a member of a deputation to a meeting at Eckington.[32] In defiance of the Executive's ruling—which was moved by G. W. Sharman, one of the Sheffield militants—he declared that if there were two candidates, one of whom would vote for Sunday Closing but not for Local Option and the other would do nothing for temperance, he would not abstain but would support the former. This firmly aligned him with Edward Whitwell and Thomas Whittaker who had in recent years been leading a campaign at Council to get exactly this policy adopted in place of the rigid insistence on supporting only the candidate who was right on one particular type of temperance reform. It was a revival of the 'better man' approach to voting.

A meeting of the Sheffield Auxiliary's Committee was then called and a motion proposed regretting what Clegg had said as opposed to Alliance and Auxiliary policy. This ended in great confusion with the chairman declaring that the motion had been lost. But at the next meeting its supporters were in a majority and had the minutes altered to state that it had been carried. Clegg then wrote to the Alliance Executive to ask for whom one should vote in the situation to which he had referred at Eckington, but, on the advice of the Parliamentary and Electoral Committee, they replied that the determination of such a question did not fall within their province. All this was explained by Clegg in a circular convening a meeting of the Auxiliary on 6 September. The militants of the T.E.A. countered with a circular of their own explaining that the February resolution had not been intended to force anyone to speak in favour of the electoral policy. If Clegg had preserved silence on the matter at Eckington, all would have been well. But where he did violate the Auxiliary's policy was in publicly denouncing that policy and thwarting the efforts of loyal members of it who were 'advocating its electoral policy and pledge'. At the meeting Clegg made it plain that he stood for a policy of working within and seeking to influence the choice of candidates by the existing political parties. If the resolution passed by the Committee were not rescinded, he would resign as President of the Auxiliary. J. W. Wilson, one of the stalwarts of Sheffield Nonconformist Liberalism, moved a vote of confidence in Clegg. Henry Gallimore, one of the militants, then moved an amendment expressing concurrence in the Committee's resolution. After an extremely heated debate the amendment was heavily defeated and the resolution carried.

Clegg had retained his control over the Auxiliary. But the Sheffield T.E.A. remained defiant. At their meetings they now made a special point of explaining 'that if both candidates were against the direct veto, and one was in favour of Sunday Closing, those who signed the electoral pledge would have to abstain altogether from voting'.[33] Clegg, for his part, was determined not to let the matter rest but to destroy his opponents utterly. On 10 September he wrote to the Alliance's Secretary, saying that he now considered that the members of the Alliance in Sheffield had decided that they did not 'intend to be bound to form an organisation to advocate and support the Direct Veto Pledge'. Then he added: 'I should be glad to know what the Executive intend to recommend to the Annual Meeting on the subject, as I and the members who are acting with me do not intend to let the matter drop.' Clegg was threatening to put the Executive in an extremely embarrassing position. He had written to all the Vice-Presidents of the Alliance to ask if they were prepared personally to 'carry out the Direct Veto Pledge', and so far only two had said that they were.[34]

The whole business of 'Direct Veto parties' was now becoming a nightmare for the Executive. In its Annual Report it had to admit that, although a special sub-committee had been set up to look after 'the formation, maintenance, and development of Direct Veto Associations', not a great deal of progress had been made. It implored the Council to appreciate that this was 'slow, laborious, and somewhat expensive' work. The passing of resolutions was not enough. In normal circumstances much money and labour were needed, but just occasionally—and here they must have had Sheffield and Liverpool in mind—strong associations could be formed, without any great expenditure of money, 'where a number —it need not be a large number—of zealous, energetic men, thoroughly convinced of the necessity for such associations, and willing to make the management of the Association their life-work, take the matter up in good earnest'.[35] The implication that the work might be better left entirely to such men in future was clear.

The sensation of the Council meeting on 22 October was Clegg's counter-attack. It took the form of an attempt to have A. R. Ecroyd and J. Thornley, two of his main antagonists in Sheffield, removed from the Alliance's Consultative Committee and replaced by others nominated by a special meeting of the Sheffield Auxiliary. J. Wycliffe Wilson, one of his principal supporters, informed delegates—to mingled cries of 'Yes' and 'No'—that underlying this proposal was a great principle: 'whether the Alliance as an Alliance should advocate the sending of the Direct Veto pledge into every constituency'. After much debate a compromise was arrived at. Clegg's amendment was rejected, but John Kempster withdrew his name from the Committee so that Councillor Rawson, another of Clegg's supporters, could be added to it. It was now the turn of the Liverpool militants to strike back at Clegg. Hargrove nominated one of their men for the place vacated by Kempster because 'there was a great principle involved in the point, and that was loyal adherence to the electoral policy of the Council'. Rawson was being put up as an opponent of that policy. Guy Hayler agreed that they should not elect 'the

representatives of men who said that they would vote against and
speak against the Direct Veto'. But the vote was taken and Rawson
won.

There were two electoral resolutions. The first was a very moderate one moved by F. R. Lees which pledged the Council to help the
Executive 'in organising the Temperance Electorate in each constituency' and did not specifically mention Direct Veto Parties. This
passed easily, no one being prepared to second an attempt by Jones
of Liverpool to add a rider urging friends to join the organisations of
their parties and influence the choice of candidates. The second
resolution was a different matter. It reaffirmed previous resolutions
on electoral organisations and urged the friends of the Alliance to
combine electors pledged not to vote for candidates who would not
promise to vote for a Direct Veto. Its mover, F. H. Smith, said that
it was necessary because in the past party-minded temperance men
had allowed too many candidates to get elected on the basis of weak
pledges and unsatisfactory answers in the hope that they 'would vote
right when the time came'. The knowledge of the existence of
pledged voters who could not be weak in this way often obliged
candidates to come out for the Direct Veto. But then Whitwell
moved an amendment which would have allowed support for candidates who promised to vote for Sunday Closing or some other important restriction of the liquor traffic but not Local Option. A London
delegate, J. G. Alexander, claimed that he understood the resolution
to reflect the advanced state of temperance opinion in the North and
that it could be interpreted to allow people in the more backward
areas of the South to accept candidates who would not go quite as
far as the Veto but were generally sympathetic. Whittaker aligned
himself with Clegg and delivered his customary attack on pledges.
D. S. Collin explained that it was the new voters that the policy of
pledging and special Associations was aimed at. They wanted to
secure them 'before they got entangled in the ranks of any political
party'. Pope summed up by acknowledging that this was probably a
good point. There was no intention, he said of forcing members of
the Alliance to join these Electoral Associations or of forcing
Auxiliaries to form them. Members were merely recommended to
form them and were bound by their rules only if they chose to join.
Thus soothed, delegates threw out Whitwell's amendment and passed
the resolution by a very large majority.[36]

The trouble in Sheffield continued unabated. The Committee of
the Auxiliary, which was now firmly under the control of the Clegg

faction, had rescinded the resolution of 15 February instructing agents and deputations to form new associations on the basis of the electoral pledge. This seemed to the Alliance Executive to be taking the reaction altogether too far, and they wrote anxiously to inquire whether the Auxiliary was now going to stop the formation of Direct Veto Associations. R. Clift Horner replied on behalf of the Auxiliary that

> the *largely prevailing* opinion of our members is that *here* the pledge is undesirable. The position of the Executive now is that while they will not take the initiative in forming *pledge* associations themselves, if in any portion of our district there is a general desire to form such they will send deputations to assist in such formation. What we intend to practice is Local Option in the promotion of the Direct Veto, and shall not force the pledge upon any organisation; every member of our deputations will be at liberty to express his own views on electoral policy and not be committed to any specified course.

The Alliance Executive regarded this reply as highly unsatisfactory and informed the Sheffield Auxiliary that it was not carrying out the policy laid down by the General Council.[37]

Meanwhile the Sheffield T.E.A. continued its campaigning. By mid-February 1890 it claimed to have 3,350 members and was still busy taking pledges—for total abstinence as well—at its meetings. When temperance workers inquired about the schism in Sheffield temperance politics, A. R. Ecroyd replied that both sides did support the Direct Veto, 'the difference being that they, the progressist wing, took their stand upon the platform that, believing this to be the most important question, they refused to vote for candidates who were opposed to Direct Popular Veto'.[38] The Liverpool and Sheffield Temperance Electoral Associations announced an essay competition on the following theme:

> That the United Kingdom Alliance electoral policy of forming Direct Veto Associations to consist of persons pledged not to vote for or support any Parliamentary candidate who will not promise to vote for a measure giving the people Direct Veto power over the issue and renewal of all licences to sell intoxicating liquors in their respective localities, is right in principle, and the best for the present stage of the Prohibition movement.[39]

This competition was won by W. Canning of Manchester who wrote a very fine essay advocating abstention as an electoral strategy and denouncing the policy of voting for 'the better man'.[40]

There were now signs that the Sheffield people wished to crusade on behalf of their cause, which they regarded with an almost evangelistic zeal, not only in their own area but throughout the country. G. W. Sharman called for the unfurling of 'the Direct Veto flag' at every election, 'heedless of consequences', and A. R. Ecroyd attended the inaugural meeting of a Prohibition League in Edinburgh, and, 'on behalf of the advanced wing of the English Direct Veto party, wished God-speed to the Scottish Prohibitionists'. The Sheffield T.E.A. even established a journal for the 'forward' party, the *Temperance Vanguard*,[41] In August 1890 a T.E.A. was set up in Birmingham after 105 men and 15 women had signed the pledge.[42] The involvement of women was characteristic of this movement. They did not have the vote but were regarded nevertheless as having electoral influence. Ecroyd's wife was herself very prominent as a canvasser and speaker at Direct Veto meetings. The Ecroyds moved from Sheffield to Liverpool in September 1890 when Ecroyd was appointed Secretary of the new Liverpool and District Direct Veto League which combined various existing groups of signatories of the pledge. In keeping with the great enthusiasm which the movement felt for abstention as an electoral strategy—as expressed in Canning's prize essay, for instance—a clause was inserted in its constitution specifying that no member was obliged to vote for or support any Direct Veto candidate. All that was asked was abstention from voting for hostile candidates.[43]

As the Alliance's Annual Report had foreshadowed in 1889, most of the work of promoting 'Direct Veto parties' had to be performed in this way—by local zealots. The 1890 Report laid great stress on the difficulty of the work and pointed out that its agents and superintendents had a great deal else to do and could not devote much of their time to it.[44] When the special sub-committee met the agents on 22 October, several of them said that they were finding it very hard to maintain these associations once they had been started.[45] This prompted F. H. Smith to make an urgent appeal at the council meeting for increased funds for this work. Lawson, he said, should be able to lead a temperance party 'like Mr. Parnell leads the Irish party'. 'We want to make an electoral Temperance sentiment.' The Liberals and Tories wished to fight on Home Rule alone and only the existence of pledged voters in these Associations would make them take notice of the Veto question. Grier moved a resolution reaffirming existing policy on electoral organisation and asking the Executive to instruct agents, superintendents, and auxiliaries to make the combining of electors 'and others' 'an essential portion of their duties during the coming winter'. This was passed, but only after the officers had had to soothe the ruffled feelings of a Sheffield delegate who disliked the reference to 'instructing Auxiliaries' and warned that this could lead to more trouble at Sheffield.[46] Sheffield, however, was now fading into the background. Once the Ecroyds had moved to Liverpool, it seemed to replace it as the new headquarters of the 'forward movement'. Alliance headquarters gave what help it could. Direct Veto pledge books were available, for instance, from the offices.

Another centre of enthusiasm was Manchester where F. H. Smith and Canning were the dominant figures. The zeal with which these people entered into this work is typified by this pronouncement by Smith: 'Temperance electoral organisations were capable of doing immense work in education, in agitation, and in elections, and they were the pioneers of a great political party which would make social and Temperance reform the basis of all political action.'[47] Leeds, by contrast, was slow to react, largely owing, no doubt, to the strong position which the temperance section had acquired in Liberal politics there since 1874. But in April 1891 a Leeds Direct Veto Association was established.[48]

Statements such as the one by Smith just quoted indicate that quite a few of the people involved in the Direct Veto Association movement had ideas of forming these Associations into a complete new party, perhaps not electing its own members—for that strategy was not very much in vogue at this time—but at least mobilising temperance voters into a structure that at once imitated and was distinct from that of the Liberal and Conservative parties. The word 'party' was often used very loosely, of course, but the Alliance, knowing that its employment might be seen by many temperance Liberals as a declaration of independence from, even war upon, the Liberal party, carefully avoided using it in all its pronouncements on the new policy, although the militants themselves had no such compunction. The official line on the idea of a temperance or prohibition party was that it would be dangerous for the interests of the movement which would be split as a result of its formation because so many temperance supporters would decline to desert their own parties. The price that had to be paid for the preservation of temperance unity was the avoidance of action that might thus break up the movement. The derisory support given to independent temperance candidates was a warning against action that might appear to expose the movement as having pitifully small support. Another reason for official opposition to the idea was that a national party went against the spirit of the Local Option policy and was in fact espoused particularly by advocates of national prohibition.

When Grier first promoted the idea of special Associations at the London convention in February 1887, the term which he used in his resolution was 'organisations to unite the electors'. But he then accepted an amendment moved by the Rev. J. Mackenzie which replaced this by 'a prohibition party in every constituency'. Mackenzie had at first wished this to read 'a national prohibition party', but he withdrew this form of words on the understanding that steps would be taken to amend the Constitution of the Alliance to enable it, in effect, to act as a national party machine. This compromise did not satisfy Axel Gustafson, an extreme prohibitionist, who moved his own amendment in favour of a national party. He argued that, as things stood, their forces were divided between the political parties and therefore weakened and that the emphasis on local temperance action contributed to this weakness by leaving untouched many places where the drink traffic happened to be strong and temperance feeling unorganised. The Rev. G. M. Murphy attacked this idea, however, pointing to the chaos which would result if every other pressure group did the same and had its own national convention and party. Gustafson's amendment was overwhelmingly defeated.[49] In fact, support for the idea of a prohibition party was marked in some areas of the kind referred to by Gustafson, for example Staffordshire, Grier's own territory and the centre of the brewing industry. It was also strong in the International Order of Good Templars.

Gustafson himself now tried to found a National Prohibition Party and convened a conference in London in May 1887 which set up a provisional committee to prepare a plan. This issued a manifesto which declared: 'The policy of this Party will be to contest every seat in Parliament, on Prohibition lines, where there is a reasonable prospect of success, and where no Prohibition pledge can be obtained from either of the candidates. The Prohibition Party will thus secure a balance of power in Parliament.' Gustafson, however, had resigned from the committee and dissociated himself from the manifesto because he believed that a prohibition party was meaningless unless prepared to run candidates even where the party candidates were pledged to prohibition.[50] Little more was heard of this organisation.

It may be asked why, in view of the very close involvement by this period of temperance politics in Liberalism, there was never-theless so much independent temperance electoral action, so much antagonism to the strategy of working within the Liberal party. One answer is that the involvement was at the institutional level only in one part of the Liberal party and that electorally this really did begin to matter. The Liberal Unionist temperance voter was felt to be a reality for all the efforts of the Liberal Unionist leaders to dis-courage the raising of the issue, and he started to become a most important element in the political game. For their part, the tem-perance leaders began to sense that he could restore to their cause that electoral freedom and flexibility, that ability to play the parties off against each other, which they seemed largely to have lost as a result of the total identification of the Conservatives with the drink interest. But he would be available to be used in this way only if the Alliance made as conspicuous as possible a disengagement from its own identification with the Gladstonian Liberal party so that he could be reassured that he was not being made a mere pawn in the struggle over Home Rule. This was not a disengagement with which the Gladstonians themselves could afford to quarrel. If it succeeded, it could in effect deliver to them considerable numbers of Liberal Unionist voters who would not have been won back on the Home Rule issue. This prospect in its turn enhanced the leverage of the Liberal Unionist temperance supporters with their Conservative allies. If the Unionist government offended temperance sentiment, temperance voters would drift back to the Gladstonians and the cause of the Union would itself be endangered.

From a very early stage the Liberal Unionist temperance vote was claimed to be a critical factor in by-elections. One of the most sensa-tional of the early by-elections was that at Burnley in February 1887 when the Gladstonian, J. Slagg, won the seat which had been gained by P. Rylands for the Liberal Unionists at the general election only seven months before. At that time both Rylands and his Gladstonian opponent had given the Direct Veto pledge, and the local temperance people were reported to have divided their votes, one-third going to Rylands who won by a majority of 43. But in 1887 only Slagg pledged himself to the Veto. The Conservative, J. Thursby, refused to give a pledge and lost by the impressive margin of 540. It was claimed that on this occasion 96 per cent. of the temperance vote went to Slagg.[51]

For Liberal Unionists such as W. S. Caine who had endured a great deal of abuse within the temperance movement because of their opposition to the Gladstonians the crisis came in 1888 when the government's proposals for compensating publicans who lost their licenses aroused a storm of temperance indignation. Caine wrote a letter to *The Times* pleading with the government to withdraw the compensation clauses or else face the loss of the Liberal Unionist temperance vote to the Gladstonians.[52]

One now finds the exceedingly novel phenomenon emerging of Conservative wrath over faddism within their own ranks. For the first time they were subjected to electoral action of a kind to which Liberals had been accustomed for many years. Thus the *Saturday Review* stormed in a leading article on 30 June 1888:

The pitch of incivism—to use a word too convenient not to deserve naturalisation—to which a fad can drive faddists has rarely been better illustrated than in the events of the last three or four weeks. We have seen persistent temperance propaganda achieve the reversal of the verdict of one large constituency (Southampton), play a great part in the reversal of that of another (Ayr), and threaten at least to influence a third. The result of the Thanet election will not be known till some time after we write; but it has been asserted, and not contradicted, that a body of six or seven hundred electors has been guided in its vote solely by a consideration which has absolutely nothing to do with the duty of a voter, properly understood.

It referred to 'this faction of avowed bad citizens (for there can be no worse citizenship than a preference of a private fad to the public good)' and to 'the complete forgetfulness of reason and decency which this intoxication of non-intoxication induces in its victims'. Conservative politicians were just as horrified and began to sound like echoes of their Liberal counterparts. For example, W. H. Smith wrote to Caine:

I think your friends are treating us badly. It must be admitted we propose to do a great deal to advance temperance, but because we do not go all the way with you, you reject *all* our proposals, and threaten us with all kinds of mischief.
It is not a temperate way of dealing with the question, and is calculated to make one regret that any attempt is being made to deal with this difficult question.[53]

The message for the Alliance in all this was clear: the avoidance of any appearance of Gladstonian Liberal bias. In June 1889 the Executive ordered its agents and superintendents not to take office in any party organisations.[54] Liberals who took for granted an identity of outlook between themselves and the Alliance were

ostentatiously rebuffed. In the promotion of the policy of Temperance
Electoral Associations constant reference was made to the objective
of mobilising a temperance vote that was separate from the Liberal
party. At by-elections which were delicately poised and a Liberal
Unionist vote was critical great care was now taken to appear to be
impartial. An example is North St. Pancras which went Liberal in
1885 by 465 votes but Conservative in 1886 by 261. Here there were
reputed to be 600 voters on the register in 1890 who supported the
Veto. J. Hilton made sure that the committee at the by-election in
March 1890 'determinedly set the Temperance question above party
political considerations' and acted 'with the utmost impartiality'.
Both candidates were interviewed and then a decision made to
recommend the Liberal, T. H. Bolton. He gained the seat by a
majority of 108. This was widely attributed to his having gained the
temperance vote.[55] The Conservatives began to take protective
action. At Stamford in the same month H. J. C. Cust, the Conservative candidate, promised to vote for Local Option, and this
was said to have saved him from desertion by Unionist temperance
voters. He held the seat for the Conservatives.[56] At Stoke-on-Trent
both candidates accepted the Alliance programme, the Liberal
Unionist being W. S. Allen, a Vice-President of the Alliance.[57] This
was, however, a Gladstonian stronghold. The Alliance leaders were
delighted at this development. The parties were once again competing for the temperance vote.

Every effort was made to explain away the appearance of bias
towards the Gladstonians. When Lloyd George won the Caernarvon
Boroughs with temperance backing, the Conservatives were given
the blame for the frequency with which Liberals had to be supported:
'until the politicians of both parties agree to reduce the Temperance
vote in this way to a negligible quantity, by liberating the Temperance men from all need to choose between the candidates on
Temperance grounds, the Alliance will have to bear the disadvantage of seeming to be more favourable to one political party than it
is to another.'[58] When Herbert Gladstone chaired an Alliance
meeting at Chester and pleaded with the movement to come to
terms with the Liberal party, he was informed that it 'knows, and
can know nothing, of mere party considerations. It is not free, nor
able, to shape its course by anything of the kind. . . . it may not,
without distinct protest, allow itself to be invited to become the
mere appendage of any political party.'[59]

Suddenly, in the midst of all this the Alliance was confronted and greatly embarrassed by the complicated electoral situation which arose as the result of the decision by Caine to resign his seat at Barrow and fight a by-election on the basis of protest against the Conservative government's liquor licensing policy. He hoped now to make his peace with the Liberal party and end the intolerable dilemma in which his attempt to reconcile devotion to temperance and opposition to Home Rule had placed him. But the Barrow Liberal 'caucus' refused to have him back and put up their own candidate, J. A. Duncan, who also supported Local Option. In the ensuing three-cornered contest Duncan won and Caine came bottom of the poll. The Alliance itself was deeply divided over what to do in this situation. The Alliance Executive decided to recommend Caine as 'a man of sincere conviction and great force of character, willing to stand free of all political party considerations, and to appeal to a constituency simply as a real Temperance reformer'. It saw here a good opportunity to prove that the Alliance was not a mere Gladstonian organisation—even if, in doing so, it had to snub a perfectly sound Gladstonian candidate. But Caine did look very much like an independent temperance candidate, and his low place in the poll was something of a setback to independent temperance politics. Much more damaging, however, was the conduct of Sir Wilfrid Lawson, the President of the Alliance and a Liberal MP for a neighbouring constituency. Lawson refused to go to Barrow to speak on Caine's behalf. Caine begged him to come. The Executive sent a deputation to him to plead with him to do so. But it was to no avail. Just when the Alliance was striving to present an image of neutrality, of not being the tool of Gladstonianism, Lawson insisted on behaving in what appeared to be a very partisan manner. 'If I had been a Home-Ruler', lamented Caine, 'he would have been down long since.' Lawson supplied a variety of reasons for his action—that, as a Liberal MP, he could not 'run counter' to a local Liberal Association; that to have asked for votes for Caine instead of Duncan would have shifted enough from Duncan, the stronger candidate, to let in the Conservative enemy; that the result was a victory for Local Option because Duncan also supported it and therefore the 'Local Option vote' was the vast majority of the electorate; and that he was the true observer of neutrality in the situation since it was an Alliance rule, which he as President always observed, not to intervene in any election where there were two Local Option candidates. The Executive had, after all, deliberately preferred one Local Option candidate to another to prove a point. The appearance of divided counsels and of Gladstonian bias on Lawson's part, was however, very damaging.[60]

What was impressive about Barrow was that Caine gained as many votes as he did. He had not been its MP for very long, and his 1,280 votes in a total poll of about 5,000 were evidence of a reasonable 'temperance vote'. In other constituencies this vote seemed to continue to have an influence on results. At Eccles in October 1890, when H. J. Roby gained the seat for the Liberals, a number of Unionist temperance voters were reported to have pledged him their votes. At Hartlepool in January 1891 both the Liberal and the Unionist candidates promised to vote for the Direct Veto.[61]

The Annual Report presented to the Alliance Council in October 1891 includes a discussion of strategy in relation to the Unionist temperance vote. The great danger before the Alliance was, it warned, that of assuming that the parties were monolithic in their attitudes to the temperance question. It was natural to assume this, but appearances were deceptive. Some of the staunchest temperance men in the country were Unionists, but this fact was often overlooked for the reason that 'in most of the constituencies they are not strong enough to compel their party to select candidates who would at all adequately represent themselves on the Temperance question'. Because they existed, the Alliance must observe strict impartiality and not let Liberal candidates off with pledges that fell short of the Alliance demand on the assumption that theirs was the better party.[62]

In some constituencies Liberal Unionists did not find it very easy to support rather Radical Liberal candidates just because they happened to support the Direct Veto. In January 1892 at Hartington's old seat of Rossendale the Alliance decided to give strong backing to J. H. Maden, the Gladstonian. Some local Unionist temperance people then issued a manifesto protesting against this. It was believed that some of them abstained altogether in the end.[63] Maden won by 1,225 as compared to Hartington's 1886 majority of 1,450.

Another irritant which came in the way of good relations between the temperance movement and the Liberals in this period was the problem of the selection as candidates by some local Liberal caucuses of persons connected with the brewing industry. This divided the Alliance between those who argued that such men had to be accepted as long as they would constitute another vote for

Local Option in the House of Commons and those who found something very suspicious in Local Optionist brewers and began to sense a plot to deceive them. As a result, Liberal brewer candidatures became very divisive and weakened the electoral force of the 'temperance party'—a major reason why some temperance people became so hostile to them.

There was controversy within the temperance ranks at Southampton when one of the Liberal candidates in 1886, J. H. Cooksey, although supporting popular control over the liquor traffic, was himself revealed to own shares in a brewery.[64] The dilemma was to decide whether such men were sincere and altruistic or hypocrites who wished to worm their way into the Liberal party in order to erode its commitment to licensing reform. The next controversy, and one which foreshadowed one of the most bitter disputes of the 1890s, was over the support given by Lawson and an Alliance agent, H. J. Osborn, to a Liberal brewer, Mark Beaufoy, at Kennington in 1889. There was some doubt as to whether Beaufoy did in fact support the Direct Veto, and Lawson was accused of lowering his and the Alliance's standards and accepting a brewer just because he was a Liberal.[65]

By 1890 this question was being taken up seriously by the militants. The inaugural meeting of the Prohibition League in Edinburgh passed a motion of opposition to any candidate who was opposed to the Direct Veto *or* was engaged in the sale or manufacture of liquor. This was significant as showing that even brewers who supported Local Option would not be acceptable. The reasoning behind this was explained by Sheriff Guthrie Smith:

It was disappointing, notwithstanding the many pledges of members of Parliament, that the Temperance question had made so little progress in the House of Commons. There seemed to be a lack of earnestness in the House of Commons, and the time had therefore come when they should consider the methods and principles on which this movement was in the future to be conducted. The first lesson that was suggested to them was that they should be more careful in the selection of Parliamentary candidates. There was something intensely grotesque in Temperance voters sending a brewer to Parliament to stop the sale of beer, and he sympathised with the declaration signed by most present that henceforth there would be a signal change in their attitude in that respect.[66]

The first opportunity to demonstrate this change of attitude came in Birmingham in January 1891 when the Liberal Association selected as its candidate for East Birmingham at the general election H. G. Fulford, a wealthy brewer. At a meeting on 23 January the

Birmingham T.E.A. passed a resolution protesting against this. J. Moseley wrote of the dilemma which this candidature posed: 'I fear Mr. Fulford *would promise* us support for our Alliance policy if we approached him, and I could not vote for him or work for him whatever he promised. . . . I almost think we should let him alone or run an independent candidate.' The Liberal Association in Birmingham was of no help, although it contained many temperance people. An amendment to the motion endorsing Fulford's nomination proposed opposition to any candidate connected with the liquor traffic but was overwhelmingly rejected. The Alliance itself was divided. The Executive of the Auxiliary came out in opposition to Fulford, but E. C. Brambley, the Alliance agent, wrote a letter to the *Birmingham Daily Post* saying that he should at least be asked whether he supported Local Veto legislation. 'If he does,' wrote Brambley, 'then I for one should certainly vote for him, because the vote of a brewer counts for as much on a division in Parliament as that of any other hon. member, and would be far preferable to the opposition of the Home Secretary.' The Auxiliary Executive passed a resolution deploring this letter.[67] But Brambley was not alone in holding this opinion. A prominent Scottish temperance reformer agreed that 'votes in Parliament are not valued, but counted'.[68]

Controversy now began to form around a second proposed Liberal brewer candidate, Captain H. T. Fenwick, at Houghton-le-Spring. Efforts started to find an independent temperance candidate to run against him. In September 1891 Jonathan Hargrove announced that he would come forward as that candidate if no agreement could be reached between the local Liberals and teetotallers.[69] On 1 October a deputation met the Executive of the Houghton-le-Spring Liberal Association, but, after some members of the Executive had argued that the teetotallers in their districts were in favour of Fenwick's candidature, a resolution was passed declining to alter the Association's position. It was argued that the proper time for temperance people to make such objections was while the Liberal candidate was being selected and not afterwards, when it looked like dictation by an outside body. The Alliance Executive now advised the local temperance party that they should run their own candidate, and so Hargrove proceeded to test the ground to see how much support he might get. Hayler and other militants toured the district holding anti-Fenwick meetings. But at some of them pro-Fenwick votes were carried. The drink interest may have seen to this, but people who claimed to be supporters of temperance did stand up and declare support for Fenwick. Nevertheless, Hargrove did announce his candidature in late January 1892. He was careful to state that he was standing as a Radical and not just as a temperance candidate.[70]

The reason why the Alliance Executive had decided to encourage Hargrove's candidature was that it had persuaded the Council meeting in October 1891 to pass a resolution making it Alliance policy not to support any candidate who would not promise to vote for the Direct Veto *or* who was 'a licensed common brewer, or distiller, or liquor-seller'. The Rev. James Clark who moved this acknowledged that he did so with some misgivings because it raised the very vexed question of how far it would be right or feasible to carry such proscriptions. Should one also exclude candidates who had shares in brewing concerns? Some delegates thought that they should, but Joseph Malins of Birmingham, although reiterating his well-known opposition to brewers even if they supported Local Option, urged the Council not to get itself into that morass. This move to withdraw support from a certain category of candidates who did support the Alliance's programme was a major change in Alliance electoral strategy and was bound to complicate electoral matters considerably. Henry Hibbert put the case against it when moving deletion of the clause concerning brewers:

He did not care whether a man were a brewer or distiller if he would give the power of destroying the traffic. . . . Let us get help from wherever we could, and not tie our hands. It was sufficient if the resolution declared that we would not vote for any man who would not give the Direct Veto. The less complexity the better. Let the issue be clearly stated that these men could deliver us from this evil, and, if they did not, the responsibility was with them. We might get bad men to pass good laws, if good men would not. The question was—What was the most effectual way of getting this law on the statute book?

He was supported by E. A. Davis who 'thought it would be a great mistake to narrow our ground of action' and pointed out that accusations of hypocrisy might just as well be made against Liberals who drank and also supported Local Option. In his reply in defence of the motion Caine made much of the 'Trojan horse' argument: 'We were engaged in a great fight, and we wanted to take care that we were not beguiled by a simple promise to do a single action into letting into our ranks men who were likely to give us trouble afterwards.' The Liberal 'liquor men' voted for second readings but then created all kinds of difficulties when the Bills were in committee. Another reason was that the question 'was smashing up the Temperance party in some constituencies, and we had to keep it together'. Hibbert did not appreciate this because he came from an area where the problem did not arise, 'but there were other districts where the whole Temperance party was torn by dissension and did not know what to do, and they had a right to look to us and to the united wisdom of the United Kingdom Alliance in council to let them know exactly what line they ought to take'. The Council then gave this guidance by rejecting Hibbert's amendment and passing the motion.[71]

Action against Liberal brewers concentrated on two places, Houghton-le-Spring and East Birmingham, where independent temperance candidatures were promoted. In neither place did this have the united support of the local temperance party. In Birmingham George Cadbury was a particularly outspoken critic, arguing that an Alliance candidate would get only a very small proportion of the Alliance votes and would thus expose the movement to ridicule.[72] However, there was some divergence of views even among the militants. Hargrove, who was standing against Fenwick at Houghton-le-Spring, made it plain that he did so because Fenwick was against the Direct Veto and not because he was a brewer. He was therefore not prepared to go as far as the Council resolution and rebuked those temperance people who wanted to scrutinise the motives of all Liberals who said that they supported the Direct Veto: 'It would be mad folly if we were at present to set up the standard that we must only support total abstaining candidates that can prove they have been duly and honestly converted to advanced Temperance principles, and that have proved themselves earnest advocates and ready to fight for our principles.' The main thing was that they should vote right and therefore he, for his part, was very much in favour of any brewer who supported the Alliance programme.[73]

Hargrove and D. S. Collin, the temperance candidate at East Birmingham, co-operated closely and spoke at each other's meetings. Here was the nucleus of a temperance political party, it seemed. But the Liberals had no cause for alarm, and Lawson could safely come to Houghton-le-Spring and speak for Hargrove and use his doing so to prove that the Alliance was not just a section of the Liberal party.[74] For Houghton-le-Spring and East Birmingham were both party strongholds, for the Liberals and Unionists respectively, and nothing that the Alliance did there was likely to make any difference to the results. Hargrove won 814 votes, and Fenwick's majority was 1,433, while at East Birmingham the Conservatives retained the seat by 2,209 and Collin secured a derisory 296. Cadbury appeared to be vindicated in his prediction that the candidatures would only discredit the Alliance by showing that many of those whom it claimed as its supporters in fact put party before temperance when given a choice between them.

The Alliance and the temperance movement generally appeared to become in the years after 1886 a formidable electoral force—on paper, at least. Paton and others carried on extensive canvassing for pledges in different parts of the country, and many constituencies acquired their small and well organised groups of pledged voters who might well make all the difference in an evenly balanced contest. How dependable the pledges would be in the heat of a contest and under the pressure of appeals to party loyalty was debatable. Some Alliance leaders thought that the work should be concentrated on the large numbers of new electors who were not committed to any party. Whether the Liberal Unionist temperance voters who appeared to vote for the Gladstonian candidates or to abstain between 1888 and 1892 because they gave priority to the temperance question did so because they were pledged to act in this way is not clear. After all, many of them must have voted in 1886 for Unionist or Conservative candidates who opposed Local Option against Gladstonians who supported it. The promoters of the pledge were sometimes perfectly happy to allow it to be given a flexible interpretation. When the Carlisle Temperance Federation in December 1890 debated a motion that temperance electors should refuse to vote for any candidate who would not vote for the Direct Veto, some delegates were worried that such a pledge might 'land them in a position of extreme difficulty' if an election happened to 'turn upon something of greater moment'. But D. S. Collin assured them that they could not be expected to violate their conscience and 'the pledge could be withdrawn at any time'.[75] The knowledge of the existence of this pledged vote introduced into the calculations of candidates and party managers an element of uncertainty, something which they abhorred and which made them very nervous. W. Canning analysed the psychological consequence of this: 'When the strain is sufficient the weakest link yields. A candidate can lose an election in a day, though reforms are not carried in one fight; the reformers may wait the result of their abstinence, but he must not play a trial game and let his decision tarry.'[76]

On the other hand, there were many, such as Cadbury, who were strongly in favour of working in and with the Liberal party. Their position seemed to be abundantly vindicated by the incorporation in the 1891 'Newcastle programme' of the National Liberal Federation of the item, popular control over the liquor traffic, and the subsequent endorsement given to this programme as a whole by the Liberal leaders, including Gladstone. There was something in this development to please everybody. It enabled Temperance Liberals to feel a harmony between their two loyalties. It enabled the militants in the movement to claim that the N.L.F. had only done this because of the success of pledge-taking and the threat posed for Liberal candidates by their electoral militancy. It gave Liberal candidates themselves an excuse for not giving any more pledges to specific pressure groups but simply announcing that they supported the Newcastle programme, the commitment in which to popular control over the liquor traffic was very vaguely phrased and left the maximum freedom for the later working out of details. And the Liberal leaders not merely thus preserved control over the details, in other words were not specifically pledged to the Alliance's own policy, but could also determine the timing of legislative action on the question, since items in the Newcastle programme, apart from Irish Home Rule, were not listed in any order of priority. Consequently all—or nearly all—was harmony in the general election of 1892. Liberal candidates stood as supporters of the Newcastle programme and in return received the backing of the local temperance 'parties'. Even Hargrove, when he stood against Fenwick, claimed to do so as a true Liberal because, unlike Fenwick, he accepted the whole of the Newcastle programme.[77]

However, the strong temperance support for Liberal candidates provoked the publicans and the 'trade' into giving very active aid and encouragement to their Unionist opponents, and this led some unsuccessful Liberals in what was generally a disappointing result for their party to blame 'beer' for their setback and to express the opinion that the question ought to be less prominent in future elections. Herbert Gladstone gave this as his reason for insisting that high priority must be given to legislation on the question before the end of the new Parliament.[78] Temperance people replied by arguing that the Liberals had done disappointingly because many temperance enthusiasts did not trust them and therefore had not rallied to them at the election. If the Liberals now proved their sincerity and devotion to the temperance cause, these people could be expected to give them their full support and thus considerably boost the Liberal vote.[79]

Thus there began the next great phase of temperance electoral politics—the battle to control the way in which Liberals interpret their election results.

CHAPTER XIII

The United Kingdom Alliance, 1892–1900

The political position of the temperance question was transformed by the National Liberal Federation's inclusion of popular control over the liquor traffic in its Newcastle programme of 1891, the acceptance of this programme by Gladstone and other Liberal leaders, the way in which it then formed the basis of the Liberal party's campaign in the general election of 1892, the Liberals' return to office as a result of that election, and the government's promotion of Local Option Bills in 1894 and 1895. The status of the question was now transformed. It was now the Liberals' question just as much as it was the Alliance's. The Alliance's role became one of supporting the government and conducting a campaign of publicity and propaganda on behalf of this particular item in its programme.

As a result, the electoral landscape is very much altered. Almost every Liberal candidate is endorsed and given Alliance support in his campaigning while needing, for his part, to go no further than declare his loyalty to the party programme as a whole. The day of demanding specific pledges on Local Option seems to have passed. This is reflected in the virtual extinction of that side of the Alliance's electoral work which was concerned with canvassing and pledge-taking. Threats to withhold votes from Liberal candidates now seem to belong to a bygone era and to have no place in the temperance politics of the 1890s. It was a sign of the times that in 1893 the Liverpool and District Veto League, which only a few years before had been an intensely active centre for canvassing for electoral pledges, changed its policy from one in which the pledge was its basic purpose to the general policy of the Alliance and that in 1895 it dissolved itself and was incorporated into the Alliance.[1] There are now very few instances of such canvassing. In November 1895 the

Hampstead Local Option Union held a house-to-house canvass for signatures to an electoral pledge and subsequently convened a meeting of the signatories.[2] In 1895 the London Auxiliary carried out a canvass of ten constituencies but only for signatures to a declaration of support for a Local Option Bill. No pledge concerning candidates was sought.[3] Otherwise, the only evidence of a revival of this kind of electoral action came in the aftermath of a few by-elections when Alliance agents worked very hard on behalf of a candidate and in the process succeeded in reawakening interest in electoral politics. An example is the Plymouth by-election of January 1898 when John Newton, the very energetic Alliance district superintendent, persuaded 150 voters to sign a declaration that they would vote only for a candidate who supported the Direct Veto and then organised them into a Plymouth Temperance Electoral Association for the purpose of compiling a register of temperance electors.[4] This must have been one of the very last such organisations to be founded. Many of the others had long since disappeared. Two years later this Plymouth body was still active.[5] A similar result flowed from the work done for the Liberal candidate at the Exeter by-election in November 1899. Newton and E. C. Brambley formed the temperance workers into a brand new Exeter T.E.A. on the basis of the Direct Veto pledge.[6] The only other stimulus to a revival of interest in electoral organisation was opposition to brewer candidates which had this effect in the Midlands, especially in Derbyshire.

The general decline in electoral militancy and distinctive temperance electoral organisation was symptomatic of a wider problem which affected the Liberation Society as well in this period. This was the tendency for temperance people to feel that it was now primarily the responsibility of the Liberals to carry Local Option and that everything could now be left in their hands. At the Council meeting in October 1892 W. S. Caine pleaded with delegates not to trust MPs but to continue to keep themselves very much in evidence in their constituencies.[7] It was difficult for members of a pressure group to appreciate and make allowances for the problems which a political party—a very different type of organisation—encountered when it took up their question and then had to try to make it acceptable to public opinion. This required techniques very unlike those to which the enthusiasts were accustomed and which they therefore tended to treat with hostility.

The electoral strategy in which the Alliance now found itself engaged was of a novel kind. It concerned the interpretation of election results. What the Alliance now had to do was to demonstrate statistically to the Liberal party that its identification with the Local Option issue was an electoral asset and that any move to drop or 'shelve' that policy would lose more votes than it would gain. From the beginning there were those in the party, of whom Herbert Gladstone was the most prominent, who believed that on balance the policy was an electoral liability. The results of the general election of 1895 appeared to support this view, and an unremitting struggle to interpret the figures ensued.

When Liberal electoral setbacks occurred, as in 1892 and 1895, and some were disposed to attribute this to the identification with temperance, the Alliance responded with a variety of more or less ingenious arguments. The Liberals had not been whole-hearted or convincing enough to bring out the full temperance vote. The role of other questions was exhaustively analysed and much of the blame was transferred to Home Rule, disestablishment, and the machinations of the I.L.P. The derisory votes given to Hargrove and Collin as temperance candidates in 1892 were claimed to prove how little support there was for the Veto, but the Alliance denied this. Many temperance people voted for the Liberal because his party as a whole was seen as sound on the question and deserving therefore of strengthening in the House. If the Liberals abandoned the Veto, they would lose the vote of many people, including Unionists, who were prepared to vote for them only because of their support for this reform. It was the one question in the Liberal programme which attracted votes across the party lines. In compensation the Liberals would not gain the public-house vote. That had gone for good. By-election defeats were customarily attributed to the alleged lukewarmness of the candidate or his attempt to suppress the question which alienated large numbers of temperance workers and voters.[8]

The election defeat of 1895 was particularly shocking to the Liberals and was widely blamed on the unpopularity of the Local Option legislation. The Alliance had to engage in a massive campaign of letters to the press to explain why this assumption was false.[9] Its explanations were not, however, always consistent. On the one hand, efforts were made to prove that other questions were mainly to blame and that Local Option had been only a minor issue in the campaign. On the other hand, it was natural for temperance enthusiasts to attribute as much evil and vigour as possible to 'the enemy', the drink trade. This was dangerous ground since it could be taken by Liberals to prove that the forces opposed to Local Option were electorally too strong for them ever to be able to win with it in their platform. The election results were analysed in order to show that the Liberals had not in any case done nearly as badly as they thought and that the stronger the identification of the candidate with temperance and the Alliance the better he tended to do. W. S. Caine became a specialist in this sort of analysis, partly because of an intense controversy which raged over the causes of his defeat at East Bradford where the local Liberal Association asked him not to offer himself again as a candidate because of his over-close relationship to the Alliance.[10] Another election result which was the subject of seemingly endless debate was the defeat at Derby of Sir William Harcourt, chief architect of the Local Option Bills. Caine drew up a table of statistics which purported to prove the electoral superiority of strong temperance candidates and urged Alliance members to use it as ammunition in their arguments with local Liberals. He assured them that the Liberal party managers, who had time to pore over the statistics, had come to the same conclusion. In October 1896 he told the Council that he had asked one of the leading Liberal organisers about the chances of a Liberal candidate who was a tee-totaller and supporter of the Alliance. ' "Well," replied he, "he is handicapped to some slight extent; but my experience of Temperance candidates is that they throw into the contest so much fire, and awaken so much enthusiasm in their constituencies, that they could carry ten times the handicapping of the Veto and yet do better than other people." '[11]

A great deal of emphasis was placed on the possibility of regaining a portion of the Liberal Unionist vote if only the Liberals would show themselves to be strongly committed now to the achievement of temperance reform. Those who expressed scepticism about this floating temperance vote were told that, although the number of votes might not be very great, it was 'nevertheless of great importance when compared with the number composing the majorities by which, in a large proportion of cases, candidates are returned to Parliament'. Besides, went on the Alliance's 1894 Annual Report, 'when it is remembered that, in changing sides the numbers are deducted from the one side and added to the other, the importance to electioneerers of securing such voters becomes obvious'.[12] With Gladstone's retirement in 1894, the evident inclination of Rosebery, the new Liberal leader, to shelve the question of Home Rule, and the decisive defeat of the Liberals in the general election of 1895, the threat of the enactment of Home Rule for Ireland receded very much into the background, and there are renewed reports of Liberal Unionists, and even Conservatives, voting Liberal on the temperance question, as if it was felt to be safe to put that question first now. When Sam Woods won Walthamstow in February 1897, many Liberal Unionist voters were claimed to have supported him. His opponent was T. R. Dewar, the whisky distiller, and until Woods entered the contest A. F. Hills had been intending to stand against Dewar as a Unionist temperance candidate.[13] There were also reports of Unionist backing for S. F. Mendl at Plymouth in January 1898. There was obviously sufficient of a non-Liberal temperance vote here to enable J. Newton to form the new Temperance Electoral Association. Ten prominent Unionists were said to have signed Mendl's nomination paper, including one who said that he stopped canvassing for the Conservative candidate as soon as he heard his views on the liquor question. The Liberals held the seat by a margin of 164 votes compared to 26 in 1895; 36 Unionist abstentions on the temperance question were claimed.[14] When in the same month J. Richardson regained South-East Durham for the Liberals by 275 votes compared with a Liberal Unionist majority of 114 in 1895, Unionist temperance votes were again reported to have played a part in the swing.[15] The Liberals also recaptured Cricklade, won by the Liberal Unionists in 1895 by 99 votes or 1 per cent. Many Liberal Unionist and Conservative temperance votes were said to be included in Lord Edmond Fitzmaurice's majority of 489 in February 1898.[16] Southport was another important Liberal gain in 1898. Curzon had held it for the Conservatives since the general election of 1886, but, when he was appointed Viceroy of India, a by-election was held in August 1898 and his 1895 majority of 763 (8 per cent.) was turned into a majority of 272 (2·8 per cent.) for the Liberal, Sir H. S. Naylor-Leyland. A special temperance election committee made a canvass of all Unionist abstainers, and Joseph Spraggon, a member of the Executive of the local Liberal Unionist Association, was reported as claiming that 500 Unionists had abstained this time or voted Liberal on the temperance question. They would, he added, once again vote primarily on the Home Rule issue should it re-emerge as 'a test question'.[17]

This evidence must, of course, be treated with caution, since it was in the interests of the temperance movement to show the Liberal Unionist temperance vote as a substantial and decisive electoral factor that was available to the Liberals as long as they adhered to the Local Option policy. In all probability it was only one of a

number of influences at work at this time loosening the bonds between the Conservatives and Liberal Unionists, a process which was
to culminate in the Liberal Unionist reaction against the Education
Act of 1902. Nevertheless, it was something which the Liberals could
ignore at their peril, as they had great need of every vote that they
could possibly regain.

What the Alliance had to do from 1892 on was to prove to the
Liberals that they benefited electorally from identifying themselves
with the temperance cause. The danger that they would arrive at
the opposite conclusion was greatly increased by the mobilisation of
the electoral influence of the liquor interest. Liberal candidates, now
that their party had made Local Option part of its official programme, desperately needed help against this, and only the Alliance
was in a position to give it to them. Therefore, Alliance policy came
to be to fling all its resources into any campaign where a Liberal was
standing, for a Liberal was now regarded as being, by definition, a
supporter of his party's legislative programme and commitments and
therefore a Local Optionist. Such intervention in its turn only increased the electoral fury of the drink trade, and many election
contests became in effect struggles between the forces of drink and
anti-drink, with the candidates being caught, more or less helplessly,
in the middle.

The first by-election at which this policy of making an all-out
effort to prove that the temperance question could make the difference between winning and losing a seat was tried was Wisbech in
April 1894. This was a very marginal seat—Liberal in 1885, Conservative in 1886, regained by the Liberals in 1891 by 260 votes (3·4
per cent.), and held by them in 1892 by only 122 (1·4 per cent.). In
1894 the Hon. A. G. Brand had to seek re-election on being appointed a junior government Whip. The local Liberals tried to suppress
the drink question, but E. C. Brambley, the very energetic Alliance
superintendent for the area, ignored them and went into the constituency and stirred up the question. The result of the by-election
was that Brand held the seat by 136 votes (1·6 per cent.). Brambley
claimed much of the credit for this and seemed to get Brand's concurrence in this interpretation—an important admission in view of
Brand's official position. Brambley wrote to the Alliance Executive
urging them to 'impress upon all district supts. and supporters of the
Alliance the imperative importance of their paying much more
attention to *practical electioneering*':

The politicians of the country have but one opinion of the so-called temperance party as an electioneering force—that is, that it is of but little value. Unfortunately there is much truth in this conviction. The Wisbech Election however afforded us an opportunity to do something more than 'shout' and issue 'manifestoes', for this policy—the Wisbech policy—has not only opened the eyes of local politicians but its influence has reached Cabinet Ministers and the Lobby of the House of Commons. Mr. Brand is an additional 'Whip', and he promised to tell his colleagues what we did to prevent the loss of his seat. . . . At elections candidates *want* votes and *we must* be prepared to supply them at every contest, then they will respect us as politicians as well as philanthropists. . . .[18]

The problem now was that, since Local Option was the official policy of the Liberal government, electoral intervention on behalf of that policy had to be intervention on behalf of *all* Liberal candidates, not just individuals who were selected because of their own personal adherence to it, as had been the case in the past. This made the Alliance seem much more like an adjunct of the Liberal party and ultimately led to serious strains within the movement—as well as to resentment among Liberals who were uneasy about having so close an identification with the Alliance foisted upon them.

There was one asset above all which the Alliance claimed to have available in abundance to deliver to the Liberals—enthusiasm. It was argued that 'in every constituency the backbone of the Liberal Party is with the Temperance elector' and that he supplied a large part of the help with canvassing and other election chores without which the Liberals could not hope to win.[19] The challenge was to prove this. Brambley wanted to maximise the involvement of temperance people in local Liberal organisations, but other Alliance leaders preferred to retain independence.[20] However, in by-election after by-election from 1895 on, and also in the general election of 1895, Alliance agents were poured into the constituencies to help Liberal candidates. This was undoubtedly much more of an external operation than Brambley would have liked. Too much depended on a few energetic superintendents and agents such as himself.

Many Liberal constituency organisations were very hard pressed for funds and anxious to accept voluntary aid in electioneering. When after 1895 some Liberal candidates showed a disposition to 'shelve the Veto', they were advised that this help was available to them—at a price. Thus J. M. Skinner wrote on the Brixton by-election of January 1896: 'Liberal canvassers were very much needed, and the Temperance party avowed willingness to furnish 80 volunteers for that work if Mr. Nunn would promise to support an efficient Local Control Bill.'[21] Nunn refused and was overwhelmingly defeated. By contrast, by-elections where Liberal candidates came out strongly in favour of Local Option and received Alliance backing and then did very well, were given great publicity. An example is Halifax in March 1897. The Liberals had held both Halifax seats in 1885, 1886, and 1892, but lost one of them as soon as the I.L.P. began intervening. In 1895 the I.L.P. took over 20 per cent. of the vote, and in 1897 Tom Mann decided to stand on their behalf when the Liberals were defending the one seat which they had won in 1895. The Alliance supported the Liberal candidate, A. Billson, and he went out of his way to cultivate the temperance vote. He spoke at an Alliance meeting, while the Alliance lent him five of its agents for the duration of the election, held meetings on his behalf, and did a great deal of canvassing work for him. The Alliance opposed Mann because he favoured municipalisation of the drink traffic. The result, the Liberal retention of the seat by 412 votes (3·1 per cent.) with the I.L.P. vote falling 5 per cent., was hailed by the Alliance as proof that the Liberal party, far from losing, actually gained by a close identification with the Alliance and the Direct Veto.[22] J. M. Skinner explained it this way when writing about the temperance enthusiasts: 'It is not merely the votes such men give, it is the work they do which wins elections. When the others are smoking and drinking in public-houses and clubs the teetotallers are hard at work canvassing, and winning the election.'[23] The evidence is that in the majority of cases the local Liberals welcomed this help. This was particularly the case, of course, where many of them were strong temperance people, but the temperance workers usually had so much to offer that it was foolish to turn them down. The drink interest had so much to fear from a Liberal *government* that trimming on the part of an individual Liberal candidate was not likely to abate their hostility to him as a Liberal. Therefore, as the Alliance argued, he had nothing to lose and everything to gain by securing all the countervailing influence that he possibly could.

The growing Labour political movement caused some embarrassment to the Alliance. Temperance sentiment was strong in the labour world. Keir Hardie was a good friend of the Alliance, often spoke at temperance meetings, and received Alliance endorsement at South West Ham in 1892.[24] In the 1880s he had been an electoral superintendent for the Order of Good Templars and had abstained from voting because of the views of the candidates in his constituency on the drink question.[25] Some of the temperance militants saw the rise of the I.L.P. as providing the chance for the Alliance to regain electoral manoeuvrability by threatening to support its candidates if the Liberals weakened in their commitments.[26] In December 1893 one of the superintendents asked for instructions as to what action he should take in cases where both the Liberal and Labour candidates were in favour of the Direct Veto. The ruling given by the Executive was that he should 'ask the electors to vote for such of the favourable candidates whom the electors themselves deem the likeliest to be returned'.[27] The Alliance's aim had to be to minimise the risk of a rift between pro-Veto candidates occurring in such a way as to let in the third anti-Veto candidate. But, inevitably, in the 1890s in most constituencies such a formula had a built-in bias in favour of the Liberals. The Executive reiterated this advice in June 1894 in connection with the I.L.P. candidature at Sheffield Attercliffe.[28] Support was, however, given to I.L.P. candidates who stood in tandem with Liberals in two-member boroughs, for example Fred Brocklehurst at Bolton in the general election of 1895.[29] There was great controversy when in November 1896 the Executive abandoned its previous formula of advising support for the candidate most likely to win and passed a resolution calling for support for either A. Billson, Liberal, or Keir Hardie, I.L.P., at the East Bradford by-election. Both men supported the Direct Veto, but the Alliance's advice was obviously influenced by the refusal of the local Liberals to re-adopt W. S. Caine following his loss of the seat in 1895 and their attempt to suppress the question at the by-election. The Alliance came under attack for its impartiality as between Billson and Hardie when the Conservative won the seat by 395 votes and Keir Hardie came third with 1,953. This by-election was controversial for other reasons. Relations between the Liberals and the I.L.P. were very strained in Bradford, and the I.L.P. had believed itself to be entitled to at least one of the seats. The Alliance wisely refrained from offending Labour in a situation where the Liberals were acting so offensively. The circumstances made it certain that the temperance vote would be divided, since some Labour temperance men were incensed against the Liberals, and the Alliance did well not to pretend to hold a solid temperance vote 'in the hollow of its hand'.[30] However, Billson stood again in February 1897 as Liberal candidate at Halifax and was rewarded for a much more definite commitment to the Veto by being given Alliance endorsement against Tom Mann, standing for the I.L.P. Quite a few I.L.P. candidates now, including Mann, favoured municipalisation of the drink traffic. This earned them the opposition of the Alliance which detested any policy of regulation instead of prohibition. Some said that they supported the Veto as well, but the Alliance could not countenance any endorsement of regulation. Peter Curran was opposed for this reason at Barnsley in October 1897.[31]

In September 1898 the annual conference of the North of England Temperance League debated whether Liberals who were sound on the Veto should be supported even against Labour candidates who were equally sound because of the loyalty of the Liberal party as a whole to the cause. Leif Jones argued that the time might have come when, in order to appease those elements in the Liberal party who were opposed to them and strengthen their friends in the party, they might offer to support any Liberal against all comers as long as he was sound on the temperance question. But J. M. Skinner thought that this would be going too far in allying themselves to a party. It was best to settle such cases as they arose.[32]

By the 1890s some sort of equilibrium had been arrived at in the relations between the Liberals and the temperance 'party' in most constituencies. On the one hand, temperance men were usually influential enough in local Liberal Associations to exercise a virtual veto over the choice of Liberal candidates. For example, early in 1894 H. Whitbread decided to abandon his candidature at South Bedfordshire because of hostility to him over his views on the Veto question. When the Liberal Association offered the nomination to T. G. Ashton, he accepted only on condition that he was guaranteed the undivided support of the temperance party.[33] In December 1894 it was reported that two successive Liberal candidates at Huntingdon had been obliged to withdraw mainly because of their unwillingness to pledge themselves on the Veto.[34] So strong was temperance feeling in Plymouth by 1898 that B. F. Hawksley refused to accept the Liberal nomination there until he had been pronounced as acceptable by the temperance section.[35]

Trouble arose in particular over the ban which some temperance people wished to impose on one special category of Liberal candidate —the men connected with the brewing industry. This policy, which was formulated prior to 1892, caused seemingly endless difficulties throughout the decade. Such men were still found who, in spite of their personal stake in the continuation of the drink trade, professed to be in favour of the Direct Veto. But there were more and more of them who preferred to go on to the offensive and strike back at the temperance influence within the Liberal party, taking the view that it was better in their own interest to try to do this as Liberals than to secede and leave the party entirely under temperance control and therefore certain to promote temperance legislation whenever it held office. This aggressiveness in its turn further provoked the temperance section, and some very nasty confrontations developed.

The 1891 Alliance Council resolution proscribing brewer candidates, even if they supported the Veto, was still Alliance policy. Indeed, in July 1894 the Executive passed a resolution recalling its terms and urging that it continue to be observed.[36] Action was then taken to put it into effect. Whitbread, and Thomas Earp at Grantham, were both brewers who had been docilely accepted by the local temperance people. Earp at the time of his selection had made it quite plain that he could not support the government's Liquor Traffic (Local Control) Bill. The Executive instructed its agents to do all they could to stir up resistance to both men. Two of them managed to persuade a group of temperance electors from Grantham to join them in a deputation to Tom Ellis, the new Liberal Chief Whip, to urge him to induce Earp to retire in the interests of Liberal unity.[37] The man who caused the greatest difficulties, however, was C. H. Fulford, the chairman of the Holt Brewery Company and the arch-enemy of the temperance 'party' in Birmingham. He made no secret of his opposition to the government's Bill and yet was adopted as candidate by the Liberals in Lichfield in December 1894 by a vote of 115 to 43. This so angered the Birmingham temperance militants that they at once set about finding an independent candidate to run against him.[38]

A few months later another brewer was in the news—Mark Beaufoy, the member for Kennington, whose selection back in 1889 had been the starting-point for the entire anti-brewer crusade.[39] Beaufoy had announced that he intended to retire at the next general election, and a successor who was in favour of the government's bill had been chosen. Unfortunately he had to retire because of ill health, whereupon Beaufoy began to have second thoughts about his intention to stand down. When the Kennington Liberal Association met to make another selection, it found that the Executive had, on the casting vote of the chairman, resolved to invite Beaufoy himself to address the meeting. He did so in extremely aggressive terms, attacking the temperance party and the Veto Bill and declaring that in future he would vote against all such measures and for compensation for publicans who lost their licenses. A resolution adopting Beaufoy was then carried by 127 to 99. Beaufoy had in fact supported Local Option in both 1889 and 1892 but had announced in 1893 that, owing to 'trade pressure', he had completely changed his position. He had offered to resign at that time, but a compromise—to which W. S. Caine was a party—had been arrived at by which he would stay neutral for the remainder of that Parliament and not stand for Kennington at the next election. The temperance party was most indignant at his having now broken this compact. The Kennington Temperance Council launched a campaign of protest, and numerous temperance meetings passed resolutions in opposition to Beaufoy. It is symptomatic of the rift in Kennington Liberalism that at the biggest of these, when 400 people voted for such a resolution, the chair was taken by the Treasurer of the Kennington Liberal Association. The Liberals themselves held a mass meeting at which Caine moved an amendment opposing Beaufoy's candidature. This was defeated by 900 to 600.

There was now some disagreement amongst the temperance forces as to what to do next. Caine, who was back in the House as a Gladstonian MP, clearly wanted to have nothing more to do with independent candidatures and was scrupulous about observing the Liberal rules. Beaufoy's offence was, he insisted, an offence against Liberalism primarily as he was repudiating one major item of Liberal policy. His opponents would not themselves break with Liberalism and thus commit a similar crime and leave the party in the hands of such men. They would 'run no rival candidate'. But a section of the Kennington temperance people did not agree and proceeded to bring out as a temperance candidate W. Wightman, a former honorary secretary of the London Auxiliary and editor of the *Temperance Times*. Wightman took 730 votes or 10·1 per cent. of the poll, but Beaufoy lost the seat by the slightly larger margin of 995. A similar problem loomed at Houghton-le-Spring which Hargrove had contested against Captain Fenwick in 1892. On 1 May 1895 the Alliance Executive agreed to send an agent there 'to prepare the villages for opposition' to his re-election. But Fenwick decided not to stand again.[40] No temperance candidate in the end stood against Fulford at Lichfield and he won the seat for the Liberals, only to lose it when the election was declared void on petition. Debarred from standing again, Lichfield then arranged for the candidature at the by-election to go to one of his associates, T. Courtenay Warner, who had been elected for Mid-Somerset in 1892 as a supporter of the

K

Veto but was now, like Beaufoy, strongly opposed to it and to Sunday Closing. Warner held the seat for the Liberals with a majority increased from 44 (0·6 per cent.) to 528 (6·2 per cent.). The Liberal vote was up by nearly 600. *The Times* claimed that this was accounted for by the return to the fold of 500 teetotallers who had abstained the previous July because Fulford was a brewer. The fact that Warner was not a brewer seemed to suffice to bring them back even though he was just as antagonistic to temperance legislation. The *Alliance News* deplored the example set by this weak conduct but had to admit that there was now one very vulnerable point in the position of Liberal Associations—their desperate need for wealthy candidates. 'The brewers, on one condition, are ready to find such candidates.' It was more important than ever to free the Liberals from such dependence on tainted money by offering instead the services of enthusiastic temperance agents and election workers.[41]

It was never easy to know how to handle brewer candidates, especially when their Tory opponents were backed by the 'trade'. In January 1897 John Fuller, a brewer, stood as Liberal candidate at Salisbury. The local superintendent wrote to the Alliance Executive seeking advice on what to do if Fuller returned favourable replies to the temperance deputation, for even if he did, 'the fact of his being a Brewer will prevent any enthusiastic support being given on his behalf, by the *thorough going* Tempce. friends'. The Executive instructed J. Hilton to go to Salisbury, 'meet our leading friends there, and state to them why it was impossible for the Alliance to support Mr. Fuller's candidature'. On hearing of this Lawson wrote a letter of protest to the Secretary. He had never liked the Council's anti-brewer resolution, partly no doubt because he had regarded it as a vote directed at himself after his support for Beaufoy in 1889.[42] The Executive was unrepentant and advised abstention against J. Bonham Carter, a Liberal brewer, at the Petersfield by-election of June 1897. Carter was a strong advocate of compensation.[43] Much more controversial was the instruction given to the agents to stop working for J. Barker, the Liberal candidate at the Maidstone by-election of March 1898, even though he had expressed support for the Alliance programme. His offence was that he was the son of a brewer, had married into the Gilbey family, had a brother who had just retired from a wine and spirit business, and—worst of all—himself owned a general store in one department of which liquor was on sale. The Executive had to back down when J. M. Skinner, one of their most active superintendents, wrote in pleading not to be required to withdraw. The local Grand Lodge of the Good Templars voted, however, not to support Barker who thus found himself under attack from both sides, since the Licensed Victuallers' Association were also hard at work against him. It is not surprising that he lost, although he did reduce the Conservative majority.[44]

The next centre of controversy was South Derbyshire where the Liberals chose a member of the Haig distilling family to stand against the Tory brewer MP, Gretton. The Liberals argued, first, that, although he opposed 'popular control', he was prepared to do a good deal more for temperance reform than Gretton, and, secondly, that they 'had had great difficulties in obtaining a candidate' and 'were bound to have a wealthy candidate in the division'. The temperance Liberals, or at least a section of them, formed a Temperance Electoral Council and promoted an independent candidature until Haig finally announced his withdrawal on grounds of ill health.[45] Another conflict of this kind occurred in Edinburgh. At the South Edinburgh by-election in June 1899 the Liberals selected Arthur Dewar, a member of the famous whisky-manufacturing family. He indicated that he was 'favourable to a certain measure of popular control of the liquor traffic' and did indeed promise to vote for the Scottish Local Veto Bill. But the Executive of the Scottish Permissive Bill and Temperance Association refused to recommend him owing to his connection with the liquor traffic. However, at a meeting of temperance electors a resolution of support for him was carried by 28 to 11. Its mover, Wallace Ross, the secretary of the Free Church Temperance Association, said: 'They could not get many ideal men, and therefore they must just do the next best thing. . . . He had very great sympathy with the view of those who could not vote for a man directly or indirectly connected with the liquor traffic. This was a question of politics, and he thought it would not be wise, if they wanted Temperance legislation at all, to stick at a matter of that kind.' The temperance movement in Scotland was obviously deeply divided over what happened at South Edinburgh. The bitter recriminations went on for months afterwards in the correspondence columns of various temperance journals.[46]

The policy of voting for a brewer so long as he could be persuaded to make some gesture of sympathy with temperance reform was very controversial. Some saw safety as residing only in adherence to a fixed rule never to vote for anyone connected with the liquor traffic. Such a man should not be asked to give a pledge to vote against his own interest or to deprive himself of some or all of his income.

If he sees nothing morally wrong in obtaining income by such means, it is
unfair to him to ask him to give it up. He may not think that our policy will
have such an effect; but we hope that it will, nay, we believe that it will, and
we ask him to vote blindly for his own destruction. If he holds brewery
shares with the knowledge that the income derived from them is ill-gotten
gain, a man with such a moral twist in his character is not the man to be
entrusted with the duty of carrying out the aim of the U.K.A. . . . So long
as Temperance electors are invited to support candidates who are connected with the liquor traffic, so long will there be division in the Alliance
camp, and division means weakness. Temperance men as a rule possess
consciences, and in thousands of cases conscience will not allow a vote to be
recorded which, however remotely, countenances the liquor traffic.[47]

Such was the case against brewer candidates. It was predominantly
moral but with an element of practicality in its emphasis on the
divisive effect of any such candidature on the temperance movement.
The opposite point of view was essentially practical: if such men are
willing to lend their aid, then no questions need be asked about their
motivation. A fixed rule had been laid down by the Alliance Council
but was not universally observed. Division did not disappear as a
result of any attempt to enforce it but was usually only intensified.[48]

There were then certain limits beyond which it was hazardous for
the Liberals to press if they wished to maintain harmonious relations
with the temperance section of the party. But these limits were usually
very ambiguous and ill-defined, and a great part of the temperance
politics of the 1890s was bound up with efforts by the Liberals,
harassed by the drink trade whenever the drink question assumed
political prominence, to test how far they could safely go in extending the limits and modifying or blurring their commitment to the
cause of temperance reform. The Alliance had rules governing electoral conduct, but the practical operation of these depended almost
entirely on temperance people in the constituencies, and here, as the
history of the question of Liberal brewer candidates showed, there
was often an abundance of readiness to compromise and concede and
interpret the rules in a 'soft' or elastic way. The reasons for this are
three-fold: first, the involvement of many temperance enthusiasts in
local Liberal politics which made them concerned first and foremost
for Liberal unity and success and therefore disinclined to give serious
thought to ideas of 'breaking with Liberalism' unless extreme temperance demands were fully met; secondly, the local pressures which
were so strong in any electoral contest and against which very
general principles embodied in Council resolutions were of little

assistance; and, thirdly, the fact that Local Option was now official policy of the Liberal party and government and so *any* Liberal candidate could be regarded as acceptable, even if his own views on the temperance question might not bear close scrutiny, because his election would help on the day when the Liberals as a whole would have a majority and would be able to enact Local Option legislation.

The Grantham situation in 1894 is typical. When J. B. Thornley, the District Superintendent, went to investigate why the local temperance people had accepted a candidate as thoroughly unsatisfactory as Earp, he discovered that 'the leading men in the Dissenting Churches, in the Liberal Executive, and in the Temperance League have thrown every other consideration to the winds, save that of *Party*.' The temperance section was very small, only about 130, but only 20 of these would sign a pledge not to vote for any candidate who did not support the government's Bill. 'There are so many prejudices arising from considerations of party feeling and miserable selfishness, that have first to be broken down.' When John Newton, another Superintendent, went to see the Liberal Chief Whip to urge him to get Earp replaced by someone 'who would unite all sections of the party', he had to be careful not to let Ellis know how few temperance electors were actually pledged to do anything if such action were not carried out.[49]

At West Dorset in the by-election of May 1895 the 'Independent Farmers' candidate, G. Wood Homer, was proposed by the Rev. G. T. Turnbull, 'one of the best Temperance workers in the constituency' and a member of the Alliance in spite of Homer's refusal to go further than a pledge of neutrality on the Veto Bill.[50]

It is clear that in the general election of 1895 quite a few very weak pledges or evasive pronouncements were accepted from Liberal candidates simply because they were Liberals and temperance people were anxious to do all they could to secure the re-election of a Liberal government in view of the Liberal leaders' commitment to Veto legislation. A good example of this is Bolton. Both seats at Bolton had been held by Conservatives since 1885. However, there appeared to be a good chance that the Liberals could gain one of them in 1895. Since the 1860s temperance had not been a popular issue with the working-men of Bolton, but there was a strong local teetotal 'party'.[51] As was usual in such a situation, the Liberal candidates tried to evade or fudge the issue, so as to offend neither side. The views of the Liberal candidate in 1895, G. Harwood, were far from clear or satisfactory, but there was strong pressure on the

Liberal temperance men to come to an understanding with him and so not frustrate this crucial Liberal bid to gain a seat. Finally Harwood gave a deputation from the Bolton Temperance Union an unofficial assurance that he would vote for the second reading of the Veto Bill but reserved the right to move amendments in committee and vote against the third reading if these were not adopted. The temperance people then decided that this was sufficient to earn him their endorsement. Their suspicions ought to have been aroused by the fact that two hours after giving the assurance Harwood, probably in a mood of panic, wrote a private note to their president requesting him to give no publicity to what he had said. Even this was agreed to. The *Alliance News* later made a sarcastic comment on the whole affair:

it [Harwood's concession] had one striking effect—it enabled the Temperance Union to vote Liberal without breaking the letter of their bond. . . . The Temperance Union had been straining, as it were, on the leash, ardently longing to vote for Mr. Harwood, and now the buckle had broken and they were free. And very much pleased they were accordingly.

So was Harwood. He won the seat, one of the few Liberal gains in 1895, and was to hold it until his death in 1912. But hardly was the election over before he became the first Liberal MP to speak out in favour of 'dropping the Veto'. He denied having made any compact in 1895 and declared total war on all Local Veto legislation. Bitter were the recriminations against the spineless conduct of the Bolton Temperance Union whose president could only assure an angry Alliance meeting that 'the Temperance party of Bolton would not be cajoled next time. (Hear, hear.)' There was not to be a next time.[52]

In some constituencies temperance people seemed prepared to put up with almost anything. Thomas Hardy claimed that they had accepted Fulford's nominee, Warner, at Lichfield in February 1896 simply because their leaders could not face 'being left off the Liberal committees and in other ways boycotted' if they resorted to action against him.[53] At the Alliance Council meeting in October 1896 T. P. Whittaker denounced these men as 'craven cowards' and persuaded the Council to pass a resolution which urged upon supporters 'increasing vigilance and steadfastness in refusing political support to any Parliamentary candidate who may decline to vote for' Local Option.[54]

Bolton was not the only place where failure to insist on definite pledges led to trouble later. In 1896 a bitter dispute erupted between J. E. Johnson-Ferguson, Liberal member for Loughborough, and his Liberal Association's Executive where teetotal influence was very strong. He had begun openly to take the side of the publicans. Investigation showed that the Temperance Liberals had accepted him far too readily in 1895 on the basis of some very vague and weak statements.[55] The problem at places such as Loughborough was that the temperance party had been too strong and as a result had 'captured' Liberalism with the consequence that it tended too easily to assume an identity of interests between the Liberal party and the temperance cause. The temperance factor in politics was likely to remain most independent where it was neither so predominant as to be able to acquire virtual control of, and therefore identification with, the local Liberal party nor so weak as to be safely ignored by Liberal candidates.

When the Liberals gained South Norfolk in May 1898, an immense amount of assistance was given to their candidate, A. W. Soames, by local temperance people. Yet a day or two before the poll he said that he had never been a supporter of the Local Veto. What transpired was that he was being supported because he was remembered to have endorsed it in 1892. But when some research was done into this, it was discovered that even then he had been very evasive and had actually preferred elected licensing boards, a version of the hated alternative of regulation. As so often, Soames was being supported as the 'better man', his opponent being backed fully by the liquor trade.[56] The vigour of the endorsement given to Conservative candidates in the 1890s by 'the trade' naturally made temperance people all the readier to work and vote for Liberals no matter how vague might be the latter's professions of sympathy with the temperance cause. Liberal candidates knew this and exploited it. For example, at York in January 1898 Sir Christopher Furness was a far from satisfactory candidate, but when the licensed victuallers announced that they would support his Conservative opponent, Lord Charles Beresford, the report in the *Alliance News* read simply: 'Sir Christopher Furness is therefore likely to get the Temperance vote.'[57]

There can be no doubt that many Liberal politicians longed to see the end of the drink question as a prominent issue in politics. The identification of the Liberal party with the Local Option meant that, whether they personally favoured that reform or not, they were subjected at every election to all the formidable antagonistic pressures that the public-house interest could bring to bear. At least in 1894 and 1895 the Liberal government did try to legislate on the question so as to clear it out of the political arena, but after the electoral débâcle of 1895 there was no prospect of any such legislation being proposed by a government, let alone enacted, for many years to come, and so a Liberal 'revolt against the Veto' began to gather momentum.

Liberal candidates often found themselves in an intolerable dilemma, torn between the conflicting pressures of the drink interest and the temperance movement and continually uncertain which it would be the less hazardous to offend. The agony was particularly acute in marginal seats where even a few votes could make a great deal of difference and candidates and their agents had to indulge in the finest calculations as to which side carried the bigger electoral guns and was more in need of being appeased. For example, Pontefract was a very marginal seat which the Conservatives won in 1892 by only 40 votes (1·8 per cent.). At the by-election in February 1893 the Liberal candidate gained the seat by 63 votes but only after having wobbled on the drink question right through the campaign and said quite different things to temperance and licensed victuallers' deputations. The Liberals at Pontefract were reported to be 'very much afraid of any mention of the Temperance question; the malting and brewing interest is very strong there'.[58]

It is not surprising that Liberal candidates increasingly did their very best to ensure that the temperance question was not mentioned at elections so that as little provocation as possible might be offered to the drink interest. Determined efforts were often made by them and their campaign managers to keep the question suppressed. The Alliance was not deterred by this, however. It recognised that, in order to attract the non-Gladstonian temperance voter to the cause of the Local Option candidate, it still needed to mount some kind of independent campaign and not leave everything in the hands of the Liberal politicians. When the Liberals began to manifest a disposition to turn Local Option into a non-issue at election contests, these efforts simply needed to be reinforced. Thus Liberal candidates who tried to ignore the question found that the Alliance and other temperance organisations went ahead and poured workers into the constituencies in order to make it an issue.

In October 1894 at Birkenhead W. H. Lever was the Liberal candidate but was also 'adopted candidate of the Temperance party' who then ran an entirely separate campaign on his behalf.[59] By this time Liberal party managers were often not at all anxious to have the prohibitionist sympathies of candidates publicised. At the Alliance Council meeting in the same month a delegate from Nottingham said that, when he helped to bring forward the man who was subsequently adopted as Liberal candidate in his constituency, the local 'wire-pullers' tried to suppress the fact that this man was a prohibitionist in case it should jeopardise his selection. 'Now, that was going on in more than one constituency', he added.[60]

One of the most disappointing by-election results experienced by the Rosebery government was the loss of Brigg, a normally Liberal seat, by a margin of 77 votes in December 1894. Some Liberal leaders blamed the government's Veto Bill for this setback, but the Alliance pointed out that the Liberal candidate, H. J. Reckitt, and his agent had done their very best to play down the temperance question and highlight other issues. An Alliance agent was given 'the cold shoulder' when he interviewed them. Reckitt asked that no temperance literature be issued on his behalf. The Alliance's representatives nevertheless worked hard for him, 'but', claimed the *Alliance News*, 'with a freer hand and less restraint from the party leaders more might have been accomplished, and the result of the election would probably have been much different to what it is'.[61] The Alliance was so angered at what happened at Brigg that the Executive sent a letter of complaint to Tom Ellis, the Liberal Chief Whip. He expressed regrets, but when other agents sent in reports of similar unsympathetic receptions by Liberal managers Whyte, Lawson, and Whittaker went along as a deputation to see Ellis on the subject. All that Ellis seemed able to do was to give the following advice to temperance workers: 'Don't worry about speaking at Liberal meetings, but hold your own meetings and use every influence in your power.'[62] This was in effect the independent but parallel campaigning which the temperance people had already engaged in at Birkenhead. Such advice was sensible, for Ellis must have recognised that the enthusiasm of the temperance reformers was not something that the Liberals could simply turn on and off like a tap and expect to suppress itself whenever it was convenient to them that it should be suppressed.[63]

The situation continued to deteriorate. In the by-elections at Oxford and Mid-Norfolk in April 1895 the Veto Bill was kept in the background and as far as possible hidden away by the candidates and their agents. An attempt was made to do the same at East Leeds, but in the end the candidate, T. R. Leuty, decided that he should make the question more prominent because he needed temperance support. On 10 May the *Alliance News* devoted an editorial to the very peculiar behaviour of some Liberal candidates:

whilst knowing the need of all the help they can get, they have sometimes done all they could to throw the cold blanket upon a very valuable portion of it. Belonging to the Liberal party, they hold themselves bound to accept its programme in full; and yet whilst engaging to support each plank contained in it, and to receive help from each plank's special upholders, they regard some one or more of the planks with so cold an eye as if it were 'like some near related guest, who may not rudely be dismissed,' yet who is sadly in the way, and would thankfully be got rid of. . . .
In more than one recent instance the agents and friends of the Alliance have found themselves received by a candidate pledged to vote for the Veto Bill—or if not by the candidate in person, yet by some prominent election agent or leading local friend of his—as if they were rather his enemies than his friends. They receive assurances that his election will secure a vote for the Government and its Veto Bill, but at the same time they are exhorted in the name of heaven to say as little as possible about it. They are begged not to encumber the candidate with any help except such as shall be inaudible and invisible. . . . In Mid-Norfolk and in Oxford, for example, the friends of the Alliance were received by the Liberal candidates or their leaders as shyly and as though they were conspirators unsafe to talk aloud or walk abroad. Any attempt to speak out what they had come to say was deprecated and, as far as possible, suppressed.[64]

Constituencies seemed frightened now to have anything to do with men who were publicly identified with the Alliance. W. S. Caine had been Liberal member for East Bradford from 1892 to 1895, but his loss of the seat was widely attributed to his particularly conspicuous and well-publicised Alliance connections. Late in 1896 the Conservative member died and a by-election was to be held. But Caine was not the Liberal candidate. He received a letter from the secretary of the East Bradford Liberal 200, saying that there was on its executive

a very strong feeling that it would be at once unfair to yourself and to the constituency to ask you to come forward. At the root of this feeling is the belief that you would inevitably in East Bradford produce a combination in the opposition camp which we could not at the present time hope to defeat, and as one speaker put it, your very strength would be a source of weakness to the party.

When Caine offered to come to help the new Liberal candidate, he was warned off. His presence 'would rouse the demons'. Caine was especially aggrieved not to be invited to come even by the candidate, A. Billson, 'my oldest political friend, who was election agent in my two first election contests at Liverpool'. He then retaliated by publishing statistical analyses purporting to prove that in 1895 men prominently linked with the Alliance had done better than other Liberal candidates. Billson himself did not know how far he could safely go in suppressing the question. According to Henry Hibbert, the area Superintendent for the Alliance, he at first told him: 'If you wish me to win this seat, in my judgment your best policy is to be quiet.' Then later he came to Hibbert and begged him to put out a manifesto calling on the Alliance's friends to vote for him. He was defeated but seemed to have learned his lesson, for several months later, when he was candidate at Halifax, he asked for Alliance help, was given it in abundance, and won the seat easily.[65]

Constant vigilance was required. In September 1897 the Alliance Executive received a report that S. Moss, the Liberal candidate at East Denbighshire, had declared in favour of the Veto and against Compensation but was referring to neither subject in his address and speeches. The Executive at once gave instructions for the holding of meetings and demonstrations in the constituency in support of the Veto, and a week later news arrived that the question was now well to the front.[66]

In the majority of cases down to 1900 the Liberal candidates supported the Veto and the other points in the Alliance programme and such disputes as did arise mainly concerned the emphasis given to this commitment in the candidate's campaigns. However, it was the minority of hostile candidates who were really important, for the Alliance knew that if they were permitted to get away with their opposition the floodgates could well be opened to the large numbers of candidates who were harassed by the electoral efforts of 'the trade' and felt coerced into adherence to the Alliance programme. Every by-election in which a conspicuously antagonistic Liberal was standing became a test case, a trial of strength between the Alliance and those forces in the Liberal party who were working for the abandonment or 'shelving' of the post-1891 commitment to securing popular control over the liquor traffic. In addition every effort had to be made to make Liberal MPs who looked like reneging on their support for this part of the Liberal programme feel that they were thereby courting electoral disaster. An early example of an MP who became the target for this sort of pressure was Hugh Hoare, member for Chesterton (West Cambridgeshire). An intensive campaign was mounted in the villages in his constituency to get motions of no confidence in him passed by meetings of temperance electors.[67]

The movement to 'shelve the Veto' became serious after the 1895 elections. The initial Alliance reaction was to try to prove to the Liberals that the Veto was not the main cause of their great election defeat, but some thought was given to what should be done if the Liberals should nevertheless decide that it was and proceed to abandon it. At the Council meeting in October 1895 Charles Roberts urged preparation of a campaign to persuade supporters to 'consecrate their votes to the promotion of Temperance reform' should this happen.[68] When G. Harwood, member for Bolton, spoke out against the Veto, there was much talk of initiating electoral action to make his constituency position untenable.

Alliance leaders claimed that during the first year or so after the 1895 elections the Liberal party managers deliberately put forward a series of anti-Veto candidates in an effort to assess how far it was electorally safe to go in shelving the Veto commitment.[69] At some by-elections, such as Lichfield, the temperance electors appeared to be thoroughly spineless and prepared to accept almost any insult. At others, for example Brixton in January 1896, abstention campaigns were initiated and were claimed to have contributed to the candidate's defeat. This resort to recommendations of abstention was an ominous development in that it indicated that Liberals now felt indifferent enough to temperance electoral strength to be prepared to risk selecting a candidate who was not sound on the Veto. It also seemed to demonstrate that at the stage of candidate-selection temperance influence was no longer what it had once been. As early as 1894 E. C. Brambley had warned of the dangerous consequences of the 'indisposition on the part of so many of their friends to go inside those parties who had the selection of the candidates'. But he was attacked by other delegates to the Council when he proposed that something be done about this.[70] A new organisation formed in December 1896, the London Teetotal Federation and Advocates' League, issued a manifesto setting out an electoral policy that explicitly condemned abstention from voting as 'futile and cowardly, and injurious to the Temperance cause, for when suggested it invariably indicates that our voting strength has not been properly organised'. Its own policy was to bring full influence 'to bear at the *right moment* upon the representative Associations entitled to select candidates'. Temperance advocates should not allow their principles 'to be ignored during the preliminary stages of selection, and then expect, by inconsequential threats, to achieve your object'.[71]

Whether militant electoral action based on organised abstentions was any longer a practicable strategy for the temperance movement was extremely doubtful. The setting up of the Teetotal Federation was evidence of a rift in the London temperance 'party' over this issue. The London Auxiliary at its annual meeting in January 1897 passed a resolution endorsing a policy of abstention from voting for unsatisfactory candidates. This seems to have been inspired by the Brixton by-election which gave some London temperance enthusiasts a new taste for electoral militancy and led one of them to write: 'One thing is clear: We in London must prepare ourselves to fight the Liberal official leaders, tooth and nail, at every bye-election at which they may attempt to repeat the Brixton experiment.'[72] But the Alliance could scarcely be said to have an electoral policy any more. Temperance electoral organisation in the constituencies had withered to such an extent that any strategy was now certain, if formulated, to prove virtually unenforceable. At the Alliance Council meeting in October 1897 John Kempster called for 'more definite direction' in this area 'so that the Tory and Liberal parties may know that they have a well-organised and determined power to meet at the next general election'.[73] But the time for such effective independence was now past. The temperance question was now the Liberals'—or it was nobody's. If the Liberals should choose to amend, shelve, or give up their commitment, it was unlikely that the Alliance any longer possessed enough independent electoral leverage to be able to counteract such a decision. The Liberal party had only to act decisively on the conviction that 'the supporters of the Temperance party being Liberals would have voted for the Liberal interest, Local Veto or no Local Veto',[74] and the Alliance's bluff would almost certainly be called.

From the beginning of 1898 by-elections exposed the decayed condition of temperance electoral policy and organisation and thus made it virtually inevitable that before very long a Liberal leader would persuade his colleagues to defy the Alliance's alleged electoral power and undertake a fundamental reconsideration of Liberal temperance policy. This was unlikely as long as Sir William Harcourt remained Liberal leader, for he was the architect of the Bills of 1894 and 1895 and felt himself committed to the cause. But he resigned in December 1898. His successor was Sir Henry Campbell-Bannerman who took the line increasingly favoured by Scottish Liberals of supporting their own Local Veto Bill, which seemed to have a better chance of being enacted, and not worrying too much about the wider campaign for the Veto in England as well. Even more important was the accession to the office of Chief Whip of Herbert Gladstone following Tom Ellis's death early in 1899. Gladstone had become the chief advocate of 'shelving the Veto' and attempting to promote more immediate and generally acceptable temperance legislation.[75]

The extreme electoral disorganisation and impotence of the temperance movement in many constituencies by this time is well illustrated by an account of the York by-election of January 1898 given by Ambrose Bramley, a former secretary of the York Auxiliary. He was a man who could remember former more militant days and now felt that all that militancy seemed to have been to no avail. He began by admitting that, although the Liberal candidate, Sir Christopher Furness, gave no pledge to the Alliance deputation and refused to avow himself a supporter of the Veto, he did indicate in answering questions that he supported various lesser principles of temperance reform.

Now all these things are very good, so far as they go, and as Lord C. Beresford declared himself opposed to the Veto and all similar legislation, twenty years ago we should have been justified in rallying round the Liberal candidate as the best of the two. But has not the principle been affirmed and re-affirmed year after year at the annual Councils of the U.K.A. that the Alliance can give its support to no candidate who is not prepared, at the least, to vote for the measure then before the country, whether under the name of Direct Veto or Local Option? We have therefore been in a peculiar position in York. (1) The Liberal candidate, in neither election address nor speech, has declared himself a supporter of the Veto. (2) Not a single leaflet, pamphlet, or placard, amongst the thousands with which the city has been flooded by the Liberal committee, has alluded to the Veto or stated that the candidate would support it. (3) Of the few Temperance Liberals who have spoken for Sir C. Furness at his meetings, not one has mentioned the Veto. (4) The speeches of Unionists, and placards, etc., issued by that party, are all the evidence we have that Sir C. Furness is a supporter of the Veto. Such evidence is, however, discounted by the fact that at nearly every meeting some speaker or other has taunted him with his silence on this question. As for the deputation previously referred to, if its object was to induce Sir C. Furness to declare himself fully and openly, it was foredoomed to failure, so many of its members having already in public meetings pledged their support to him, as a Liberal, and intending to support him whatever his attitude towards the Veto. This was not the way we proceeded in bygone days, when the Temperance party was a real power in this city. But in no sense can the Veto be said to be a factor in this election. No meeting of Temperance electors was summoned, and no one authorised to issue a manifesto, or speak on behalf of the Temperance party. In fact, as a party, it may be considered to have fallen to pieces. The Liberal Temperance voters generally supported their party's candidate. Many of the Unionist Temperance men supported their party man. But not a few of them, including myself (though I have voted and worked for the Liberal candidates for twenty years), stood aloof, and let the party men fight their own battle; whilst the great number of independent electors, bound by no ties of party, and to whom we have appealed with so much effect in past years, were left to drift hither and thither, some of whom, to my knowledge, not voting at all [*sic*].[76]

Trouble arose next at the West Staffordshire by-election in May 1898. Staffordshire had long been a difficult area for the temperance movement, and this was not the first by-election there in which the Alliance found itself forced into militant action after the selection of an unsatisfactory Liberal candidate.[77] On this occasion, the candidate was W. Adams, a Primitive Methodist who was opposed to the Veto and was pronounced acceptable by the licensed victuallers. The Alliance put considerable pressure on him to change his views but without avail. Therefore a manifesto was issued calling on temperance voters to abstain. It declared:

In the present election we are witnessing the evolution of a plot to reduce the Liberal party to the same abject position [as the Unionists], and a section of this party has been already captured, and is toiling under the whip of its captors to bring the rest of the party into subjection to the monopolists. . . . They calculate that the mass of Christian and Temperance men are so half-hearted or so stupid that they will vote for their political party whatever action it may take with respect to temperance reform.

Some Liberal subscribers to the Alliance were so offended by this that they discontinued their subscriptions. Adams lost, but since West Staffordshire was a Liberal Unionist stronghold this was not unexpected. Part of the temperance indignation may have stemmed from the fact that it was in West Staffordshire that the Rev. Prebendary Grier had been so active in the 1880s and early 1890s in trying to develop temperance electoral organisation. When the seat was last contested in 1892, the Liberal candidate had been someone strongly identified with the Alliance—John Kempster. He had been introduced by Grier when it seemed as if, as in 1886 and again in 1895, West Staffordshire would elect Hamar Bass unopposed. But by 1898 Grier was dead, and the choice of Adams exemplified the extinction of that temperance militancy which had been so dependent on Grier's own personal energy and appeal. Kempster had done very badly in 1892, winning only 35·5 per cent. of the vote. Adams, significantly, did much better, winning 10 per cent. more. The turn-out of voters was actually 4 per cent. higher than in 1892 when a specifically temperance candidate had been standing. These statistics cast considerable doubt on the effectiveness of the Alliance's call for abstention from voting.[78]

The following month produced another challenge to the Alliance —the City of Durham by-election. Durham was a highly marginal seat. The conservatives had won it in 1885 and 1886, but the Liberals had gained it in 1892 by 75 votes (3·6 per cent.) and held on in 1895 by only 3 (0·2 per cent.). The Liberal candidate in June 1898, H. F. Boyd, was an opponent of the Veto. The Alliance therefore organised a campaign to get temperance voters to abstain, and when Boyd lost by 65 votes (2·8 per cent.) many Liberals were disposed to blame the Alliance. The emotional atmosphere was heightened both by the fact that Boyd collapsed and died just after the election, worn out by his exertions,[79] and by the advice that some temperance militants, notably E. Tennyson Smith, gave to their supporters to go further than abstention and actually vote for the Liberal Unionist in order to make Boyd's defeat more certain. Since Boyd did show some sympathy for temperance reform and his opponent was given the support of the liquor interest, this action was highly controversial and was vigorously condemned by the veteran Thomas Whittaker. Whether many did abstain or change sides is not clear. Turn-out was almost the same as it had been in 1895, and the seat stayed with the Liberal Unionists in 1900 and at every election thereafter down to the First World War. But the appearance was of the loss of a seat to a 'representative of the liquor party' as the result of Alliance electoral action. This exposed a serious rift within the temperance movement.[80]

By this stage the Alliance leaders had evolved a 'plot' theory to explain the growing electoral resistance to the Veto. According to this, in the mid-1890s Fulford, Warner, Hoare, and a few other anti-Veto Liberals had, with the tacit approval of Herbert Gladstone, embarked on a deliberate campaign to destroy the morale and expose the electoral impotence of the temperance party by putting up anti-Veto candidates at by-elections and showing how many Liberals, including alleged temperance supporters, were still prepared to vote for them.

For a time the issue seemed doubtful. It appeared as if the staunch adherents of the movement were too few or too supine to form a sufficiently powerful electoral force to check the progress of disintegration in the party. Men of whom better things were to be expected were induced, on the strength of promises on the Temperance question which were vague and useless, to give the whole of their strength in support of men who had been selected as Liberal candidates mainly in order that they might break the power of the Temperance party in the constituencies.

Therefore the Alliance finally decided to fight back and recommend abstention from voting for anti-Veto candidates. Durham proved that this policy worked and that Liberals who turned against the Veto incurred the risk of electoral defeat.[81]

Down to 1895 Alliance electoral policy had been relatively easy to determine and to maintain. It was based on adherence to whatever was the form of prohibitory legislation favoured at the time by the Alliance—the Permissive Bill, Local Option, the Direct or Popular Veto. 1895 was the turning-point, when the election indicated that public opinion was far from ready for prohibition along these lines and that it was futile to continue to insist exclusively on this particular form of temperance legislation. After 1895 there was a growing volume of support, not just in the Liberal party but also in the temperance movement itself, for concentration on working for other temperance reforms which fell short of the Veto demand but might have a considerably greater chance of being enacted. The Alliance's aim had always been to achieve prohibition and it had steadfastly refused to allow itself to be diverted from that objective or to support reforms which involved the regulation of the liquor traffic and therefore implied condoning its continued existence. But by 1898 rigid adherence to the doctrine that support for the Direct Veto was the only acceptable temperance policy which a Liberal candidate could hold was alienating the Alliance not only from many of the Liberal sympathisers on whom it now ultimately depended for any legislative action but also from the large numbers of temperance reformers who longed for something practical to be done about the evil of drink. It now seemed madness to manipulate tiny numbers of voters, as at Durham, to ensure the defeat of a man pledged to some form of temperance legislation by one who was totally opposed, especially when it was all for the sake of a measure which was manifestly highly unpopular and could clearly not be enacted for many years to come. Enthusiasts such as Tennyson Smith talked of persuading temperance voters to abstain or even vote Conservative as 'a question of tactics, adopted in order to defeat the policy of a section of the Liberal party which advocates dropping the Veto'.[82] This assumed that 'dropping the Veto' was merely the game of a malevolent group of conspirators in the Liberal party and that temperance people who hesitated to take electoral steps to defeat them were their dupes or victims. Such an interpretation entirely ignored the wider political realities of the situation and the fact that the hesitations of Liberals and temperance people about now enforcing support of the Veto on candidates were based fundamentally on awareness of the absence of general political and popular enthusiasm for that policy.

At its meeting in October 1898 the Alliance Council passed a resolution calling on temperance electors to decline to vote for any candidate who would not give a clear pledge to vote for a Local Veto. The speakers in support of it mostly dwelt in cloud-cuckoo land. Leif Jones admitted that, when he asked 'a leading political organiser of one of the great parties' what he thought of the temperance elector, the reply was, ' "The Temperance elector is a very uncertain quantity." ' But Jones's response to this was to ask delegates to let the politicians know that 'there is a strong compact body of opinion, the votes of which they can have if they will grant the reforms for which we are asking, but which they can get on no other condition'. Thomas Whittaker, in his last appearance at the Alliance Council, opposed the resolution. He favoured voting for the better party and candidate and condemned 'inundating the constituencies with men from a distance to work out a certain theory'.[83]

The unwillingness of local temperance people to support coercive action in any significant numbers against 'unsatisfactory' Liberal candidates was further exemplified by the North Norfolk by-election of March 1899. The Alliance recommended that no temperance support be given to Sir Brampton Gurdon, the Liberal candidate in this seat where the Liberals were defending an 1895 majority of 508 (6·4 per cent.). But a local temperance party meeting passed a resolution condemning this advice, while George White, one of the temperance and Nonconformist leaders in Norfolk for many years, said that, since the Conservative was a great deal worse than Gurdon and was connected with the hotel business, he would do all he could to promote Gurdon's return and hope that he would vote right in Parliament. The local Nonconformist ministers liked Gurdon's views on disestablishment and mostly gave him their support. Not only did Gurdon win, but his majority was nearly 8 per cent. higher than that obtained in 1895 and the turn-out of voters rose by 3·2 per cent. It looked as if the Alliance's call to abstain had been completely ignored. The *Alliance News* was furious and resorted once again to the 'conspiracy' theory.

... the effort that is being made is to render the Liberal party as completely subject to the liquor interest as the Unionist party has for a considerable time been; and Liberal candidates, like Sir B. Gurdon, and Temperance electors who vote for such candidates are, whatever their motives or objects, the instruments of a conspiracy, having for its object the political ruin of the Temperance party and the indefinite postponement of *all* effective Temperance legislation.

[Abstention] would at any rate have been a proclamation to those Liberals who are eagerly watching for an opportunity and excuse to eliminate Local Veto from the party programme, that they could not secure the votes of Liberal Temperance reformers without paying the proper price for them. As it is the North Norfolk electors have lent colour, if not strength, to the contention of the malcontents within the Liberal party, that the Liberal Temperance men will be sure to vote for Liberal candidates, even though they deny the ordinary demands of the Temperance voters, provided, of course, some show is made of conceding 'Temperance' legislation. We need only further mention that the liquor monopolists were looking on and playing a game of their own, which is somehow to manipulate the situation so as to induce the Temperance electors in two or three successive contests to act after the fashion of those at Norfolk, before offering such instances to the Liberal party managers as proof positive that the Temperance people, to all intents and purposes place considerations of party before those of principle, and that being the case the party might now safely ignore them and back down on its former professions in the matter of advanced Temperance legislation.[84]

A few months later subscribers to this theory were given what they believed to be startling confirmation of its accuracy by events which took place in the Osgoldcross constituency. Osgoldcross was a strongly Liberal seat in the West Riding of Yorkshire which had been held since 1886 by Sir John Austin. After 1895 a serious rift developed between Austin and the local Liberal Association. Temperance was not his only ground of offence, but what brought matters to a head was a vote of censure which the Association passed following his opposition in Parliament to the Scottish Local Veto Bill in 1898. When this occurred, Austin resigned and stood for re-election as a member for Osgoldcross with the support of one section of the Liberal Association. The anti-Austin faction formed itself into a separate Liberal and Radical Association. The Alliance claimed that Austin's resignation and bid for re-election were unnecessary and represented a new move in the anti-Veto 'conspiracy'. Although Austin had quarrelled with one section of the local Liberals on many issues, the Veto was elevated into the main issue on which he sought the verdict of his constituents. The Alliance was almost certain to be the loser whatever its response. If it ran its own candidate, Austin was the probable winner because he would receive the support not only of the local Conservatives but also of many Liberals for reasons quite unconnected with the Veto. But if he was left alone and was re-elected unopposed, this would be held to prove that the 'temperance party' was now so impotent electorally that it was unable to do anything about even a challenge to the Veto as provocative and unequivocal as this one. What tipped the balance between these unpalatable options was the fact that what was also involved was a bid by Austin to determine who was master in local Liberal politics. The Liberal and Radical Association responded to the challenge by nominating Charles Roberts to stand against Austin. Roberts had been Liberal candidate for Wednesbury in 1895 and was later to be Liberal member for Lincoln. But in 1898, although he stood as a Liberal and Radical candidate, he placed the Veto first in his campaign and it quickly became the leading issue. The Alliance poured in aid on his behalf. Both Caine and Lawson addressed meetings in support of his candidature. It turned out that this was yet another case in which temperance people had weakly accepted an anti-Veto candidate in 1895 just because he was a supporter of the Liberal government and were now told by him that he was in no way breaking any pledge by voting against the Veto. The result was a victory for Austin who defeated Roberts by 5,818 to 2,893. Both sides claimed the moral victory. Austin and the anti-Vetoists saw the result as a decisive popular verdict against the Veto. The Alliance analysed the figures and argued that, since obviously the Conservative vote went entirely to Austin, Roberts must have taken just over half the Liberal vote. This was taken to prove that in any future straight fight with a Tory a Liberal candidate would have to support the Veto. Austin was admitted to be popular locally and to have gained some votes from 'credulous' temperance people after he had announced that he would follow any lead given by Campbell-Bannerman on temperance legislation.[85]

Osgoldcross might not prove much one way or the other, but what was now unmistakable were the cries for relief issuing from harassed Liberal candidates. In July 1899 the Liberals were defeated at East St. Pancras, and their candidate, B. F. C. Costelloe, gave an interview to the *Westminster Gazette* in which he blamed this result on 'the influence of the liquor trade on the slum vote':

I am firmly persuaded that this is one of the most serious questions with

which the country at large is confronted at the present time—the growth in
power of the liquor trade as a political organisation, employed not for
political ends, but from purely sectional and interested motives.
My experience in East St. Pancras, both during the recent contest and at
the last General Election, has convinced me that this is the question of
questions to which Liberals must address themselves if they are ever to
exercise their legitimate influence and obtain their proper representation in
the councils of the nation. . . . Here you have an enormously powerful
organisation throwing the whole of its influence from purely interested
motives into one scale and against one party because that party alone
threatens to deal effectively with the giant evil upon which the trade in
question subsists. . . . unless Liberals take active steps to put an end to a
state of things so deplorable, the outlook for the party is very dark indeed.
. . . I think there can be no doubt that Sir William Harcourt committed a
tactical error in placing Local Veto in the forefront of the Liberal programme. That measure is regarded by the trade as nothing less than Prohibition and confiscation, and has increased a thousandfold the virulence of
their opposition to the party in consequence. So much so, indeed, that,
ardent Temperance reformer as I am, I firmly believe the anti-liquor cause
would benefit if some mode of attack could be devised which excited less
furious hostility on the part of the trade.

Costelloe urged that an attempt be made to take the question out of
party politics by discovering some minimum amount of reform on
which there was general agreement.[86]

The answer was very shortly provided—as many Liberals were expecting and hoping that it would be—by the publication of the Report
of the Royal Commission on the Licensing Laws, set up in April 1896
under the chairmanship of Lord Peel.[87] This Report rejected the
Local Veto, at least for England, but did suggest some other quite
sweeping reforms including a considerable reduction of the number
of licenses with compensation paid out of funds provided by the
trade itself, not the taxpayer. T. P. Whittaker and W. S. Caine, who
had both been members of the Commission, decided to make an all-
out effort to rally the Liberal party and the temperance movement
behind the Peel proposals and so ensure that at last there was a good
chance of some practical reform being accomplished. But this meant
an indefinite postponement of the Local Veto for England. Some
temperance leaders consequently saw Whittaker and Caine as
'traitors', and the movement was torn apart by bitter recriminations
and controversy. In the process the last pretensions of the Alliance
to have a coherent and credible electoral policy were shattered.

The official electoral policy of the Alliance was support only for
candidates who were in favour of the Local Veto. The problem
which now arose was what was to be done about candidates who

went as far as the Peel proposals which were, after all, recommended by two of the Alliance's most respected leaders. At the Alliance Council meeting in October 1899 total silence reigned on the subject of electoral policy. Lawson asked that no resolution be moved reaffirming the Veto as the basis of electoral policy, and Kempster, who wished to move such a resolution, acquiesced most reluctantly, complaining that the result of the failure to make this pronouncement would be that 'many of our leaders will be disheartened throughout the country'.[88] The main division which now appeared was between the Alliance and the International Order of Good Templars in which Kempster was a prominent figure. The Good Templars continued to take a very hard line on electoral policy. In December J. M. Skinner, their Grand Electoral Superintendent, sent a circular to all district electoral superintendents reaffirming the Order's policy of not supporting any candidate who was not in favour of the Local Veto. A bitter dispute broke out between Kempster and Dawson Burns when Burns advocated leaving Alliance supporters to vote as they liked with regard to any candidate who opposed the Veto but favoured the Peel reforms.[89]

The Peel Report provided an admirable basis for a rapprochement between the Liberal party and its temperance adherents, and this proceeded to take place in many constituencies. Although he believed that the Peel recommendations went too far in some respects, Herbert Gladstone, the new Liberal Chief Whip, encouraged this trend because he saw an opportunity for splitting the temperance forces and destroying their electoral cohesiveness once and for all.[90] In Scotland candidates who endorsed Peel and agreed to vote for the Scottish Local Veto Bill were accepted by temperance people even if they could not support the full Local Veto policy.[91] In England many Liberal candidates took shelter behind the Peel Report and declined to give a pledge to Local Veto. In most cases they had no difficulty in receiving temperance endorsement. The great majority of temperance Liberals clearly wanted to be at peace with their party, and the Peel proposals provided an opportunity for this as welcome as had been the switch to the Local Option Resolution in the late 1870s. A good example of the new atmosphere in the constituencies is the following report sent to the Alliance Executive by F. Cowley, one of the superintendents, on the Liberal candidate for King's Lynn, F. Handel Booth:

When at Lynn this week I had an interview with Mr. Alfred Jermyn, J.P.

and others about Mr. H. Booth's position on a Direct Local Veto &c. Mr. Booth has not pledged himself either for or against, and will not at present; but contents himself, and satisfied local temperance friends by saying he is in favour of practical temperance legislation and would support legislative proposals submitted by his political party. He would support legislation on the lines of Lord Peel's Report.

Mr. Jermyn, Mr. Perry and others told me that the local Temperance party were satisfied with the assurances of Mr. Booth and cautioned me not to interfere or disturb them.

Our chat was of a most friendly character, as Mr. Jermyn is fully with our principles, but he is also a strong Liberal and wishes a change in the parliamentary representation.[92]

The virtual abandonment of an electoral policy based on the Direct Veto or other form of popular local vote on the question of liquor licenses was a break with a tradition which went back almost half a century. Not surprisingly, therefore, it met with some resistance and disagreement. For instance, it reawakened the slumbering embers of the feuds in the Sheffield temperance movement. On 30 November 1899 R. Clift Horner, Honorary Secretary of the Sheffield Auxiliary, wrote to Lawson assuring him of 'our unswerving adhesion to the Alliance Electoral policy, for we feel that this old policy is endangered by the agitation for Lord Peel's proposals'.[93] However, this proved to be a false rendering of the feelings of the members of the Auxiliary. At a special meeting held on 9 February 1900 to debate the Peel Report a motion calling for the retention of the Local Veto as the Alliance's electoral policy was rejected by 37 votes to 17, with 17 abstentions. The line-up was almost the same as that of the late 1880s: on the 'radical' side, in favour of the motion, G. W. Sharman and J. Thornley; on the 'moderate' side, opposing it, the Clegg family, F. P. Rawson, and H. J. Wilson, now MP for Holmfirth. The president, John Parker, two past presidents (G. W. Sharman and James Melling), a vice-president, and five members of the executive, then submitted their resignations because they declined to take responsibility for giving effect to 'a proposition which, in our judgement, is not in accordance with the constitution of the Alliance, and is an alteration of its electoral policy'.[94]

In a few places, extremists, especially people associated with the Good Templars, determined to carry on the fight for the Veto and nothing but the Veto. The trouble was that their wrath was now directed particularly at alleged 'traitors' within the temperance movement itself. W. S. Caine found himself harassed so much by the Good Templars in the Kilmarnock Boroughs that he withdrew from

his Liberal candidature there.[95] The Good Templars alone seemed
to wish to take an unequivocal line on electoral policy. Most other
temperance organisations were so worried by the potentially divisive
effects of the issue that they tried to ignore it and thus abandoned
any pretence of having a clear electoral policy. Temperance voters
were left in most places without specific guidance to vote as they
thought best. On the one hand, the old policy was not explicitly
given up, unless its advocates deliberately forced an attempt to
reaffirm it, as at Sheffield; on the other hand, no new policy was
explicitly defined. For example, the annual meeting of the Newcastle and Gateshead Auxiliary endorsed a resolution passed by its
Executive which included the following statement:

It is also unwise to define the attitude which the United Kingdom Alliance
should assume towards Parliamentary candidates with reference to this
particular proposal [reduction of licenses]. This Auxiliary is of opinion that
the declaration of an electoral policy by the United Kingdom Alliance,
which would allow Parliamentary candidates to shelve the Veto, would be
disastrous to the organisation.[96]

The electoral policy was seldom if ever rewritten, and attempts to
do this were usually rejected. The divergences within the movement
were fudged over. Thus an electoral policy was officially maintained
which many ignored in practice and which was clearly now quite
unenforceable and lacking in credibility. A façade of unity was preserved by trying to suppress controversial attempts to amend the
status quo. At the annual meeting of the National United Temperance Council, an 'umbrella' organisation, on 9 July 1900,
L. G. S. Gibbard sought to amend its constitution by deleting a
section binding it to refuse support for any candidate who declined
to support Local Veto and Sunday Closing and replacing this with
a new form of words, 'The Council will seek as far as possible to
obtain pledges from candidates to vote for these reforms'. This, he
said, was to enable support to be given to candidates who were in
favour of the numerous 'desirable reforms' in the Peel Report. W.
Sutherland of the Good Templars 'urged uncompromising adherence to the electoral platform of the organisation as it stood'. But
Lee Warner of Norfolk 'considered they would be committing
"political suicide" if they refused to support the candidates favourable to Temperance reforms, although they fell short of all they
required'. Nevertheless, Gibbard's proposal was decisively rejected.[97]

In practice, relations between the Liberal party and the temperance section were settled in a spirit of give and take far removed

from the dogmatic illusions of the advocates of 'uncompromising adherence' to the electoral policy based on the Veto. Herbert Gladstone helped to persuade J. E. Johnson-Ferguson, the member for Loughborough who had become so unacceptable to the local temperance Liberals, to move to another constituency, Burton-on-Trent, the very heart of the brewing industry.[98] In South Derbyshire Haig gave ill health as his excuse for abandoning his Liberal candidature, W. Bingham gave up his own temperance candidature, and the local temperance party, after some hesitation, decided to give full support to Haig's replacement, H. H. Raphael, against the Tory brewer, Gretton, even though Raphael went only as far as the Peel proposals and refused to pledge himself to the Local Veto.[99]

The general election of 1900 was largely overshadowed by the South African War. Temperance electoral militancy on behalf of a cause as manifestly unpopular and remote from practical realisation as the Local Veto would have been futile, even if a campaign to organise it had been attempted. Numerous Liberal candidates who promised to support legislation along the lines of the Peel Report were given temperance support. Instances of independent temperance electoral action were very rare. In Leeds efforts that were made to have temperance votes withheld from Herbert Gladstone were conspicuously unsuccessful.[100] More success was claimed at Middlesbrough and Christchurch. The Middlesbrough contest was most unusual. This seat was won, normally by large majorities, by Liberal or Liberal-Labour candidates at every election between 1885 and 1910—with one exception, 1900. The member since 1892 had been the Lib.-Lab., J. Havelock Wilson. He supported the Peel proposals but had greatly angered the local temperance people by going to Osgoldcross in 1899 to speak on behalf of Sir John Austin. In 1900 his Conservative opponent, Colonel S. A. Sadler, saw an opportunity to exploit this rift. He declared that he favoured the Local Veto and other temperance reforms, and, although his views were not completely clear or satisfactory, he was in the end given temperance endorsement. In 1895 in a straight fight with Wilson he had lost by 2,020 votes (17·6 per cent.). In 1900 in another straight fight Sadler won by 55 (0·4 per cent.). For this remarkable swing the temperance party claimed much of the credit, although Labour dissatisfaction with Wilson was probably the most important factor.[101]

Christchurch had been held by the Conservatives since 1885, always with small majorities. The Liberal candidate in 1900, as in 1895, was T. A. Brassey. His constantly wavering attitude on the temperance question was characteristic of that of many Liberals in very marginal seats where even a handful of votes could make all the difference. Brassey appears to have supported the Veto in 1892 (when a candidate at Epsom) and in 1895 but to have tried to evade the question thereafter and to have met with no resistance from the temperance Liberals when he did so. However, the Good Templars persuaded a few of their people to threaten to abstain. Brassey wavered right through the election campaign. He declared in favour of the Veto and then told the licensed victuallers' deputation that he favoured full compensation for publicans deprived of their licenses. On polling day about ten Good Templars were known to have abstained. Brassey lost by 8 votes.[102]

CHAPTER XIV

Labour and Irish Electoral Strategy

CHARTISM

As a movement the principal aim of which was to obtain the vote for non-voters, Chartism could not rely to any great extent on electoral techniques. Nor was the prospect of its demands being granted substantial enough to induce politicians to pay respect to it as an organisation representing *potential* electors. The major agitational methods resorted to by the Chartists were therefore non-electoral and traditional. Petitions were revealed as being now a singularly barren form of pressure on Parliament because unaccompanied either by the ability to call on force as an effective sanction if they were not acceded to or by the possibility of translating the signatures on them into votes which could be employed against the hostile parliamentarians at election time.

Nevertheless, electoral strategy does have a place even in the history of Chartism. In the first place, the Chartists did twice summon what they regarded as their own Parliaments, the Conventions of 1839 and 1842, and they conducted elections of delegates to these in what was almost a parody of the national electoral system. A similar electoral strategy related to 'anti-Parliaments' had been seen earlier in the Radicalism of the period after 1815.[1] Secondly, there were Chartist sympathisers who did possess the vote, and they were at times given an opportunity to use it in order to promote the interests of the movement. This was particularly the case in 1841 when there were Chartist-Tory alliances in some constituencies, the factor which linked them being antagonism to the new Poor Law. Some Tory candidates were said to have been elected partly with the aid of Chartist votes. The most celebrated example of this was the Nottingham by-election of April 1841 when John Walter gained the seat for the Conservatives with Chartist backing. He lost it again in the general election, but his by-election success encouraged some Chartist leaders to think in terms of a much more general strategy of using such electoral strength as they could muster to support the Tories in order to destroy the hated Whigs. Thomas Cooper claimed to have said to Walter: 'Don't have a wrong idea of why you are to have Chartist support. We mean to use your party to cut the throats of the Whigs, and then we mean to cut your throats also.' Feargus O'Connor took up the idea with great enthusiasm. He advised Chartists to vote Tory in the general election. His argument was that it was necessary to use all available means to prevent the Whigs from having another seven years in office and that a Tory Government was bound to be weaker and therefore anxious not to alienate any of the support that it had received. Bronterre O'Brien thought that this strategy was complete madness. The Tories if elected would be merciless to the Chartists. He believed it to be an immoral strategy as well. It made the Chartists the mere tools of the Tories. Undoubtedly there was some exploitation of it by the Tories: in Leicester, for instance, they paid some Chartists to attend the hustings and hold up their hands for the Tory candidate. This action seriously divided the Leicester Chartists, and, according to Gammage, it divided Chartists in many other places as well.

There were numerous Chartist candidatures, but only one Chartist candidate ever secured election to Parliament. This was Feargus O'Connor at Nottingham in 1847 when he stood in lieu of a second Tory candidate and John Walter headed the poll. Candidatures had to be linked to some broader movement of opinion in Tory or Radical politics to have any hope of succeeding. By far the most enterprising and imaginative form of electoral action which the Chartists engaged in was what was known as 'hustings candidatures'. In the nineteenth century nominations were called for at the hustings, an open public meeting. If there was more than one candidate nominated, then a show of hands was called for, and the candidate who received the largest number of votes by this count was declared elected. However, if any one of the candidates made a request for a poll, then a poll had to be held at which, unlike with the show of hands in which anyone who attended the meeting could take part, only registered voters could record a vote. Hustings elections afforded a unique opportunity for non-voters to make a dramatic and symbolic gesture concerning their electoral status. They could attend the hustings and put up their hands for a candidate of their choice and so by their numbers have him declared 'elected', only to have another candidate who had been in the minority on this occasion subsequently elected when the much smaller number of registered voters were able to have the final say. MPs could thus be shown to be unrepresentative of 'the people'.

Some Chartists wished to make this form of electoral strategy the corner-stone of their entire campaign and the solution to that most vexing of all their dilemmas, what to do when Parliament rejected their petitions. But, whereas action at the hustings was constitutional and a highly dramatic non-violent way of making a point, what some of them proposed then to do with the point involved the threat of violent revolution.

The Chartist leader principally associated with giving the scheme this wider application was Bronterre O'Brien. His plan, which he first elaborated in 1837, was that there should be a systematic nominating and electing of 'people's candidates' at the hustings, and that these 'MPs' should then present themselves at Westminster, accompanied by some of their unrepresented 'constituents', and claim the right to take their seats. Nothing was done along these lines in 1837, apart from a few hustings candidatures, but in 1839 O'Brien tried to persuade the Convention—without success—to adopt his plan and turn the local Chartist organisations into electoral bodies that would promote such candidatures at the next general election. George Julian Harney had a more clearly revolutionary plan. He proposed a great march on London following the election of hustings candidates who would take their seats, by force if necessary, and aided by 'a body-guard of sturdy *sans-culottes* some thousands strong'. In 1840 the National Charter Association commended O'Brien's plan to Chartists and left unclear the question of what action should be taken following the election of their hustings candidates. O'Brien seems to have envisaged some form of anti-Parliament consisting of these 'representatives' rather than an attempt to overthrow the existing Parliament. He wished to use the immense moral force of the existence of large numbers of men who had been elected by many more people than had chosen the MPs at Westminster. But O'Connor had different ideas and, much to O'Brien's anger, recommended instead his own plan of voting for Tories.

Nevertheless, although no scheme for exploiting the fact of their existence was ever implemented, numerous Chartist candidates were proposed and 'elected' at the hustings in 1837, 1841, and 1847. O'Brien himself won on the show of hands at Manchester in 1837. Chartists were sometimes scrupulous in observing the democratic proprieties. When on one occasion two lost at the hustings in Leeds, they scored a publicity point by accepting this as the verdict of the people. Hustings were excellent occasions on which to make speeches and secure publicity for the cause. The most famous such occasion was at Tiverton in 1847 when Harney challenged Palmerston and beat him on the show of hands. Palmerston helped matters by making a spirited response and thus attracting national attention to the incident.[2]

THE REFORM LEAGUE

The Reform League, being likewise an organisation for the enfranchisement of workingmen, was not able to employ electoral techniques to any great extent in its agitation. Nevertheless, there are two fundamental differences between it and Chartism in this respect. In the first place, its chances of achieving at least a good measure of the enfranchisement for which it was asking were infinitely greater. Indeed, for most of its existence the parties in Parliament seemed to be competing with one another in the production of more and more generous Reform Bills. Consequently, its relations with Liberal politicians in particular were strongly influenced by its claim to speak on behalf of large numbers of men who were certain soon to be voters. At first, some of its leaders, still under the influence of the old Chartist ideas, thought of reviving the 'Anti-Parliament' strategy. In September 1865, when the Executive Committee was debating the convening of a national conference, W. R. Cremer suggested that delegates to it 'should be formally elected by the present Non-Electors and sent to the House of Commons with instructions to take their seats'. At this stage the idea was given a welcome and set down for further discussion. But a year later a motion to set up a committee to 'consider a plan for a people's Parliament' was rejected by a large majority.[3] It was simply not necessary to think in such terms any longer.

A second difference was that in some places the Reform League replaced Non-Electors' Committees which had become accustomed to work at elections and express their views as to the candidates who were standing. As early as 1847 such a Committee appears in Birmingham. It regularly endorsed Liberal candidates. In 1859 many artisan non-voters campaigned actively in Birmingham for the Liberals who welcomed their support and treated them as if they were already voters. The close collaboration between the Birmingham branch of the Reform League and the Birmingham Liberal

Association was simply a continuation of this.[4] In Bradford too there was a Non-Electors' Committee which at once formed itself into a branch of the League.[5]

At first, some electoral work of the traditional kind was carried out, especially deputations to candidates. But such work was not for some time included among the duties of the League's lecturers and agents.[6] It was not until early 1867, as a general election under an extended franchise began to become a serious possibility in the near future, that the first thoughts were given to turning the League into an electoral organisation. On 20 March a delegate meeting passed a resolution calling on members to form election committees.[7] This was, in fact, a move by an organisation representing men who were shortly to become electors to bring electoral pressure to bear on MPs during the struggle over the Reform Bill. One of the purposes of these committees was stated to be the replacement of Liberal MPs who refused to support certain principles of reform on which the League was then insisting. The next stage was to set in hand an investigation as to which constituencies were most likely under the new system to return advanced Liberal candidates. The decision in July 1867 to set up a committee for this purpose represented a decision to convert the League from a pressure group for achieving a specific reform into one aiming to influence the first general election at which that reform would be put into effect.[8]

The League entered into this work with some trepidation. George Howell, the secretary, was most anxious that they should not, whatever they did, 'fall into the old evil of Election Agents with the corruption &c which have for so long held sway'.[9] Instead, contact was made with the constituencies through special agents appointed by the League and an extensive correspondence carried on by Howell himself.[10] Some of the League's supporters were somewhat perturbed when it appeared in this way to change its nature. Howell had to assure them that the League still thought 'Manhood Suffrage and the Ballot' important and would go on agitating for them, 'only we think that by operating upon the constituencies we shall be able to arrive at the goal sooner'.[11] Others, however, welcomed and adapted to the new course of action with the greatest enthusiasm. At a delegate meeting on 19 August 1867 an Exeter representative said that

the Reform party in Exeter were fully alive to their duties now that the Reform Bill had passed. The Exeter Branch of the Reform League had decided on forming themselves into a registration society, and had determined that any candidates they should select for the representation of Exeter should pledge themselves to support the ballot, justice to Ireland, and an improved system of education. They had selected as a candidate for the next election the son of Sir John Bowring.[12]

On 28 August the Council debated a manifesto on future policy. This was carefully worded to preserve the two concepts which members had of the League's role as a pressure group. On the one hand, electoral purposes were defined, but, on the other, in order to meet the objections of delegates such as Guedella who thought that they 'should guard against the League being regarded as a mere electioneering agency', the manifesto left open the possibility of using the League to promote further parliamentary reform.[13] This is a transitional phase. The League is poised to make the same transition as had occurred in Cobden's politics in the late 1840s— from pressure group devoted to achieving a single reform to one whose main purpose is to influence elections not for any specific reform but in the belief that in that election activity itself lies the secret of further advance.

In May 1868 the League made a major move towards converting itself into a full-scale 'electioneering agency' when it set up a Parliamentary Sub-Committee 'for registration and electoral purposes'. This included not only Cremer and Guedella but also James Acland, a professional election agent with experience going back to the Anti-Corn Law League. A year earlier a proposal to make Acland the League's Honorary Election Agent or Election and Registration Adviser to the Executive had met with considerable resistance, but the inhibitions had now been removed, perhaps because Acland had been engaged as agent for the candidature at Tower Hamlets of Edmond Beales, president of the League. Under Acland's guidance the League now began to produce large quantities of electoral statistics designed to show how and where the highly complex clauses of the Reform Act had improved the chances of getting 'advanced' candidates returned. Howell himself became a most enthusiastic electioneer. 'If some of the candidates did but know it,' he wrote, 'we could save them hundreds of pounds and do the work more efficiently in many instances than the local agent.'[14]

One important aspect of the League's election work was the sending out of agents to investigate and report on the situation in selected constituencies. As many of these constituencies were new or enlarged out of all recognition, and as the League did not content itself with short, single visits to them but sent agents back and kept up

a flow of correspondence to and about them, it acquired an understanding of local situations which undoubtedly excelled that of the
Liberal party and probably also of most purely local agents—where
such existed.[15]

To what purpose was all this electioneering activity devoted? In
the first place, much of it was designed to make a reality of the reform for which the League had fought. This involved educating the
new voters in the technicalities of the Reform Act and helping them
to get registered. Much of the literature put out by the League, and
much of the work done by the agents, was aimed at instructing
working-people in the mysteries of registration and qualification for
the borough franchise. The reports sent back by the agents showed
just how raw the new voters were and how desperately they needed
guidance and instruction.

Secondly, the Reform League used its electoral influence and
machinery to help certain candidates. There were two strategies
open to the League with regard to candidatures. One was to promote
its own in constituencies where they had a good chance of success.
The other was to work for candidates of other parties who were
regarded as 'advanced' enough to be worthy of receiving the workingman's vote. In practice, it was the latter of these which was
adopted, but policy was always very confused and sometimes
decidedly controversial.

The idea of independent League candidatures was approached
by the League's leaders very warily. There was an unfortunate early
experience when J. Baxter Langley stood as an independent at
Greenwich in 1865 and sought the League's endorsement. Beales
was opposed to giving him it, being 'rather inclined to believe that
unless the Candidate polled a large number it would rather tend to
weaken our influence and importance'. But the Executive overruled
him, and Langley received the endorsement. Beales's judgment was
vindicated when he gained only 190 votes.[16] The question was again
raised when the Executive began devising an electoral plan early in
1867. On 15 March 1867 it passed a resolution, proposed by Langley
himself, that an attempt be made to 'get League candidates for the
next General Election'.[17] A definition of such candidates was made
in a resolution passed at the delegate meeting five days later.
Existing MPs who accepted all or most of the League's programme
should be supported, but, where MPs refused to come up to this
standard, measures should be commenced to have them replaced by
'more advanced Reformers'.[18] The strategy was very flexible. This

L

was reinforced by the brief given to a committee set up by the Executive in July 1867. It was asked to report on 'the places where they believe it possible to get candidates returned at the next General Election, pledged to advanced Liberal principles, and to suggest the names of gentlemen as candidates for such places'.[19]

When Radicals announced their candidatures for seats, the League began to endorse them. The language used to describe acceptable candidates remained fluid. In the manifesto of 28 August 1867 they were 'persons qualified to represent the feelings, opinions, and interests of the working classes'. Local branches were hesitant about putting forward independent working-class candidates. However, in December 1867 the Council of the League passed a resolution calling on them to take energetic steps 'in conjunction with the Trades, Friendly, Temperance, and other Societies to secure the return at the next General Election of a number of working men proportionate to the other interests and classes at present represented in Parliament'.[20]

George Howell, who supervised many of the negotiations connected with candidatures, came to feel that this policy was impracticable and premature and must be replaced by a pragmatic one of support for sympathisers from outside the working class. 'I wish the workmen of your good old town could send in a working man,' he wrote to a correspondent in Exeter; 'but of course you must walk first and then run.'[21] To another correspondent he wrote: 'As to working men representatives as a rule our time is not yet come. We want *good men* no matter whence they come or what they are.'[22] In practice the League did not resort to independent candidatures as a major feature of its strategy. Indeed, Howell did his best to discourage them. Reform League candidatures were suppressed or opposed at Kidderminster, Brighton, Nottingham, Halifax, Hackney, and Northampton. In the case of Halifax E. O. Greening had been chosen by the local branch but was refused support by the Executive.[23]

The reasons for this attitude to League candidatures have been hotly debated. To some it reflects the subservience of the League's leaders, especially Howell, to Liberal party interests, a subservience that was paid for by the sums which Samuel Morley and other Liberals were willing to supply on the condition that they should be used to promote Liberal candidates and suppress divisive working-class candidatures. That the money was used for this purpose and would not have been available had the League been proposing an electoral campaign to disrupt Liberal politics is undoubted. But what is doubtful is whether policy can be entirely dismissed as a result from the range of influences on the League's electoral conduct. Most nineteenth-century pressure groups, when they ran their own candidates, did so for tactical reasons, not expecting them to win, knowing full well that they would get only a small minority of the votes, half hoping that they would not have to be carried the full distance, and looking on them essentially as a lever to frighten the Liberal party into concessions. It is in this respect that labour is most sharply to be differentiated from the pressure groups. Labour candidatures were normally intended to be successful. This is a theme which runs right through nineteenth-century labour electoral strategy and must be borne in mind in any assessment of Howell and the Reform League. In analysing other pressure groups we have seen that there was often a section, particularly Nonconformists, who disliked tactics—such as abstention or voting for candidates who were expected to lose—which were regarded as tantamount to the disfranchisement of the people who engaged in them.[24] This feeling seems to have been especially strong in labour politics. Acquisition of the right to vote had been the major demand of nineteenth-century working-class Radicalism, notably the Charter, and any strategy which suggested using this right frivolously, once acquired, or throwing it away does not appear to have been popular. Howell, like other labour politicians, wanted the workingman's vote to be used to get elected to Parliament practical men who would do the workingman some good. This meant giving support to candidates who had a good chance of winning if given such support and discouraging 'divisive' candidatures which might well have the effect of letting a Tory in. Howell's entire strategy was directed towards getting into the House as many sympathisers with advanced Liberalism as possible. He was not interested in tactical or unpractical candidatures.

Throughout his career Howell was opposed to coercive electoral tactics.[25] He wanted members who really believed in helping working-people or who would help them because they were grateful for the help given them by the leaders of the working class, not members who had been coerced and bullied into professing support and who would then abandon it as soon as the intimidatory pressure was removed. Therefore, in 1867 and 1868 he and his associates devoted themselves entirely to helping Liberal and Radical candidates and spent no time whatever in organising the negative and coercive tactics of which other pressure groups were sometimes very fond. At one stage Howell did suggest that he might recommend such tactics against the 'Whigs' who 'have ever been our Enemies, and are now'. He wrote that '*if the Whig is doubtful* I personally should prefer a Tory' but then added that 'of course this is a delicate matter and one which requires care in the working out'.[26] In the end it never was worked out. The Reform League mounted no electoral strategy against 'Whigs'. Instead they went in for the strategy of voting for the 'better man', even if he by no means came up to their ideal. Liberal candidates, accustomed to the coercive tactics of other pressure groups, were agreeably surprised to discover how very different the Reform League was. For example, when the Reform League approached W. Rathbone, candidate for Liverpool, his initial reaction was to treat this as yet another demand for a pledge with the threat of electoral coercion implied. Howell wrote back to reassure him:

You are quite mistaken as to the import of my letter. You are not supposed to *endorse anything, only tell us how to serve you.* . . . We think we can give great aid, if you think we cannot there the matter I suppose will end.[27]

The League used its influence against other pressure groups which did resort to intimidation of candidates who did not come completely up to a standard. Howell wrote to Sir Wilfrid Lawson in July 1868:

. . . do try and prevent our temperance friends acting as foolishly as they did at Bristol. Mr. Morley did not feel justified in giving his pledge *absolutely* to the Permissive Bill. But Mr. Miles absolutely went against it yet they either voted for Miles or not at all.
We have done good service in this matter as far as Bristol is concerned as we sent a good Temperance lecturer down there but there is a fear that the Temperance people will act unwarily in other Boroughs.[28]

Howell's strategy was a positive one. 'We must be busy between now and the General Election,' he wrote, 'so that *every good Liberal* can be made perfectly secure of his seat, and good seats secured for other good candidates'.[29] When it was suggested that Liberal candidates who were less than completely satisfactory should be opposed, his response was to lay emphasis on the negative consequences of such tactics: 'If we advised any contest the Liberal Party would say that we were dividing the "liberal interest" and we should thereby lose friends.'[30] It was his view that 'liberal fighting liberal is not sound policy, but rather, as it appears to me, a contention for personal ambition without regard to the principles at stake'.[31]

A great deal of the Reform League's work involved mediating in local disputes and endeavouring to unify local progressive forces so as to ensure that Liberals would not be denied victory as a result of the quarrels of their adherents.[32] An important aspect of this was helping to bring about agreement to a coalescing of forces between separate and sometimes hostile middle-class and working-class Liberal or Reform Associations.[33] The League was particularly concerned over surplus Liberal candidatures. In October 1868 its Council adopted a plan for a preliminary ballot to select the Liberal candidates where an excess number was in the field, and George Odger showed the way by accepting the verdict of such a ballot at Chelsea and standing down.[34] As an electoral strategy this action to 'close up the Liberal ranks' may have been paid for by Samuel Morley's money but it did also correspond to the basic political aims of the movement. In endorsing the manner in which the Liberals in Nottingham had chosen their candidates and deprecating the independent candidature of J. J. Merriman there, the Executive referred to its belief 'that the surest and quickest mode of ensuring the triumph of our principles is to be found in the most complete organisation of the [Liberal] Party'.[35]

THE IRISH NATIONALISTS IN GREAT BRITAIN

From the late 1870s the bloc vote of the Irish who lived in Great Britain was a significant factor in the politics of Home Rule for Ireland. Most pressure groups dreamed of being able to organise a bloc vote that was largely isolated from all other political issues and influences and could be depended upon to be available for whatever strategy the leaders decided on. But few went so close to achieving the ideal as the Irish Nationalists in Great Britain.[36]

The Irish voters were not very numerous but they possessed many other attributes which made them excellent material for an effective election strategy. They were sufficiently concentrated to make them a meaningful electoral factor in a number of urban constituencies. Their very presence in such places sometimes increased the electoral support of the non-Irish population for the Conservative party and so made them more attractive as a compensating asset for the Liberals. Their habit of living in their own districts made them easily organisable for electoral purposes. Their way of life was already so different in so many respects from that of the rest of the population that an extension of this differentiation into electoral behaviour encountered few obstacles, especially since it was paralleled and inspired by a similar trend in politics in Ireland itself. It was not only an Irish, but also a Roman Catholic, bloc vote and could be mobilised at times, occasionally and confusingly the same times, by the Church for Catholic reasons, notably in the realm of educational policy. It was also exceptionally raw material, as many of the Irish voters in Britain only became involved in voting when requested to do so by the organisers of the movement. The element of enthusiasm, of devotion to the cause of emancipating Ireland, also made them a formidable electoral force.

The potential of the Irish vote was probably dramatised first by the Liverpool by-election of February 1880 when the Irish Home Rulers protested against the vagueness of the views on their question of Lord Ramsay, the Liberal candidate, and then gave him their full support when he made a much more explicit promise. Under the leadership of various national organisations, especially the Irish National League of Great Britain from 1882, the Irish vote became very thoroughly organised in many parts of the country.

The Irish tactics were fairly similar to those of other pressure groups. They hardly ever ran their own candidates, the only major exception being T. P. O'Connor who represented the Scotland division of Liverpool for many years and was never opposed by a Liberal. The major strategy involved balancing between the parties and encouraging them to compete for the bloc vote. This tactic reached its climax in the general election of 1885 when the Irish National League, on Parnell's instructions, issued a manifesto calling on the Irish voters in Great Britain to abstain from voting for most Liberal and Radical candidates. Contrary to legend, they were not called upon to vote for Conservatives. It was a classic instance of an abstention strategy aimed primarily at influencing Liberal politics. Immense efforts were made to publicise this advice among Irish voters, and the election results were generally interpreted as demonstrating that the advice had been taken. The extent of Irish obedience to it has, however, been questioned by C. H. D. Howard. He sees it as having been disobeyed in places where the advice to vote for or abstain from supporting certain Liberals conflicted with advice being given by the Roman Catholic Church on the education question. What mattered at the time was the general impression, and this was that the Irish had switched votes to the Tories—which was not technically true—and thus delivered perhaps 25 or 30 urban seats to them and deprived Gladstone of an overall majority.

When Gladstone himself shortly afterwards embarked on the promotion of a Home Rule Bill, there were many who argued that this electoral pressure had been a principal factor in his 'conversion'. Thus a most potent myth was born, rivalling that created by the alleged role of the Anti-Corn Law League's electoral activities in bringing about the repeal of the Corn Laws.

The history of the Irish vote in Great Britain after 1886 is very similar to the history of the electoral influence of other pressure groups once the Liberal party had committed itself to their cause. On the one hand, every effort was made to increase this vote and devote it to the election of Liberal candidates. That this opened up a 'new frontier' for the Liberals of people who would otherwise not have voted at all or even might have voted Conservative on religious grounds, is undoubted. J. R. Denvir wrote that in London a canvasser for a branch of the National League or a Church collector could nearly always 'get an apathetic friend to sign a claim to be put on the register of voters, where the English Liberal agent, however zealous, signally fails, because he is so often taken for a School Board visitor, a broker's man, or some other equally obnoxious individual'. Denvir claims that the Irish vote was now crucial at by-elections. He gives two instances. At Coventry and Burnley the Gladstonians regained seats won by Unionists in 1886, and he attributes this to the balancing factor of the Irish vote. The temperance people would have disputed his claim for Burnley at least and pointed out that the Irish vote had not saved the seat in 1886.[37]

For the Irish, on the other hand, the adoption of their cause by one party robbed them of the ability to repeat their 1885 strategy of playing off the parties against each other. The Irish vote was never again so powerful a factor in British politics, partly because there was nowhere else for it to go if the Liberals abandoned their commitment, partly because of the schisms in the Irish Nationalist party itself, and partly also because Irish voters in Britain were subjected to increasing counter-pressures from the environment into which they were settling, especially from the growing Labour political movement.

LABOUR AND SOCIALIST POLITICS, 1870–1900

The basic principle of labour electoral action in the late nineteenth century remained that which had underlain the work of George Howell and the Reform League—to engage only in action of a positive kind with the objective of getting candidates elected. Negative and disruptive electoral tactics continued to be opposed. The policy of the Labour Representation League in the early 1870s was to discover those constituencies in which labour candidates would have a good chance of being elected and then to concentrate its efforts on them. Right through until the foundation of the Labour Representation Committee in 1900 the main aim of *labour* electoral politics was to get working-class representatives into the House of Commons, not to coerce other parties into adopting a specific programme or policy. The Labour Electoral Association, which originated as a committee of the T.U.C., opposed candidatures that were 'propagandist' or not intended to be successful. In 1890 it adopted a resolution declaring that 'the action of any few men in forcing a candidate on a constituency where the general feeling of the working class is hostile to such a candidate is an error of judgment, as such a course of action is likely to bring the cause into disrepute'.[38] The secret pact between Ramsay MacDonald, secretary of the L.R.C., and Herbert Gladstone, Liberal Chief Whip, in 1903 represented a reversion to a non-coercive relationship with Liberalism which had mainly characterised labour electoral politics during the nineteenth century. Labour Representation League candidatures were seldom used or intended to deprive the Liberal party of seats. When at Bristol Odger came last in a ballot for Liberal candidate, he observed the rules and withdrew. Howell gave up a candidature at Norwich in 1871 when requested to do so by the Liberal Association.[39] The policy of the Labour Electoral Association was to work for decision of Liberal candidatures by test ballot. It was opposed to Labour intervention in contests between a Conservative and a Liberal and refused to support Keir Hardie's candidature at Mid-Lanark in 1888. In 1892 it supported Alfred Illingworth in West Bradford against the socialist, Ben Tillett, as it was opposed to any course of action that might hand over a Liberal seat to the Tories.[40] T. R. Threlfall who was largely responsible for setting it up as a committee of the T.U.C. in 1886 took as the guiding principle of Labour electoral politics that 'they could not contest any seat without declaring their adherence to one of the other of the great political parties'.[41] Even at Mid-Lanark, one of the justifications for Keir Hardie's breach of this principle was that the Liberals themselves had broken their own and the L.E.A.'s rules by refusing to have a preliminary ballot to which Hardie had agreed to submit himself and by the result of which he had promised to abide.[42]

Very different, however, was the philosophy of socialists, both middle- and working-class, and indeed other middle-class sympathisers. When in 1870 at Southwark Odger did intervene in a contest between Tory and Liberal and enable the former to win a normally Liberal seat, it is significant that he was incited to do so by John Stuart Mill who wanted Labour candidatures that were not likely to be successful but that would probably let in Tories to be used tactically to force the Liberals to give more candidatures to workingmen.[43] In 1873 another intellectual who sympathised with the labour movement, Frederic Harrison, had the idea of organising the working-class voters to vote for such candidates as would accept the trade unions' programme and to abstain or run their own men wherever none of the candidates would do this.[44] Middle-class people tended to think in terms of the tactics adopted by middle-class pressure groups. Harrison was a prominent lecturer and adviser of the Liberation Society in the 1870s.

The socialist had his own reasons for favouring coercive and disruptive electoral tactics. To him there was no essential difference between the Tory and the Liberal and so action which helped to prevent a Liberal from being elected was no worse than action which kept out a Tory. Both represented the class enemy and their very competition was a sham designed to deceive and divide the working class. Furthermore, if only a Liberal and a Tory were standing, abstention was the only conceivable response for a true socialist. This argument may be illustrated by the following extract from Robert Tressell's *The Ragged Trousered Philanthropists* in which he describes the action taken by Socialists at a by-election in which a Liberal was standing against a Conservative:

In their attempts to persuade others to refrain from voting for either of the candidates, they were opposed even by some who professed to believe in Socialism, who said that as there was no better Socialist candidate the thing to do was to vote for the better of the two. . . .
One man said that if he had his way, all those who had votes should be compelled to record them—whether they liked it or not—or be disenfranchised! Barrington asked him if he believed in Tariff Reform. The man said no. 'Why not?' demanded Barrington.
The other replied that he opposed Tariff Reform because he believed it would ruin the country. Barrington inquired if he were a supporter of Socialism. The man said he was not, and when further questioned he said that he believed if it were ever adopted it would bring black ruin upon the country—he believed this because Mr. Sweater [the Liberal candidate] had said so. When Barrington asked him—supposing there were only two candidates, one a Socialist and the other a Tariff Reformer—how would he

like to be compelled to vote for one of them, he was at a loss for an answer.[45]

Socialists showed themselves much readier to engage in devious or coercive electoral tactics. These were sometimes too devious for their own good, as in the notorious 'Tory gold' affair of 1885 when the Social Democratic Federation put up two candidates for Hampstead and Kennington, both seats where they had no chance of winning, and it was discovered that these candidatures had been paid for by Tory money from Maltman Barry.[46] This episode only served to confirm the deep hostility felt by many Labour leaders to candidatures of this kind.

The official line of the Labour Electoral Association was that working-class representation in Parliament should be promoted only by agreement with the Liberal party or through the machinery provided by that party for the selection of its candidates. The exclusion both of coercive methods and of testing of candidates on questions of policy was challenged from within the Association by the socialist, H. H. Champion, who ran its Metropolitan Section and was enabled through the possession of private sources of finance to organise an electoral policy of his own that was at variance with the Association's. Champion was inspired in particular by the example of the Irish Home Rulers. In January 1888 he declared: 'I find that Home Rule is "practical politics" because the Irish vote counts, and that the Labour problem is not "practical politics" because the Labour vote is not effectively organised.' In 1892 he planned a highly disruptive campaign of electoral intervention in order to 'make the Labour question in general and 8 hours in particular what the Irish question has been made by similar tactics.' Champion was, however, essentially a pragmatist. In other words, unlike the L.E.A., he did not explicitly exclude electoral coercion, but nor did he wish to resort to it under all circumstances. The basis of his strategy was to judge candidates according to their answers to questions on Labour policy and, where such a criterion was relevant, whether they were 'good' or 'bad' employers of labour. At least in the late 1880s, he seems to have regarded independent Labour candidatures as only a last resort and to be used mainly as tactical weapons in the pre-election manoeuvring. Threats of candidatures were employed to extract concessions from Liberal candidates. For example, he announced his own candidature at Deptford in January 1888 and then withdrew after the Liberal had made some concessions. At five by-elections between 1887 and 1889 he did support the Liberal candidate, while at another, Holborn, he recommended abstention. In the early 1890s his by-election interventions became more ambitious—and more irritating to Lib.-Lab. politicians. He himself stood at South Aberdeen in 1892 and took nearly 16 per cent. of the vote, although this did not affect a very easy Liberal victory. In 1892 he financed H. R. Taylor as S.D.F. candidate at Bethnal Green, North East, against George Howell and a Conservative. Taylor took 2 per cent. of the vote. He wrote to J. L. Mahon after the 1892 elections: 'It is possible, given pluck to put out 50 Liberals at the next election by running men in 10 seats and voting Tory in the other 40. That will cause some little fuss, and will probably put in a Tory Govt. holding power at the sweet will of the I.L.P.'[47]

The Independent Labour Party, which was founded at Bradford in 1893, was a socialist organisation, but, because it made serious overtures to trade unionists and wanted their political support, its electoral strategy showed an interesting combination of the labour and socialist attitudes to elections—a combination which often led to confusion or conflict. The I.L.P. was ready to put up candidates where they had no chance of succeeding but where their intervention might let a Tory in. But the motivation was sometimes ambiguous. Was the aim to create a genuinely independent party with men being supported who would have a good prospect of being elected, or was it tactical, to force the Liberal party into concessions on policy and working-class candidatures? Men looked back to Keir Hardie's 1888 candidature at Mid-Lanark as the first great gesture of labour electoral independence, but at the time Hardie had seen it very much in the same light as most nineteenth-century pressure groups had seen their action at by-elections. 'Better split the party now, if there is to be a split, than at the general election; and if the labour party only make their power felt now, terms will not be wanting when the general election comes.' Some of the action taken by the I.L.P. was openly intended to have the effect of replacing a Liberal by a Unionist. At Grimsby in 1893 it spoke and worked against the very prominent Lib.-Lab., H. Broadhurst, and claimed credit for his defeat by the Liberal Unionist, E. Heneage, who had lost the seat the year before. At Halifax, also in 1893, an I.L.P. candidate, J. Lister, took 25 per cent. of the vote but still could not prevent the Liberals from holding the seat. The officers of the I.L.P. did, however, on this occasion try to make a deal with the Liberals so that they could withdraw the candidature. In 1895 the I.L.P. ran 28 candidates and all lost.

The most hotly debated issue of I.L.P. electoral strategy, and one which reflected the division between labour and socialist attitudes, was that of whether or not members and supporters should abstain in contests where there was no socialist candidate. This became known as the 'Fourth Clause' controversy. The Manchester I.L.P., which was founded in May 1892, pledged its members by the fourth clause in its constitution to abstain from voting for any Liberal, Liberal Unionist, or Conservative candidate. When the inaugural conference of the national I.L.P. was held at Bradford the Manchester delegates moved the addition of a similar clause to its constitution. This was not a congenial idea to those who were in the 'labour' electoral tradition, for it implied that most members would in fact have to abstain from voting and thus 'disfranchise themselves' since the I.L.P. would not for some time have the resources to give more than a small number of constituencies the chance to vote for an I.L.P. candidate. Robert Blatchford, the socialist writer and a founder of the Manchester I.L.P., spoke strongly in favour of the proposal: 'He regarded Liberals and Tories as the enemies of the people. When he said a man was his enemy he meant he hated him, and would fight him to the death. . . . He considered it a stain on the Labour Party to have any dealings with the Liberals. He would as soon have dealings with the devil.' Tressell's socialists would have cheered this very loudly. James Sexton of Liverpool proposed to make adoption of the resolution optional for each branch but was ruled out of order. Instead the conference carried by 62 to 37 a Bradford proposal that, in the absence of an I.L.P. candidate, members should act in an election on the directions of their local branch.

Blatchford argued that the I.L.P. could hope to grow only by attracting the support of Tory and Liberal workers and that this could not be done if they were going to be asked on occasions to vote for a candidate of the opposite party in the traditional two-party conflict. On the other hand, the 'Fourth Clause' was strongly opposed not only by many Labour men but also by one group of middle-class socialists, the Fabians, who were strongly attached to the alternative strategy of 'permeating' the Liberal party. At the I.L.P. conferences of 1894 and 1895 the 'Fourth Clause' was again rejected, but at a special conference in 1895 the decision was taken to recommend members at this particular election to abstain where there was no socialist candidate. This caused a great deal of controversy.[48]

The new Labour party in the early twentieth century adopted a predominantly 'labour' type of electoral strategy, that is it concentrated on getting workingmen into the House of Commons where Taff Vale and other developments made their presence seem urgently needed. It was therefore prepared to come to terms with the Liberal party to minimise electoral conflict between them and maximise the chances of the election of Labour candidates. Confrontation with Liberals was most likely to occur where the Liberals themselves appeared to be breaking their own rules and denying workingmen a fair chance to get elected to Parliament.

Conclusion

By 1900 the political parties dominated the political scene, and the days were gone for ever when reform movements could utilise electoral pressure of the kind described in the foregoing pages to force the parties to attend to their legislative demands.

The passing of the politics of electoral pressure was obviously intimately associated with the decline of Nonconformity as a coherent, identifiable, and effective influence in the political life of the nation.[1] In asking electors to use their voting power for the advancement of some great moral cause, such as the repeal of the Corn Laws or the crusade against the drink trade, pressure groups had clearly appealed mainly to Nonconformists, while in two instances—the National Education League and the Liberation Society—the cause specifically related to the interests of that section of the community.

There was a substantial revival of Nonconformist interest in politics after the production of the Balfour government's Education Bill in 1902. The electoral aspect of this was a vigorous campaign to persuade Nonconformists, including those who had been abstaining or voting Liberal Unionist over recent elections, to rally to the Liberals and secure the overthrow of the Balfour government. Most analysts of the 1906 election now agree that Nonconformist antagonism to the Education Act played a major part in the Liberal landslide which then occurred.[2] On the surface it would therefore have appeared that Nonconformity was now a more powerful electoral force than ever.

But this superficial appearance proved to be an illusion. There was clearly still no problem about rallying Nonconformists against a Conservative government which was promoting legislation to discriminate against Nonconformists and to entrench the privileged position of the Church of England. But there was not to be another Conservative government in Britain until 1922. From 1906 on the real test for Nonconformity as a political and electoral force lay in its ability to put pressure on the Liberal party and Liberal government. What became apparent was that it no longer possessed such a capability. In other words, Nonconformity had ceased to have any substantial political and electoral independence. When there was a Conservative government, it could offer additional reserves of political enthusiasm to a Liberal opposition. But, once there was a Liberal government, electoral sanctions could no longer credibly be invoked as a way of forcing it to satisfy Nonconformist demands. The era when there existed a Nonconformist or a temperance vote that could be manipulated in this way had now passed. The very success of earlier tactics of electoral coercion and pressure had contributed to the ultimate onset of political impotence. The Liberal party had been obliged to take steps to absorb these sectional interests and accommodate them within the structure of its own organisation and programme, but the result was that over the years those people who had to be the mainstay of any strategy based on the threat of the withholding of votes became less and less easily detachable from that party with which they had come to identify themselves politically and support for which was the only way of keeping out of office the party which was the protector of the interests of the Church of England and the drink trade.

It was much more difficult now to arouse support for the upholding of the doctrine that, in exercising his vote, an elector should place the promotion of great moral principles above mere considerations of party politics. For by the late nineteenth and early twentieth centuries party politics could no longer be regarded in this contemptuous manner. In the mid-nineteenth century the parties had had little in the way of extra-parliamentary organisation and had drawn their support from only a very limited section of the population. They could both be regarded as representing portions of the same very small and aristocratic ruling class. Their manoeuvres looked like little more than the intrigues of members of that class for power and place, the battles of the 'ins and outs', into which considerations of principle entered very slightly, if at all. It was quite easy, therefore, to persuade somebody—especially a new voter of Nonconformist background—that in his use of the vote he should rise above this 'immoral', aristocratic type of politics if he believed in the furthering of some great moral reform and that he should withhold his vote from such parties unless they promised to assist this cause. But the political parties of the late nineteenth and early twentieth centuries were very different organisations. They had developed a broad popular appeal and a substantial extra-parliamentary dimension. Their competition and their alternation in office were clearly no longer just a matter of 'ins versus outs' but involved basic differences in political philosophy, policy, and sources of support in the nation at large. Government was playing an ever larger role in the regulation of the economic and social life of the country, and the parties were inviting the people to see and to support basic principles, such as the maintenance of free trade or of the structure of the Union or the Empire, in the policies which they put forward for implementation by government. In these circumstances it is not surprising to discover the declining appeal and relevance of strategies which assumed that principles could be injected into party politics only from outside and by the employment of techniques of electoral coercion.

It is clear that the systematic organisation of abstention and *bloc* voting on behalf of the interests of particular reform movements or pressure groups belonged to an early stage of the development of the party system and disappeared as changes in the relationship between that system and the electorate rendered impossible the mobilising of sufficient numbers of voters to give such strategies continued effectiveness as an influence over the conduct and the policies of politicians. Once doubts as to the effectiveness of techniques of electoral pressure began to set in, the decline in recourse to them was bound to be rapid, for their application, if it was to be of any value at all, had to be based on elaborate organisation sustainable, for instance, over the lengthy periods between general elections and requiring to be constantly ready for activation in the case of by-elections, and such organisation depended in its turn on the enthusiasm of adherents and their conviction that their efforts and sacrifices were soon going to bring about the achievement of the desired goal. The triumph of the Anti-Corn Law League in 1846 had bred expectations as to the effectiveness of organised electoral pressure which inspired other movements for several decades thereafter to engage in similar strategies. But their pressure had remarkably little success. The Church of England was not disestablished, the 1870 Education Act was not amended along the lines favoured by the militants of the National Education League, Local Option legislation was not enacted. Lack of success bred weariness and frustration and an inability to sustain the organisation and effort necessary for a credible strategy of electoral pressure.

At first the electoral activities of the pressure groups undoubtedly had a positive relationship to the development of democracy in Great Britain. These groups were pioneers in the discovery and exploitation of ways of using electoral power for the achievement of goals desired by voters. They therefore helped to promote the democratisation of British politics. They encouraged participation in electioneering and showed voters, especially the large numbers who were granted the franchise during the nineteenth century, how they could employ the vote to force politicians and governments to take heed of their wishes and to give them the legislation which they required as distinct from the legislation which the ruling class thought was good for them. The Anti-Corn Law League and its successors pioneered and perfected a new, democratic form of relationship between government and governed. Indeed, in certain respects they endeavoured to put into operation an understanding of democracy which went significantly beyond that which is now established in Britain. The range of uses of the power to vote that were open to the voter was assumed to be much wider than that which now obtains. Most modern voters vote for the candidate of one of a small number of national political parties, and that is as far as their active role in democracy goes. Abstention or non-voting is customarily regarded as a mindless exercise, usually the product of apathy or boredom or bad weather. But the nineteenth-century pressure groups tried to make a positive and constructive use of the power to withhold one's vote and to turn it into an instrument for helping to determine the policies of the parties. What they stood for and tried to base their strategy on was the independence of the voter, his right not to be taken for granted but to be able to impose certain conditions in return for the disposal of his vote. Unfortunately, however, in time the negative aspects of this approach to participation in the electoral process came to predominate. The manipulation of small *bloc* votes in order to coerce or tempt politicians into promising to promote certain policies became an anti-democratic tendency, especially when it threatened the enactment by a pledged majority of MPs of reform legislation, for example prohibition of the sale of liquor, which went well beyond what public opinion in general was prepared to accept or tolerate.

Electoral pressure of the kind discussed in this book has not been an agitational technique much favoured by twentieth-century

M

pressure groups. In determining their policies and drawing up their election manifestoes the parties are, of course, still very mindful of the relevance of what they are doing to the gaining or losing of the votes of particular sections or enthusiasts for particular causes. But in arriving at their calculations as to how many votes may actually be at stake they are not given the kind of assistance offered by the nineteenth-century pressure groups. The pressures on a modern voter at election time are so great, and the policies which he is invited to consider when casting his vote are so numerous, that it would be virtually impossible for a pressure group now to organise and sustain in electoral isolation a *bloc* vote of any meaningful proportion. The shrinkage of the dimensions of the techniques which have been the subject of this book may be indicated by the sole reference to them in a study of one modern election. It is a footnote: 'As usual, local and national pressure groups, ranging from old-age pensioners' associations to bee-keepers, and from nuclear disarmers to public-decency vigilantes, used the election to seek promises from candidates. But it is hard to attribute much significance to their activities.'[3] Modern MPs have little experience of this kind of pressure, and when it does occur it is a great surprise. In January 1975 MPs reported 'unusually fierce constituency pressure over a private member's Bill on the abortion law', and the note of surprise was unmistakable in one Labour MP's statement that 'some of the letters in his postbag virtually amounted to the threat: if you don't vote for this Bill we will never vote for you again.'[4]

Appendix

The following are some basic facts concerning the main pressure groups discussed in this book.

A. THE ANTI-CORN LAW LEAGUE

1. *Date of formation.* 1839

2. *Objective*
   The 'total and immediate' repeal of the Corn Laws.

3. *Organisational structure*
   Its offices were in Manchester, although in 1843 the official head-quarters were transferred to London. There was a Council, whose chairman was George Wilson. It met regularly and transacted most of the League's business. Membership was open to all who had paid £50 or more to the League's funds, some 500 by 1845: only a small minority—Manchester residents—regularly attended meetings. The League itself was a federation of local Anti-Corn Law Associations. But it developed its own autonomous organisation. In 1842 it established a structure of 12 districts each with a full-time agent.

4. *Income*
   This was derived partly from subscriptions, partly from the proceeds of bazaars, tea-parties, and other such functions, and partly from special appeals—for £50,000 in 1842, £100,000 in 1844, and £100,000 in 1845.

5. *Membership figures, etc.*

The League's Council had nearly 500 members by 1845. The weekly circulation of *The League* was 20,000.

6. *Sources*

The J. B. Smith, George Wilson, and other League Papers in the Manchester City Library.

The League (weekly newspaper published in London from September 1843).

John Bright and Richard Cobden Papers in the British Library.

H. D. Jordan, 'The Political Methods of the Anti-Corn Law League'. *Political Science Quarterly*, XLII, 1 (March 1927).

N. McCord, *The Anti-Corn Law League 1838–1846*, 1958.

J. Morley, *The Life of Richard Cobden*, 1881.

A. Prentice, *History of the Anti-Corn Law League*, 1853.

D. Read, *Cobden and Bright. A Victorian Political Partnership*, 1967.

B. THE LIBERATION SOCIETY

1. *Date of formation*

1844—as the British Anti-State-Church Association. In 1853 its title was changed to the Society for the Liberation of Religion From State Patronage and Control. It became generally known as the Liberation Society.

2. *Objectives*

These were summarised in 1887 as follows:

'1. The abrogation of all laws and usages which inflict disability, or confer privilege, on ecclesiastical grounds.

2. The discontinuance of all payments from public funds, and of all compulsory exactions, for religious purposes.

3. After an equitable satisfaction of existing interests, the application of the national property now held in trust by the established Churches of England and Scotland to other and strictly national purposes; and, concurrently therewith, the liberation of those Churches from State-control.' (*The Liberal Year Book 1887*, p. 115, reprinted 1973, The Harvester Press, Hassocks.)

3. *Organisational structure*

The Society's offices were in London. A conference of delegates from local associations was held once every three years. This elected a Council of 600 (originally 500) members plus the Executive Committee, the 75 (originally 50) members of which were members of the Council *ex officio*. The main officers were the Treasurer, the Secretary (at times both these posts were shared between two men), and the Chairman of the Parliamentary Committee. The Executive Committee met regularly and transacted the business of the Society. Attendance was small—on average 6 to 7 members—as most members did not live in London. A substantial portion of the minutes of the Executive and Parliamentary Committees are now held in the Greater London Record Office at County Hall, London. The Council met every year. The Society had a network of agents throughout the country. In 1875 there were 30 such agents, including 4 in London and 3 in Wales. This system was established in 1859. Electoral work was organised by the Parliamentary Committee (a separate Electoral Committee was merged with it in 1857). Its Chairman from 1865 was J. Carvell Williams.

4. *Income*

The Society's annual income was £8,564 in 1867–8, £16,353 in 1877–8, and £9,075 in 1881–2. Funds were raised partly from subscriptions, partly from legacies, and partly from special Campaign Funds. The 1874 Triennial Conference launched an appeal for a special fund of £100,000. Five years later £84,063 had been raised for this. By contrast, when in 1890 a fund of £5,000 over a three-year period was asked for, only half of this was realised.

5. *Membership figures, etc.*

In 1868 there were 10,000 subscribers. The circulation of the *Liberator* in the mid-1870s was 10–12,000 copies.

6. *Sources*

Minute Books in the Greater London Record Office.
The Nonconformist.
The Liberator (the Society's own journal, published monthly).
S. M. Ingham, 'The disestablishment movement in England 1868–74', *Journal of Religious History*, 3 (June 1964).
J. G. Jones, 'The Liberation Society and Welsh Politics, 1844–68', *Welsh History Review*, 1, no. 2 (1961).

W. H. Mackintosh, *Disestablishment and Liberation. The Movement for the Separation of the Anglican Church from State Control*, 1972.

K. O. Morgan, *Wales in British Politics 1868–1922*, revised edition, Cardiff, 1970.

D. M. Thompson, 'The Liberation Society, 1844–1868', in P. Hollis (ed.), *Pressure from Without in early Victorian England*, 1974.

J. Vincent, *The Formation of the Liberal Party 1857–1868*, 1966, 2nd edition 1976, The Harvester Press, Hassocks.

C. THE UNITED KINGDOM ALLIANCE

1. *Date of formation.*   1853

2. *Objective*
   To create a public opinion 'in favour of such legislation as would secure the suppression of intemperance by the removal of its legislative causes', in particular 'a well-considered and efficient measure of Local Option, which would enable the inhabitants of various districts to protect themselves from the ravages of drunkenness and its resultant evils'. (*The Liberal Year Book 1887*, p. 127, reprinted 1973, The Harvester Press, Hassocks.)

3. *Organisational structure*
   The Alliance had offices in London and Manchester. It was a federation of local organisations, known as Auxiliaries. These sent delegates to a meeting of the General Council once a year. This elected the President, Vice-Presidents, and an Executive Committee of about 25 members which met regularly and transacted the business of the Society. The office of Vice-President was honorific and was bestowed on noted public figures (bishops, MPs, etc.) who supported the cause and also on substantial donors to the Alliance's funds. The Alliance's officers were the Chairman of the Executive, the Vice-Chairman, the Treasurer, the Hon. Secretary, and the Secretary. Among holders of offices during the period covered by this book were:

   President: Sir W. C. Trevelyan, 1853–79
                     Sir Wilfrid Lawson, 1879–1906

   Chairman of the Executive:
                     William Harvey, 1853–70
                     B. Whitworth, 1870–89

A. McDougall, 1889–1909

Treasurer: W. Armitage, 1856–88

Sir W. J. Crossley, 1888–1911

Secretary: T. H. Barker, 1853–84

J. Whyte, 1884–1903

Hon. Secretary: S. Pope, 1853–1901

The Alliance organised a system of agents to carry out its work throughout the country. This became increasingly complicated as time went on, and there were numerous different kinds of agent: deputational and general, i.e. sent out from the Executive Committee to undertake specific assignments and act as a deputation from it to local Auxiliaries; electoral; district; and superintendents who supervised the work of the district agents within regions. By 1869 there were eleven superintendents. The Alliance also had a full-time parliamentary agent from 1860 whose duty it was to expedite in all possible ways, including the organisation of electoral pressure, the passage of the Alliance's legislation through Parliament and to advise on and implement action with regard to all other legislation that might have a bearing on the Alliance's objectives. This position was held by J. H. Raper from 1860 to 1878 and then by John Hilton (who combined it with the post of Metropolitan superintendent). The district agents were under the direct control of the Executive Committee and were assigned a multiplicity of tasks including the collecting of funds, the promotion of petitions, and the organisation of electoral activity. For electoral purposes the most important of the general agents was the full-time electoral organising secretary. This post was created in 1873 and held by J. W. Owen until his death in 1880.

4. *Income*

This was raised through subscriptions, donations, legacies, and from special appeals for 'guarantee funds'. The first two of these aimed at raising £50,000 and £100,000 respectively within five years (1865–70, 1871–5). Both were successful. £90,000 was raised or promised towards the second within the first year. The Alliance spent its money mainly on salaries (£4,551 in 1868–9) and pamphlets, advertising, etc. (£6,887) with smaller sums spent on office expenses (£685), meetings (£1,152), and parliamentary and election expenses (£611). The last item consisted mainly of subsidies asked for by local Auxiliaries who raised their own income and were responsible for expenditure on elections within their own areas. The income of the Alliance for 1881–2 was £13, 548 and for 1885–6 £17,471.

5. *Membership figures, etc.*

The number of signatures to petitions organised by the Alliance on behalf of the Permissive Bill rose from 482,413 in 1864 to 898,456 in 1871 and 1,388,075 in 1872. In the 1870s the *Alliance News* had a circulation of about 25,000 copies a week.

6. *Sources*

The Minute Books of the Executive Committee, held in the Offices of the U.K. Alliance, Alliance House, Westminster (these survive only from 1871).

The *Alliance News*.

H. Carter, *The English Temperance Movement: A Study in Objectives,* 1933.

B. Harrison, *Drink and the Victorians. The Temperance Question in England 1815–1872,* 1971.

M. H. C. Hayler, *The Vision of a Century 1853–1953. The United Kingdom Alliance in Historical Retrospect,* 1953.

7. *Note also: The Independent Order of Good Templars*

This was an American movement devoted to total abstinence and prohibition. Its first English Lodge was founded by Joseph Malins in Birmingham in 1868. It took an active interest in electoral matters and had its own electoral agents who often also carried out agency work for the Alliance. The Good Templars' electoral policy may be seen from the Manifesto issued in 1873 (quoted in H. Carter, *The English Temperance Movement,* p. 193):

'That members of our Order do their utmost to obtain as candidates in connexion with their respective political parties only such as are favourable to the prohibition of the liquor traffic.

'That our members shall under no circumstances vote for those who are hostile to the object for the accomplishment of which our Order exists. That in any contest where all candidates are hostile to prohibitory legislation on the liquor traffic, our members shall refuse to aid them, and so prove true to the spirit and purpose of our Order and organization.'

D. THE NATIONAL EDUCATION LEAGUE

1. *Date of formation.* *1869*

2. *Objective*
To obtain a state-aided, nation-wide, compulsory education system, the education to be given where necessary in new non-sectarian schools supported by local rates and grants from Parliament. In this connection it sought certain amendments in the 1870 Education Act. In 1872 it demanded universal School Boards to control all existing schools and to provide secular instruction, with the various denominations being at liberty to provide religious instruction in out-of-school hours.

3. *Organisational structure*
Its offices were in Birmingham. It had a Council which met once a year and an Executive Committee. Delegates to the Council were appointed by the League's local branches of which there were 315 by late 1871. Among the officers of the League were George Dixon, Chairman of the Council, and Jesse Collings, secretary.

4. *Income*
By 1870 this was reaching £6,000 a year. In 1871–2 it was £6,486. By 1876 it had declined to £3,741. The main source of funds was donations, chiefly from Birmingham businessmen and manufacturers.

5. *Membership figures, etc.*
The League's monthly newsletter was selling about 20,000 copies a week on average by 1870.

6. *Sources*
National Education League Monthly Paper.
F. Adams, *History of the Elementary School Contest in England,* 1882, reprinted with J. Morley, *The Struggle for National Education,* 1873, and edited with an introduction by A. Briggs, The Harvester Press, Hassocks, 1972.

Notes

ABBREVIATIONS

A.N.	*Alliance News*
E.C.	Executive Committee
H.C.	Howell Collection
L.	*The Liberator*
Lib. Soc.	Liberation Society
N.	*The Nonconformist*
N.Ed.L.	National Education League
N.I.	*The Nonconformist and Independent*
N.S.	New Series
P.C.	Parliamentary Committee
Ref. L.	Reform League
U.K.A.	United Kingdom Alliance

All books are published in London unless a different place of publication
is stated. The sources for election statistics are J. Vincent and H. Stenton
(eds.), *McCalmonts Parliamentary Poll Book British Election Results 1832–1918*,
8th ed., The Harvester Press Ltd., Hassocks, 1971, and F. W. S. Craig
(ed.), *British Parliamentary Election Results 1885–1918*, 1974.

I. THE FADDISTS AND VICTORIAN LIBERAL POLITICS

1 See R. Harrison, *Before the Socialists. Studies in Labour and Politics 1861–
   1881*, 1965, pp. 137–209.
2 See below, pp. 299–302.
3 B. Harrison, *Drink and the Victorians. The Temperance Question in England
   1815–1872*, 1971, pp. 253–4.
4 D. A. Hamer, introduction to J. Chamberlain and others, *The Radical
   Programme* [1885], The Harvester Press, Hassocks, 1971, pp. xxxi–
   xxxiii.
5 D. A. Hamer, *Liberal Politics in the Age of Gladstone and Rosebery. A Study
   in Leadership and Policy*, Oxford, 1972, pp. 57–9, 63–4, 67–9, 74, 89–90,
   130–1, 185, 206–7.

II. ELECTORAL STRATEGIES

1 A pioneering study in this regard was H. Jephson, *The Platform, Its
   Rise and Progress*, 1892. There is a considerable amount of very useful

comparison with other movements in B. Harrison, *Drink and the Victorians. The Temperance Question in England 1815–1872*, 1971.

2　T. Lloyd, 'Uncontested Seats in British General Elections, 1852–1910', *The Historical Journal*, Vol. VIII, No. 2 (1965), pp. 260–5.

3　See below, pp. 63–64.

4　Among the most useful surveys of the history of electoral registration in the nineteenth century are C. Seymour, *Electoral Reform in England and Wales. The Development and Operation of the Parliamentary Franchise 1832–1885*, Newton Abbot, 1970 [reprint of 1915 edition], esp. Chapter V, N. Gash, *Politics in the Age of Peel. A study in the Technique of Parliamentary Representation 1830–1850*, 2nd ed. 1977, The Harvester Press, Hassocks, esp. Chapters 4 and 5; J. Alun Thomas, 'The System of Registration and the Development of Party Organisation, 1832–1870', *History*, Vol. 35, pp. 81–98.

5　See below, pp. 61, 80.

6　See below, pp. 305–8.

7　See below, pp. 27–28.

8　A. W. W. Dale, *The Life of R. W. Dale of Birmingham*, 2nd ed., 1899; A. Briggs, *Victorian Cities*, Harmondsworth, 1968, Chapter 5; E. P. Hennock, *Fit and Proper Persons. Ideal and Reality in Nineteenth-Century Urban Government*, 1973, Part II; D. M. Thompson (ed.), *Nonconformity in the nineteenth century*, 1972.

9　A. Miall, *Life of Edward Miall Formerly Member of Parliament for Rochdale and Bradford*, 1884, pp. 125–6.

10　*N.*, 944 (2 Dec. 1863), p. 965. See below, p. 107.

11　J. Vincent, *The Formation of the Liberal Party 1857–1868*, 2nd ed. 1976, The Harvester Press, Hassocks, 1966, p. xxix.

12　See below, p. 26.

13　See below, pp. 81–82, 317–23.

14　*A.N.*, XIX, 40 (4 Oct. 1873).

15　*N.*, 1702 (3 July 1878), p. 672; 1706 (31 July 1878), p. 762.

16　For example, T. Whittaker at meetings of the Alliance Council. See below, pp. 183, 229.

17　See below, pp. 182–83.

18　E.g. *N.*, 1472 (4 Feb. 1874), p. 97. This point was often made by T. Whittaker at Alliance meetings.

19　*N.*, 1628 (31 Jan. 1877), p. 97.

20　See below, pp. 210–15.

21　For Edward Miall's handling of this problem, see below, p. 105.

22　See below, pp. 47, 194.

23　See below, pp. 104–8. This was also the strategy of Samuel Morley and his Dissenters' Parliamentary Committee in 1847. See below, pp. 92–93.

III. TYPES OF ELECTORAL ACTION

1　*A.N.*, XL, 43 (27 Oct. 1893), p. 727.

2　See below, pp. 69–76, 82–83

3　See below, pp. 178–79.

4   See below, pp. 125, 147–51.
5   Cf. *N.*, 1367 (31 Jan. 1872), p. 121.
6   See below, pp. 124–25.
7   On this theme see D. A. Hamer, *Liberal Politics in the Age of Gladstone and Rosebery. A Study in Leadership and Policy*, Oxford, 1872, *passim*.
8   *N.*, 1707 (7 Aug. 1878), p. 791.
9   *N.*, 959 (16 March 1864), p. 203.
10 J. Guinness Rogers, *An Autobiography*, 1903, p. 214.
11 See below, pp. 103–4.
12 See below, pp. 67–76, 82–83.
13 See below, pp. 74–75.
14 An outstanding example of this is the Bath by-elections of 1873, for which see below, pp. 131–33. When in 1900 the Derby and District Temperance Electoral Council put forward William Bingham for South Derbyshire against the official Liberal candidate, Haig, who was a distiller, Bingham 'said that he had not come forward with any desire to split the Liberal party, nor had he any real desire to be returned as member for the division. . . . his position was this, that if the party would withdraw the man who was now their candidate, if they would select a man who would be acceptable to them, without the slightest compunction or the slightest hesitation he would stand on one side.' *A.N.*, XLVII, 22 (31 May 1900), p. 345.
15 *A.N.*, XI, 544 (3 Dec. 1864).
16 *N.*, 945 (9 Dec. 1863), p. 981.
17 It is printed in *A.N.*, XXXVII, 15 (11 April 1890), p. 229.
18 See below, pp. 108, 313.
19 *N.*, 943 (25 Nov. 1863), p. 959.
20 *A.N.*, XXXI, 42 (17 Oct. 1885). The speaker was T. C. Rayner.
21 *A.N.*, XIX, 41 (11 Oct. 1873).
22 *A.N.*, XVIII, 42 (19 Oct. 1872).
23 For examples see reference to meetings organised by the Sheffield Temperance Electoral Association in *A.N.*, 1889–91. See below, pp. 246–47, 252.
24 U.K.A. Exec. Minutes, 19 Aug. 1874.
25 For an attempt to make the Alliance's pledge positive, see U.K.A. Exec. Minutes, 26 Jan. 1898.
26 See below, pp. 252–53.
27 *A.N.*, XXXVII, 15 (11 April 1890).
28 For testimony to this see *A.N.*, XII, 585 (16 Sept. 1865).
29 Cf. *A.N.*, XXI, 28 (10 July 1875); 36 (4 Sept. 1875).
30 *A.N.*, XIX, 40 (4 Oct. 1873).
31 Cf. *A.N.*, XIV, 40 (5 Oct. 1878).
32 Cf. J. H. Raper in *A.N.*, XII, 565 (29 April 1865).
33 See below, pp. 166–69.
34 *A.N.*, XLV, 31 (5 Aug. 1898).
35 *A.N.*, XLV, 32 (12 Aug. 1898).
36 *N.*, 1370 (21 Feb. 1872), p. 190.
37 *N.*, 1444 (23 July 1873), p. 742.
38 Cf. *N.*, 1707 (7 Aug. 1878), p. 791; *A.N.*, XIX, 51 (20 Dec. 1873).

39 On this point see Harrison, *Drink and the Victorians*, p. 381.
40 *A.N.*, XXXIX, 44 (28 Oct. 1892).
41 *N.*, 1328 (4 May 1871), p. 417; Cf. W. S. Allen's observations in *N.*, 1641 (3 May 1877), p. 434.
42 See below for Mason Jones's views on this, p. 131.
43 *L.*, 225 (1 Jan. 1874), p. 8. This was a constant theme in the 1890s when the disestablishers became aware of differences between their approach to the question and that of the politicians who had 'taken it up'. Cf. *L.*, N.S., 65 (May 1892), p. 69; 66 (June 1892), p. 97; 72 (Dec. 1892), p. 192.
44 *A.N.*, XXI, 28 (10 July 1875).
45 *N.*, 945 (9 Dec. 1863), p. 981. See below, p. 42.
46 On this cf. C. Pease in *A.N.*, XVIII, 42 (19 Oct. 1872), and a debate on the subject analysed in an editorial in *A.N.*, XI, 544 (3 Dec. 1864).
47 On the politicians' view of this see below, pp. 49–51.
48 Cf. *N.*, 794 (16 Jan. 1861), p. 41; 1512 (11 Nov. 1874), p. 1082. But cf. the Rev. G. Reaney's argument that 'in politics gratitude was grossly immoral'. *N.*, 1512, p. 1103.
49 *A.N.*, XIX, 42 (18 Oct. 1873).
50 *A.N.*, XXXII, 42 (16 Oct. 1886).
51 *N.*, 1688 (27 March 1878), p. 307.
52 Howell to N. Steal, 25 July 1868, H.C. MS. 4129, f. 567; *N.*, 1778 (17 Dec. 1879), p. 1256; Cf. S. Morley on the same theme in *ibid.*, p. 1267.
53 D. T. Ingham to H. J. Wilson, 12 April 1873, H. J. Wilson MSS. (M.D. 5922), Sheffield Public Library.
54 Cf. Harrison, *Drink and the Victorians*, pp. 260–1.
55 Lib. Soc. Exec. Minutes, A/LIB/3, f. 286.

IV. PRESSURE GROUPS AND LIBERAL POLITICS

1 See below, pp. 104, 107.
2 See below, p. 129.
3 See below, pp. 153, 269–71.
4 *N.*, 1444 (23 July 1873), p. 742.
5 These arguments were prominent in the debates in the Liberation Society in the late 1870s on their future strategy. They formed the basic theme of Charles Miall's 1877 paper on electoral action. 'Early preparation', wrote Miall, 'is the most effectual antidote to division, and the best reply to the charge of dividing the Liberal interest; and success can be better achieved in the committee room, where candidates are chosen, than in the polling-booth.' *N.*, 1641 (3 May 1877), p. 438.
6 See below, pp. 234, 236.
7 See below, pp. 241–43.
8 Harrison, *Drink and the Victorians*, p. 243.
9 On this theme see D. A. Hamer, *Liberal Politics in the Age of Gladstone and Rosebery, passim.*
10 See below, pp. 230–31.
11 *N.*, 1525 (10 Feb. 1875), p. 164.

12   The reverse was also true. Cf. Rosebery's reaction to attending a sermon by Spurgeon in 1873: 'Here is a great multitude, powerful, wealthy, devoted, with a perfect organization and independence, with a leader of genius, as completely unknown to the world in which I live as if it did not exist. Its aims are not our aims, its language is not our language, its aspirations and ideas are wholly alien to our aspirations and ideas. Would it not be well for "society" to ponder this?' R. Rhodes James, *Rosebery. A Biography of Archibald Philip, Fifth Earl of Rosebery*, 1963, pp. 57–8; Cf. Harrison, *Drink and the Victorians*, p. 29; B. Harrison, ' "A World of Which We had No Conception." Liberalism and the English Temperance Press: 1830–1872', *Victorian Studies*, XIII, 2 (Dec. 1969), p. 125.

13   Cf. H. Richard's paper on 'The Political Relations of the Nonconformists to the Liberal Party', read to the Manchester Conference of Nonconformists on 25 Jan. 1872: 'There seems some ambiguity in speaking of the relations of the Nonconformists to the Liberal party, seeing that the Nonconformists themselves, to a large extent, constitute the Liberal party in this country. (Hear, hear.) But by the "Liberal party" probably it was intended we should understand the leaders of that party in Parliament, whether in or out of office; and it is in that sense that I shall use the expression in this paper.' *N.*, 1367 (31 Jan. 1872), p. 115. Cf. also Samuel Pope in 1873: 'It does not necessarily follow that the Government represents the party. (Hear.) That is the precise difficulty we are in at this moment. (Hear.)' *A.N.*, XIX, 42 (18 Oct. 1873).

14   Cf. Edward Jenkins: 'The League and Nonconformists were still, and would remain, the true Liberal party, one and indivisible. His belief was that the true Liberal party were at this moment existing outside the Government and outside the House of Commons; and he believed that something more must be done before the real Liberal party could be brought *en rapport* with the Government and the House of Commons.' *N.Ed.L. Monthly Paper*, 37 (Dec. 1872).

15   See below, pp. 139–40, 205–10.

16   *A.N.*, XXI, 42 (16 Oct. 1875).

17   For examples see below, pp. 209, 279.

18   *N.*, 1707 (7 Aug. 1878), p. 791. The letter does not give the name of the constituency, but the internal evidence proves that it must be Dudley. According to an account in *A.N.*, XXIII, 17 (28 April 1877), what happened was that electors who had signed a declaration to vote only for a Permissive Bill candidate met to form an organisation, 'and seeing that there was no Liberal Association in the borough, and that nearly all who had signed the declaration were Liberals in politics, they decided that the organisation should be called the Dudley Liberal and Permissive Bill Association. . . . Since the formation of the association efforts have been made by a few persons in the borough who have no sympathy whatever with temperance legislation, and who are anxious to continue the representation as at present, to form another Liberal Association. . . .'

19   See below, pp. 146, 152.

20 See above, pp. 26, 39.
21 *N.*, 944 (2 Dec. 1863), p. 967. The Rev. R. Bruce expressed the fear in 1864 that separation from the Liberal party would lead to their becoming 'a clique in the state'; *N.*, 953 (3 Feb. 1864), p. 83. See also *L.*, 104 (1 Jan. 1864), p. 9.
22 *A.N.*, XX, 14 (4 April 1874). The agent was W. Mart.
23 Cf. W. S. Caine on this in *A.N.*, XLII, 20 (17 May 1895).
24 Cf. below, p. 230.
25 Quoted in W. H. G. Armytage, *A. J. Mundella 1825–1897. The Liberal Background to the Labour Movement*, 1951, p. 131.
26 See below, pp. 273–75.
27 *A.N.*, XXXII, 19 (8 May 1886).
28 *A.N.*, XXII, 23 (5 June 1886); 26 (26 June 1886).
29 *N.*, 1641 (3 May 1877), p. 434.
30 Cf. Walter Morrison's repudiation of his Permissive Bill pledge at Plymouth in the early 1860s and Colonel Coke's interpretation of his pledge on the Church Rates question at East Norfolk. *A.N.*, XII, 575 (8 July 1865), and below, pp. 108–9.
31 This theme is examined in Hamer, *Liberal Politics in the Age of Gladstone and Rosebery.*
32 *Ibid.*, p. 26.
33 Mundella to R. Leader, 4 July 1874, Mundella MSS. Folio IX.
34 *A.N.*, XXXI, 42 (17 Oct. 1885). For the relevance of this to Caine's later career, see below, pp. 242–43.
35 *N.*, 1694 (9 May 1878), p. 454. See below, pp. 227, 313.
36 Cf. Hugh Mason: 'Generally speaking, he was no friend of pledges, and would rather let a man take his own unbiassed course in determining every case upon its own merits.' *N.*, 943 (25 Nov. 1863), p. 959.
37 *N.I.*, 264 (15 Jan. 1885), p. 59.
38 *N.*, 1003 (18 Jan. 1865), p. 42. See below, p. 113.
39 *N.*, 1315 (1 Feb. 1871), p. 100. See below, p. 128.
40 *N.*, 1745 (1 May 1879), p. 439. This issue came up in the Alliance in connection with Liberal brewer candidates. See below, pp. 260–64.
41 *N.*, 1708 (14 Aug. 1878), p. 815.
42 Sir William Harcourt's phrase in 1895: 'W.V.H. said he supposed that they would all say that they stuck to the old programme, but that each man would have liberty for his individual *italics*.' L. V. Harcourt's Journal, 27 June 1895, quoted in A. G. Gardiner, *The Life of Sir William Harcourt*, II, 1923, p. 366.
43 See below, pp. 117, 148, 222.
44 *N.*, 1635 (21 March 1877), p. 274.
45 *N.*, 1179 (17 June 1868), p. 599.
46 *A.N.*, XVII, 42 (21 Oct. 1871).
47 *A.N.*, XIX, 51 (20 Dec. 1873). Hoyle told the Alliance Council in 1882 that, 'so long as the liquor traffic existed some of the reforms which might be carried on in the country, instead of being a benefit to the country, were a mischief to it. Whilst he recognised the great importance of many reforms, he was driven to the conclusion that,

good as they were in themselves, if they were carried out before this reform they would be a mischief to the country and not a blessing. . . . Ours was the reform that ought to be attended to first.' *A.N.*, XXVIII, 42 (21 Oct. 1882).

48 *A.N.*, XXII, 6 (5 Feb. 1876).
49 *N.*, 1639 (18 April 1877), p. 378.
50 *N.*, 1367 (31 Jan. 1872), p. 121.
51 *N.*, 1745 (1 May 1879), p. 441.
52 *A.N.*, XXXIII, 9 (26 Feb. 1887).
53 *A.N.*, XXXVIII, 44 (30 Oct. 1891).
54 *A.N.*, XXXI, 42 (17 Oct. 1885).
55 *A.N.*, XXIII, 43 (27 Oct. 1877).
56 Baines to W. Arthur, 6 March 1874, Baines MSS. 45/19. See also the letter quoted in Vincent, *Formation of the Liberal Party*, pp. 124–6.
57 'Our Torrington correspondent thinks that candidates holding anti-state-church views had better either wait till the licensing question be settled, or not mix up the two questions in the same context.' *L.*, 201 (1 Jan. 1872), p. 8.
58 See below, pp. 131–32, 185–89.
59 *N.Ed.L. Monthly Paper*, 44 (July 1873), p. 9.
60 On this see a letter by Samuel Tomkins in *N.*, 1391 (17 July 1872), p. 739. Cf. Vincent, *Formation of the Liberal Party*, p. 92.
61 H. J. Wilson to his brother, 4 Dec. 1872, H. J. Wilson MSS., Sheffield Public Library (M.D. 6008).
62 Harrison, *Drink and the Victorians*, Chapter 7.
63 Wilson to Mundella, 22 March 1873, H. J. Wilson MSS., Sheffield University Library (Box 1).
64 Harrison, *Drink and the Victorians*, p. 155; Cf. H. J. Hanham, *Elections and Party Management*, 1959, pp. 238–9.

V. THE ANTI-CORN LAW LEAGUE

1 E. C. Black, *The Association. British Extraparliamentary Political Organization 1769–1793*, Cambridge, Mass., 1963, p. 13; I. R. Christie, *Wilkes, Wyvill and Reform. The Parliamentary Reform Movement in British Politics 1760–1785*, 1962, pp. 52–60; S. Maccoby, *English Radicalism 1762–1785. The Origins*, 1955, p. 84.
2 Black, *The Association*, pp. 43–54; Christie, *Wilkes, Wyvill and Reform*, pp. 92, 106, 111–12, 117–18; T. M. Parssinen, 'Association, convention and anti-parliament in British radical politics, 1771–1848', *English Historical Review*, 88 (1973), p. 504; H. Butterfield, 'The Yorkshire Association and the Crisis of 1779–80', *Transactions of the Royal Historical Society*, 4th Series, XXIX (1947), p. 69.
3 The requirement that the holders of certain offices had to offer themselves for re-election upon appointment was abolished by the Re-election of Ministers Act of 1926. An Act of 1919 had considerably modified the requirement.
4 Cobden to Smith, 3 Feb. 1839, J. B. Smith MSS.
5 N. McCord, *The Anti-Corn Law League 1838–1846*, 1958, p. 81.

6   *Ibid.*, p. 83.
7   *Ibid.*, pp. 84–9.
8   *Ibid.*, pp. 91–2.
9   E.g. G. Wilson to Cobden, 29 Aug. 1841: 'North Lancashire would only be a failure. There is not a single man in that division of the County who has public spirit sufficient even to make enquires into our strength there and Livesey says that there is no chance but attending to the Register.' Cobden MSS., Add. MS. 43,663, f. 131.
10 McCord, *Anti-Corn Law League*, pp. 93–4; J. Morley, *The Life of Richard Cobden*, 1893 (1 vol. edition), pp. 173–4.
11 McCord, *Anti-Corn Law League*, p. 86.
12 Cobden to Wilson, 9 Oct. 1841, Wilson MSS.
13 As Cobden put it in the same letter: 'Leeds ran away after a political *ignis fatuus*. Glasgow deserted us for tariff reform. Birmingham has never had a lucid interval yet.'
14 9 Nov. 1841, Wilson MSS.
15 On this cf. R. Greg to G. Wilson, 30 Jan. 1840, Wilson MSS.: 'I am not sanguine as to any impression being made upon the County *Constituencies*, on the contrary, I think we shall have them more & more against us for the present at least, & thus must redouble our efforts to win all the Representatives of Boroughs. . . . Our field of action is, boroughs, & towns generally. The population of them has the same interest as ourselves, & more power to assist us. . . .' Cobden to Wilson, 17 March 1842, Wilson MSS.: 'Our work must be directed towards the boroughs.'
16 27 Feb. 1842, Wilson MSS.; Morley, *Cobden*, pp. 228–9.
17 McCord, *Anti-Corn Law League*, pp. 148–53.
18 *Ibid.*, p. 155.
19 12 Oct. 1842, Cobden MSS., Add. MS. 43,663, ff. 24–7.
20 *The League*, 1 (30 Sept. 1843), pp. 1, 5.
21 *The League*, 88 (31 May 1845), p. 571.
22 *The League*, 42 (13 July 1844), p. 676.
23 25 Oct. 1842, Cobden MSS., Add. MS. 43,663, ff. 40–1.
24 28 Jan. 1841, Cobden MSS., Add. MS. 43,656, ff. 1–2.
25 *The League*, 2 (7 Oct. 1843), p. 21.
26 *The League*, 4 (21 Oct. 1843), p. 53.
27 *The League*, 6 (4 Nov. 1843), p. 84.
28 12 May 1842, Cobden MSS., Add. MS. 43,649, f. 31.
29 *The League*, 6 (4 Nov. 1843), p. 81.
30 Cf. Cobden to G. Wilson, 24 Feb. 1842, Wilson MSS.: 'One thing is certain, unless we can strike a bold blow *now*, we shall be superseded very materially by the suffrage people.'
31 Cf. James Wilson's letter, quoted above, p. 65.
32 *The League*, 8 (18 Nov. 1843), pp. 116–17.
33 *The League*, 9 (25 Nov. 1843), p. 133.
34 22 Oct. 1843, Wilson MSS.
35 *The League*, 10 (2 Dec. 1843), pp. 146, 154.
36 16 Nov. 1843, Wilson MSS.
37 4 April 1844, Wilson MSS.

38 3 Nov. 1843, Wilson MSS.

39 Cf. McCord, *The Anti-Corn Law League*, pp. 156–60.

40 'I feel anxious about the possible predicament in which the League
    may be placed on the anticipated vacancy for Morpeth. The League
    is pledged to contest every borough, & our enemies will watch our
    course very narrowly to impeach our consistency, & establish proofs
    of political partisanship. I wish you would try to see Lord Morpeth,
    & prevail on him to frame his address in such a manner as to save us
    from any difficulty. He might use the peace maker "if" & thus leave
    himself free to vote for Mr. Villiers' motion. Peel's declaration opens
    the door for him.' Cobden to Baines, 6 Feb. 1844, Cobden MSS., Add.
    MS. 43,664, ff. 149–50.

41 *The League*, 20 (10 Feb. 1844), p. 318.

42 *The League*, 27 (30 March 1844), p. 432.

43 *The League*, 28 (6 April 1844), pp. 445–6. Cf. R. Moore to Wilson,
    25 April 1844, Wilson MSS.: 'it is impossible to overrate the impor-
    tance of those Electioneering agitations.'

44 *The League*, 29 (13 April 1844), p. 461.

45 9 April 1844, Wilson MSS.

46 *The League*, 29 (13 April 1844). p. 461.

47 *The League*, 30 (20 April 1844), p. 479.

48 *The League*, 30 (20 April 1844), p. 485.

49 *The League*, 31 (27 April 1844), p. 493.

50 Wilson MSS.

51 *The League*, 32 (4 May 1844), p. 516.

52 For details see McCord, *The Anti-Corn Law League*, pp. 148–53, 173;
    H. D. Jordan, 'The Political Methods of the Anti-Corn Law League',
    Political Science Quarterly, XLII, 1 (March 1927), pp. 58–76.

53 Quoted in A. Prentice, *History of the Anti-Corn Law League*, 1968 ed., II,
    pp. 220–1.

54 *The League*, 33 (11 May 1844), p. 530.

55 Thomas Bazley wrote to G. Wilson urging him to make a classification
    of the voters. 'An important *moral* and *intelligent majority* I am sure we
    can establish in our favor.' 28 May 1844, Wilson MSS.

56 *The League*, 36 (1 June 1844), pp. 577–8. Cf. Cobden to Baines, 24
    June 1844: 'South Lancashire, the West Riding, & Middlesex, may
    & must be won. *They* will be regarded by all politicians as the testing
    points of public opinion. Our friends in Lancashire are sanguine of
    being able to place us out of danger by the next revision.' Cobden
    MSS., Add. MS. 43,664, f. 153.

57 *The League*, 38 (15 June 1844), p. 615.

58 Wilson MSS.; D. Read, *Cobden and Bright. A Victorian Political Partner-
    ship*, 1967, p. 30. Cf. Cobden to Bright [21–25 April], 1842: 'Nothing
    will frighten the aristocracy into Free Trade measures so soon as a
    threatened union of the classes upon the suffrage.' Cobden MSS.,
    Add. MS. 43,649, f. 27.

59 *The League*, 45 (3 Aug. 1844), p. 722.

60 *The League*, 57 (26 Oct. 1844), pp. 67–8.

61 E.g. *The League*, 60 (16 Nov. 1844), p. 113.

62 For details of the plan and how it operated see Jordan, 'Political Methods of the Anti-Corn Law League'; McCord, *The Anti-Corn Law League*, pp. 148 ff.; F. M. L. Thompson, 'Whigs and Liberals in the West Riding, 1830–1860', *English Historical Review*, 74 (1959), pp.214 ff.

63 *The League*, 61 (23 Nov. 1844), p. 132.

64 *The League*, 63 (7 Dec. 1844), pp. 165–6; 68 (11 Jan. 1845), p. 245.

65 *The League*, 69 (18 Jan. 1845), p. 264.

66 *Ibid.*

67 *The League*, 74 (22 Feb. 1845), p. 337.

68 *The League*, 73 (15 Feb. 1845), pp. 321–2.

69 Cobden to Wilson, 20, 23 April 1845, Wilson MSS.

70 *The League*, 89 (7 June 1845), p. 577; 91 (21 June 1845), p. 609. On this theme see also 74 (22 Feb. 1845), p. 337. Cf. James Heywood to C. Wilson, 19 July 1844, Wilson MSS.: 'In the warfare of the registration the solicitors rise to the rank of Generals, and the policy of the government of the country greatly depends on their talent & energy in the right formation of the constituencies on the register.'

71 *The League*, 73, p. 322.

72 *The League*, 75 (1 March 1845), p. 353.

73 *The League*, 99 (16 Aug. 1845), pp. 741, 750. On the background to this by-election see Lord Grey to Cobden, 21 July 1845, Cobden MSS., Add. MS. 43,667, ff. 122–4, and an extensive correspondence in the Wilson MSS.

74 *The League*, 108 (18 Oct. 1845), p. 17.

75 *The League*, 110 (1 Nov. 1845), pp. 52–3.

76 Thompson, 'Whigs and Liberals in the West Riding', p. 227.

77 *The League*, 110 (1 Nov. 1845), p. 54; Jordan, 'Political Methods of the Anti-Corn Law League', p. 71.

78 *The League*, 110 (1 Nov. 1845), p. 53.

79 *The League*, 112 (15 Nov. 1845), p. 81.

80 *The League*, 113 (22 Nov. 1845), p. 97.

81 *The League*, 121 (17 Jan. 1846), p. 225.

82 *The League*, 118 (27 Dec. 1845), p. 182. Cf. Cobden to J. B. Smith, 3 Jan. 1846, J. B. Smith MSS.: 'I hope the attention of our friends in the League Council rooms will now be given exclusively to the registration. *All depends on it.* The two leading rival statesmen will be both ready & willing to do our work when we can give them votes enough. But they will look to the majority in the House. . . .'

83 *The League*, 121 (17 Jan. 1846), p. 237.

84 Cf. his views as expressed to Prince Albert in Dec. 1845 and quoted in H. J. Hanham, *The Nineteenth-Century Constitution 1815–1914 Documents and Commentary*, Cambridge, 1969, p. 305.

85 'But for the League & its organization, & especially its 40/– freehold *bludgeon*, the aristocracy would have cashiered Peel or any other statesman who dared to propose the total repeal of their darling monopoly, with as little ceremony as they would discharge a groom or a gamekeeper; and I am much mistaken if we shall not live to hear Peel declare that the League alone enabled him to do the good work.' Cobden to J. B. Smith, 18 March 1846, J. B. Smith MSS.

86   Morley, *Life of Cobden*, p. 501.

87   Read, *Cobden and Bright*, p. 56.

88   Hanham, *Elections and Party Management*, p. 309; N. McCord, 'Cobden and Bright in Politics, 1846–1857', in R. Robson (ed.), *Ideas and Institutions of Victorian Britain. Essays in honour of George Kitson Clark*, 1967, pp. 100–1.

89   Cf. Cobden to Wilson, 4 Nov. 1845, Wilson MSS.: 'The qualification & registration movements have done it, & we must go [on] with both as vigorously as ever.' Others in the League's organisation were not so keen. W. Evans wrote to Wilson from the League's Manchester offices, 19 May 1846: 'Turn over in yr. mind the best plan for continuing the registration—individually I confess I feel now little interest in it, and I find that feeling pervading all our friends. I know however how much you value it and in deference should be glad to hear your views.' Wilson MSS.

90   S. Maccoby, *English Radicalism 1832–1852*, 1935, p. 435. Cobden refers to such a discussion with other Radicals, in this case Hume, Fox, and Milner Gibson, in a letter to Bright, 3 Jan. 1849, Cobden MSS., Add. MS. 43,649, ff. 130–1.

91   28 Aug., 8, 16 Sept., 1, 23 Nov., 25, 27 Dec. 1848, 22 Jan,. 1 Oct., 8 Dec. 1849, Cobden MSS., Add. MS. 43,649, ff. 71–2, 75, 79, 88, 98–100, 119–20, 127, 130–1, 136, 141–6, 150–3; Morley, *Life of Cobden*, pp. 503, 515–17, 520–1.

92   28 Sept. 1848, Cobden MSS., Add. MS. 43,656, ff. 60–4.

93   14 Sept. [1848], Cobden MSS., Add. MS. 43,656, ff. 45–6.

94   28 Sept. 1848, Cobden MSS., Add. MS. 43,656, f. 61.

95   McCord, 'Cobden and Bright in Politics', *Ideas and Institutions*, pp. 96–9.

96   28 Aug. 1848, Cobden MSS., Add. MS. 43,649, ff. 71–2.

97   Cobden to Bright, 27 Dec. 1848, Cobden MSS., Add. MS. 43,649, f. 127.

98   Cobden to Bright, 8 Dec. 1849, Cobden MSS., Add. MS. 43,649, ff. 150–3; Morley, *Life of Cobden*, pp. 520–1.

99   Morley, *Life of Cobden*, p. 566.

100   D. Martin, 'Land Reform', in P. Hollis (ed.), *Pressure from Without in early Victorian England*, 1974, pp. 150–1; F. E. Gillespie, *Labor and Politics in England 1850–1867*, 1966, pp. 84–95.

VI. NONCONFORMIST ELECTORAL POLICY PRIOR TO 1870

1   R. G. Cowherd, *The Politics of English Dissent. The Religious Aspects of Liberal and Humanitarian Reform Movements from 1815 to 1848*, New York, 1956, pp. 31, 57–8, 84.

2   On the subject of Nonconformity and politics in the 1830s and 1840s see N. Gash, *Reaction and Reconstruction in English Politics 1832–1852*, Oxford, 1965, Chapters III and IV; Cowherd, *The Politics of English Dissent*; G. I. T. Machin, 'The Maynooth Grant, the Dissenters and Disestablishment, 1845–1847', *English Historical Review*, LXXXII (1967), pp. 61–85; Salter, 'Political Nonconformity in the eighteen-

thirties', *Transactions of the Royal Historical Society*, 5th Series 3 (1953), pp. 125–43.

3 Miall, *Life of Edward Miall*, p. 108.

4 Machin, 'The Maynooth Grant', p. 76.

5 'Voluntarists' were Nonconformists who totally opposed State control over education.

6 Machin, 'The Maynooth Grant', p. 76; Miall, *Life of Edward Miall*, pp. 108–10.

7 E. Hodder, *The Life of Samuel Morley*, 3rd ed., 1887, pp. 98–105.

8 E.g. E. Miall, C. Gilpin, Apsley Pellatt, W. Ackroyd, Jacob Bright, G. Hadfield, Henry Ashworth. See above, pp. 18–19.

9 Cowherd, *The Politics of English Dissent*, pp. 162–3; W. H. Mackintosh, *Disestablishment and Liberation. The Movement for the Separation of Anglican Church from State Control*, 1972, p. 32; Machin, 'The Maynooth Grant', pp. 77–83; Gash, *Reaction and Reconstruction*, pp. 100–6.

10 Mackintosh, *Disestablishment*, p. 57.

11 Lib. Soc. E.C. Minutes, 9 Feb. 1854, A/LIB/2.

12 Lib. Soc. E.C. Minutes, 23 June, 3 July, 4, 16 Oct. 1854, A/LIB/2, ff. 90–2, 110, 244.

13 Lib. Soc. E.C. Minutes, 11 Oct. 1854, A/LIB/2, f. 111.

14 Lib. Soc. E.C. Minutes, 2, 16 March 1855, A/LIB/2, ff. 329, 344; *L.*, 1 (July 1855), p. 7; 2 (Aug. 1855), p. 29.

15 *L.*, 3 (Sept. 1855), p. 42.

16 *L.*, 7 (Jan. 1856), pp. 9, 10, 19. In July 1856 the *Liberator* (14, p. 138) published a letter from 'A Hertfordshire Freeholder' suggesting that county as a suitable place on which to concentrate efforts for the purchase of new qualifications. 'The registration is thoroughly attended to, and has been so for several years, so that nothing that is done will be thrown away. The county is intersected by the North-Western, the Great Northern, and the Eastern Counties Railways, and is, therefore, easily accessible, not only from London, but from most of the provinces.' He lists ways of purchasing a qualification: buying a freehold rent-charge, buying a piece of land from the National Freehold Land Society, joining with others to buy a house, taking care that the rent produces at least 40/- a year for each person after payment of repairs. Leading friends who have already become freeholders, of Hertfordshire are named. They include S. Morley, Gilpin, Pellatt, Courtauld, and Finch, and, amongst the 'advanced Liberals', Cobden, Scholefield, Ricardo, and Travers.

17 *L.*, 12 (15 May 1856), pp. 90–8.

18 Lib. Soc. E.C. Minutes, 30 June 1856, A/LIB/2, f. 604; *L.*, 14 (July 1856), p. 140.

19 Lib. Soc. E.C. Minutes, 19 Jan., 2 Feb. 1857, A/LIB/2, ff. 662, 664.

20 Lib. Soc. E.C. Minutes, 23 March, 6 April 1857, A/LIB/2, ff. 685, 687.

21 Vincent, *Formation of the Liberal Party*, p. 72.

22 *L.*, 24 (May 1857), p. 84.

23 *L.*, 25 (June 1857), p. 96.

24 *L.*, 25 (June 1857), pp. 106–7; 27 (Aug. 1857), p. 133.

25 Miall, *Life of Edward Miall*, p. 218. In 1859 the Electoral Committee reported that it had been trying to find him a seat 'but while, in more than one constituency, a strong desire for his return has been manifested, from a determination to be represented by local men, & other causes, a preference has been given to other candidates.'; Lib. Soc. E.C. Minutes, 27 April 1859, A/LIB/2, f. 946.

26 *L.*, 25 (June 1857), p. 94.

27 Mackintosh, *Disestablishment*, pp. 57–9; Lib. Soc. E.C. Minutes, 15 June, 14 Aug. 1857, 4 Feb., 14, 25 March, 1859, A/LIB/2, ff. 725, 742, 902, 926, 937.

28 *N.*, 758 (9 May 1860), p. 363. After Sir William Clay lost his seat in 1857, Sir John Trelawny, MP for Tavistock, undertook the annual moving of a Bill to abolish Church Rates. In 1858 this passed its second reading by 214 to 160 but was eventually rejected by the House of Lords. Early in 1860 the second reading was again carried, and, after 5,281 petitions bearing 582,386 signatures had been presented, the third reading was carried by 9 votes. The Bill met the same fate as in 1858 at the hands of the Lords.

29 *N.*, 798 (13 Feb. 1861), p. 145.

30 *N.*, 798 (13 Feb. 1861), p. 132; 799 (20 Feb. 1861), p. 146.

31 *N.*, 813 (29 May 1861), p. 421. Cf. *N.*, 800 (27 Feb. 1861), p. 171.

32 *N.*, 821 (24 July 1861), pp. 581, 594; 822 (31 July 1861), pp. 601, 607.

33 Lib. Soc. E.C. Minutes, 27 Sept., 4, 18 Oct. 1861, A/LIB/2, ff. 1204, 1208, 1213, 1217.

34 *N.*, 845 (8 Jan. 1862), pp. 22–3; 849 (5 Feb. 1862), p. 132.

35 *N.*, 864 (21 May 1862), p. 441; 883 (1 Oct. 1862), pp. 827, 829; 887 (29 Oct. 1862), p. 908; 889 (12 Nov. 1862), p. 947.

36 Lib. Soc. E.C. Minutes, 16 Jan. 1863, A/LIB/3, f. 171.

37 In 1861 the Bill passed its second reading by 281 to 266 but was lost on the third reading by the Speaker's casting vote. In 1862 the Bill was defeated by 287 to 286 and in 1863 by 285 to 275. It was not moved in either 1864 or 1865. Mackintosh, *Disestablishment*, Chapters 5 and 13.

38 Lib. Soc. E.C. Minutes, 15 May 1863, A/LIB/3, f. 225.

39 *N.*, 915 (13 May 1863), pp. 366–7.

40 *N.*, 931 (2 Sept. 1863), p. 697.

41 Lib. Soc. E.C. Minutes, 26 June 1863, A/LIB/3, ff. 253–4.

42 Lib. Soc. E.C. Minutes, 23 Oct. 1863, A/LIB/3, f. 286. The paper was subsequently given at various conferences. See, e.g., *N.*, 943 (25 Nov. 1863), p. 937.

43 Lib. Soc. E.C. Minutes, 13 Nov. 1863, A/LIB/3, f. 297; *N.*, 942 (18 Nov. 1863), pp. 918–19.

44 *N.*, 943 (25 Nov. 1863), pp. 940–1, 957–9.

45 *Ibid.*, p. 942.

46 *N.*, 944 (2 Dec. 1863), pp. 961, 963.

47 *Ibid.*, pp. 963–7.

48 *N.*, 945, p. 981.

49 *N.*, 949 (6 Jan. 1864), pp. 3–4.

50 *L.*, 104 (Jan. 1864), p. 9.

51 *N.*, 950 (13 Jan. 1864), p. 21.

52 *L.*, 105 (Feb. 1864), pp. 25–6.
53 *N.*, 952 (27 Jan. 1864), pp. 62–3.
54 *N.*, 953 (3 Feb. 1864), p. 83.
55 *N.*, 956 (24 Feb. 1864), p. 142.
56 *N.*, 957 (2 March 1864), pp. 163–4.
57 *N.*, 958 (9 March 1864), p. 182.
58 *N.*, 959 (16 March 1864), p. 203.
59 *N.*, 967 (11 May 1864), p. 381.
60 *N.*, 977 (20 July 1864), p. 588. Cf. *N.*, 975 (6 July 1864), p. 547; *L.*, 105 (Feb. 1864), p. 26.
61 *N.*, 977 (20 July 1864), pp. 588–9; 978 (27 July 1864), p. 601.
62 *N.*, 980 (10 Aug. 1864), pp. 642–3, 647, 651; 983 (31 Aug. 1864), p. 697; *L.*, 112 (Sept. 1864), p. 136; 113 (Oct. 1864), p. 152.
63 *N.*, 984 (7 Sept. 1864), p. 722.
64 *N.*, 985 (14 Sept. 1864), p. 743; 988 (5 Oct. 1864), p. 797; *L.*, 113 (Oct. 1864), pp. 149–50; Lib. Soc. E.C. Minutes, 23 Sept., 7 Oct. 1864, A/LIB/3, ff. 421, 428; Lib. Soc. P.C. Minutes, 5, 12 Oct. 1864, A/LIB/13.
65 *N.*, 989 (12 Oct. 1864), p. 823.
66 *L.*, 114 (Nov. 1864), p. 171.
67 Lib. Soc. E.C. Minutes, A/LIB/3, ff. 429, 433.
68 Lib. Soc. E.C. Minutes, 18 Nov. 1864, A/LIB/3, f. 444; Lib. Soc. P.C. Minutes, 16 Nov. 1864, A/LIB/13.
69 *N.*, 1003 (18 Jan. 1865), pp. 41–2; *L.*, 117 (Feb. 1865), p. 26.
70 Mackintosh, *Disestablishment*, p. 123.
71 *N.*, 1018 (4 May 1865), pp. 346–7.
72 *N.*, 1020 (17 May 1865), p. 389.
73 Lib. Soc. E.C. Minutes, 26 May 1865, A/LIB/3, f. 543.
74 Lib. Soc. P.C. Minutes, 15, 21 June 1865, A/LIB/13.
75 *L.*, 122 (July 1865), pp. 119, 121.
76 Lib. Soc. E.C. Minutes, 21 July 1865, A/LIB/3, f. 563.
77 *L.*, 123 (Aug. 1865), p. 138.
78 *N.*, 1047 (29 Nov. 1865), p. 954.
79 *L.*, 123 (Aug. 1865), p. 136.
80 Lib. Soc. E.C. Minutes, 22 June 1866, A/LIB/3, f. 729.
81 *N.*, 1090 (26 Sept. 1866), pp. 771–3; 1091 (3 Oct. 1866), pp. 789, 798; Vincent, *Formation of the Liberal Party*, p. 71; K. O. Morgan, *Wales in British Politics 1868–1922*, 2nd ed., Cardiff, 1970, pp. 17–18, 28; I. G. Jones, 'The Liberation Society and Welsh Politics, 1844–68', *Welsh History Review*, 1, No. 2 (1961).
82 *N.*, 1120 (2 May 1867), p. 348.
83 *N.*, 1124 (29 May 1867), p. 437; 1146 (30 Oct. 1867), p. 891.
84 *N.*, 1167 (28 March 1868), pp. 289, 301.
85 *L.*, 155 (April 1868), p. 58; 156 (May 1868), pp. 75–6.
86 *N.*, 1178 (10 June 1868), p. 582; 1179 (17 June 1868), p. 599; 1180 (24 June 1868), p. 624; 1181 (1 July 1868), p. 645.
87 Lib. Soc. E.C. Minutes, A/LIB/4, ff. 121–2.
88 *L.*, 159 (Aug. 1868), p. 146; Lib. Soc. E.C. Minutes, 11 Sept. 1868, A/LIB/4, f. 167.

89 Mackintosh, *Disestablishment*, pp. 124–5; Lib. Soc. E.C. Minutes, 4 Dec. 1868, A/LIB/4, f. 202.
90 *L.*, 174 (Nov. 1869), pp. 179–80.
91 *L.*, 185 (Oct. 1870), p. 165; Lib. Soc. E.C. Minutes, 8 Sept. 1870, A/LIB/4, f. 895. Miall's motion was defeated by 374 to 89.
92 *N.*, 1328 (4 May 1871), p. 417.
93 *L.*, 198 (Oct. 1871), p. 184; Lib. Soc. E.C. Minutes, 3, 17 July, 18 Sept., 1871, 29 Jan., 9 Dec. 1872, A/LIB/4, ff. 1057, 1068–9, 1091, 1154, 1514.
94 *L.*, 217 (May 1873), p. 68.

VII. THE NATIONAL EDUCATION LEAGUE AND THE 'REVOLT OF THE NONCONFORMISTS'

1 J. L. Garvin, *The Life of Joseph Chamberlain*, I, 1932, pp. 117–18.
2 See Appendix.
3 *N.Ed.L. Monthly Paper*, 23 (Oct. 1871).
4 *N.Ed.L. Monthly Paper*, 24 (Nov. 1871).
5 *N.*, 1355 (8 Nov. 1871), p. 1094.
6 Clause 25 permitted the School Boards to pay the fees of poor children out of the rates and was objected to because it meant that rates paid by Nonconformists might be used to enable children to attend Church schools. It was seen as further bolstering the position of those schools. Clause 74 permitted School Boards to make attendance compulsory and to remit all or part of the fees of any child where the parent satisfied the Board that he could not pay.
7 For the text see *N.*, 1358 (29 Nov. 1871), p. 1185.
8 *N.*, 1367 (31 Jan. 1872), pp. 115–21.
9 *N.*, 1369 (14 Feb. 1872), p. 163.
10 *N.*, 1377 (10 April 1872), p. 363.
11 *N.*, 1368 (7 Feb. 1872), p. 144.
12 *N.*, 1369 (14 Feb. 1872), p. 167.
13 *N.*, 1370 (21 Feb. 1872), p. 190.
14 Cf. *N.*, 1358 (29 Nov. 1871).
15 *A.N.*, XVIII, 5 (3 Feb. 1872). Isaac Holden complained that the League's 'new programme' 'had interfered very much with the smooth current of political matters in Yorkshire'; *N.Ed.L. Monthly Paper*, 37 (Dec. 1872).
16 *N.Ed.L. Monthly Paper*, 31 (June 1872).
17 Garvin, *Chamberlain*, I, pp. 129–30.
18 *N.Ed.L. Monthly Paper*, 32 (July 1872).
19 Garvin, *Chamberlain*, I, p. 132; A. Briggs, Introduction to the Harvester Press edition of F. Adams, *History of the Elementary School Contest in England*, 1972, p. xxxvi. For Winterbotham see also above, p. 50.
20 Garvin, *Chamberlain*, I, p. 118; *N.Ed.L. Monthly Paper*, 34 (Sept. 1872).
21 *N.Ed.L. Monthly Paper*, 34 (Sept. 1872).
22 *N.Ed.L. Monthly Paper*, 37 (Dec. 1872).
23 *N.*, 1421 (12 Feb. 1873), pp. 157–8.
24 The following account is based on *N.Ed.L. Monthly Paper*, 44 (July

1873); and Adams, *History of the Elementary School Contest*, pp. 292–4.
25 *N.*, 1444 (23 July 1873), p. 742.
26 *N.Ed.L. Monthly Paper*, 44 (July 1873).
27 *Ibid.*
28 Cf. Morley to Chamberlain, 15 July 1873; Chamberlain to Morley 19 July 1873, Chamberlain MSS., JC 5/54/2, 3. Morley wrote to Frederic Harrison, 15 Aug. 1873: 'The League agent has been down to Hastings to sound the people there. They decide in a fortnight whether they, i.e. the Radicals, will break off with the Whigs and run me to lose, or will persuade the Whigs to throw over Shuttleworth, and run me with Brassey as the regular candidate. The agent saw three Radical leaders; one a Baptist minister, the other an Independent ditto, the third a Rationalist contractor in the building line.'; F. W. Hirst, *Early Life & Letters of John Morley*, I, 1927, p. 279.
29 Chamberlain MSS., JC 5/54/3.
30 Chamberlain to Morley [10 Aug. 1873], Chamberlain MSS., JC 5/54/7.
31 *N.Ed.L. Monthly Paper*, 46 (Sept. 1873).
32 *Ibid.*, quoting the *Congregationalist*: 'We have fought too long under the chiefs of the old Liberal party not to feel a thrill of satisfaction in thinking once more of the policy of the party as our own policy, and of regarding its struggles and its triumphs as our own.'
33 Hirst, *Early Life of Morley*, I. p. 279.
34 *N.*, 1449 (27 Aug. 1873), p. 849.
35 *N.Ed.L. Monthly Paper*, 47 (Oct. 1873).
36 *L.*, 221 (Sept. 1873), p. 152.
37 *N.Ed.L. Monthly Paper*, 48 (Nov. 1873).
38 *L.*, 221 (Sept. 1873), p. 152; 223 (Nov. 1873), p. 186.
39 *N.Ed.L. Monthly Paper*, 51 (Feb. 1874).
40 *N.*, 1472 (4 Feb. 1874), p. 97.
41 Dale, *Life of R. W. Dale*, p. 728.
42 *L.*, 227 (March 1874), p. 36.

VIII. THE LIBERATION SOCIETY, 1874–1900

1 *N.*, 1512 (11 Nov. 1874), pp. 1082, 1101–3.
2 See Appendix. Mackintosh, *Disestablishment*, pp. 217–21.
3 *N.*, 1525 (10 Feb. 1875), pp. 163–4.
4 Cf. *N.*, 1564 (10 Nov. 1875), p. 1121.
5 *N.*, 1578 (16 Feb. 1876), p. 153.
6 *N.*, 1621 (13 Dec. 1876), p. 1236.
7 *N.*, 1668 (7 Nov. 1877), p. 1115.
8 *N.*, 1672 (5 Dec. 1877), p. 1212.
9 *Ibid.*, p. 1217.
10 *N.*, 1778 (17 Dec. 1879), pp. 1265–7, 1255–6.
11 *N.*, 1626 (17 Jan. 1877), p. 49; 1628 (31 Jan. 1877), p. 97; 1637 (4 April 1877), p. 321; 1641 (3 May 1877), p. 438.
12 *N.*, 1630 (14 Feb. 1877), p. 149.
13 *N.*, 1631 (21 Feb. 1877), p. 175.

14 *N.*, 1637 (4 April 1877), p. 321.
15 *N.*, 1641 (3 May 1877), pp. 434, 438–9.
16 *N.*, 1670 (21 Nov. 1877), p. 1163. Cf. Hamer, *Liberal Politics in the Age of Gladstone and Rosebery*, pp. 47–51.
17 *N.*, 1668 (7 Nov. 1877), p. 1121.
18 *N.*, 1677 (9 Jan. 1878), p. 25.
19 Lib. Soc. E.C. Minutes, 8 July 1878, A/LIB/6, f. 227.
20 Lib. Soc. E.C. Minutes, 22 July 1878, A/LIB/6, f. 239.
21 *N.*, 1721 (13 Nov. 1878), pp. 1128–33.
22 J. G. Kellas, 'The Liberal party and the Scottish church disestablishment crisis', *English Historical Review*, LXXIX (Jan. 1964), pp. 31–46.
23 *N.*, 1773 (12 Nov. 1879), pp. 1120–1.
24 R. T. Shannon, *Gladstone and the Bulgarian Agitation 1876*, 2nd ed., Harvester Press, Hassocks, 1976.
25 Lib. Soc. E.C. Minutes, 8 July, 14, 28 Oct., 18 Nov., 30 Dec. 1878, A/LIB/6, ff. 228, 270, 277, 290, 306.
26 *N.*, 1720 (6 Nov. 1878), p. 1105.
27 *N.*, 1722 (20 Nov. 1878), p. 1151.
28 *N.*, 1732 (29 Jan. 1879), p. 101; Lib. Soc. E.C. Minutes, 27 Jan. 1879, A/LIB/6, f. 817.
29 *N.*, 1701 (26 June 1878), pp. 642–3; 1706 (31 July 1878), p. 762; 1707 (7 Aug. 1878), p. 791.
30 *N.*, 1745 (1 May 1879), pp. 439–41.
31 *N.*, 1770 (22 Oct. 1879), p. 1041; 1761 (20 Aug. 1879), p. 822.
32 *N.*, 1772 (5 Nov. 1879), p. 1096.
33 *N.*, 1773 (12 Nov. 1879), pp. 1113, 1120–1; 1778 (17 Dec. 1879), p. 1241.
34 *N.*, 1778 (17 Dec. 1879), p. 1265.
35 Lib. Soc. E.C. Minutes, 24 Nov. 1879, A/LIB/6, f. 1021; Mackintosh, *Disestablishment*, p. 232; *N.I.*, 1 (1 Jan. 1880), p. 21.
36 Lib. Soc. E.C. Minutes, 5 Jan. 1880, A/LIB/6, f. 1042.
37 Lib. Soc. E.C. Minutes, 12 April 1880, A/LIB/6, f. 1102. Cf. Hanham, *Elections and Party Management*, p. 124.
38 *N.I.*, 9 (26 Feb. 1880), pp. 222–3; 12 (18 March 1880), pp. 290–1.
39 Hanham, *Elections and Party Management*, p. 124. Cf. Hamer, *Liberal Politics in the Age of Gladstone and Rosebery*, pp. 82–3.
40 *N.I.*, 10 (4 March 1880), p. 231.
41 *N.I.*, 11 (11 March 1880), p. 265.
42 *Ibid.*, p. 257.
43 *N.I.*, 12 (18 March 1880), p. 279.
44 *N.I.*, 25 (17 June 1880), pp. 645–51.
45 *N.I.*, 110 (2 Feb. 1882), p. 98.
46 *Ibid.*, p. 99.
47 *N.I.*, 173 (19 April 1883), p. 355.
48 *N.I.*, 175 (4 May 1883), Suppl., p. 12.
49 *N.I.*, 110 (2 Feb. 1882), p. 99.
50 *N.I.*, 201 (1 Nov. 1883), p. 1000.
51 *N.I.*, 160 (18 Jan. 1883), p. 60; Kellas, 'The Liberal party and the Scottish church disestablishment crisis'.

52 *N.I.*, 260 (18 Dec. 1884), p. 1203; 261 (24 Dec. 1884), p. 1228; Lib. Soc. P.C. Minutes, Circulars dated Dec. 1884 and Jan. 1885, A/LIB/14.
53 Lib. Soc. P.C. Minutes, 19 Jan. 1885, A/LIB/14; Lib. Soc. E.C. Minutes, 12, 26 Jan. 1885, A/LIB/7, ff. 454, 465.
54 *N.I.*, 264 (15 Jan. 1885), p. 57.
55 'Whether the Liberation Society was to have any political weight in the future depended upon the action it should take at the next General Election.' C. McLaren, MP. *Ibid.*, p. 58.
56 *N.I.*, 265 (22 Jan. 1885), p. 80.
57 *N.I.*, 274 (26 March 1885), Suppl., pp. 1–3.
58 *N.I.*, 280 (7 May 1885), Suppl., p. 6.
59 *N.I.*, 281 (15 May 1885), Suppl., p. 2.
60 *N.I.*, 216 (14 Feb. 1884), p. 158.
61 *N.I.*, 281 (15 May 1885), Suppl., p. 3.
62 *Ibid.*, p. 6.
63 E.g. J. J. Colman, *N.I.*, 287 (25 June 1885), pp. 618–19.
64 As acknowledged by J. Guinness Rogers, *N.I.*, 308 (19 Nov. 1885), p. 1117.
65 *L.*, 372 (March 1886), pp. 35–6.
66 *N.I.*, 324 (11 March 1886), p. 249.
67 *L.*, 376 (July 1886). Cf. Hamer, *Liberal Politics in the Age of Gladstone and Rosebery*, pp. 131–2.
68 Mackintosh, *Disestablishment*, pp. 295–6.
69 Lib. Soc. E.C. Minutes, 11 Aug., 22 Sept. 1890, A/LIB/8, ff. 156, 167.
70 *L.*, N.S., 43 (July 1890), pp. 104–5; 65 (May 1892), p. 71; 66 (June 1892), p. 97; 72 (Dec. 1892), pp. 191–3.
71 *L.*, N.S., 46 (Oct. 1890), p. 153.
72 *L.*, N.S., 51 (March 1891), p. 44.
73 *L.*, N.S., 54 (June 1891), p. 84.
74 *L.*, N.S., 61 (Jan. 1892), p. 9.
75 *L.*, N.S., 63 (March 1892), p. 46. Cf. *L.*, N.S., 64 (April 1892), p. 62.
76 *L.*, N.S., 65 (May 1892), p. 69.
77 *Ibid.*, pp. 70–4.
78 Mackintosh, *Disestablishment*, pp. 301–2; *L.*, N.S., 86 (Feb. 1894), pp. 19–20, 25–6; Lib. Soc. E.C. Minutes, 1, 4, 22 Jan., 12 Feb. 1894, A/LIB/8, ff. 739–46, 754, 759.
79 Mackintosh, *Disestablishment*, p. 295; Lib. Soc. E.C. Minutes, 20 July, 10 Aug. 1891, A/LIB/8, ff. 418, 425.
80 *L.*, N.S., 86 (Feb. 1894), p. 26.
81 *L.*, N.S., 150 (June 1899), p. 86.
82 *Ibid.*, pp.86–7; *L.*, N.S., 151 (July 1899), p. 110; Memo. by H. Gladstone, 14 June 1899, Viscount Gladstone MSS., Add. MS. 41,215, ff. 70–2.
83 *L.*, N.S., 162 (June 1900), p. 87.
84 *L.*, N.S., 163 (July 1900), pp. 109–10; Lib. Soc. E.C. Minutes, 9, 26 July, 10 Sept. 1900, A/LIB/9, ff. 460–1, 466, 468, 475.

IX. THE UNITED KINGDOM ALLIANCE, 1859–1874

1 For a history of the founding and early years of the Alliance see Harrison, *Drink and the Victorians*.
2 See Appendix.
3 Harrison, *Drink and the Victorians*, pp. 215–17.
4 *Ibid.*, pp. 239–40, 245 ff.
5 *Ibid.*, pp. 239–40.
6 See above, pp. 10, 29–30.
7 E.g. *A.N.*, 250 (16 April 1859).
8 *L.*, 227 (March 1874), p. 36.
9 E.g. *A.N.*, 560 (25 March 1865).
10 *A.N.*, 570 (3 June 1865).
11 *A.N.*, 575 (8 July 1865).
12 *A.N.*, 621 (26 May 1866).
13 *A.N.*, 537 (15 Oct. 1864).
14 *A.N.*, 546 (17 Dec. 1864).
15 *A.N.*, 591 (28 Oct. 1865).
16 *A.N.*, 565 (29 April 1865).
17 *A.N.*, 513 (30 April 1864).
18 *A.N.*, 572 (17 June 1865).
19 *A.N.*, 545 (10 Dec. 1864); 617 (28 April 1866); 639 (29 Sept. 1866); 649 (8 Dec. 1866); 674 (1 June 1867).
20 *A.N.*, XVI, 34 (20 Aug. 1870).
21 *A.N.*, XVII 7 (18 Feb. 1871).
22 *A.N.*, 513 (30 April 1864).
23 *A.N.*, 551 (21 Jan. 1865).
24 *Ibid.* Cf. 545 (10 Dec. 1864); 572 (17 June 1865).
25 *A.N.*, 565 (29 April 1865).
26 *A.N.*, 591 (28 Oct. 1865).
27 *A.N.*, 617 (28 April 1866).
28 *A.N.*, 523 (9 July 1864).
29 *A.N.*, 527 (6 Aug. 1864). See above, p. 111.
30 *A.N.*, 536 (8 Oct. 1864).
31 *A.N.*, 575 (8 July 1865).
32 *A.N.*, 602 (13 Jan. 1866).
33 *A.N.*, 699 (23 Nov. 1867); 700 (30 Nov. 1867).
34 *A.N.*, 537 (15 Oct. 1864).
35 *A.N.*, 565 (29 April 1865).
36 *A.N.*, 591 (28 Oct. 1865).
37 *A.N.*, 602 (13 Jan. 1866).
38 *A.N.*, 572 (17 June 1865).
39 *Ibid.*
40 *A.N.*, 575 (8 July 1865).
41 *A.N.*, 585 (16 Sept. 1865).
42 *A.N.*, 591 (28 Oct. 1865).
43 For which see *ibid.* and 593 (11 Nov. 1865).
44 E.g. Newcastle-on-Tyne: *A.N.*, 602 (13 Jan. 1866).

45 *A.N.*, 640 (6 Oct. 1866); 641 (13 Oct. 1866).
46 See below, pp. 210–15.
47 *A.N.*, 643 (27 Oct. 1866).
48 *A.N.*, 657 (2 Feb. 1867).
49 *A.N.*, 672 (18 May 1867); 691 (28 Sept. 1867). See above, pp. 78–85.
50 *A.N.*, 668 (20 April 1867).
51 *A.N.*, 699 (23 Nov. 1867).
52 *A.N.*, XV, 13 (28 March 1868); 25 (20 June 1868).
53 Howell to Sir W. Lawson, 10, 15 July 1868, Howell MSS., 4129, ff. 542, 549.
54 E.g. *N.*, 1178 (10 June 1868), p. 582; 1179 (17 June 1868), p. 599.
55 *A.N.*, XV (2), 43 (23 Oct. 1869).
56 *A.N.*, XV, 29 (18 July 1868); 30 (25 July 1868).
57 *A.N.*, XVI, 20 (14 May 1870); 24 (11 June 1870); 34 (20 Aug. 1870); 42 (15 Oct. 1870).
58 *A.N.*, XVII, 7 (18 Feb. 1871); 12 (25 March 1871); 26 (1 July 1871); 43 (28 Oct. 1871); 51 (23 Dec. 1871).
59 *A.N.*, XVI, 35 (27 Aug. 1870); XVII, 42 (21 Oct. 1871); 47 (25 Nov. 1871).
60 *A.N.*, XVII, 46 (18 Nov. 1871); U.K.A. E.C. Minutes, 8, 15 Nov. 1871.
61 *A.N.*, XVIII, 5 (3 Feb. 1872); U.K.A. E.C. Minutes, 17 Jan. 1872.
62 *A.N.*, XVIII, 23 (8 June 1872).
63 *A.N.*, XVIII, 28 (13 July 1872).
64 *A.N.*, XVIII, 29 (20 July 1872).
65 U.K.A. E.C. Minutes, 31 July 1872.
66 *A.N.*, XVIII, 33 (17 Aug. 1872).
67 *A.N.*, XVIII, 34 (24 Aug. 1872).
68 *A.N.*, XVIII, 37 (14 Sept. 1872); 38 (21 Sept. 1872); U.K.A. E.C. Minutes, 28 Aug. 4, 11 Sept. 1872.
69 *A.N.*, XVIII, 36 (7 Sept. 1872).
70 U.K.A. E.C. Minutes, 25 Sept. 1872.
71 *A.N.*, XVIII, 42 (19 Oct. 1872).
72 *A.N.*, XVIII, 43 (26 Oct. 1872).
73 *A.N.*, XVIII, 47 (23 Nov. 1872), 48 (30 Nov. 1872); U.K.A. E.C. Minutes, 13 Nov. 1872.
74 *A.N.*, XIX, 10 (8 March 1873).
75 U.K.A. E.C. Minutes, 20 Nov. 1872, 29 Jan. 1873; J. Newton, *W. S. Caine, M.P. A Biography*, 1907, p. 52.
76 This is based on the 1868 Report on Bath for the Reform League by G. Davis and W. Osborne in Howell MSS. 4060.
77 *A.N.*, XIX, 9 (1 March 1873).
78 *A.N.*, XIX, 20 (17 May 1873); U.K.A. E.C. Minutes, 18, 25 June 1873.
79 U.K.A. E.C. Minutes, 30 April, 7 May 1873.
80 *A.N.*, XIX, 22 (31 May 1873).
81 *A.N.*, XIX, 27 (5 July 1873); U.K.A. E.C. Minutes, 18, 25 June 1873. Cf. above pp. 131–32.
82 U.K.A. E.C. Minutes, 25 June 1873.

83   *A.N.*, XIX, 31 (2 Aug. 1873); 32 (9 Aug. 1873); U.K.A. E.C. Minutes, 30 July, 6 Aug. 1873. The matter was further complicated by the fact that the Liberal candidate was Treasurer of the National Education League. The Alliance's conduct greatly angered Chamberlain. He wrote to the Secretary of the U.K.A. 'asking him to define the Electoral policy of the Alliance'. At the meeting of the U.K.A. Executive Committee on 15 Sept., a letter was read 'from Mr. Jesse Collings, Birmingham intimating that he did not agree with the policy of the Alliance, that he had felt constrained to withdraw, and asking questions as to the scope of the Permissive Bill and the test put to Candidates.'; U.K.A. E.C. Minutes, 10, 15 Sept. 1873.

84   *A.N.*, XIX, 33 (16 Aug. 1873). Cf. the Reform League Report on Stamford in 1868, Howell MSS. 4060.

85   *A.N.*, XIX, 38 (20 Sept. 1873); 40 (4 Oct. 1873); 41 (11 Oct. 1873); U.K.A. E.C. Minutes, 24 Sept., 8 Oct. 1873.

86   *A.N.*, XIX, 38 (20 Sept. 1873); 39 (27 Sept. 1873); 40 (4 Oct. 1873); 41 (11 Oct. 1873).

87   *A.N.*, XIX, 42 (18 Oct. 1873).

88   *A.N.*, XV, 39 (26 Sept. 1868).

89   *A.N.*, XIX, 44 (1 Nov. 1873); U.K.A. E.C. Minutes, 3, 8, 22 Oct. 1873.

90   U.K.A. E.C. Minutes, 24, 29 Oct., 3 Dec. 1873, 21 Jan. 1874.

91   The following account is derived from the Minutes of 26, 27, 28, 29, 30, 31 Jan., 2, 3, 4 Feb. 1874.

92   *A.N.*, XX, 1 (3 Jan. 1874).

93   On Denbigh see also *A.N.*, XX, 4 (24 Jan. 1874).

94   *A.N.*, XX, 11 (14 March 1874).

95   *A.N.*, XX, 8 (21 Feb. 1874).

96   *Ibid.*

97   *A.N.*, XXI, 6 (6 Feb. 1875); 7 (13 Feb. 1875). See below, pp. 216–18.

X. THE UNITED KINGDOM ALLIANCE, 1874–1880

1   U.K.A. E.C. Minutes, 23 Feb. 1874.

2   *A.N.*, XXI, 11 (13 March 1875); U.K.A. E.C. Minutes, 3 March 1875.

3   *A.N.*, XXI, 32 (7 Aug. 1875); U.K.A. E.C. Minutes, 28 July 1875.

4   *A.N.*, XXII, 10 (4 March 1876).

5   *A.N.*, XXII, 17 (22 April 1876), 18 (29 April 1876).

6   U.K.A. E.C. Minutes, 8, 15 Nov. 1876.

7   U.K.A. E.C. Minutes. Report dated 5 April 1880.

8   U.K.A. E.C. Minutes, 18 March 1874.

9   *A.N.*, XX, 41 (17 Oct. 1874).

10   *A.N.*, XXI, 17 (24 April 1875).

11   *A.N.*, XXII, 53 (30 Dec. 1876); XXIII, 1 (6 Jan. 1877); U.K.A. E.C. Minutes, 6, 20 Dec. 1876.

12   *A.N.*, XXIII, 43 (27 Oct. 1877).

13   *A.N.*, XXIV, 40 (5 Oct. 1878).

14   *A.N.*, XXIV, 43 (26 Oct. 1878).

15   *A.N.*, XXIV, 44 (2 Nov. 1878).

16 *A.N.*, XXIV, 48 (30 Nov. 1878).
17 *A.N.*, XXV, 44 (25 Oct. 1879).
18 *A.N.*, XXV, 50 (6 Dec. 1879).
19 U.K.A. E.C. Minutes, 12 Jan. 1876. The new atmosphere may be
    illustrated by the following letter which H. J. Wilson received from
    J. Lacon, 25 Nov. 1875, H. J. Wilson MSS., Sheffield Public Library,
    M.D. 5889: 'Whilst coming away from the Hotel this morning Mr.
    G. W. Sharman expressed his disappointment that in the Liberal
    Demonstration on the 15th prox.° there was no speaker, among those
    you mentioned as likely to be present, who would be accepted by the
    Alliance Party as representing their views. He thought that Sir
    Wilfrid or Trevelyan ought to have been invited. I told him I under-
    stood it was a meeting not for the purpose of upholding principle so
    much as to celebrate the union between the hitherto divided sections
    and that in selecting speakers more consideration had been paid to
    the "natural leaders" of the party than that all parties shd. be repre-
    sented. In other words, that the head & tail were now about to be
    reunited after an unsuccessful cruise apart, & that the tail as was to be
    expected was taking its natural place *behind* the head while at the
    same time it furnished the motive power to the united body. Mr. S.
    seemed to think however it would be well to take into consideration
    the Alliance party if it was desired that they should give their
    cooperation to the union. If you think this worth considering you
    might arrange for an Alliance speaker.'
20 U.K.A. E.C. Minutes, 9 Sept. 1874.
21 *A.N.*, XXI, 42 (16 Oct. 1875).
22 *A.N.*, XXI, 52 (25 Dec. 1875).
23 *A.N.*, XXII, 7 (12 Feb. 1876); U.K.A. E.C. Minutes, 9 Feb. 1876.
24 U.K.A. E.C. Minutes, 26 April 1876.
25 *A.N.*, XXII, 18 (29 April 1876).
26 This was after F. R. Lees had said that he would stand again as an
    independent if Baines secured the Liberal nomination. *A.N.*, XXII,
    33 (12 Aug. 1876).
27 *A.N.*, XXII, 46 (11 Nov. 1876).
28 *A.N.*, XXIII, 6 (10 Feb. 1877); 7 (17 Feb. 1877); 8 (24 Feb. 1877);
    U.K.A. E.C. Minutes, 31 Jan. 1877.
29 *A.N.*, XXIII, 50 (15 Dec. 1877); XXIV, 3 (19 Jan. 1878).
30 U.K.A. E.C. Minutes, 30 Jan. 1878.
31 U.K.A. E.C. Minutes, 18 Dec. 1878.
32 *A.N.*, XXIV, 29 (20 July 1878).
33 *A.N.*, XXIV, 45 (9 Nov. 1878).
34 *A.N.*, XXIV, 8 (23 Feb. 1878).
35 *A.N.*, XXII, 44 (28 Oct. 1876).
36 *A.N.*, XXV, 44 (25 Oct. 1879).
37 *A.N.*, XXI, 51 (18 Dec. 1875).
38 See above, pp. 176–77.
39 *A.N.*, XX, 41 (17 Oct. 1874).
40 *A.N.*, XLIV, 43 (22 Oct. 1897).
41 U.K.A. E.C. Minutes, 10 Feb. 1875.

42 U.K.A. E.C. Minutes, 30 June 1875.
43 *A.N.*, XXI, 28 (10 July 1875).
44 *A.N.*, XXI, 42 (16 Oct. 1875).
45 U.K.A. E.C. Minutes, 12 Jan. 1876.
46 U.K.A. E.C. Minutes, 19 Jan., 2, 16 Feb. 1876.
47 *A.N.*, XXII, 44 (28 Oct. 1876).
48 *A.N.*, XXII, 16 (15 April 1876).
49 U.K.A. E.C. Minutes, 5 July 1876.
50 U.K.A. E.C. Minutes, 4 Oct. 1876.
51 *A.N.*, XXII, 44 (28 Oct. 1876).
52 U.K.A. E.C. Minutes, 22 Nov. 1876.
53 U.K.A. E.C. Minutes, 31 Jan., 7, 14 Feb., 28 March 1877; *A.N.*, XXIII, 17 (28 April 1877). For Dudley, see above, pp. 144, 179.
54 U.K.A. E.C. Minutes, 7 Feb. 1877; *A.N.*, XXIII, 33 (18 Aug. 1877).
55 *A.N.*, XXIII, 8 (24 Feb. 1877).
56 *A.N.*, XXIII, 43 (27 Oct. 1877).
57 *A.N.*, XXIII, 50 (15 Dec. 1877); 51 (22 Dec. 1877); 52 (29 Dec. 1877).
58 U.K.A. E.C. Minutes, 20 March 1878.
59 *A.N.*, XXIV, 34 (24 Aug. 1878).
60 *A.N.*, XXIV, 38 (21 Sept. 1878).
61 *A.N.*, XXIV, 44 (2 Nov. 1878); 50 (14 Dec. 1878).
62 *A.N.*, XXIV, 44 (2 Nov. 1878); 49 (7 Dec. 1878); XXV, 1 (4 Jan. 1879).
63 *A.N.*, XXV, 1 (4 Jan. 1879).
64 *A.N.*, XXI, 7 (13 Feb. 1875).
65 *A.N.*, XXI, 21 (22 May 1875).
66 *A.N.*, XXII, 14 (1 April 1876). Chamberlain did, however, vote for the Permissive Bill when he entered Parliament. When John Morley wrote regretting that he had done so, he replied, 20 Nov. 1876: 'There is much in what you say about the Permissive Bill, yet as a matter of *policy* I am convinced that I am right. Nothing can be done *without* the Alliance—if they were actively hostile as they have hitherto been to all similar proposals, I could not hope to succeed.' Chamberlain MSS., JC 5/54/130.
67 *A.N.*, XXII, 12 (18 March 1876).
68 U.K.A. E.C. Minutes, 5, 12 April 1876.
69 *A.N.*, XXII, 46 (11 Nov. 1876).
70 *A.N.*, XXV, 12 (20 March 1880); U.K.A. E.C. Minutes, 22 Jan. 1879, 16 March 1880.
71 *A.N.*, XXIV, 32 (10 Aug. 1878); 50 (14 Dec. 1878).
72 *A.N.*, XXIV, 50 (14 Dec. 1878). See above, p. 189. For Norwood's hostility to the Bulgarian agitation see Shannon, *Gladstone and the Bulgarian Agitation*, p. 128.
73 U.K.A. E.C. Minutes, 3, 10 Sept., 29 Oct. 1879; *A.N.*, XXV, 27 (5 July 1879).
74 *A.N.*, XXVI, 3 (17 Jan. 1880); 7 (14 Feb. 1880); 9 (28 Feb. 1880); 14 (3 April 1880). See below, pp. 227, 236.
75 See above, pp. 117-18, 178-79.

76 H. Carter, *The English Temperance Movement: A Study in Objectives*, 1933, pp. 171–2, 200–1.
77 *A.N.*, XXV, 44 (25 Oct. 1879).
78 *A.N.*, XXVI, 8 (21 Feb. 1880).
79 Dale, *Life of R. W. Dale*, pp. 429–30; *A.N.*, XXVI, 12 (20 March 1880).
80 *A.N.*, XXVI, 9 (28 Feb. 1880); U.K.A. E.C. Minutes, 16 March 1880; L. A. Atherley-Jones, *Looking Back. Reminiscences of a Political Career*, 1925, p. 21.
81 E.g. at Exeter: R. Newton, *Victorian Exeter 1837–1914*, Leicester, 1968, p. 199.

XI. THE UNITED KINGDOM ALLIANCE, 1880–1885

1   U.K.A. E.C. Minutes, 22 Feb., 2 March 1881.
2   *A.N.*, XXVII, 41 (8 Oct. 1881).
3   *A.N.*, XXVII, 47 (19 Nov. 1881).
4   *A.N.*, XXVII, 53 (31 Dec. 1881). For Howell's attitude to pledges, see above, p. 50 and below, p. 313.
5   *A.N.*, XXVIII, 21 (27 May 1882).
6   *A.N.*, XXVIII, 42 (21 Oct. 1882); 45 (11 Nov. 1882).
7   *A.N.*, XXVIII, 21 (27 May 1882).
8   U.K.A. E.C. Minutes, 22 Nov. 1882.
9   *A.N.*, XXIX, 20 (19 May 1883).
10 *A.N.*, XXIX, 42 (20 Oct. 1883).
11 *A.N.*, XXX, 12 (22 March 1884).
12 U.K.A. E.C. Minutes, 24 Sept., 15 Oct. 1884.
13 *A.N.*, XXX, 43 (25 Oct. 1884).
14 U.K.A. E.C. Minutes, 25 Feb. 1885.
15 E.g. a letter from S. Pope included in U.K.A. E.C. Minutes, 4 March 1885.
16 *A.N.*, XXXI, 40 (3 Oct. 1885).
17 U.K.A. E.C. Minutes, 11, 18, 25 Feb. 1885.
18 *A.N.*, XXXI, 7 (14 Feb. 1885); 8 (21 Feb. 1885); U.K.A. E.C. Minutes, 18 March 1885.
19 *A.N.*, XXXI, 11 (14 March 1885); U.K.A. E.C. Minutes, 25 March 1885.
20 *A.N.*, XXXI, 11 (14 March 1885).
21 *A.N.*, XXXI, 12 (21 March 1885); U.K.A. E.C. Minutes, 1 April 1885.
22 *A.N.*, XXXI, 14 (4 April 1885).
23 *A.N.*, XXXI, 18 (2 May 1885).
24 *A.N.*, XXXI, 22 (30 May 1885).
25 *A.N.*, XXXI, 40 (3 Oct. 1885).
26 *A.N.*, XXXI, 22 (30 May 1885).
27 *A.N.*, XXIX, 48 (1 Dec. 1883).
28 U.K.A. E.C. Minutes, 12, 19 Nov. 1884.
29 *A.N.*, XXXI, 36 (5 Sept. 1885).
30 *A.N.*, XXXI, 11 (14 March 1885).
31 *A.N.*, XXXI, 17 (25 April 1885).

32 *A.N.*, XXXI, 26 (27 June 1885).
33 *A.N.*, XXXI, 27 (4 July 1885). On Billany's candidature see also M. Barker, *Gladstone and Radicalism. The Reconstruction of Liberal Policy in Britain 1885–94*, The Harvester Press, Hassocks, 1975, p. 18.
34 *A.N.*, XXXI, 32 (15 Aug. 1885); XXXII, 5 (30 Jan. 1886).
35 *A.N.*, XXXI, 42 (17 Oct. 1885).
36 *A.N.*, XXXII, 2 (9 Jan. 1886).
37 *Ibid.*

XII. THE UNITED KINGDOM ALLIANCE, 1886–1892

1 E.g. U.K.A. E.C. Minutes, 13 March 1889.
2 U.K.A. E.C. Minutes, 18 Sept. 1889.
3 U.K.A. E.C. Minutes, 5 March 1890.
4 *A.N.*, XXXVII, 43 (24 Oct. 1890).
5 U.K.A. E.C. Minutes, 26 Nov. 1890, 28 Jan. 1891.
6 *A.N.*, XXXVIII, 42 (16 Oct. 1891).
7 Newton, *W. S. Caine*, pp. 167–8.
8 *A.N.*, XXXII, 42 (16 Oct. 1886).
9 Newton, *W. S. Caine*, p. 180; *A.N.*, XXXIII, 13 (26 March 1887).
10 Newton, *W. S. Caine*, pp. 180–2.
11 U.K.A. E.C. Minutes, 23, 30 March 1887.
12 U.K.A. E.C. Minutes, 21 Nov. 1888.
13 *A.N.*, XXXVIII, 44 (30 Oct. 1891).
14 E.g. *A.N.*, XXXII, 18 (1 May 1886).
15 *A.N.*, XXXII, 42 (16 Oct. 1886).
16 *A.N.*, XXXIII, 9 (26 Feb. 1887).
17 U.K.A. E.C. Minutes, 2 March 1887.
18 U.K.A. E.C. Minutes, 9 Feb. 1887.
19 *A.N.*, XXXIII, 11 (12 March 1887).
20 *A.N.*, XXXIII, 13 (26 March 1887).
21 *A.N.*, XXXIII, 14 (2 April 1887).
22 *A.N.*, XXXIII, 21 (21 May 1887); 33 (13 Aug. 1887); U.K.A. E.C. Minutes, 20 July, 31 Aug., 7 Sept. 1887.
23 *A.N.*, XXXIII, 42 (15 Oct. 1887).
24 U.K.A. E.C. Minutes, 7 Dec. 1887.
25 *A.N.*, XXXV, 3 (21 Jan. 1888).
26 *A.N.*, XXXV, 4 (28 Jan. 1888).
27 *A.N.*, XXXV, 10 (10 March 1888); 17 (28 April 1888).
28 *A.N.*, XXXV, 18 (5 May 1888).
29 These are frequently referred to in *A.N.*, XXXVI (1889).
30 U.K.A. E.C. Minutes, 13 Feb. 1889.
31 U.K.A. E.C. Minutes, 27 March 1889.
32 What follows is derived from *A.N.*, XXXVI 37 (13 Sept. 1889).
33 *A.N.*, XXXVI, 39 (27 Sept. 1889).
34 U.K.A. E.C. Minutes, 18 Sept. 1889.
35 *A.N.*, XXXVI, 42 (18 Oct. 1889).
36 *A.N.*, XXXVI, 43 (25 Oct. 1889).
37 U.K.A. E.C. Minutes, 20, 27 Nov. 1889, 8 Jan., 5 March 1890.

38 *A.N.*, XXXVII, 9 (28 Feb. 1890).
39 *Ibid.*
40 *A.N.*, XXXVII, 15 (11 April 1890). See above, p. 25.
41 *A.N.*, XXXVII, 12 (21 March 1890); 14 (4 April 1890); 37 (12 Sept. 1890).
42 *A.N.*, XXXVII, 35 (29 Aug. 1890).
43 *A.N.*, XXXVII, 38 (19 Sept. 1890).
44 *A.N.*, XXXVII, 42 (17 Oct. 1890).
45 U.K.A. E.C. Minutes, 5 Nov. 1890.
46 *A.N.*, XXXVII, 43 (24 Oct. 1890).
47 *A.N.*, XXXVIII, 13 (27 March 1891).
48 *A.N.*, XXXVIII, 15 (10 April 1891).
49 *A.N.*, XXXIII, 9 (26 Feb. 1887).
50 *A.N.*, XXXIII, 32 (6 Aug. 1887); 50 (10 Dec. 1887).
51 *A.N.*, XXXIII, 10 (5 March 1887).
52 Newton, *W. S. Caine*, pp. 196–7.
53 *Ibid.*, pp. 198–9, 215.
54 U.K.A. E.C. Minutes, 5 June 1889.
55 U.K.A. E.C. Minutes, 26 Feb. 1890; *A.N.*, XXXVII, 11 (14 March 1890).
56 *A.N.*, XXXVII, 11 (14 March 1890).
57 *A.N.*, XXXVII, 12 (21 March 1890).
58 *A.N.*, XXXVII, 16 (18 April 1890).
59 *Ibid.*
60 U.K.A. E.C. Minutes, 2 July 1890; *A.N.*, XXXVII, 27 (4 July 1890); 28 (11 July 1890); Newton, *W. S. Caine*, pp. 224–7.
61 *A.N.*, XXXVII, 42 (17 Oct. 1890); XXXVIII, 2 (9 Jan. 1891).
62 *A.N.*, XXXVIII, 43 (23 Oct. 1891).
63 *A.N.*, XXXIX, 5 (29 Jan. 1892); U.K.A. E.C. Minutes, 20 Jan. 1892.
64 *A.N.*, XXXII, 29 (17 July 1886).
65 U.K.A. E.C. Minutes, 20 March, 10 April 1889.
66 *A.N.*, XXXVII, 14 (4 April 1890).
67 U.K.A. E.C. Minutes, 28 Jan., 25 March 1891; *A.N.*, XXXVIII, 5 (30 Jan. 1891); 11 (13 March 1891).
68 *A.N.*, XXXVIII, 26 (26 June 1891).
69 *A.N.*, XXXVIII, 31 (31 July 1891); 37 (11 Sept. 1891).
70 *A.N.*, XXXVIII, 41 (9 Oct. 1891); 43 (23 Oct. 1891); 52 (25 Dec. 1891); XXXIX, 5 (29 Jan. 1892).
71 *A.N.*, XXXVIII, 44 (30 Oct. 1891).
72 *A.N.*, XXXVIII, 33 (14 Aug. 1891).
73 *A.N.*, XXXIX, 17 (22 April 1892).
74 *A.N.*, XXXIX, 20 (13 May 1892).
75 *A.N.*, XXXVII, 52 (26 Dec. 1890).
76 *A.N.*, XXXVII, 15 (11 April 1890).
77 *A.N.*, XXXIX, 5 (29 Jan. 1892).
78 *A.N.*, XXXIX, 31 (29 July 1892); 33 (12 Aug. 1892).
79 *A.N.*, XXXIX, 32 (5 Aug. 1892); 43 (21 Oct. 1892); 44 (28 Oct. 1892).

XIII. THE UNITED KINGDOM ALLIANCE, 1892–1900

1   *A.N.*, XLII, 45 (8 Nov. 1895).
2   *A.N.*, XLII, 49 (6 Dec. 1895).
3   *A.N.*, XLIII, 27 (3 July 1896).
4   *A.N.*, XLV, 5 (4 Feb. 1898).
5   *A.N.*, XLVII, 13 (29 March 1900).
6   *A.N.*, XLVI, 46 (16 Nov. 1899).
7   *A.N.*, XXXIX, 44 (28 Oct. 1892).
8   For these arguments see the Alliance's Annual Reports for 1892, 1894, and 1895.
9   See *A.N.*, during July and Aug. 1895.
10   See below, pp. 276, 288–89.
11   *A.N.*, XLIII, 43 (23 Oct. 1896).
12   *A.N.*, XLI, 42 (19 Oct. 1894).
13   *A.N.*, XLIV, 4 (22 Jan. 1897); 6 (5 Feb. 1897); 7 (12 Feb. 1897); U.K.A. E.C. Minutes, 20 Jan. 1897.
14   *A.N.*, XLV, 1 (7 Jan. 1898); 2 (14 Jan. 1898); 3 (21 Jan. 1898); 5 (4 Feb. 1898).
15   *A.N.*, XLV, 6 (11 Feb. 1898); 7 (18 Feb. 1898).
16   *A.N.*, XLV, 9 (4 March 1898).
17   *A.N.*, XLV, 35 (2 Sept. 1898).
18   *A.N.*, XLI, 14 (6 April 1894); U.K.A. E.C. Minutes, 11 April 1894.
19   *A.N.*, XLI, 43 (26 Oct. 1894). (W. S. Caine.)
20   *Ibid.*
21   *A.N.*, XLIII, 7 (17 Feb. 1896).
22   *A.N.*, XLIV, 11 (12 March 1897).
23   *A.N.*, XLV, 3 (21 Jan. 1898).
24   *A.N.*, XXXIX, 26 (24 June 1892).
25   *A.N.*, XL, 7 (17 Feb. 1893). For Hardie's temperance background see F. Reid, 'Keir Hardie's Conversion to Socialism', in A. Briggs and J. Saville (eds.), *Essays in Labour History 1886–1923*, 1971, pp. 23–4; and K. O. Morgan, *Keir Hardie radical and socialist*, 1975, pp. 9–10.
26   *A.N.*, XXXIX, 45 (4 Nov. 1892).
27   U.K.A. E.C. Minutes, 13 Dec. 1893.
28   U.K.A. E.C. Minutes, 27 June 1894.
29   U.K.A. E.C. Minutes, 11 July 1895.
30   *A.N.*, XLIII, 46 (13 Nov. 1896); 47 (20 Nov. 1896).
31   *A.N.*, XLIV, 41 (8 Oct. 1897); U.K.A. E.C. Minutes, 24 Feb., 13 Oct. 1897.
32   *A.N.*, XLV, 39 (30 Sept. 1898).
33   *A.N.*, XLI, 10 (9 March 1894).
34   *A.N.*, XLI, 52 (28 Dec. 1894).
35   *A.N.*, XLV, 39 (30 Sept. 1898).
36   *A.N.*, XLI, 28 (13 July 1894).
37   U.K.A. E.C. Minutes, 30 May, 13, 20 June, 11 July, 22 Aug. 1894.
38   U.K.A. E.C. Minutes, 9 Jan. 1895; *A.N.*, XLI, 52 (28 Dec. 1894); XLII, 1 (4 Jan. 1895).

39 What follows is based on *A.N.*, XLII, 14 (5 April 1895); 15 (12 April 1895); 18 (3 May 1895); 20 (17 May 1895). See above, p. 261.

40 U.K.A. E.C. Minutes, 1 May 1895.

41 *A.N.*, XLII, 7 (14 Feb. 1896); 10 (6 March 1896); 11 (13 March 1896); U.K.A. E.C. Minutes, 29 Jan. 1896.

42 U.K.A. E.C. Minutes, 20, 27 Jan. 1897.

43 U.K.A. E.C. Minutes, 26 May 1897.

44 U.K.A. E.C. Minutes, 23, 30 March 1898; *A.N.*, XLV, 13 (1 April 1898); 16 (22 April 1898).

45 *A.N.*, XLVI, 7 (17 Feb. 1899); 33 (17 Aug. 1899); 37 (14 Sept. 1899); XLVII, 22 (31 May 1900); 31 (2 Aug. 1900).

46 *A.N.*, XLVI, 25 (22 June 1899); 28 (13 July 1899).

47 *A.N.*, XLVI, 28 (13 July 1899).

48 W. Blackwood of Dundee wrote: 'The subject is attended with considerable difficulty, especially when Temperance bodies are not in a position to bring forward candidates of their own, or when they are not able to bring pressure to bear on caucuses where candidates are selected.' *A.N.*, XLVI, 32 (10 Aug. 1899).

49 U.K.A. E.C. Minutes, 30 May, 13 June, 11 July 1894.

50 U.K.A. E.C. Minutes, 7 May 1895.

51 On this cf. the Reform League report on Bolton, 4 Sept. 1868 (compiled by T. Sanders and C. Wade), Howell MSS., 4060: 'The political position in this borough is peculiar. Liberalism is very strong, but the liberal candidates, Pope and Barnes, being Teetotallers, many of the Liberals will be opposed to them on that account. The Magisterial Bench is mostly composed of teetotallers, and in some cases which have been brought before them they exhibited a very intolerant spirit.'

52 *A.N.*, XLII, 44 (1 Nov. 1895); XLIII, 22 (29 May 1896); 24 (12 June 1896).

53 *A.N.*, XLIII, 7 (14 Feb. 1896).

54 *A.N.*, XLIII, 43 (23 Oct. 1896).

55 *A.N.*, XLIII, 48 (27 Nov. 1896).

56 *A.N.*, XLV, 20 (20 May 1898).

57 *A.N.*, XLV, 1 (7 Jan. 1898).

58 *A.N.*, XL, 6 (10 Feb. 1893).

59 *A.N.*, XLI, 40 (5 Oct. 1894); 41 (12 Oct. 1894).

60 *A.N.*, XLI, 43 (26 Oct. 1894).

61 *A.N.*, XLI, 50 (14 Dec. 1894).

62 U.K.A. E.C. Minutes, 9, 16 Jan., 24 April, 7 May 1895.

63 Cf. T. P. Whittaker: 'In this country the issue has been raised by the masses of the people; and as the result of two generations of persistent and self-sacrificing labours, such as this country has never seen surpassed, it has now been forced into the very front rank of political questions, and the great popular party and the Government of the day have embodied it in their programme. The issue and the policy have not been forced downward from the top. They have grown upward from the very bottom. They can no more be thrust back now than the hen can be put back again into the egg from which it came.' *A.N.*, XLII, 19 (10 May 1895).

64 *Ibid.*
65 *A.N.*, XLIII, 47 (20 Nov. 1896); 51 (18 Dec. 1896).
66 U.K.A. E.C. Minutes, 15, 22 Sept. 1897.
67 *A.N.*, XLI, 30 (27 July 1894); 42 (19 Oct. 1894); XLII, 14 (5 April 1895).
68 *A.N.*, XLII, 43 (25 Oct. 1895).
69 *A.N.*, XLV, 41 (14 Oct. 1898).
70 *A.N.*, XLI, 43 (26 Oct. 1894).
71 *A.N.*, XLIII, 52 (25 Dec. 1896).
72 *A.N.*, XLIII, 6 (7 Feb. 1896); XLIV, 6 (5 Feb. 1897).
73 *A.N.*, XLIV, 43 (22 Oct. 1897).
74 *A.N.*, XLIV, 51 (17 Dec. 1897).
75 For an account of the position of the temperance question in politics at this time see D. M. Fahey, 'Temperance and the Liberal Party—Lord Peel's Report, 1899', *The Journal of British Studies*, X, 2 (May 1971), pp. 132–59.
76 *A.N.*, XLV, 3 (21 Jan. 1898).
77 See above, p. 187.
78 *A.N.*, XLV, 18 (6 May 1898); 20 (20 May 1898); U.K.A. E.C. Minutes, 27 April 1898.
79 As did Henry Hibbert, veteran U.K.A. agent.
80 *A.N.*, XLV, 26 (1 July 1898); 27 (8 July 1898); 31 (5 Aug. 1898); 42 (21 Oct. 1898).
81 *A.N.*, XLV, 41 (14 Oct. 1898).
82 *A.N.*, XLV, 31 (5 Aug. 1898).
83 *A.N.*, XLV, 42 (21 Oct. 1898).
84 *A.N.*, XLVI, 11 (16 March 1899); 12 (23 March 1899).
85 *A.N.*, XLVI, 25 (22 June 1899); 26 (29 June 1899); 27 (6 July 1899); 28 (13 July 1899); 41 (12 Oct. 1899).
86 *A.N.*, XLVI, 29 (20 July 1899).
87 For which see Fahey, 'Temperance and the Liberal Party—Lord Peel's Report, 1899', *loc. cit.*
88 *A.N.*, XLVI, 42 (19 Oct. 1899).
89 *A.N.*, XLVI, 47 (23 Nov. 1899); 49 (7 Dec. 1899).
90 Fahey, 'Temperance and the Liberal Party'. H. Gladstone to Sir H. Campbell-Bannerman, 12, 23 Dec. 1899, Campbell-Bannerman MSS., Add. MS. 41, 215, ff. 171–2, 190.
91 E.g. *A.N.*, XLVI, 51 (21 Dec. 1899).
92 U.K.A. E.C. Minutes, 28 March 1900.
93 *A.N.*, XLVI, 51 (21 Dec. 1899).
94 *A.N.*, XLVII, 7 (15 Feb. 1900); 10 (8 March 1900). They were later persuaded to withdraw their resignations.
95 *A.N.*, XLVII, 14 (5 April 1900); 17 (26 April 1900); Newton, *W. S. Caine*, p. 286.
96 *A.N.*, XLVII, 14 (5 April 1900).
97 *A.N.*, XLVII, 28 (12 July 1900).
98 Which he lost. *A.N.*, XLVI, 47 (23 Nov. 1899); XLVII, 31 (2 Aug. 1900).

99 *A.N.*, XLVII, 31 (2 Aug. 1900); 32 (9 Aug. 1900); 34 (23 Aug. 1900); 36 (6 Sept. 1900); 39 (27 Sept. 1900).
100 *A.N.*, XLVII, 42 (18 Oct. 1900).
101 *A.N.*, XLVII, 41 (11 Oct. 1900).
102 *A.N.*, XLVII, 44 (1 Nov. 1900).

XIV. LABOUR AND IRISH ELECTORAL STRATEGY

1 T. M. Parssinen, 'Association, convention and anti-parliament in British radical politics, 1771–1848', *English Historical Review*, 88 (1973), pp. 515 ff.
2 A. Briggs (ed.), *Chartist Studies*, 1962, p. 136; R. G. Gammage, *History of the Chartist Movement 1837–1854*, 1969 [reprint of 1894 ed.], pp. 192–5; M. Hovell, *The Chartist Movement*, 2nd ed., Manchester, 1925, pp. 149, 193, 197–8, 238–9; G. D. H. Cole, *Chartist Portraits*, 1941, pp. 196, 248–9, 253, 255, 277, 279, 285; J. Ridley, *Lord Palmerston*, 1970, pp. 323–7; A. Plummer, *Bronterre. A Political Biography of Bronterre O'Brien 1804–1864*, 1971, pp. 83–4, 112–15, 157–9.
3 Ref. L.E.C. Minutes, 29 Sept. 1865, 12 Oct. 1866, Howell MSS. 4052.
4 T. R. Tholfsen, 'The Origins of the Birmingham Caucus', *The Historical Journal*, II (1959), pp. 171–3, 180–4; A. Briggs, *Victorian Cities*, 1963, p. 191.
5 Ref. L.E.C. Minutes, 9 May 1865, Howell MSS. 4052.
6 Ref. L.E.C. Minutes, 27 Oct. 1866, Howell MSS. 4053.
7 Ref. L. Council Reports, Howell MSS. 4056.
8 Ref. L.E.C. Minutes, 8, 12, 17 July 1867, Howell MSS. 4054.
9 Howell to E. Lyulph Stanley, 16 July 1867, Howell MSS. 4128, f. 797.
10 Hanham, *Elections and Party Management*, pp. 333 ff.; R. Harrison, *Before the Socialists. Studies in Labour and Politics 1861–1881*, 1965, Chapter IV.
11 Howell to G. Lynes, 23 July 1867, Howell MSS. 4128, f. 815.
12 Report in Howell MSS. 4056.
13 Report in Howell MSS. 4056.
14 Ref. L.E.C. Minutes, 5, 8 July, 11 Oct. 1867, 9 May 1868, Howell MSS. 4054; Howell to W. Hargreaves, 22 July 1868, Howell MSS. 4129, f. 555. For Acland see Hanham, *Elections and Party Management*, p. 237.
15 The Reports are collected in Howell MSS. 4060 and analysed by Hanham, *Elections and Party Management*, pp. 333 ff.; and Harrison, *Before the Socialists*, Chapter IV.
16 Ref. L.E.C. Minutes, 30 June 1865, Howell MSS. 4052.
17 Ref. L.E.C. Minutes, 15 March 1867, Howell MSS. 4053.
18 Report in Howell MSS. 4056.
19 Ref. L.E.C. Minutes, 8 July 1867, Howell MSS. 4054.
20 Report in Howell MSS. 4056.
21 Howell to W. Payne, 24 Feb. 1868, Howell MSS. 4129, f. 313.
22 Howell to F. Clayton, 28 Feb. 1868, Howell MSS. 4129, f. 319.
23 Hanham, *Elections and Party Management*, pp. 337–41; Harrison, *Before the Socialists*, pp. 170–81.

24 See above, p. 26.

25 'Some of us have to stand in the character of obstructives because we will not consent to the revival of the old Chartist practice[,] that of opposing all parties except those pledged to Labour questions.' Howell to J. Stansfeld, 8 Nov. 1869, Howell MSS. 4130, f. 226. See above, pp. 35, 50, 227.

26 Howell to G. Jackson, 11 May 1868, Howell MSS. 4129, f. 436.

27 27 Oct. 1868, Howell MSS. 4129, f. 764.

28 10 July 1868, Howell MSS. 4129, f. 542. See also his letter to Lawson of 15 July, f. 549. On 12 Aug. 1868, f. 599, he wrote to S. Morley: 'The Temperance people have called a meeting for next Tuesday [in Bristol], and some of them, I hear, are for pressing the question of the Permissive Bill at all hazards. This we must try to avoid. I have done something towards throwing oil on their troubled waters.'

29 Howell to W. Malleson, 28 July 1868, Howell MSS. 4129, f. 570.

30 Howell to L. Butcher, 28 Sept. 1868, Howell MSS. 4129, f. 661.

31 Howell to J. Thompson, 28 Oct. 1868, Howell MSS. 4129, f. 775.

32 E.g. the Reports on Bath, Exeter, Kidderminster, and Tiverton in Howell MSS. 4060.

33 E.g. the Reports on Boston, Newcastle-under-Lyme, Maldon and Whitby in Howell MSS. 4060.

34 Ref. L. Council Reports, 7, 28 Oct. 1868, Howell MSS. 4056; Harrison, *Before the Socialists*, p. 182.

35 Ref. L.E.C. Minutes, 4 Nov. 1868, Howell MSS. 4054.

36 For what follows see J. Denvir, *The Irish in Britain From the Earliest Times to the Fall and Death of Parnell*, 1892, pp. 287–8, 317–28, 334, 391, 428; C. H. D. Howard, 'The Parnell Manifesto of 21 November, 1885, and the Schools Question', *English Historical Review*, 62 (1947), pp. 42–8; T. W. Moody, 'Michael Davitt and the British Labour Movement 1882–1906', *Transactions of the Royal Historical Society*, 5th Series, 3 (1953); C. C. O'Brien, *Parnell and his Party 1880–90*, Oxford, 1957, pp. 104–5, 193–4.

37 See above, p. 256.

38 A. W. Humphrey, *A History of Labour Representation*, 1912, p. 100.

39 *Ibid.*, pp. 39–40.

40 *Ibid.*, pp. 100–1; G. D. H. Cole, *British Working Class Politics 1832–1914*, 1941, pp. 114–15.

41 H. Pelling, *The Origins of the Labour Party 1880–1900*, 2nd ed., Oxford, 1965, p. 57.

42 *Ibid.*, p. 65; F. Reid, 'Keir Hardie's Conversion to Socialism', *loc. cit.*, pp. 45–6, challenges the view that this was the most important reason for his action; Morgan, *Keir Hardie*, pp. 22–3.

43 Cole, *British Working Class Politics*, p. 56. Mill's advice to Howell in a letter of 27 Dec. 1868 (copy in Howell MSS., original at the L.S.E.) appears an exact replica of the strategy of Miall and the Liberation Society: 'I hope the working classes will learn from their present failure a lesson of organisation, and, as the Liberal party can never succeed at a general election without their active support, will henceforth make such support conditional on being allowed an equal voice

in the selection of the Liberal candidates, so that whenever a constituency returns two members, one of these may be a man designated by, and specially acceptable to, the Liberals of the "working classes".'

44 H. W. McCready, 'The British Election of 1874: Frederic Harrison and the Liberal Labour Dilemma', *The Canadian Journal of Economics and Political Science*, 20, 2 (May 1954), p. 168.

45 R. Tressell, *The Ragged Trousered Philanthropists*, 1965, pp. 536–7.

46 Cole, *British Working Class Politics*, p. 91; Pelling, *Origins of the Labour Party*, pp. 40–1.

47 Pelling, *Origins of the Labour Party*, pp. 58–9; A. E. P. Duffy, 'Differing Policies and Personal Rivalries in the Origins of the Independent Labour Party', *Victorian Studies*, VI, 1 (Sept. 1962), pp. 47–9; E. P. Thompson, 'Homage to Tom Maguire', in A. Briggs and J. Saville (eds.), *Essays in Labour History*, 1967, p. 315.

48 Pelling, *Origins of the Labour Party*, pp. 69, 73, 95–7; Duffy, 'Differing Policies and Personal Rivalries', *loc. cit.*, pp. 58–63; Cole, *British Working Class Politics*, pp. 143–6.

CONCLUSION

1 Some valuable studies of this decline are S. Koss, *Nonconformity in Modern British Politics*, 1975; J. F. Glaser, 'English Nonconformity and the Decline of Liberalism', *American Historical Review*, LXIII, no. 2 (Jan. 1958); P. F. Clarke, *Lancashire and the New Liberalism*, Cambridge, 1971; P. F. Clarke, 'Electoral Sociology of Modern Britain', *History*, vol. 57, no. 189 (Feb. 1972); P. Thompson, *Socialists, Liberals and Labour. The Struggle for London 1885–1914*, 1967; H. Pelling, *Social Geography of British Elections, 1885–1910*, 1967; E. Halévy, *Imperialism and the Rise of Labour*, second ed., 1961; E. Halévy, *The Rule of Democracy, 1905–1914*, second ed., 1961.

2 A. K. Russell, *Liberal Landslide. The General Election of 1906*, Newton Abbot and Hamden, Connecticut, 1973; S. Koss, *Nonconformity in Modern British Politics*, Chapters 2 and 3.

3 D. E. Butler and R. Rose, *The British General Election of 1959*, 1960, p. 138 n.

4 Quoted in *The Guardian*, 30 Jan. 1975.

NOTE: LOCATION OF MANUSCRIPTS

Edward Baines Papers, Leeds City Archives.
Joseph Chamberlain Papers, Birmingham University Library.
George Howell Papers, Bishopsgate Institute.
A. J. Mundella Papers, Sheffield University Library.
J. H. Wilson Papers, Sheffield Public Library.
For location of other collections, see Appendix.

Index

Baines—*cont'd*

Leeds P.B.A., 1865, 173; temperance opposition to at Leeds, 1873-4, 186, 196, 197; and Leeds by-election, 1876, X: n. 26

Baines, George H., 145

Baker, R. B. Wingfield, 117

Banbury, general election, 1865, 114; temperance electoral canvass at, 214

Barker, J., 280, 281

Barker, T. H., and Leeds election, 1874, 196, 197

Barnard, Rev. J. F., 233

Barnes, Thomas, XIII: n. 51

Barnsley, by-election, 1897, 277

Barnstaple, S. Waddy chosen for, 1873, 186

Barran, J., 207

Barrow, by-election, 1890, 259, 260

Barry, Maltman, 320

Bass brewing interest, 187

Bath, the 1873 situation in, 44, 56, 195, III: n. 14; the third by-election, 1873, 44, 187-9; the second by-election, 1873, 56, 131, 132, 186, 188; Roebuck beaten at, 1847, 93; relations at between Liberals and the temperance people, 1868-73, 184, 185; creation of P.B.A. at, 1873, 184; the first by-election 1873, 185; general election, 1874, 190, 192, 193; Liberal-temperance harmony at, 1880, 224, 225

Batley, 228

Bazley, Sir Charles, 194

Bazley, Thomas, V: n. 55

Beales, Edmond, 310, 311

Beaufoy, Mark, 261, 278-80

Bedford, 215

Bedfordshire South, 277

Bell, I. Lowthian, 201

Beresford, Lord Charles, 285, 292

Berkshire, general election, 1857, 97

Berwick, general election, 1874, 193

Bethnal Green, North-East, general election, 1892, 321

Billany, N. B., 237

Billson, A., 275, 276, 288, 289

Bingham, W., 303, III: n. 14

Birkenhead, general election, 1865, 167; by-election, 1894, 286, 287

Birmingham, and purchase of county freehold qualifications, 85, 90; Lib. Soc. and Liberals at, 1880, 152; Alliance Electoral Organisation formed at, 1870, 171, 180; Liberals and the temperance party and question at in the 1870s, 180, 197, 216-18; general election, 1874, 194-99; temperance conflict at in 1870s, 209, 217, 218; general election, 1880, 218; conflict over Liberals' selection of brewer as candidate at, 1882, 228; T.E.A. set up at, 1890, 253; conflict over Liberals' selection of brewer as candidate at, 1891, 261, 262, 264; C. H. Fulford and temperance party at, 278; electoral action by non-voters at, 308; relations between Ref.L. and Liberal Association at, 308; and the A.C.L.L., V: n. 13

Birmingham East, temperance opposition to Liberal brewer candidate at, 1891-2, 261-5

Birmingham Daily Post, 180

Blackburn, general election, 1874, 195; temperance politics at, 1885, 236

Blackwood, W., XIII: n. 48

Blatchford, Robert, 322

Boal, Alfred E., 31

Bodmin, 215

Bolckow, H. W. F., 209

Bolton, general election, 1895, 283, 284; Ref.L. report on, 1868, XIII: n. 51

Bolton, T. H., 258

Bompas, H. M., 225

Booth, F. Handel, 300, 301

Bootle, general election, 1885, 237

Bowring, Sir John, 309

Boyd, H. F., 294

Bradford, competition of pressure groups at, 56; Nonconformists and choice of Liberal candidates at in late 1870s, 146; formation of T.E.A.s at, 1885, 232; relations between I.L.P. and Liberals at, 276; Non-Electors' Committee at, 309

Bradford East, Caine's defeat at, 1895, 271, 276, 288, 289; Liberals opposed to Caine as candidate, 271, 276, 288, 289; by-election, 1896, 276, 288, 289

Bradford West, general election, 1892, 318

Brambley, E. C., temperance electoral work of, 215, 228, 244, 246, 269; advocates working within Liberal party, 240, 274, 290; supports pro-Local Veto brewer candidates, 262; and Wisbech by-election, 1894, 274

Elections—*cont'd*
 sure groups and, 20–2, 67; 1865, 21,
  113–16, 173, 175, 176; 1837, 307;
  1874, 21, 137–40, 144, 190–200, 229;
  1780, 61; 1841, 64, 71, 305–7; 1847,
  93, 307; 1852, 94; 1857, 97, 166; 1859,
  98, 166; 1868, 117–19, 122, 178, 179,
  315; 1880, 139, 147–52, 222, 228;
  1886, 241; 1885, 155–7, 237, 238, 316;
  1892, 159, 160, 267, 268, 270; 1895,
  162, 270, 274, 283, 286, 289, 290,
  295, 322; 1900, 164, 303
Elgin District, temperance electoral
 strength in, 1876, 213
Elimination of Corrupt Practices Act,
 1883, 4
Ellis, Tom, and the pressure groups, 7;
 and Earp's candidature at Grantham, 278, 283; and Liberal treatment of temperance question at by-
 elections, 1894–5, 287; death of,
 1899, 292
Essex, general election, 1865, 114
Essex, East, Lib. Soc. and, 1879, 144
Essex, South, registration campaign in,
 96; general election, 1868, 117
Evans, Rev. David, 129
Evans, W., V: n. 89
Evesham, general election, 1874, 192
Exeter, by-election, 1844, 75; by-
 election, 1864, 111, 173; general
 election, 1865, 115; by-election, 1899,
 269; Reform League and, 309, 312;
 general election, 1880, X: n. 81

Fabians, 322
Falkirk, general election, 1874, 194
Farish, William, and U.K.A. electoral
 policy, 1878, 203; and electoral can-
 vassing, 212, 214, 224
Fawcett, H., 208
Fenwick, Capt. H. T., 262, 264, 266,
 279
Finsbury, Lib. Soc. organisation at,
 143; temperance electoral pledge at,
 215
Firth, J. F. B., 143
Fisher, John, 158, 160
Fitzmaurice, Lord Edmond, 272
Fitzwilliam, Hon. J. W., 209
Fletcher, J., 109
Flower, Rev. J. E., 162
Forster, W. E., refuses to give pledges,
 50; and Lib. Soc. electoral strategy

in 1860s, 108; Education Bill of, 1870,
 122, 132; Nonconformists and at
 Bradford in 1870s, 146
Foster, Dr. C. J., 94–7, 102
Fox, W. J., 77, 82, V: n. 90
Freeholders, forty-shilling, creation of
 by Catholic Association, 61; A.C.L.L.
 and registration of, 77 ff.; Cobden
 advocates strategy based on registra-
 tion of after 1846, 87 ff.; the move-
 ment for registration of in the late
 1840s and early 1850s, 90
Freehold Land Societies, 90, 95, 98
Freeman, The, 161
Frome, by-election, 1854, 94; general
 election, 1865, 115; general election,
 1874, 191; by-election, 1876, 201
Fulford, C. H., 278–80, 284, 294
Fulford, H. G., 261
Fuller, John, 280
Furness, Sir Christopher, 285, 292

Gallimore, H., 249
Gamble, R. W., 207
Gammage, E., 306
Gateshead, A.C.L.L. canvass at, 68
German, Major, 181
Gibbard, L. G. S., 302
Gibbon, Rev. J. Morgan, 163
Gibson, Milner, V: n. 90
Gilbey family, 280
Gilpin, Charles, 190, VI: n. 8, 16
Gladstone, Herbert, and the sections
 after 1899, 7; advises against disestablishment as an election issue, 1899,
 163; urges U.K.A. to reach accom-
 modation with Liberal party, 1890,
 258; urges high priority for licensing
 legislation, 1892, 266; sees Local
 Option as electoral liability for
 Liberals, 270; advocates substituting
 more immediate and acceptable
 temperance reform for the Veto, 292;
 encourages 'revolt against the Veto',
 294; and the Peel report, 1899–1900,
 300; encourages Johnson-Ferguson's
 move from Loughborough, 303; temperance opposition to at Leeds, 1900,
 303; and Lib-Lab electoral pact,
 1903, 318
Gladstone, W. E., and the faddists, 7;
 praises Nonconformists, 1880, 21,
 151; suspected of 'shunting' disestablishment, 22; seen as 'squeezable',

Hughes, John, 208

Hull, by-election, 1873, 189; general election, 1868, 189; search for Liberal candidate for, 1873, 189; Liberal Association and temperance party at in late 1870s, 219–22; general election, 1880, 221, 222; harmony at after 1880, 227; general election, 1885, 236; Prohibition League at, 245

Hulme, Obadiah, 59

Hume, Joseph, V: n. 90

Hume, Major, 49

Hunter, Ex-Bailie, 147

Huntingdon, A.C.L.L. and, 74, 75, 77; Liberal candidates withdraw from, 1894, 277

Hutchinson, J. D., 207

Hutton, Rev. Dr., 147, 154

Illingworth, Alfred, as MP, 8; and Nonconformist electoral strategy in 1870s, 119, 123, 131, 141, 142; candidature of for Bradford in 1870s, 146; and Lib. Soc.-Liberal co-operation, 1882, 153; and Nonconformist strategy, 1885, 156; U.K.A. seeks candidatures for, 1874, 194; candidature of at West Bradford, 1892, 318

Independent Labour Party, blamed for Liberal electoral setbacks in 1890s, 270; and temperance politics in 1890s, 275–7; electoral strategy and conduct of, 321–3

Iredale, J., 177

Irish bloc vote and British elections, 315–17

Irish Church, disestablishment of, 53, 117–20, 179

Irish Home Rule, pressure groups ask supporters to ignore, 41; split in U.K.A. over, 41, 243; polarises politics, 158; Lib. Soc. and, 158; effect on Liberal party of split over, 240; opposition to, 241; in the Newcastle Programme, 266; blamed for Liberal electoral setbacks in 1890s, 270; position of after Gladstone's retirement, 271; Liberal Unionist temperance people and, 272; Gladstone's conversion to, 317

Irish Home Rule Party, 30, 168, 253, 320

Irish Nationalists in Great Britain,

electoral policy and behaviour of, 315–17

Isle of Wight, general election, 1865, 115; general election, 1874, 192

Jackson, Stanway, 145

Jacobs, E., 53

Jaffray, W., 135

Jenkins, Edward, candidature of at Truro, 1871, 123; and the N.Ed.L.'s electoral strategy, 129; candidature of at Dundee, 1873, 133; on relationship between Liberal party and government, 1872, IV: n. 14

Jermyn, A., 300, 301

Johnson-Ferguson, J. E., 285, 303

Jones, J. R., 49

Jones, Leif, 277, 296

Jones, Mason, 131

Jones, William, 213, 217

Judge, Thomas, 171

Kane, John, 209

Kempster, John, candidature of for West Staffordshire, 1892, 8, 293; and Nonconformist electoral policy, 1900, 163; and U.K.A. electoral policy, 203, 204, 229, 291, 300; withdraws from U.K.A. Consultative Committee, 1889, 250

Kennington, by-election, 1889, 261; controversy over Beaufoy's candidature for, 1893–5, 278, 279; S.D.F. candidature for, 1885, 320

Kent, West, by-election, 1857, 96; general election, 1865, 115

Kerr, R., 196

Kidderminster, Ref.L. and, 312

Kilmarnock, Caine's candidature for 1899, 301

King's Lynn, F. Cowley's report on situation at, 1899, 300

Kingston, general election, 1885, 237

Kirkcaldy, by-election, 1875, 202

Knox, Thomas, 176

Labour, electoral behaviour of, 26, 313, 317–23

Labour Electoral Association, 318, 320

Labour Party, electoral strategy of, 323

Labour Representation Committee, 318

Labour Representation League, 318

Lacon, J., X: n. 19

Nottingham—*cont'd*
suppression of prohibitionist sympathies of Liberal candidate for alleged, 1894, 287; by-election, 1841, 305; general election, 1847, 306; Ref.L. and, 312, 315
Nottinghamshire, A.C.L.L. and, 63
Nunn, E. H., 274, 275

O'Brien, Bronterre, 306, 307
O'Connell, Daniel, 61
O'Connor, Feargus, 306, 307
O'Connor, T. P., 316
Odger, George, 315, 318, 319
Oldham, by-election, 1872, 180; by-election, 1877, 213; general election, 1885, 238
Oldroyd, M., 243
Osborn, H. J., 261
Osgoldcross, by-election, 1899, 297, 298 303
Otter, F., 239
Owen, J. W., U.K.A. electoral secretary, 183; electoral work of, 187, 188, 205, 212
Oxford, general election, 1874, 191, 195, 200; by-election, 1874, 200; Prohibition League at, 245; by-election, 1895, 288
Oxford Tests Bill, 114

Paisley, temperance canvass at, 211
Palmer, George, 54
Palmerston, Lord, 88, 308
Parker, J., 301
Parkes, Joseph, 83
Parnell, C. S., 253, 316
Paton, John, and Ayrshire election, 1874, 191; temperance electoral canvassing by, 211–15, 223, 247, 265
Peace movement, 88
Peace Society, 54
Pearson, Rev. S., 152
Pease, Arthur, U.K.A. suggests for York, 1874, 194; candidature suggested for Hull, 1878, 219; antagonism to in U.K.A. after 1885, 243
Peel Commission, 5, 299–301, 303
Peel, Frederick, 114
Peel, Sir Robert, 84, 86, 87, V: n. 40, 85
Pellett, Apsley, VI: n. 8, 16
Permissive Bill Electoral Associations, formation of, 166; function of, 171

Peterborough, general election, 1874, 195, 196; by-election, 1878, 209; formation of T.E.U. at, 1887, 245
Petersfield, by-election, 1897, 280
Picton, J. A., on disestablishment, 52, 53
Plancke, J. H., 167
Pledges, and the temperance movement, 13, 27; Nonconformists and, 21; as an electoral technique, 27 ff.; given by candidates, 49 ff.
Plymouth, by-election, 1871, 127, 180; debate on electoral policy in temperance movement at, 1868, 179, 180; by-election, 1898, 269, 272; T.E.A. at, 269, 272; choice of Liberal candidate at, 1898, 277
Pontefract, N.Ed.L. and, 129; by-election, 1872, 129, 180; general election, 1892, 286; by-election, 1893, 286
Pope, Samuel, candidature of at Stoke, 1857, 166; on the publicans' power at elections, 172; on the difficulty of breaking party ties, 175; on U.K.A. electoral policy, 1872–3, 182, 183, 188; supports U.K.A. rapprochement with Liberals, 206, 207; on U.K.A. electoral policy, 1877, 214; moves U.K.A. electoral resolution, 1883, 229; and proposal for Direct Veto parties, 1885, 232; moves U.K.A. electoral resolution, 1885, 237; opposes Hargrove's resolution, 1887, 246; and T.E.A.s, 1889, 251; on relationship between Liberal party and government, 1873, IV: n. 13; candidature of at Bolton, 1868, XIII: n. 51
Portsmouth, U.K.A. canvass at, 1878, 214
Potter, G., 195, 196
Preston, by-election, 1872, 129, 181, 182
Priestley, A., 239
Pryce, E. S., electoral work of for Lib. Soc., 94–7; proposed candidature of at Hull, 1880, 221, 222

Ragged Trousered Philanthropists, The (R. Tressell), 319
Ramsay, Lord, 316
Raper, J. H., candidature of at Peterborough, 1878, 8, 209; opposes abstention policy of U.K.A., 1885,